Instructional Methods for Students with Learning and Behavior Problems

■ Patrick J. Schloss
The Pennsylvania State University

■ Robert A. Sedlak
University of Wisconsin-Stout

Allyn and Bacon, Inc.
Boston London Sydney Toronto

To our families,
Cindy, Patrick, Rebecca, and Tarah
and
Denise, Robert, and Wendy

Series Editor: Jeffery W. Johnston
Senior Production Administrator: Jane Schulman
Editorial-Production Services: TKM Productions
Interior Designer: Judith Ashkenaz
Cover Coordinator: Linda K. Dickinson
Cover Designer: Lisa Tedeschi

Library of Congress Cataloging-in-Publication Data

Schloss, Patrick J.
   Instructional methods for students with learning
and behavior problems.

   Includes index.
   1. Handicapped children—Education—United States—
Curricula.   2. Handicapped children—United States—
Testing.   3. Criterion-referenced tests—United States.
4. Individualized instruction—United States.   I. Sedlak,
Robert A., 1947–   .   II. Title.
LC4031.S36   1986   371.9   85-27509
ISBN 0-205-08735-3

Printed in the United States of America

10 9 8 7 6 5 4 3 2 1   91 90 89 88 87 86

Brief Contents

A Note on This Book

I believe this methods text has a clear, no-nonsense bottom line: *results* —how teachers go about the task of obtaining, maximizing, and retaining results with their students.

The authors state the familiar theme a bit differently. Effective educational interventions must be functionally related to student achievement; that is, the initiated procedure must produce data to demonstrate its positive effect on student performance. This effectiveness is underlined by recent legislation and litigation requiring a honest and lawful effort on the part of educators in: (1) selecting strategies that maximize the educational potential of the learner, (2) monitoring students' progress during the educational program, and (3) revising the program based on objective data. The text sees Special Education as an empirical process—the selection of intervention methods built on the relationship of the methods and resulting student performance.

The focus is on the principles and practices that have a strong learning theory foundation. Strategies are highlighted that have been demonstrated in the professional literature to produce objective changes in student performance. The text presents a model of instruction for the purposes of:

1. Assessing special learners
2. Establishing goals and objectives
3. Implementing data-based educational approaches
4. Evaluating outcomes

As a result, teachers will be better prepared to develop and implement instructional programs that may be verified as having a positive effect on special learners.

Jeff Johnston
Series Editor

Contents

Foreword

Instructional Methods for Students with Learning and Behavior Problems reflects substantial gains and improvements in the instruction of children with mild handicaps over the past two decades. An effective program for exceptional children depends on two major components being in place: (1) policy, and (2) differential curriculum and instructional strategies.

Since the 1960s, substantial attention in special education has been focused on *policy*, which may be defined as actions that deliver the right resources to the right place at the right time for the handicapped child. That is what Public Law 94-142, The Education for All Handicapped Children Act, attempts to do—create a learning environment that is rich and potentially productive and assure that the resources will be sufficient to get the job done. In a way, it is like an owner of a baseball team assembling the best players and using the best equipment. In the end, the players still have to play the game and win. In special education, having all the necessary resources will be insignificant if the teacher cannot provide effective instruction.

Robert Sedlak and Patrick Schloss address the second goal for effective programs—the nature of the differential curriculum and instructional strategies. Through their concern for individual assessment, instructional goals and objectives, and data-based educational procedures, they deal directly with the hands-on problems of the special education teacher and bring to bear the recent developments in learning theory and information processing to the instructional process.

The degree of specificity with which the authors approach skills development, task analyses, and the design of useful exercises, for example, should be of substantial help to practicing special education teachers, regular classroom teachers, and those who are preparing for such critical roles. In addition to chapters on reading, writing, and arithmetic, the authors provide a discussion of criterion-referenced measurement—a useful device for the type of formative evaluation that teachers need. Such measurement provides information and feedback to the teachers on how successful their instruction has been with a given student or with a given task. Another useful chapter focuses on the roles to be played by the new technologies of the microcomputer, videotape, and calculators.

Although sound theory is discussed in the book, it is in the translation of that theory to the classroom plans and activities that will be appreciated by the front-line practitioners—the teachers. The authors' own classroom experience with mildly handicapped children has served them well, as demonstrated by the examples and exercises suggested in this book.

Many years ago it was popular to pose the question, "What's special about special education?" *Instructional Methods for Students with Learning and Behavior Problems* provides some very clear answers to that question.

James J. Gallagher

Preface

Special education is defined by federal law as "specially designed instruction, at no cost to the parent, to meet the unique needs of a handicapped child" (U.S. Office of Education, 1977, p. 42480). "Specially designed instruction" is interpreted by professionals and parents in many different ways. Some advocate instruction directed at presumed underlying pathology, such as auditory discrimination deficits and visual perception problems. Others emphasize the development of discrete skills, such as reading and math, to the exclusion of potential underlying problems. What is generally not argued is that specially designed instruction that does, in fact, meet the unique needs of the learner, will produce a change in the learner's performance. Regardless of teachers' orientation to the education of handicapped learners, it is generally agreed that instructional tactics should produce objective changes in learners' performance.

Therein lies the focus of *Instructional Methods for Students with Learning and Behavior Problems.* The text describes special education as an empirical process. Empiricism implies that the selection of educational methods is based on the relationship between those methods and student performance. Therefore, this text includes procedures for (1) assessing special learners, (2) establishing instructional goals and objectives, (3) implementing data-based educational procedures, and (4) evaluating the impact of those procedures on the instructional goals and objectives. Upon completion of the text, readers will be able to develop and implement instructional programs that will have a positive effect on special learners.

Organization

Instructional Methods for Students with Learning and Behavior Problems comprises three parts. The first, "Educational Perspectives," begins with a chapter on the historical and legislative foundations of empirical special education methods. This chapter includes a set of principles that underlie the text. The second chapter presents an empirical approach for classifying learner characteristics. Emphasis is placed on translating these characteristics into instructional objectives. The third chapter discusses the coordination of services for handicapped learners. This chapter describes potential special education services and settings, identifies potential members of the multidisciplinary team and their roles, and discusses the Individualized Education Program (IEP) document as a planning tool.

The second part, "Educational Approaches," describes empirical special education methods that are applicable to general instruction situations. Chapter 4 forms the basis of empirical educational practices by describing a sequence of direct instructional activities. The following chapters discuss criterion-referenced evaluation tactics. Chapter 5 describes paper-and-pencil measures, and chapter 6 presents systematic observation tactics. Chapter 7 discusses strategies for classroom management. Emphasis is placed on techniques that increase the amount of time students are engaged in progress toward objectives. Chapter 8 discusses both old and new technology that is suited to educational programs for the mildly handicapped and highlights ways in which technology can be adapted to specific curricular areas.

The final part, "Educational Competencies," provides specific educational activities for each of the major content areas. Respective chapters are on spoken language, written language, reading, arithmetic, vocational skills, and interpersonal skills. These chapters review specific curricular concerns, educational strategies, assessment procedures, and instructional materials. Emphasis is placed on the application of the general instructional strategies discussed in part II to each of the specific content areas.

Features

Instructional Methods for Students with Learning and Behavior Problems includes several distinctive features that are intended to enhance its value as a course textbook and as a reference book.

DID YOU KNOW THAT... Each chapter begins with a set of *cognitive competency statements*, which establish the scope of information contained in the chapter. Cognitive competencies highlight the knowledge base that readers should acquire from each chapter.

CAN YOU... The chapters are also prefaced by *performance competency statements*, which identify the specific strategies discussed in each chapter. The performance competencies target specific skills that readers should possess after reading the text and participating in supplemental practicum activities.

TEXT REFERENCING The *Did you know that...* and *Can you...* entries are referenced to specific content in each chapter through symbols and numbers located in the margins. This feature may be used as an advanced organizer, a study reference, an indexing system, and a mastery check. It emphasizes that persons reading the text should master both cognitive and performance objectives. In other words, after reading this book, readers should be able to *articulate principles* and *demonstrate practices* associated with empirically based instruction for mildly handicapped learners.

ACTION PLANS   Action plans are included throughout the book to further emphasize performance aspects of its content. Action plans include brief step-by-step procedures or guidelines for conducting educational interventions. In most cases, the action plans summarize activities discussed in the text without repeating the more detailed rationales.

CASES FOR ACTION   Cases for action provide opportunities for the reader to analyze instructional problems. They are generally open-ended case studies that may be resolved through plans developed from information in the text.

TECHNICAL WRITING   Special education as a discipline uses some technical terms that have a precise meaning to professionals. There are also abundant terms in the field that add little to the precision of professional activities. It would be inappropriate for a college text to exclude technical terms used in the meaningful practice of the discipline. Therefore, when appropriate, technical terms are included and defined. Jargon that does little to enhance our ability to communicate an understanding of problems or solutions has been replaced with generally accepted terms.

For Our Friends

We are deeply indebted to the people who made the writing of this text possible. Foremost, we would like to acknowledge Jeffery Johnston, editor at Allyn and Bacon. Jeff's voracious study of the field and its needs, and his frequent communications regarding the relationship between this work and those identified needs, are primarily responsible for the present form of this text. Similarly, we are indebted to Professors Sandra Cohen, Sharon Davis, Stephen McCarney, Arthur McElroy, James McLoughlin, Susan Miller, and Carlene Van Etten for their substantive reviews of early drafts of this text.

We are also indebted to our mentors and colleagues, who have provided the intellectual, experiential, and practical resources from which this project has evolved. Specifically, we would like to acknowledge Professors G. Phillip Cartwright, William I. Gardner, and David A. Sabatino.

Finally, we would like to express our appreciation to Maureen Smith for reviewing and editing the final manuscript, to Cay Freeman and Kim Mitch for developing the *Can you . . .* and *Did you know that . . .* features, and to Paul Schloss and Jeanne Kussrow-Larson for typing the manuscript.

R. S.
P. S.

To The Student

You will notice that each chapter of this text begins with two sets of questions. The first set, labeled DID YOU KNOW THAT..., highlights concepts you should learn by reading the chapter. The second set, labeled CAN YOU..., identifies performance competencies you should acquire from the chapter. Finally, in reading through each chapter, you will notice that specific DID YOU KNOW THAT... and CAN YOU... questions are referenced directly to paragraphs in the text by symbols and numbers in the margins. These features may be useful to you in several ways:

- You may use the questions as an advanced organizer before reading the chapters. Having read the DID YOU KNOW THAT... and CAN YOU... entries, you may read each chapter with a specific purpose in mind—to acquire the target concepts and skills.
- The questions may be used as a pretest to determine chapter content that is unfamiliar to you. You may scan chapters in which a majority of the DID YOU KNOW THAT... and CAN YOU... entries identify familiar information and concentrate on those that present a larger number of unfamiliar concepts or skills.
- The questions may be used as a posttest. Once you have read and studied a chapter, you may review the statements to ensure that you have mastered the relevant concepts and skills. Then you may review entries that remain unfamiliar.
- Finally, the DID YOU KNOW THAT... and CAN YOU... questions, along with references to these skills and concepts in the text, may be used as an index system. You may follow up on questions that are of particular interest by reading associated paragraphs in the text.

In sum, the DID YOU KNOW THAT... and CAN YOU... features of this text are intended as a resource for you. We hope that they will help you identify, learn, and retrieve the concepts and skills that are necessary for a teacher of mildly handicapped students.

Part I

Educational Perspectives

1

Empirical Basis for Special Education Methods

■ DID YOU KNOW THAT . . .

■ 1   . . .recognition and treatment of persons with exceptional characteristics date back to early history?

■ 2   . . .Jean Itard's treatment of a feral child in the 1800s exemplifies the period of empiricism that was the forerunner of empirical educational methodology today?

■ 3   . . .Thorndike identified various relationships between a stimulus and a response?

■ 4   . . .B. F. Skinner's laboratory studies led to the development of empirical principles currently used to explain human learning?

■ 5   . . .precision teaching methods make use of empirical learning theory principles?

■ 6   . . .a number of court cases laid the groundwork for PL 94–142, the landmark legislation that is rooted in empiricism?

■ 7   . . .the IEP is a planning and monitoring tool that is described in PL 94–142?

■ 8   . . .the IEP contains objective data that are used to communicate a student's needs, resolve differences, and evaluate pupil progress?

■ 9   . . .a good-faith effort is required of educators to use objective performance data to implement the provisions of the IEP?

■ **10** . . . the extent to which an individual will achieve depends on the interaction of the environment and the individual's inherited characteristics?

■ **11** . . . past educational and social environments greatly influence a student's current learning experiences?

■ **12** . . . learning is demonstrated when a student's performance changes as a result of educational procedures?

■ **13** . . . you cannot assume that individuals with similar characteristics will benefit from the same teaching procedures?

■ **14** . . . a student's performance may be altered by manipulating the antecedents and consequences of the behavior?

■ **15** . . . norm-referenced data are useful for student placement and program planning decisions?

■ **16** . . . criterion-referenced measures are useful for monitoring student progress during instruction?

■ **17** . . . competencies that are not practiced and reinforced may be forgotten?

○ **CAN YOU . . .**

○ **1** . . . use a current educational or psychological journal to identify procedures that use empirical learning principles?

○ **2** . . . describe an educational strategy used by teachers that incorporates empirical principles?

○ **3** . . . use a student's educational history along with other information to plan a comprehensive instructional program?

○ **4** . . . conduct a functional analysis to decide whether an educational procedure is effective?

○ **5** . . . provide arguments that refute the decision to develop a curriculum based only on the identification of a student's disability?

○ **6** . . . identify events that either enhance or inhibit student performance?

○ **7** . . . identify potential antecedents and consequences that maintain disruptive classroom behavior?

○ **8** . . . develop a data collection protocol that would outline when to take performance data and what to use them for?

HISTORICAL FOUNDATIONS

■ **1**   Special services to handicapped persons have received increased attention as the result of recent laws and court cases. Contrary to popular notions, however, attention to the characteristics and treatment of exceptional persons has not been restricted to the past several decades. Evidence dating from the start of recorded history suggests that humans have sought to explain the origins of and provide treatment for exceptional characteristics in children and youth. Prehistoric man practiced trephining (removing a small portion of the skull) so that evil spirits associated with mental illness would leave the body. Hippocrates (460–375 B.C.) and Galen (2 A.D.) postulated that epilepsy and various mental problems were the result of structural defects in the brain. Evidence from the Middle Ages suggests that deviance was explained as a function of divine or demonic intercessions (Telford & Sawrey, 1972).

The Renaissance resulted in a more humanitarian view of exceptionality. Paracelsus' (1493–1541) treatise, which advocated the use of medicine rather than spiritual rituals in treating mentally ill persons, appears as a focal point of the era. The establishment of a facility for the care and treatment of the feebleminded by Saint Vincent de Paul (1576–1660) and the first successful school for the treatment of mental defectives (1837) signaled the beginning of more scientific efforts on behalf of the handicapped (Telford & Sawrey, 1972).

■ **2**   The 1800s have repeatedly been cited as the forerunner to the modern period of empiricism in the education and treatment of handicapped persons (Cleland & Swartz, 1982; Kirk & Gallagher, 1983; MacMillan, 1977; Telford & Sawrey, 1972). Probably the most widely popularized effort of this era was Jean Itard's (1932) treatment of Victor, a feral child found abandoned in the forest in the Province of Aveyron. The 5-year endeavor resulted in publication of *The Wild Boy of Aveyron*, a classic acclaimed by the French Academy. Itard, who studied empiricist philosophy under John Locke, believed that environmental stimulation accounted for the way children developed. His student, Edouard Sequin (1866) detailed environmentally based treatments in *Idiocy, Its Treatment by the Physiological Method*. Sequin's work has had a strong impact on current educational methodology. For example, the French physician-educator Maria Montessori's (1870–1952) programs for normal children were modeled after the concrete instructional materials and sensory training activities described by Sequin.

Itard, Sequin, and Montessori each sought to identify relationships between specific events and an individual's behavior. Thus, their work was the forerunner of modern empiricism in special education. It is clear that many of their constructs (e.g., modeling, stimulus control, shaping, contingency management), though described in different terms, are currently considered fundamental to effective educational programs.

■ 3   Recent scholars have provided more precise and comprehensive accounts of the impact of specific environmental manipulations. Edward L. Thorndike, the father of modern reinforcement theory, viewed the association between a stimulus and a response as fundamental to learning. Thorndike described three empirical principles: (1) *the law of effect*, which suggests that learning is enhanced as a function of satisfying consequences; (2) *the law of readiness*, which states that the learner's physiological structure influences the extent to which the law of effect operates; and (3) *the law of connection*, which emphasizes the role of practice in learning.

■ 4   B. F. Skinner (1968) extended these views in well-controlled laboratory studies. He used two major empirical constructs to explain human learning: *respondent conditioning*, in which involuntary responses are elicited by provoking stimuli; and *operant conditioning*, in which responses are used volitionally to gain pleasant consequences and avoid aversive consequences. He and his colleagues have identified a range of corollary principles that govern human behavior. These principles emphasize (1) that behavior is learned through interaction with environmental events; (2) that behavior can be changed by carefully restructuring environmental stimuli; and (3) that functional relationships between behavior and events can be observed to operate in a stable and predictable manner.

■ 5   Researchers and practitioners over the past two decades have demonstrated the applicability of Skinner's work to a variety of applied educational settings. Haring and Phillips (1962) and Hewett (1967, 1968) developed separate model programs for behaviorally disordered students. Their efforts relied heavily on Skinner's operant principles by emphasizing the identification and utilization of stimuli and consequences that are functionally related to academic success. Clear objectives, consistent consequences, and daily monitoring of student progress were hallmarks of their programs. Lindsley (1964), and O. R. White and Haring (1980) extended the application of empirical learning theory principles to educational settings through the use of *precision teaching*. Procedures described by these authors include pinpointing behavior, monitoring and charting performance, and making data-based instructional decisions.

○ 1   Currently, commercial materials, professional literature, and model programs based on these learning principles are prevalent throughout the United States. Journals have been initiated in the past two decades solely for reporting applied operant work in education and psychology (e.g., *Journal of Applied Behavior Analysis, Applied Research in Mental Retardation, Behavior Modification, Education and Treatment of Children*). Several texts have been devoted to empirical teaching methodology (Alberto & Troutman, 1982; Carnine & Silbert, 1979; Gardner, 1977, 1978; Martin & Pear, 1978; Silbert, Carnine, & Stein, 1981; O. R. White & Haring, 1980). Numerous teacher-training programs have added courses or competency requirements in empirical teaching techniques. Finally, a variety of applied educational research programs for handicapped learners have been funded by the federal government.

LEGISLATIVE FOUNDATIONS

A series of landmark legal decisions have emphasized the importance of empiricism in the education of handicapped learners. *PARC, Bowman, et al. v. Commonwealth of Pennsylvania* (1971) resulted in a consent agreement that provided for (1) a free and appropriate public education for all mentally retarded children, (2) education in the least restrictive educational environment appropriate to the learner, (3) periodic review and evaluation of the educational program, and (4) procedural due process. In 1972, *Mills v. Board of Education of the District of Columbia* extended this mandate beyond mentally retarded students to include all handicapped children and youth. Similar rulings ensured the right to education and treatment for institutionalized severely handicapped persons (*Armstrong v. Kline*, 1980; *Halderman v. Pennhurst State School and Hospital*, 1974; *Wyatt v. Stickney*, 1972). Finally, *Diana v. State Board of Education* (1970), though settled out of court, ensured the use of proper evaluation procedures that result in the appropriate placement of potentially handicapped learners.

■ 6   These rulings collectively comprised the framework for the most comprehensive legislation authored on behalf of handicapped persons. Public Law 94-142, the Education for All Handicapped Children Act of 1975, provides for a free and appropriate education program for all children and adolescents (5–21 years). A free and appropriate education includes the provision of (1) an Individualized Education Program (IEP), (2) services in the least restrictive environment, (3) nondiscriminatory testing, (4) confidentiality, and (5) due process. (A more detailed analysis of the implications of this legislation on educational services will be provided in chapter 3.) The thread running through this litigation and legislation that is important to the present discussion is the requirement for educator accountability (empiricism).

■ 7   The focal point of PL 94-142 is the development of the IEP—a document prepared by a multidisciplinary team to ensure that educational decisions pertinent to the handicapped learner are based on objective data. The importance of empiricism in the IEP process is emphasized in a policy clarification document contained in the *Federal Register* (1981):

> (a) The IEP meeting serves as a communication vehicle between parents and school personnel, and enables them, as equal participants, to jointly decide what the child's needs are, what services will be provided to meet those needs, and what the anticipated outcomes may be.
> (b) The IEP process provides an opportunity for resolving any differences between the parents and the agency concerning a handicapped child's special education needs; first, through the IEP meeting, and second, if necessary, through the procedural protections that are available to the parents.
> (c) The IEP sets forth in writing a commitment of resources necessary to enable a handicapped child to receive needed special education and related services.

(d) The IEP is a management tool that is used to ensure that each handicapped child is provided special education and related services appropriate to the child's special learning needs.

(e) The IEP is a compliance/monitoring document which may be used by authorized monitoring personnel from each governmental level to determine whether a handicapped child is actually receiving the free appropriate public education agreed to by the parents and the school.

(f) The IEP serves as an evaluation device for use in determining the extent of the child's progress toward meeting the projected outcomes. (p. 5462)

■ 8   Underlying the statements contained in the document are three major facets relating to data-based educational programming. First, the student's needs, the services to be provided, and the anticipated outcomes are identified on the basis of valid and reliable student performance measures. The IEP is a vehicle for conveying these planning data to all members of the multidisciplinary team. Second, differences between parents' or advocates' and school agencies' views are resolved through procedural safeguards, which include presenting performance data in an impartial hearing. The adequacy of available data and the extent to which the resulting program reflects the data are reviewed. Third, the individual service providers are required to assess learner progress toward short-term objectives continuously. Short-term objectives should be revised on the basis of these data. Also, the IEP must be evaluated annually. School personnel are expected to present data that support learner progress toward the projected outcomes of the previous year's IEP. Also, an IEP revised on the basis of these data must again be developed for the next year.

■ 9   In short, the IEP is a planning and monitoring document that is firmly rooted in empirical educational philosophy. Although the *Federal Register* (1977, 1981) suggests that the IEP is not a performance contract that assures the student's mastery of the goals and objectives—that is, teachers and administrators may not be held accountable for progress anticipated by the IEP—it is clear that educational agency personnel must provide a good-faith effort in moving the learner toward the anticipated goals. A good-faith effort is often defined by the extent to which educational personnel utilize accurate pupil performance data to establish reasonable goals and objectives, prescribe services, and monitor outcomes (Turnbull, Strickland, & Brantley, 1982).

EMPIRICAL PRINCIPLES

○ 2   Current practices in special education clearly result from the convergence of scientific and legislative activities discussed in the preceding sections. Sequin, Montessori, Thorndike, and Skinner initiated interest in the careful analysis of the student and the learning environment. They sought to identify relationships between well-defined educational interventions and educational achievement. Recent legislation and litigation requires a good-faith effort on the part of educators in (1) selecting strategies that maximize the educational potential of the learner, (2) monitoring students' progress during the course of the educational program, and (3) revising the educational program on the basis of objective data.

Seven principles will be reviewed that meet the criteria implied in the empirical research and the legislative and litigation outcomes for making decisions regarding educational programs for handicapped learners (see Action Plan 1.1). Subsequent chapters will detail classroom strategies based on these principles.

ACTION PLAN 1.1   EMPIRICAL PRINCIPLES

An empirical philosophy governing special education services includes the following principles:

1. Students' learning and behavioral characteristics are a product of the interaction between their biological endowment and environmental influences.
2. Students' current learning and behavioral features are influenced by past and current environments.
3. Learning occurs through functional relationships between student responses and environmental events.
4. Students with topographically similar learning and behavioral characteristics may be influenced by different events.
5. Students' learning and behavioral characteristics may be systematically altered by manipulating the learning environment.
6. Data collection is important in designing, monitoring, and evaluating educational programs.
7. Skills that are practiced and reinforced in natural work, leisure, home, and social environments are likely to have a lasting impact on students' development and adjustment.

■ 10   *Principle 1:*   Students' learning and behavioral characteristics are a
            product of the interaction between their biological endowment and
            environmental influences.

            The nature–nurture debate has been a continuing controversy in psy-
            chology and education (Cleland & Swartz, 1982; Scarr-Salapatek, 1975).
            Proponents of the nature view argue that hereditary endowment accounts
            for a substantial degree of variability in human performance (Jensen,
            1969). Those who support the nurture viewpoint attribute achievement dif-
            ferences to external or environmental influences (Skeels, 1966; Skeels &
            Dye, 1939; Thoday & Gibson, 1970). Recent theorists have argued that
            both factors exert a considerable influence in establishing human potential.
            The learner is born with certain constitutional limitations. These
            limitations designate the ceiling of performance given optimum experi-
            ences, and they also determine the extent to which the learner will benefit
            from interactions with the environment. The quality of the environment
            (or instruction), on the other hand, determines the extent to which learners
            will achieve the upper limits of their potential.
            Although students' learning and behavioral characteristics are clearly
            associated with both of these factors, educators cannot alter the hereditary
            endowment of an individual. Therefore, educators' activities are restricted
            to establishing environments that maximize student achievement regardless
            of constitutional limitations.

            Principle 2:   Students' current learning and behavioral features are
            influenced by past and current environments.

■ 11   Beyond initial constitutional features, previous and current experi-
            ences have a substantial influence on students' cognitive, motor, social, and
            communication repertoires. There is consistent evidence that preschool ex-
            periences may have a dramatic influence on students' progress in elementa-
            ry and secondary grades (Darlington, 1980; Heber & Garber, 1975). Con-
            versely, children who are raised in deprived environments may be less able
            to benefit from subsequent learning experiences (Zigler, Butterfield, &
            Capobianco, 1970). Researchers have demonstrated that, to some extent,
            early experiences establish students' current motivational characteristics
            (Zigler, Balla, & Butterfield, 1968), language abilities (Love, Nauta,
            Coelen, Hewett, & Ruopp, 1976), intelligence (Heber & Garber, 1975),
            and other psychological characteristics. As a result, numerous authors have
            argued for the development of specialized preschool educational programs
            (Bronfenbrenner, 1975; C. A. Cartwright, 1981).

○ 3   The effect of previous learning environments on students' current
            characteristics is undeniable. Knowledge of the student's educational
            history may assist the educator in planning current programs. Achievement

gains from one year to the next may assist in establishing current annual goals. The identification of educational programs that accelerate academic gains may suggest current educational intervention approaches. Finally, motivating events utilized in past years may serve as a starting point for current motivational tactics.

Despite the importance of obtaining data from previous environments for planning purposes, educators are not able to alter student histories. Consequently, educators' efforts are limited to structuring current learning environments to maximize student success.

■ 12   *Principle 3:*   Learning occurs through functional relationships between student responses and environmental events.

○ 4   Functional relationships are defined as observable relationships between student performance and intervention procedures. Student performance and an intervention are functionally related if performance changes systematically with changes in the educational procedure (Sidman, 1960). For example, a functional relationship exists between sending notes home to parents and student performance if sending notes consistently produces increased performance. The focal point of effective educational strategies is the identification of functional relationships between learner characteristics and educational interventions. For this reason, regardless of the skill an educator seeks to develop, the overriding approach is to demonstrate the influence of the educational procedure on the student's performance. Educational procedures that can be demonstrated to have a strong impact on the learner's characteristics may be maintained or intensified. Those that do not have a demonstrated association with student growth may be removed or modified.

■ 13   *Principle 4:*   Students with topographically similar learning and behavioral characteristics may be influenced by different events.

○ 5   Although two mentally retarded, learning disabled, or behaviorally disordered students may possess highly similar learning and behavioral features, the factors that develop and maintain those features may be quite different. A variety of causes for each of these conditions have been proposed in the literature (Grossman, 1973; Kauffman, 1981). There is consistent acknowledgment that any one of these causes may be a valid explanation for the condition of a given child or youth. However, valid statements may *not* be made of a common etiology for *all* students within an area of exceptionality (Gardner, 1977). Similarly, functional relationships between instructional conditions and specific characteristics may be different for any two students within a handicapping condition. For example, constitutional and experiential differences may result in one learning disabled child progressing more rapidly when auditory cues and tangible incentives are used. Conversely, another learning disabled child's achievement may be accelerated through the use of visual cues and infrequent social praise.

In addition to interindividual (between-student) differences, intra-individual (within-student) differences may be influenced by different events. Consequences that motivate a youth to use social amenities may be ineffective in motivating homework completion, and lesson formats that are effective in developing a child's written language skills may not promote oral language competencies. These viewpoints emphasize that a priori decisions about effective teaching approaches that are based on isolated descriptions of exceptional characteristics are seldom valid. Functional analyses, as identified in the preceding principle, must be conducted to establish relationships between effective educational procedures and individual student characteristics.

○ 6   *Principle 5:* Students' learning and behavioral characteristics may be systematically altered by manipulating the learning environment.

Functional analyses that demonstrate relationships between student performance and classroom events may be used to structure future learning experiences. Events that have been demonstrated to interfere with the acquisition of skills and information (e.g., specific lesson formats, unstructured time, proximity of specific peers, excessively difficult materials) may be withdrawn from the educational program. Events that promote the student's performance (e.g., frequent and consistent feedback, active student participation, appropriate peer models, proximity of the teacher) may be arranged to occur more frequently in the classroom setting.

■ 14 ○ 7   Influencing events used in structuring the learning environment may include antecedents (events that precede a target response and influence the likelihood of its occurrence) and consequences (events that follow a target behavior and influence the likelihood of its occurrence). Potential antecedent events may include, but are not limited to, prompts used by the teacher, instructional materials, lesson formats, classroom structure, difficulty of materials, and relevance of materials to the learner. Consequences may include the student's sense of accomplishment, teacher's praise, grades, free time, high-preference activities, and notes sent home to the student's parents.

Numerous applied research reports have demonstrated the impact of various antecedent and consequence combinations on students' performance. Academic performance (Schumaker, Hovell, & Sherman, 1977), social skills (Edelstein, Elder, & Narick, 1979), self-care behaviors (Snyder & White, 1979), disruptive classroom behaviors (Marlowe, Madsen, Bowen, Reardon, & Logue, 1978), and school attendance (Schloss, Kane, & Miller, 1981) have been targets of recent investigations. As was previously emphasized, these reports do not ensure the potency of identified educational procedures for all learners. However, they do suggest potentially effective techniques. Ultimately, the educator must evaluate the extent to which suggested procedures influence the characteristics of individual learners.

○ **8**   *Principle 6:*   Data collection is important in designing, monitoring, and evaluating educational programs.

Data that reliably identify functional relationships between students' responses and educational procedures are central to the empirical teaching process (Haring, Lovitt, Eaton, & Hansen, 1978; O. R. White & Haring, 1980). Data pertaining to the students' past educational performance and current level of functioning are useful in targeting specific goals and objectives. These data may also suggest potentially effective educational procedures. Data collected immediately before and during implementation of the educational program are useful in troubleshooting and revising the approach. Finally, data collected upon conclusion of the program may be used to evaluate the extent to which the program achieved the pre-established goals.

■ **15**   ■ **16**   Data collection may involve norm-referenced measures comparing the student's performance to that of his or her peers or criterion-referenced measures contrasting the learner's skill level with the specific objectives of the educational program. Norm-referenced data are useful for establishing general goals for the educational program and for periodically evaluating the learner's progress against that of his or her peers. Criterion-referenced measures, however, are the backbone of empirical educational programs. These measures, discussed in chapters 5 and 6, may provide a daily or weekly account of learner progress toward the objectives. Because of (1) the frequency with which they are administered, (2) their sensitivity to the characteristics of the learner, and (3) their focus on precise objectives, criterion-referenced measures provide information that is directly related to daily educational programming. In short, data provided through criterion-referenced measurement procedures assist the teacher in establishing the focus, pace, and nature of the educational intervention.

■ **17**   *Principle 7:*   Skills that are practiced and reinforced in natural work, leisure, home, and social environments are likely to have a lasting and important impact on students' development and adjustment.

As a general (but not absolute) rule, mildly handicapped persons (1) learn at a slower rate and acquire less information, (2) are less likely to transfer information or strategies from one situation to another, (3) do not benefit substantially from events incidental to the learning task, and

(4) are more likely to forget acquired information (G. P. Cartwright, Cartwright, & Ward, 1985). The selection of educational goals must reflect the severity of the handicapping conditions. Two major features may enhance the lasting impact of educational goals on the development and adjustment of handicapped persons.

First, educational goals and their component objectives should be developmentally sequenced to the extent that they build logically upon one another, producing progressively more complex sets of behaviors. Prerequisites should be established (or compensated for) prior to targeting instruction at subsequent goals or objectives. Second, goals should include competencies that are practiced and reinforced in natural environments. Instruction directed toward behaviors that are not practiced and reinforced frequently may result in immediate performance gains, but these gains are likely to be forgotten by the student because of the lack of use (Stokes & Baer, 1977).

It is likely that all handicapped individuals will not progress as far in curriculum domains as their peers. Consequently, educators must be careful to select goals that have the greatest likelihood of being useful to the individual in adult life. Placing the handicapped student into a curriculum track that is designed for the general student may result in the learner leaving school at the adolescent level without addressing critical life skills. Therefore, goal sequences for the handicapped learner should be developmental within competency areas that promote adult adjustment.

SUMMARY

Early efforts on behalf of handicapped persons attributed exceptional characteristics to phenomena that were not measurable through observation or analysis. Beginning with the work of Itard and Sequin in the 19th century, explanations of deviance began to focus on more objective indices. Recent writings and research have expanded the range of instructional technology available for analyzing the learning and behavioral features of handicapped persons. Current litigation and legislation have supported the use of empirical methods in special education. Public Law 94–142, the Education for All Handicapped Children Act of 1975, requires (1) that educational goals be based on a comprehensive analysis of the learner's characteristics, (2) that school personnel be able to demonstrate the relationship between learner characteristics and educational procedures, and (3) that a continuous monitoring system be established that assesses learner progress toward the educational goals.

As the result of the combined influence of humanistic, legal, and scholarly influences, a number of principles have been advanced that underlie the empirical teaching process. The principles recognize the complexity of handicapped individuals and suggest that students with similar learning and behavioral features may be influenced by different events. Both constitutional factors and previous and current environments may account for these features. The central focus of the principles is the importance of functional relationships between student responses and educational procedures. Effective educational interventions are functionally related to student achievement; that is, data evaluating learner performance demonstrate that initiation of an intervention procedure systematically alters student performance. Finally, the principles emphasize the importance of developmentally sequenced goals and objectives that promote adult adjustment for the learner.

The principles outlined in this chapter underlie the chapters that follow. They serve as a road map for instructional procedures adopted by special educators. The next chapter will discuss in detail the complex nature of children's and youth's learning and behavioral characteristics. Special attention will be paid to translating these characteristics into functional and developmental curricula.

CASE FOR ACTION 1.1

You have applied for a position as a learning disabilities resource teacher for the Franklin and Jefferson County Special Education Cooperative. During an employment interview, the director asks you to explain your philosophy of education. You explain . . .

2

Functional Classification of Exceptional Learners

■ **1** . . . categorical labels are useful in establishing funding priorities and enable professionals to benefit from the professional journals?

■ **2** . . . an intraindividual classification approach focuses on skill and ability differences within the individual?

■ **3** . . . the Characteristic Specific Classification System divides behavior into four classes: cognitive, motor, social, and communication?

■ **4** . . . most handicapped learners' behavior deviates from social norms in degree rather than in kind?

■ **5** . . . students' performance problems may be categorized as skill, motivational, and/or discrimination deficits?

■ **6** . . . it is useful for teachers to recognize cues and motivational conditions that affect a learner's behavior?

■ **7** . . . learning and behavioral features of mildly handicapped learners require careful selection of educational objectives?

■ **8** . . . a teacher should consider a student's learning and behavioral characteristics, chronological age, and availability of instruction when selecting instructional objectives?

■ 9   . . . a student's chronological age is a critical feature in determining whether to use developmental or functional instruction?

■ 10   . . . a teacher may use prosthetics to assist students in overcoming skill deficiencies?

○ CAN YOU . . .

○ 1   . . . avoid potential adverse effects associated with an overreliance on categorical labels?

○ 2   . . . enhance instruction by identifying intraindividual differences?

○ 3   . . . facilitate instruction by determining the severity of exceptionalities?

○ 4   . . . increase instructional efficiency by identifying the nature of performance problems?

○ 5   . . . design instruction based on antecedents and consequences associated with student achievement?

○ 6   . . . select goals and objectives based on a knowledge of students' learning and behavioral characteristics?

○ 7   . . . select instructional objectives that reflect the skills needed in the student's current and/or future environments?

○ 8   . . . develop a skills checklist that evaluates students' performance before and after instruction?

○ 9   . . . identify the component skills that make up a student's performance problems?

○ 10   . . . provide educational experiences in natural and simulated environments?

■ 1   Special education is governed at the administrative level through the use of categories of exceptionality. Categorical labels are used to identify students who are eligible for specific services, and they serve numerous other functions in developing and administering special education programs. It is important, however, that practitioners recognize the limitations of exceptionality categories. Therefore, this chapter will review both positive and negative aspects of exceptionality labels, placing emphasis on how effective teachers go beyond exceptionality labels to develop instruction based on the unique features of each child and youth. Because this text focuses on mildly handicapped learners, issues in distinguishing between levels of severity (e.g., mild, moderate, severe) are avoided. The reader should recognize that service provisions based on this severity continuum are common in the field and often justified. The discussion here, however, will be limited to issues within the categories of mildly handicapped students.

Eligibility for services under PL 94-142 occurs only after the student is identified as falling in one of 11 categories (*Federal Register*, 1977). The categories and their definitions, as reported in figure 2.1, are intended to target homogeneous groups of students for whom a relatively common set of exceptional practices may be employed. Exceptionality categories, as detailed in the law, are also used by the Department of Education, Office of Special Education, to monitor the numbers and types of services provided to students within each category.

FIGURE 2.1   Definitions of Handicapped Children from PL 94-142

A) The term "handicapped children" means those children evaluated as being mentally retarded, hard of hearing, deaf, speech impaired, visually handicapped, seriously emotionally disturbed, orthopedically impaired, other health impaired, deaf-blind, multihandicapped, or as having specific learning disabilities, who because of those impairments need special education and related services.

B) The terms used in this definition are defined as follows:

1) "Deaf" means a hearing impairment which is so severe that the child is impaired in processing linguistic information through hearing, with or without amplification, which adversely affects educational performance.

2) "Deaf-blind" means concomitant hearing and visual impairments, the combination of which causes such severe communication and

Source: *Federal Register* (1977, August 22). Washington DC: U.S. Government Printing Office, pp. 42478–79.

(continued)

FIGURE 2.1   continued

other developmental and educational problems that they cannot be accommodated in special education programs solely for deaf or blind children.

3) "Hard of hearing" means a hearing impairment whether permanent or fluctuating, which adversely affects a child's educational performance but which is not included under the definition of "deaf" in this section.

4) "Mentally retarded" means significantly subaverage general intellectual functioning existing concurrently with deficits in adaptive behavior and manifested during the developmental period, which adversely affects a child's educational performance.

5) "Multihandicapped" means concomitant impairments (such as mentally retarded-blind, mentally retarded-orthopedically impaired, etc.), the combination of which causes such severe educational problems that they cannot be accommodated in special education programs solely for one of the impairments. The term does not include deaf-blind children.

6) "Orthopedically impaired" means a severe orthopedic impairment which adversely affects a child's educational performance. The term includes impairments caused by congenital anomaly (e.g., clubfoot, absence of some member, etc.), impairments caused by disease (e.g., poliomyelitis, bone tuberculosis, etc.), and impairments from other causes (e.g., cerebral palsy, amputations, and fractures or burns which cause contractures).

7) "Other health impaired" means

i) having an autistic condition which is manifested by severe communication and other developmental and educational problems; or

ii) having limited strength, vitality or alertness, due to chronic or acute health problems such as a heart condition, tuberculosis, rheumatic fever, nephritis, asthma, sickle cell anemia, hemophilia, epilepsy, lead poisoning, leukemia, or diabetes, which adversely affects a child's educational performance.

8) "Seriously emotionally disturbed" is defined as follows:

i) The term means a condition exhibiting one or more of the following characteristics over a long period of time and to a marked degree, which adversely affects educational performance:

a) An inability to learn which cannot be explained by intellectual, sensory, or health factors;

b) An inability to build or maintain satisfactory interpersonal relationships with peers and teachers;

(continued)

FIGURE 2.1 continued

c) Inappropriate types of behavior or feelings under normal circumstances;

d) A general pervasive mood of unhappiness or despression; or

e) A tendency to develop physical symptoms of fears associated with personal or school problems.

ii) The term includes children who are schizophrenic. The term does not include children who are socially maladjusted, unless it is determined that they are seriously emotionally disturbed.

9) "Specific learning disability" means a disorder in one or more of the basic psychological processes involved in understanding or in using language, spoken or written, which may manifest itself in an imperfect ability to listen, think, speak, read, write, spell, or to do mathematical calculations. The term includes such conditions as perceptual handicaps, brain injury, minimal brain dysfunction, dyslexia, and developmental aphasia. The term does not include children who have learning problems which are primarily the result of visual, hearing, or motor handicaps, of mental retardation, or of environmental, cultural, or economic disadvantage.

10) "Speech impaired" means a communication disorder, such as stuttering, impaired articulation, a language impairment, or a voice impairment, which adversely affects a child's educational performance.

11) "Visually handicapped" means a visual impairment which, even with correction, adversely affects a child's educational performance. The term includes both partially seeing and blind children.

These categories are used to establish funding priorities on the federal, state, and local levels. Also, many states certify special educators on the basis of a sequence of course work and experiences within specific areas of exceptionality. Such states follow the assumption that the skills required by a teacher working with one group of exceptional children are different from the skills required by a teacher working with another group. Therefore, the college and university experiences that lead to certification are differentiated according to the category of students with whom the preservice educator expects to work.

Aside from administrative issues, knowledge of categories of exceptionality enhance professionals' ability to benefit from the professional literature. Many journals in special education (see figure 2.2) focus on single areas of exceptionality. Others address the full range of handicapping conditions but include categorically based issues and research. Research articles in these journals report response capabilities, learning styles, behavioral characteristics, biophysical features, and environmental histories associated with the major handicapping conditions. Many researchers have attempted to evaluate the applicability of specific educational approaches to learners within the various categories.

FIGURE 2.2   Special Education Journals

General Special Education

Journal of Special Education
Exceptional Children
Topics in Early Childhood Education
Remedial and Special Education

Deaf/Hard of Hearing

American Annals of the Deaf
The Volta Review
Journal of Rehabilitation of the Deaf
Perspectives for Teachers of the Hearing Impaired

Mental Retardation

American Journal of Mental Deficiency
Mental Retardation
Applied Research in Mental Retardation
Education and Training of the Mentally Retarded
Journal of the Association for Persons with Severe Handicaps

Orthopedically Impaired

American Journal of Orthopsychiatry
American Journal of Occupational Therapy
Cerebral Palsy Journal
Cerebral Palsy Review

Seriously Emotionally Disturbed

Behavioral Disorders
Journal of Autism and Developmental Disabilities

Specific Learning Disability

Journal of Learning Disabilities
Learning Disabilities Quarterly

(continued)

FIGURE 2.2 continued

Speech Impaired

Journal of Speech and Hearing Research
Language, Speech, and Hearing Services in the Schools
ASHA
Journal of Speech and Hearing Disorders
Journal of Speech Disorders

Visually Handicapped

New Outlook for the Blind
International Journal for Education of the Blind
Education of the Visually Handicapped
Sight Saving Review

Beyond research, many of the issues in the education of handicapped learners are categorically based. A majority of the introductory level textbooks available for teacher training in special education have chapter titles representing areas of exceptionality (e.g., G. P. Cartwright et al., 1985; Cleland & Swartz, 1982; Lilly, 1979; Payne, Patton, Kauffman, Brown, & Payne, 1983; Suran & Rizzo, 1979).

○ 1   Despite the importance of exceptionality categories, recent literature has highlighted potentially adverse effects of the current diagnostic system. Miller and Schloss (1982), upon reviewing the available literature, have cited the following factors that limit the utility of exceptionality categories for providing special education services:

1. Exceptionality labels provide little treatment-relevant information. Research has failed to demonstrate that educational programs designed specifically for one group of handicapped students have a differential effect when applied to another group (Bartel & Guskin, 1980; Guskin & Spicker, 1968; Salvia & Seibel, 1983; Sindelar & Deno, 1978).

2. Exceptionality labels are often assigned on the basis of variables (e.g., race and socioeconomic status) that are not relevant to the specific definition (Franks, 1971; Gollub & Sloan, 1978; Rivers, Henderson, Jones, Lodner, & Williams, 1975).

3. Exceptionality labels have a significant and potentially adverse effect on teachers' expectations. Reduced expectations may limit the type, level, and efficacy of special education services (Gillung & Rucker, 1977; MacMillan, Jones, & Aloia, 1974; Miller, Schloss, & Sedlak, 1983; Schloss & Miller, 1982).

4. Professionals may attribute characteristics to an individual that are overgeneralized from the exceptionality label. Although current definitions for handicapping conditions include a limited number of behavioral descriptors, educators may assume additional response characteristics that are neither relevant nor valid (Reynolds & Balow, 1972).

5. Similarly, there is a substantial degree of variability between students with the same exceptionality label (Salvia & Seibel, 1983).

6. Exceptionality labels emphasize limitations of the individual, rather than behavioral features that might be at or above the average for the general population.

7. Professionals may view exceptionality characteristics identified by a label as static. People may assume that once a child or youth is identified as handicapped, the condition will remain with the individual for life (Bialer, 1966; Ysseldyke & Foster, 1978).

8. Finally, exceptionality labels may have an adverse effect on the self-esteem of students (R. L. Jones, 1970, 1972; Rivers et al., 1975).

These factors emphasize the limited empirical basis for the use of current exceptionality categories. Despite the absence of an empirical justification from a student service perspective, however, it is clear that exceptionality categories serve a sufficiently important administrative function to ensure their continued use in our educational systems. Consequently, arguing against the use of exceptionality labels may be analogous to fighting the proverbial windmill. It is hoped, however, that this and similar discussions in other texts (Gardner, 1977; R. M. Smith, Neisworth, & Hunt, 1983; Miller & Schloss, 1982) will alert professionals to the importance of adopting alternative classification procedures for direct service purposes.

INTRAINDIVIDUAL CLASSIFICATION

■ 2   One approach to classification of individuals' learning and behavioral characteristics that can result in relevant direct services involves focusing on intraindividual characteristics (Gardner, 1977; Kirk & Gallagher, 1983; Miller & Schloss, 1982; Schloss, 1983). Intraindividual differences refer to differences *within* the individual in regard to skills and abilities. A student may do average work in math but below-average work in reading. His or her word attack skills may be adequate but vocabulary and comprehension skills below average. Such comparisons produce an analysis of discrepancies within the learner's performance across relevant learning and behavioral dimensions. Program recommendations can then be based on the student's overall skill profile.

Figure 2.3 illustrates a sample intraindividual skill profile of a handicapped adolescent. Recognition that the learner's levels of social competence and spoken expressive language are substantially below those of other personal characteristics, and that these skills are particularly im-

FIGURE 2.3   Intraindividual Skill Profile

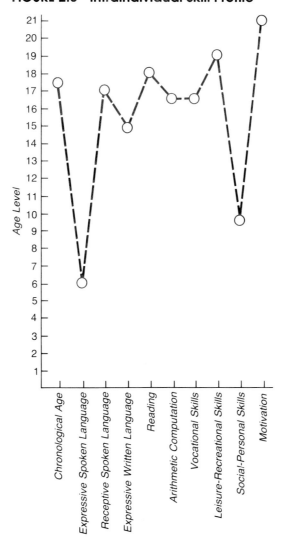

portant to the youth's career goals as a salesperson, would suggest a strong intrapersonal skill training curriculum focus. Because the youth's math and receptive language capabilities are sufficiently high to promote successful adjustment in adult life, skill training in these areas may be de-emphasized. In addition, the strong receptive language, arithmetic, and motivation skills may be used to promote expressive language and social skills.

○ **2**   Although students are placed into special education programs on the basis of interindividual differences, educators must be concerned with intraindividual variability for instructional purposes. Awareness of intra-individual differences means that we should not treat the learner the same way in all skill areas nor assume deficiencies in all areas because of deficiencies in one. Miller and Schloss (1982) and Schloss (1983) have proposed an empirical approach to classifying exceptional characteristics—the Characteristic-Specific Classification System—that is particularly relevant to direct service providers. Factors that emphasize the applicability of the approach in educational settings include the following:

1. The system describes the strengths and weaknesses of individual students, rather than contrasting individuals on the basis of one or two variables (e.g., IQ and adaptive behavior).

2. The complexity of learners' characteristics is recognized by the system. The exceptional learner cannot be adequately programmed for on the basis of one or two behavioral descriptors. Rather, the range of associated learning and behavioral dimensions must be identified and evaluated before initiating an educational program.

3. The system emphasizes the development of positive characteristics. Unproductive explanations for deviance that emphasize limitations of the individual are minimized. Also, circular reasoning that attributes performance problems to a theoretical construct defined by the performance problems is avoided.

4. The system has an empirical foundation. Objective and reliable data used to generate educational decisions are central to the operation of the system.

5. The system promotes the adoption of task-analytic methodology, which involves developing and chaining component skills to form complex behavioral repertoires.

6. Information gained from the system may be translated directly into educational goals. As was emphasized earlier, knowledge of the

learner's strengths and weaknesses provides a clear indication of the appropriateness of selected intervention targets.

7. The system is sufficiently flexible to account for change in the student's learning and behavioral features. Educational programs that successfully affect established goals alter the learner's status within the classification scheme.

8. The system highlights contemporary events associated with the student's learning or behavioral characteristics. Recognition of these events may be useful in developing instructional strategies.

Classes of Behaviors

■ 3   Figures 2.4 through 2.7 represent a modified version of the Characteristic-Specific Classification System. The system provides for four general classes of behavior: cognitive, motor, social, and communication. These classes were adapted from B. Bloom's (1956) taxonomy of educational objectives. The cognitive class of behaviors includes a range of academically related objectives. Skill clusters that comprise this class are identified in figure 2.4.

FIGURE 2.4   Characteristic-Specific Classification of Cognitive Skills

FIGURE 2.5 Characteristic-Specific Classification of Motor Skills

MOTOR SKILL CLASS	PERFORMANCE FACTORS: Degree		PERFORMANCE FACTORS: Nature			Influencing Events	
Sample skill clusters:	*Current Level*	*Expected Level*	*Skill Deficit*	*Motivational Deficit*	*Discrimination Deficit*	*Antecedents*	*Consequences*
Strength Speed Agility Dexterity Flexibility Coordination Reaction Balance Fine Motor Skill Gross Motor Skill							

It is likely that many learners currently described as mentally retarded and learning disabled have a substantial number of deficiencies in this area.

The motor class of behaviors includes responses that require fine and gross motor skills. Figure 2.5 enumerates the skill clusters that comprise this class. Students currently described as orthopedically impaired, health impaired, multiply handicapped, and visually handicapped are likely to exhibit deficiencies in this class of behaviors.

The social class of behaviors includes skills necessary for establishing and maintaining interpersonal relationships with peers, adults, employers, service providers, and so on. Disruptive social responses (e.g., irrational fears, anxiety, aggression) are also included within the social class. Skill clusters that comprise this class are identified in figure 2.6. Children and youth served in programs for the seriously emotionally disturbed are likely to exhibit excessive or deficient responses identified in this class.

The communication class of behaviors includes skills involving receptive and expressive language. Written, spoken, gestural, and other forms of

FIGURE 2.6 Characteristic-Specific Classification of Social Skills

	PERFORMANCE FACTORS							
	Degree		Nature			Influencing Events		
SOCIAL SKILL CLASS	Current Level	Expected Level	Skill Deficit	Motivational Deficit	Discrimination Deficit	Antecedents		Consequences
Sample skill clusters:								
Receptive: Positive Assertion								
Receptive: Negative Assertion								
Receptive: Questions								
Receptive: Initiating Conversation								
Receptive: Maintaining Conversation								
Receptive: Terminating Conversation								
Expressive: Positive Assertion								
Receptive: Negative Assertion								
Receptive: Questions								
Receptive: Initiating Conversation								
Receptive: Maintaining Conversation								
Receptive: Terminating Conversation								

communication are subsumed by this response class. Figure 2.7 identifies the skill clusters that are included in this class. Learners currently described as deaf, deaf-blind, hard of hearing, speech impaired, and visually handicapped often exhibit deficiencies in this class of behaviors.

Severity of Exceptionality

■ 4   The responses that set handicapped individuals apart from the general population differ in degree, not in kind (Gardner, 1977; Hallahan & Kauffman, 1976; Kauffman, 1981; L. Phillips, Draguns, & Bartlett, 1975; Quay & Werry, 1979). Handicapped individuals do not exhibit responses that are topographically different from those of an average student. From time to time, most students have sworn, have been late for class, have failed to complete assignments, have answered test items incorrectly, and so on. However, typical students do not engage in these responses at an excessive high rate of intensity or duration.

FIGURE 2.7 Characteristic-Specific Classification of Communication Skills

PERFORMANCE FACTORS

COMMUNICATION SKILL CLASS Sample skill clusters:	Degree		Nature			Influencing Events	
	Current Level	Expected Level	Skill Deficit	Motivational Deficit	Discrimination Deficit	Antecedents	Consequences
Spelling Grammar Handwriting Dictionary Skills Reading Oral Expression Aural Comprehension							

○ **3**   The severity of exceptionality—the extent to which a learner's behavior deviates from social norms—is established through a three-step process. First, for each potential skill deficit, data are obtained that provide a reliable indication of the student's performance level. Assessment data may result from criterion-referenced techniques (see chapters 5 and 6) and/or from norm-referenced measures (Salvia & Ysseldyke, 1985). When possible, multiple measures should be used to establish performance levels. Second, the multidisciplinary team determines the level of performance expected of the student. Expected levels may be drawn from normative data (e.g., the average student's level on the developmental curriculum sequence, average performance on standardized tests, rate of occurrence of observed responses from average students in mainstream classes) and from the subjective judgments of the multidisciplinary staff.

Finally, the discrepancy between measured student performance and expected performance is determined. When the discrepancy is sufficiently large, the response may be included as an objective in the learner's educational program. It should be emphasized that this discrepancy will not be the only criterion for selecting educational objectives. The chronological age, developmental level, and anticipated future environments in which the student will compete may also be considered when prioritizing objectives. The strategy is summarized in Action Plan 2.1.

ACTION PLAN 2.1   SEVERITY OF A SPECIFIC DEFICIT

We recommend the following procedures for determining the extent of a student's problem and establishing objectives:

1. Determine the student's current performance level using criterion-referenced or norm-referenced measures.
2. Determine the level of performance expected given the student's chronological age.
3. Determine the discrepancy between the student's current behavior and the expected behavior.
4. Repeat this process for all potential skill deficits exhibited by the student.
5. Prioritize the resulting discrepancies from most to least critical for the student's future adjustment.
6. Establish instructional objectives for priority deficits.

The Nature of the Deficiency

■ 5   Consistent with the views of Gardner (1977), similar performance patterns within and between individuals may result from different etiological factors. Recognition of the nature of these performance problems may assist in developing educational interventions. Therefore, it may be useful for an intraindividual classification scheme to specify the nature of performance problems.

○ 4   Skill deficits, motivational deficits, and/or discrimination deficits underlie the majority of educationally relevant exceptionality characteristics. These factors may operate separately, but it is far more likely that they will occur in combination. The associations between skill and motivational deficits (Mager & Pipe, 1984) and between motivational and discrimination deficits (Zeaman & House, 1963) have been a frequent theme of the professional literature. Recognition of skill problems may lead the educator to utilize instructional procedures (task analysis, shaping, modeling); motivational problems may be addressed through reinforcement procedures (token systems); and discrimination deficits may be addressed by teaching the conditions under which the desired behavior should occur. These strategies will be discussed in later chapters.

Skill deficits are defined by the absence of a response in the student's repertoire. They may be identified by determining whether the individual has ever performed the behavior (a review of achievement data suggests that the student has consistently missed items involving multiplication facts); whether the learner does not perform the response under highly motivating conditions (the learner adds incorrectly even when the correct response would produce highly desirable free time); and whether the student has demonstrated an inability to perform the component steps of a complex behavior (the student has demonstrated an inability to count, so it is unlikely that he or she can add).

Motivational deficits are defined by the student's failure to perform a behavior even though the prerequisite skills are present in his or her repertoire. Motivational deficits may be identified by determining whether or not the student has ever been observed to engage in the behavior. If the student has performed the behavior, one may assume that he or she possesses the skill but that the motivational conditions are not sufficiently strong to ensure performance. For example, a student may be on-task for an average of 30 minutes during math study and 10 minutes during language study. Because the student has demonstrated the ability to remain on-task for 30 minutes in math, one may assume that the attention deficit in language is a function of the motivational conditions. Similarly, a student may fail to use social amenities when addressing customers and co-workers during on-the-

ACTION PLAN 2.2   DETERMINING THE NATURE OF A DEFICIENCY

We recommend the following procedures for identifying the nature of a problem:

Skill Deficit
1. The student has never been observed to perform the skill.
2. The student does not perform the skill under the most reinforcing conditions.
3. The student is unable to perform one or more of the components of a complex skill.

Motivational Deficit
1. The student performs the skill at inconsistent times.
2. The student only performs the skill under highly rewarding conditions.

Discrimination Deficit
1. The student performs the skill under the wrong circumstances.
2. The student is unable to identify the conditions under which the skill should be performed.

job training. Because the student has often been observed to use amenities when asking for special privileges from his or her employer or teachers, we may speculate that the student is not motivated to use amenities with customers and co-workers.

Discrimination deficits result when an individual possesses the skill and motivation necessary to engage in the desired behavior but is not aware of appropriate conditions for performing the behavior. Discrimination deficits may occur through the learner engaging in an appropriate response under the wrong conditions (e.g., reading aloud during silent reading time) or failing to engage in a desirable behavior at the correct time (e.g., failing to work quickly on a timed test). In both cases, the learner's ability to discriminate appropriate performance conditions may be developed by teaching and motivating him or her to perform the behavior only under the target conditions. Procedures for determining the nature of a deficiency are summarized in Action Plan 2.2.

Events Influencing the Deficiency

■ 6   The final aspect of classifying intraindividual differences that is important to educational decisions involves the identification of influencing events—that is, cue conditions and motivational conditions that may influence the rate, duration, magnitude, or quality of the target behavior. Recognition of the influencing events provides a direct link to the design of the educational program by suggesting classroom conditions that might maximize student performance.

○ 5   *Antecedent events* are conditions that precede cognitive, motor, social, or communication responses and influence the strength or quality of their performance. Antecedent events typically involve the general instructional conditions, including interactions between teacher and student, level of difficulty of assignments, age appropriateness of materials, time of day, proximity to peers, level of prompts or assistance provided by the teacher, and so on. Although numerous conditions are present in the classroom prior to instruction, antecedent events are only those events that are functionally related to the occurrence of target responses. Materials that neither increase nor decrease the rate of a student's accurate responses are not antecedents. Conversely, materials that produce a high rate of accurate responses are considered antecedents. Similarly, low-interest materials that are associated with high off-task rates and other disruptive social responses are also considered relevant antecedents.

Consequent events are conditions that follow cognitive, motor, social, or communication responses and influence the strength or quality of their performance. Consequent events are typically described as motivational conditions. Common consequent or motivational events include praise from the teacher, pride of accomplishment, grades, free time, parental approval, and peer recognition. As with antecedents, numerous consequent events may occur in the classroom following target responses. These events are considered consequent events only if they are functionally related to the target behavior. Self-pride, praise, free time, and so on, are not identified as consequences unless their influence on the student's performance can be

ACTION PLAN 2.3   PROCEDURES FOR IDENTIFYING INFLUENCING EVENTS

We recommend that teachers identify events that influence performance problems through the following procedures:

1. Define the performance problem.
2. Observe the student during times the performance problem or related behaviors are likely to occur.
3. Record events that occur immediately prior to the occurrence of the target skill or behavior (e.g., specific instructions, materials used, proximity of peers, group size).
4. Record events that occur immediately following the target skill or behavior (e.g., peer or teacher attention, praise, feedback, removal of work).
5. After several observations, read over the recorded events and look for patterns.
6. Design instruction accordingly.

CASE FOR ACTION 2.1

During an IEP staffing, the school psychologist recommends that a student receive certain types of instruction because he or she has been diagnosed as learning disabled. You disagree with the use of this label because of the potential harm it may cause the student and the limited confidence you have in its usefulness in prescribing instruction. What will you say to the psychologist about these two issues? What alternative will you suggest?

established. For example, praise may be identified as a (reinforcing) consequence if the use of praise increases the speed and accuracy of the student's academic performance.

Antecedent and consequent events are important contributors to the classification of intraindividual characteristics. Knowing the actual exceptional characteristic provides a target for instructional objectives (e.g., the learner will print his or her first name). The degree of the exceptional characteristic indicates the criterion for mastery (e.g., nine of ten times). Finally, influencing events data provide greater detail for the instructional condition (e.g., how many successive approximations of an accurately printed name result in free time in the activity center). Procedures for identifying antecedent and consequent events are summarized in Action Plan 2.3.

SELECTION OF EXCEPTIONAL CHARACTERISTICS

■ 7   The preceding section outlined an empirical classification approach that goes beyond the study of between-student differences to consider within-student variables. The system was described as especially relevant to educational methods for mildly handicapped learners. The major feature that recommends the use of the system by classroom educators is that the data it contains are sufficiently comprehensive to be translated directly into IEP objectives.

Probably the single most critical element in using the system is the careful selection of exceptional characteristics. Exceptional children and youth vary along a number of learning and behavioral dimensions. Often, the number of excessive and/or deficient behavioral features precludes intervention that focuses on all exceptional characteristics. Consequently, the multidisciplinary staff and the learner must establish instructional priorities.

The importance of prioritizing intervention targets can be highlighted by a review of the learning and behavioral features of mildly handicapped learners. In general, data suggest the following:

- Handicapped learners do not acquire information at a rate commensurate with their nonhandicapped peers (Madle, 1983; Myklebust, 1960; N. M. Robinson & Robinson, 1976).
- Handicapped learners do not acquire the same amount of information over an extended period of instruction as nonhandicapped students (Hallahan & Kauffman, 1976, 1982; Telford & Sawrey, 1972).

- Handicapped students will forget acquired information sooner than their nonhandicapped peers. This is particularly true if the information is not used fairly often (Kirk & Gallagher, 1983; Robinson & Robinson, 1976; Telford & Sawrey, 1972).
- Handicapped individuals are less likely to acquire information that is incidental to the central learning task (A. L. Brown, Campione, & Gilliard, 1974; N. R. Ellis, 1970).
- Information gained under one set of instructional conditions is less likely to transfer or generalize to different conditions (Robinson & Robinson, 1976).

These assertions generally indicate that handicapped individuals are likely to learn less efficiently than their nonhandicapped peers, though again we must caution the reader that these generalizations *do not* apply to all special education students. When these generalizations are valid, however, the handicapped child or youth may progress through traditional developmentally sequenced curricula at a substantially slower rate than nonhandicapped students. Information acquired through the traditional curriculum sequence may be forgotten shortly after instruction (particularly if it is not utilized frequently), and health, sensory, and emotional problems may result in the student not being available for learning during critical instructional periods. The latter two events may produce gaps in the student's knowledge base. Consequently, handicapped learners are likely to enter secondary and postsecondary environments at a lower level of general academic development than the general population. They may also be more likely to have deficiencies in developmentally important competencies. Finally, the handicapped youth may be less likely to apply acquired skills across a range of critical life situations.

Careful selection of educational objectives within cognitive, motor, social, and communication domains has the potential of ensuring that the information and skills acquired are most likely to be maintained and reinforced in subsequent educational and independent living environments. In general, because less information will be acquired and retained, educators must be careful that target skills are most usable by the individual.

Unfortunately, there is no simple rule or protocol to follow in prescribing instructional objectives. Strict adherence to a curriculum sequence based on competencies acquired by the general population at various developmental levels may result in excessive exposure to basic skills training. This focus may exclude the development of functional skills that are likely to be utilized and reinforced in postsecondary environments. Conversely, application of a functional skills curriculum that matches objectives to the demands of independent living may exclude acquisition of developmentally important basic skills that are prerequisite to secondary level competencies. Therefore, several important factors must be considered when selecting instructional objectives: learning characteristics, behavioral characteristics, availability of instruction, and chronological age.

Learning Characteristics

■ 8 ○ 6   The rate at which a student acquires, retains, and generalizes information suggests the scope of knowledge that may be developed through the school years. Students who have demonstrated strong learning characteristics through previous academic performance and standardized tests may be placed in a developmentally sequenced curriculum. The expectation may be that the student will progress through the range of critical objectives that promote adult adjustment prior to graduation. Students with learning characteristics that are less well developed may be placed in curriculum sequences that are more directly focused on functional skills. Developmentally sequenced objectives for these learners may be used to the extent that they facilitate direct acquisition of functional skills.

Behavioral Characteristics

The student's current behavioral repertoire, or total number and quality of skills acquired, is an equally important factor in establishing curriculum objectives. Students with well-developed cognitive, motor, social, and communication repertoires may benefit from educational experiences that build directly on these existing skills. Individuals with poorly developed repertoires require a more analytic approach. For these youngsters, the multidisciplinary team may consider which deficit skills, if developed, would produce the greatest degree of success and satisfaction in adult environments. As with students with deficient learning characteristics, a developmentally sequenced curriculum may be secondary to training approaches focused on functional skills.

Availability of Instruction

Beyond recognition of a student's learning and behavioral features, the multidisciplinary team may consider the total time per day, semester, or year during which the student is available for instruction. Availability of instruction includes such dimensions as educational resources that affect the amount of direct instruction (e.g., tutoring programs, resource services, summer school programs), the student's rate of attendance, and the likelihood of the student exhibiting behavioral or health problems that remove him or her from the educational environment. These factors influence the level of progress that may be obtained through the student's school career. Students with limited available instructional time may benefit from direct functional skills training. Conversely, those for whom a substantial amount of available instructional time is anticipated may benefit from a more developmental orientation.

Chronological Age

■ 9   The number of years remaining in the student's educational career may be an equally important factor in establishing curriculum objectives. Young students are more likely to benefit from developmentally sequenced curric-

ACTION PLAN 2.4   FUNCTIONAL VERSUS DEVELOPMENTAL CURRICULUM

We recommend the following checklist for identifying factors that indicate adoption of a functional or a developmental curriculum:

A functional curriculum should be adopted if:

- The learner has significant difficulty learning new skills.
- The student has not kept pace with his or her peers in the total number of skills acquired.
- The student is actually engaged in instructional activities a very small portion of the day.
- The student is approaching graduation.

A developmental curriculum should be adopted if:

- The student acquires new skills fairly efficiently.
- The student has kept pace or is only slightly behind the level of his or her peers.
- The student spends a substantial part of the school day engaged in instruction.
- The student will receive a number of years of instruction before graduation.

ulum objectives, which will form the basis for functional skills to be developed in secondary educational programs. Older students, because of the limited instructional time prior to entering independent adult environments, are more likely to benefit from functional skills training activities. Because handicapped learners have difficulty applying information across a variety of dissimilar conditions, the secondary level is especially critical to the generalization of skills across functional environments. Factors that should be considered when selecting between a functional or developmental curriculum are presented in Action Plan 2.4.

CURRICULUM DEVELOPMENT

The primary philosophy of curriculum development that is advocated in this text is toward developing functional skills—the skills that are needed to interact successfully in specific environments. Examples of functional skills include writing a check, making change for a quarter, and filling in a job application.

Another curriculum philosophy fosters the teaching of developmental skills. Most regular school curricula follow this model, in which skills are developed sequentially and in predictable patterns. Developmental skills include such things as adding and subtracting, handwriting, and reading.

Our view of the two philosophies is that they are both applicable in making decisions about instructional objectives for handicapped learners. However, the age of the learner is the critical feature that determines the model to be followed in deciding on instructional objectives. Most commercial curriculum series contain the normal sequential development of skills in math, reading, and language arts. The curriculum content chapters of this book will also identify some of these sequences. A curriculum based on the development of functional skills is not so commonly available, however. Therefore, we will describe such a curriculum process in detail in this section.

Action Plan 2.5 illustrates a curriculum process designed for arriving at functional curriculum objectives. The sequence of activities is intended (1) to establish the skills required for successful adjustment in adult environments; (2) to ensure that enabling skills that underlie the functional goals are developed in developmentally sound sequences; (3) to recommend available materials and activities that correspond with the instructional objectives; and (4) to provide evaluation materials that establish the learner's level of proficiency in the target skills before and after instruction. The following sections will describe this decision-making process.

ACTION PLAN 2.5   PROCESS FOR PROMOTING FUNCTIONAL CURRICULUM OBJECTIVES

Identify current and future environments in which the learner is expected to participate.

↓

Observe others in these settings to determine necessary skills for successful participation.

↓

Develop a skills checklist that assesses learner competence in using the skills required by the setting.

↓

Apply the checklist to determine skills the student possesses and skills that are deficient.

↓

Determine skills that may be accommodated through prosthetics (e.g., calculators, charts, color codes, amplification).

↓

Delineate developmentally sound task sequences that deal with skill deficits not accommodated through prosthetics.

↓

Provide educational experiences that promote acquisition of the skill sequences.

↓

Assess the learner, using the skills checklist, to determine the effectiveness of instruction and the degree to which the learner is prepared to participate in the target environment.

Identify Current and Future Environments

○ **7**   We have repeatedly emphasized that the functional curriculum prepares learners to compete in natural environments outside the school setting. These environments generally include residential, vocational, recreational, and transportation settings. For learners of elementary school age, the future environment will be secondary school placement. Educators working with elementary school aged handicapped learners generally know the expectations for those learners in a secondary school setting, and the curriculum must focus on the skills needed to function in that environment. It is likely that the acquisition of developmentally based skills underlie much of what is needed to be successful in secondary school environments. For example, basic language, reading, and math skills are important to success in most areas of secondary school functioning and in the out-of-school environments in which a learner will participate.

For secondary school aged learners, entry-level skills required in specific occupations, living arrangements, or recreational settings can also be predicted. What may be difficult is identifying the specific jobs, living arrangements, and recreational settings. Parental involvement in the planning process is therefore critical. The importance of an accurate prediction at this point cannot be overstated. Specific vocational, residential, recreational, and transportation skills that are developed in school and used in the community will remain a lasting and important part of the learner's repertoire. Those skills that are not used periodically in natural settings will be quickly forgotten.

Observe Others

Even within similar environments, such as grocery stores or restaurants, subtle differences occur that influence skill requirements. Locating a restroom, for example, may involve recognition of the words *men/women*, *lad/lass*, *ladies/gentlemen*, or an international symbol, depending on the specific establishment. The most efficient way to ensure that the learner is prepared to compete in an environment is to identify the precise skill requirements for specific settings. One approach to accomplishing this objective is to observe and enumerate skills utilized by other individuals in these environments. For example, observing an attendant at the corner gas station may produce a list of skills that includes counting change, writing a sales slip, using a cash register, cleaning windshields, cleaning restrooms, and so on. These observed skills can become the focus of the learner's educational program.

Develop a Skills Checklist

○ **8**   The final product of this curriculum process will be the development of functional skills matched to natural environments. Commercially available criterion-referenced and norm-referenced testing materials sample from a range of generic competencies. However, many of the skills required for success in a specific functional environment are not likely to be sampled by these instruments. Consequently, the educator should devise a skills checklist based on the precise skills observed in the setting. The skills checklist may take various forms. The skill sequences may be enumerated in a single column, and functionally similar skills may be grouped for the sake of convenience (e.g., cleaning skills, social skills, language skills, math skills). Next to this column may be (1) a simple "can perform" or "cannot perform" statement, (2) a rating indicating the relative quality of performance (e.g., poor to excellent), or (3) a rating indicating the level of external prompts needed to produce performance (e.g., self-directed, verbal prompts, modeling prompts, physical prompts).

Pretest with the Checklist

The learner's preinstruction skills may be evaluated using the checklist. The most reliable method of collecting student performance data is to observe the student in the actual setting, scoring performance against the checklist criteria. A less reliable but more economical and practical method is to construct simulation exercises in the classroom, such as bagging groceries, counting change, sweeping floors, and so on. As a simple test of the reliability or accuracy of checklist data, two professionals can score the learner's performance independently. Scores for the two observers may then be compared by dividing the number of agreed-upon ratings by the total number of skills rated. For instructional purposes, interobserver agreement of .70 (representing agreement on seven of ten skills rated) is generally considered sufficient. Low reliability generally results from vague or incomplete skill descriptions or imprecise evaluation criteria. Thus, reliability is often improved by clarifying the response definition and evaluation criteria.

Determine Skills to Be Accommodated Through Prosthetics

■ 10   Skill deficiencies can be overcome through training or through prosthetics. The use of calculators, charts, and color codes may overcome the necessity for extensive instruction in many areas. However, the educator must weigh the advantages and disadvantages of the two approaches. The major question is the extent to which the anticipated amount of additional training will be offset by long-term benefit to the students. Aside from the educator's recommendations, a useful source of data for making this decision may be the opinions of significant persons in the target environment (e.g., employers, store clerks, waitresses).

Delineate Developmentally Sound Task Sequences

○ 9   The majority of skill deficits identified through the performance checklist will be too broad to be dealt with in one or two instructional periods. Therefore, it is often necessary to break these skills down into more manageable instructional steps. This process is referred to throughout the literature as a *task analysis*. Washing dishes, for example, may be broken down into steps such as scraping food from plates, drawing the water, adding soap, inserting the dishes, and so on. The size of the steps in the task sequence is a function of the learning characteristics of the student. For example, the components for changing a tire may be very large for a more gifted learner (e.g., obtain tools and spare from trunk, remove hub cap and loosen lug nuts, jack up car, etc.) but very small for a less adaptive youth (e.g., open trunk, locate spare tire, loosen tie-down from spare tire, remove spare tire, locate tire iron, etc.). Finally, depending on the nature of the skill, the skill may be forward-chained (teaching the first step, second, third, and so on, until the entire sequence is mastered) or backward-chained (teaching the last step, second to the last and last, third to the last, second to the last, and last, and so on).

Provide Educational Experiences

○ **10**   Consistent evidence in the educational literature suggests that handicapped learners are most likely to benefit from instruction presented through (1) concrete materials; (2) multiple modalities, including the auditory, visual, tactile, and kinesthetic modes; (3) distributed drill and practice; and (4) frequent feedback and reinforcement. For a majority of specific skill sequences, the actual environment in which the skills are to be applied may be the most closely matched training environment. In addition, consistent evidence in the special education literature emphasizes the limited extent to which skills trained in one setting are likely to generalize to another setting (Wehman, Abramson, & Norman, 1977). Training in the natural environment eliminates the need for generalization from school to functional settings.

Unfortunately, training in the natural environment is substantially less convenient and more costly than school-based instruction. As a result, training outside of school may be reserved for the later stages of skill development (e.g., trips to a shopping mall as a culminating experience to a consumer unit, or a work-study placement in the later phases of a vocational program). To prepare for these limited experiences in natural environments, three stages of instruction may be considered. In the first stage, basic component skills may be developed through seatwork, using the general instructional principles outlined previously. In the second, the educator may simulate the requirements of the natural setting. Students can then work to some degree of proficiency in the simulated setting. Finally, the instruction may move to the natural environment.

This process is exemplified by an instructional sequence designed to prepare learning disabled adolescents to shop in a grocery store. In the

CASE FOR ACTION 2.2

It has become apparent that the developmental curriculum used in your special education district is not applicable to many students. Therefore, you are asked to chair a curriculum committee to design a functional curriculum. The curriculum must cover an age range from 5 to 21 and must be applicable for all mildly handicapped students. What guidelines will you establish for using the functional curriculum with a given student? How will you develop this functional curriculum?

seatwork phase, the educator uses standard instructional materials to teach basic consumer skills (e.g., addition, subtraction, basic sight words, social skills). In the simulation phase, the educator arranges the classroom to resemble a grocery store, including markers requiring use of the sightwords and a checkout counter requiring math and social skills. Students may then use the skills developed through seatwork to solve problems in the simulated environment. Finally, in the last stage, the students may actually apply the skills in the natural environment.

Posttest with the Checklist

A logical final activity in the curriculum sequence involves assessing the learner to determine the extent to which skills have been acquired. The checklist described earlier is an ideal instrument for conducting this evaluation. The use of this instrument before and after instruction demonstrates the effectiveness of instruction in helping learners acquire the functional objectives. The assessment data may also indicate areas in which further instruction is required.

SUMMARY

It should be clear that the selection of goals and objectives for exceptional education programs is not an unidimensional effort. Questions that must be addressed include the following:

- Should the objectives increase or decrease the strength of the target behavior?

- What is the optimal level of performance expected for the target response?
- Should the objectives involve the acquisition of new responses (skill development), increase or decrease the rate and consistency with which responses occur (motivational development), and/or enhance the learner's ability to identify conditions in which the behaviors should be exhibited (discrimination development)?
- Under what instructional conditions are the target cognitive, motor, social, or communication behaviors likely to be acquired most efficiently?
- Finally, what specific cognitive, motor, social, or communication responses should be influenced by the educational program?

The final section of this chapter outlined a series of curriculum development and implementation activities. These procedures are intended to ensure that educational targets influence the learner's adjustment to adult environments. The following chapters will describe procedures for utilizing this curriculum process.

3

Coordination of Services

■ 1 ...teachers are usually responsible for coordinating special education services?

■ 2 ...educational environments range from normal to highly restrictive?

■ 3 ...more restrictive placements should be used only when options closer to the mainstream have not been successful?

■ 4 ...coordination among service providers is needed to identify student characteristics, performance goals, settings, and services needed?

■ 5 ...the classroom special education teacher may exert substantial influence on the decisions of the multidisciplinary team?

■ 6 ...parents are an important source of information and support at all stages of a multidisciplinary team's actions?

■ 7 ...the IEP is used to coordinate efforts across settings, over time, and among service providers?

■ 8 ...annual goals are based on a student's current performance levels and can be broken down into short-term objectives?

■ 9 ...evaluation procedures and schedules are established to directly monitor progress toward objectives?

■ 10 ...interaction with nonhandicapped peers is important to the student's adult social adjustment?

■ 11 ...the IEP must identify related services and indicate the time frame and the exact nature of these services?

○ CAN YOU . . .

○ **1**   . . . identify the data on an IEP that ensure that a least restrictive environment is used?

○ **2**   . . . select the most appropriate placement from Deno's Cascade of Services model, given a student's learning and behavioral characteristics?

○ **3**   . . . establish a procedure for objectively determining whether a change in placement is warranted?

○ **4**   . . . formulate an appropriate multidisciplinary team for a specific student and outline each member's role?

○ **5**   . . . recommend specialized support personnel who should be on a multidisciplinary team for a student with specific disabilities?

○ **6**   . . . inform parents of their rights (under PL 94–142) regarding evaluation, placement, and programming decisions?

○ **7**   . . . use the information in an IEP to implement the decisions of the multidisciplinary team?

○ **8**   . . . identify sources of assessment information that could be used·to determine current levels of performance.

○ **9**   . . . write the short-term objectives of an annual goal that include the four principal components?

○ **10**   . . . describe the types of data you would collect for an annual evaluation?

○ **11**   . . . identify possible arrangements that might be made to obtain related services not available in the school district?

■ 1   The first chapter of this text highlighted both scholarly and legislative influences supporting an empirical orientation to special education. The interaction of these two influences has produced a body of knowledge that may assist the educator in (1) identifying individuals with special needs, (2) establishing curriculum priorities, (3) adopting instructional procedures that have the greatest potential for promoting achievement, and (4) monitoring student performance to ensure the student's continued success. Teachers do not implement these procedures in a vacuum. As was emphasized in chapter 2, teachers are part of a multidisciplinary team. They must work with other professionals in developing and implementing individualized education programs. The coordination of services, from initial screening to the termination of special involvement, is a critical aspect of effective educational programs. Although practices may vary in different districts, the special educator is typically responsible for coordinating special education services. Therefore, this chapter discusses the teacher's role in coordinating the special education program.

COORDINATION ACROSS SETTINGS

Coordination of services, as discussed in this chapter, occurs within three major dimensions: across settings, over time, and among service providers. The most basic is the coordination of services across settings. Few issues have raised as much controversy as the setting in which education services should be provided (Sindelar, 1981). Researchers and writers have argued for both the positive influences (Christopolos & Renz, 1969; Ensher, 1980; MacMillian, 1971; Peterson & Haralick, 1977; Reynolds, 1962) and the adverse influences (Carlberg & Kavale, 1980; Clark, 1978; Cruickshank, 1982; Gottlieb, 1981; Gresham, 1982; Ysseldyke & Algozzine, 1982) of various special education environments. Although consensus has not been reached on this issue, federal mandates have provided rigorous guidelines for settings in which special education services are to be provided.

○ 1   With reference to special education environments, PL 94-142 requires that the Individualized Education Program (IEP) specify the extent to which the student will participate in mainstream environments with nonhandicapped peers. Also, the anticipated duration and precise nature of special placement and services must be identified. The underlying rationale for the inclusion of these data is to ensure compliance with the "least restrictive environment" provision.

In reviewing the literature, Ruhl (1983) identified three positive outcomes supporting education in least restrictive environments. First, handicapped persons educated in regular education settings perform at least as well as those in special classes. Gottlieb's (1981) review of ten efficacy studies supported this view, indicating nonsignificant differences in five studies and significant differences favoring settings other than self-contained class-rooms. Second, integration in regular education settings enhances social skills, self-esteem, and adult adjustment. Finally, nonhandicapped persons are expected to acquire greater acceptance and tolerance of handicapped persons who are mainstreamed into their classrooms.

One approach to the coordination of special education services across settings that is particularly prominent in the literature is Evelyn Deno's (1970) "cascade of services." The cascade model, depicted in figure 3.1, arranges seven service options from least restrictive (Level I) to most restric-

FIGURE 3.1   Deno's Cascade System of Special Education Service

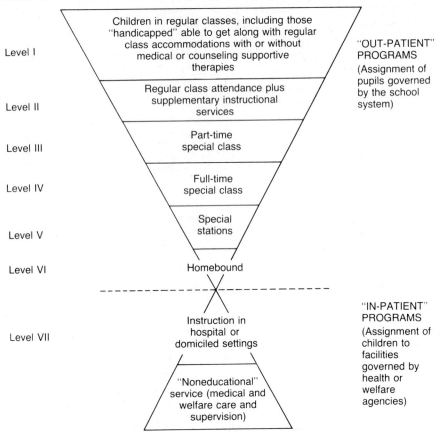

Source: From "Special Education as Developmental Capital" by Evelyn Deno. *Exceptional Children*, 1970, *37*(3), 229–237. Copyright 1970 by the Council for Exceptional Children. Reprinted by permission.

tive (Level VII). The shape of the cone emphasizes the number of service options that are available to handicapped learners. Although seven discrete services are depicted in the model, innumerable options may occur through various combinations. Mildly handicapped individuals, comprising the greatest incidence of special populations, are expected to be served closer to the upper end of the cascade. More severely handicapped learners, compromising a lower incidence, are expected to be served in the middle to lower end of the cascade. A student may move from one level to another whenever a revision is made in the learner's educational plan.

■ 2   The cascade model has four implications for special educators and ancillary service providers. These implications conform to the "least restrictive environment" mandate of PL 94-142:

1. Educational service personnel should provide a range of placements that serve the changing needs of handicapped learners. Service options for the mildly handicapped range from full-time special classes to the regular classroom, with or without support services. More severely handicapped learners may require more restrictive services in special day schools or residential school programs.

2. The greatest number of mildly handicapped students will be served in closest to normal educational settings. Placement in more restrictive settings is limited to the relatively smaller number of individuals who may not be adequately served in the upper levels of the cascade.

3. Educational service providers should continually monitor students' performance to determine whether a change in placement would enhance performance. A student's placement may change whenever the multidisciplinary team obtains data suggesting the advisability of an alternative placement.

4. An immediate goal of the educational program is to move the learner to less restrictive settings. As adaptive cognitive, social, motor, and language skills are developed, the student may become more able to compete in less restrictive settings. The multidisciplinary staff should monitor these changes and move the learner to a less restrictive setting as appropriate.

○ 2   The first level of the cascade model, *handicapped students in regular classes,* represents the least restrictive of the available options. This environment includes placement in the normal curriculum, with or without support services. Supportive services parallel those available for typical students, including guidance counseling, remedial reading, tutorial assistance, and the like.

The second level, *attendance in regular classes plus supplementary services*, involves placement in regular classes with support services beyond those considered typical for nonhandicapped students. Supplementary services may include prosthetic devices (e.g., talking books, calculators, wheelchairs) modifications in the curriculum, and the assistance of an educational consultant.

The third level, *part-time special class*, typically includes students who require more intensive instruction than can be provided in the regular education setting. Resource room programs account for the majority of services provided in this area. Instruction provided in resource rooms generally includes special tutorial assistance paralleling concepts developed in the regular curriculum, compensatory skills that overcome the student's limitations in regular curricular areas, and functional skills that prepare the student to adapt to community demands.

The fourth level, *full-time special class*, is typically reserved for students who need intensive educational assistance. Depending on the nature of students' disabilities and the availability of an instructional aide, class size may be from 6 to 17 pupils. Students served in special classes should need a degree of structure that is not available in the regular classroom. These students may also require substantially more support from related disciplines (i.e., school psychologists, social workers, recreation therapists, physical and occupational therapists, etc.).

Features and objectives unique to self-contained classes are (1) an emphasis on developing social competence, which promotes adjustment to regular education settings; (2) the inclusion of services that promote vocational, cognitive, social, and leisure skills, leading to community adjustment; and (3) the provision of increased consistency and structure, which enhances handicapped learners' social and academic performance. The major drawback of self-contained classes is the limited interaction of handicapped students with more adaptive learners (Dunn, 1968).

The fifth level, *special stations*, involves placement in a building or complex apart from the campus of regular education programs. These stations may serve students with a variety of handicapping conditions or may be limited to children and youth with one type of disability. Special stations may provide a range of cognitive, motor, social, and communication enhancing activities, or they may specialize in one area, such as vocational development.

Special stations were originally designed to centralize services for handicapped persons, so that diagnostic, medical, instructional, therapeutic, and vocational specialties could all be located in and coordinated from one setting. Special stations may also provide a degree of structure that is not available even in self-contained classes in the regular school. To a greater extent than self-contained classes, however, special stations exclude handicapped persons from appropriate models. Therefore, they may be considered only after placements closer to the mainstream have proved un-successful.

The sixth level, *homebound services*, may be used under highly un-usual circumstances for a student who is confined to his or her residence. Typically, they are required when the student is bedridden or is dependent on unusual support apparatus confined to the home. Homebound services may be provided for a short period of time (e.g., for an accident victim) or may last indefinitely in the case of a chronic condition.

The most restrictive level, *instruction in hospital, residential, or total care settings*, involves full-time services in an isolated setting. These place-ments typically include inpatient mental health services, institutions for the severely and profoundly developmentally disabled, hospitalization, and intervention in a correctional facility. Several authors have raised seri-ous questions about such placements (L. Brown, Neitupski, & Hamre-Neitupski, 1976). The most obvious limitation is the exclusion of the handi-capped persons from the mainstream of society. Residential services should be reserved for those persons who cannot adjust to placement in special sta-tions or classes without imposing a moderate threat on their own or others' physical safety. Therefore, it is highly unlikely that even moderately handi-capped learners would be considered for this level of service.

COORDINATION OF SERVICES OVER TIME

The cascade of services model is characterized by free movement between levels, as indicated by the student's performance. A major question involves guidelines for movement to less restrictive environments over time. Once a student is served for a period of time at one level in the cascade model, what criteria are used to change placement to a more or less restrictive setting? Although federal guidelines emphasize the importance of collecting assess-ment data before identifying or altering placement, little guidance is offered regarding how the data are to be used.

Sindelar (1981) has suggested an empirical approach to moving the student through successively less (or more) restrictive placements over time. His procedures, summarized in Action Plan 3.1, rely heavily on the empiri-cal principles that underlie this text:

1. *Operationalize the instructional outcomes.* This procedure in-volves clearly and completely specifying the objectives of the instructional program so that they may be reliably assessed.

2. *Establish the criterion levels of performance.* Operational out-comes may be referenced against the performance of an age-matched peer

ACTION PLAN 3.1   EMPIRICAL APPROACH FOR MOVING STUDENTS TO LESS (OR MORE) RESTRICTIVE SETTINGS

Operationalize Instructional Outcomes
Establish measurable objectives for the educational program.

Establish the Criterion Levels of Performance
Determine the level of performance expected following successful instruction.

Determine the Expected Progress Toward Criterion Performance
Specify the rate at which the learner is expected to approach the criterion performance level.

Evaluate the Extent to Which the Student's Actual Performance Coincides with the Expected Performance
Contrast the student's progress with the expected rate of achievement.

If the student's performance is below expectations, revise the program or change to a more restrictive setting.

If the student's performance is at or near expectations, continue in the current setting.

If the student's performance exceeds expectations, move to a less restrictive setting.

group in the next less restrictive setting. When these data are not available, broader-based normative data may be used. For example, Starlin and Starlin (1973), Tomaras (1975), Guthrie, Seifert, Burnham, and Caplan (1974), and Patterson, Reid, Jones, and Conger (1975) have reported normative data for a variety of cognitive, social, motor, and communication skills. In addition, criteria may be derived from standardization data of norm-referenced achievement tests.

3. *Determine the expected progress toward criterion performance.* Having operationalized the instructional outcome and having established a

criterion for performance, the teacher next determines an acceptable rate of progress toward the criterion. The expected rate of progress is determined, to a large extent, by the amount of time available for instruction, the student's learning characteristics, and the discrepancy between the student's current performance and the performance criterion. Three sources of data may be useful in specifying the expected rate of progress for handicapped students: (1) the rate of progress toward the objective for students with similar learning characteristics, (2) the student's rate of progress toward similar objectives, and (3) the student's general performance gains over his or her school history (e.g., achievement level as assessed by standardized tests, divided by the total number of months or years of instruction). O. R. White and Liberty (1976) have proposed a similar list appropriate to the general population.

4. *Evaluate the extent to which the student's actual performance coincides with the expected performance.* This final step provides evidence of the appropriateness of placement over a period of time. Performance that continually meets or exceeds the expected rate of progress (see figure 3.2) may indicate movement to a less restrictive setting. This is especially true if

FIGURE 3.2 Student Performance Meeting or Exceeding Expected Progress Line

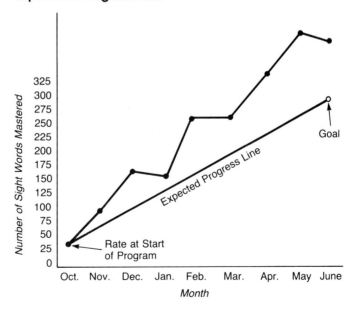

the student's expected rate of progress is within the range observed for students in the less restrictive setting. Performance that is frequently below the progress line (see figure 3.3) does not present as clear a recommendation. Consistent with the writings of Ysseldyke and Regan (1980), Sindelar (1981) argues that school personnel should systematically demonstrate that three or more program modifications in the less restrictive setting are ineffective before moving to a more restrictive placement. He cautions: "Even an empirically-based decision to move to a more restrictive environment should be made with caution because such movement does not necessarily imply improved educational progress" (p. 288).

Handicapped students' instructional programs generally include from three to seven goals. Consequently, the foregoing model may become substantially more complex. Rather than evaluating the restrictiveness of placement over time on the basis of one performance measure, data reflecting each goal should be considered. Guidelines for considering multiple goals in determining the appropriateness of placement include the following: (1) the student meets or exceeds the expected rate of progress for 75% of the goals; (2) goals that reflect social behaviors detrimental to the learner or other students exceed the expected rate of progress; and (3) resources and expertise are available in the less restrictive setting to maintain the rate of progress. These criteria are reflected in the checklist in Action Plan 3.2.

FIGURE 3.3   Student Performance Below Expected Progress Line

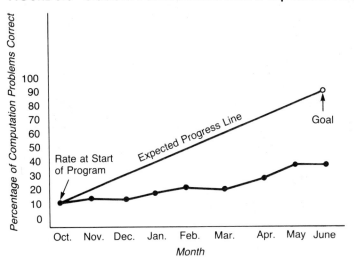

ACTION PLAN 3.2   DETERMINING THE APPROPRIATENESS OF SPECIAL EDUCATION SETTINGS

We recommend using the following checklist to determine whether a change in placement to a more or less restrictive setting is warranted:

Move to a less restrictive setting if:
- Student meets or exceeds the expected rate of progress for 75% of his or her goals.
- Social adjustment/management goals are met or exceeded.
- Resources are available in the less restrictive setting to maintain progress.

Move to a more restrictive setting if:
- Student falls below the expected rate of progress for 75% of his or her goals.
- Student falls below social adjustment/management goals to the extent that his or her behavior consistently disrupts the learning environment of others.
- Resources for carrying out an effective educational program in the present setting are not available.
- Three or more systematic attempts to enhance performance through a change in the educational program have been unsuccessful.

CASE FOR ACTION 3.1

You are an educator in an inpatient mental health center that serves adolescents with severe behavioral disorders. One of your responsibilities is to make recommendations to the diagnostic and treatment team regarding the appropriateness of reintegrating students you teach into community school settings. What information/data would you collect for each student that might be used to make this decision? What criteria would you establish for recommending the reintegration of a student into a community school?

COORDINATION AMONG SERVICE PROVIDERS

■ **4**   The preceding discussions highlight the role of a multidisciplinary team in the decision-making process. Another critical role of this team is the provision of direct services. Coordination among service providers refers to the extent to which various personnel provide complementary services directed at common goals. This may be contrasted with the provision of discrete services aimed at different goals. Coordination among service providers provides for continuous attention to relevant goals across educational settings. For example, communication skills developed by a language specialist may be reinforced by mainstream educators, by the resource teacher, by parents, and even by the bus driver.

As highlighted in Action Plan 3.3, coordination among service providers should occur in assessment, planning, and intervention processes. Coor-

ACTION PLAN 3.3   TEAM MEMBERS' RESPONSIBILITIES

We recommend the following cooperative responsibilities of team members:

Coordination during assessment:
- Team members raise assessment questions cooperatively.
- Team members provide information in their possession.
- Team members use individual expertise in obtaining missing data.
- Team members merge resulting data to provide a clear and complete picture of the student.

Coordination during planning:
- Team members jointly arrive at performance expectations.
- Team members jointly determine appropriate settings.
- Team members jointly determine appropriate services.

Coordination during intervention:
- Team members utilize individual expertise in providing instruction and supportive services.
- Team members cooperate in insuring that skills acquired in one setting are used in other settings.

dination during assessment requires (1) that educators, administrators, and ancillary service providers raise assessment questions cooperatively; (2) that each member of the team provide information already in his or her possession; (3) that efficient means for collecting missing data be identified that utilize the expertise of each team member; and (4) that the resulting data be merged so that a complete description of the student's learning and behavioral features emerges. Coordination during planning requires that the multidisciplinary team arrive at performance expectations cooperatively. These goals should reflect each team member's understanding of the learner from the perspective of his or her individual discipline. Once the goals are established, the team must collaborate in determining services and settings most likely to promote achievement. Finally, coordination during intervention requires that service providers work toward common goals. Although a guidance counselor may be primarily responsible for providing social skill training activities, all team members should promote the generalization of trained behaviors to their individual settings.

○ **4**   Having emphasized the importance of cooperative assessment, planning, and intervention, we will now describe the role of each member of the multidisciplinary team (see figure 3.4).

Regular Educator

The role of the regular educator at the elementary level may be substantially different from that at the secondary level. At the elementary level, teachers are typically child-centered, and the majority of instruction occurs through one teacher. At the secondary level, teachers are often subject-oriented. Instructors at the secondary level may be responsible for only one or two specialized classes. This difference influences the regular educator's

FIGURE 3.4 Potential Service Providers

Regular Educator
Administrator
Special Educator in a Special Class
Special Educator in a Resource Program
Vocational Personnel
School Psychologist
Speech and Language Specialist
Social Worker
Physical Therapist
Occupational Therapist
Other Professionals, as Indicated by the Student's Needs

role on the multidisciplinary team. Primary-level educators are likely to be generalists, possessing information on numerous facets of the child's educational development. Secondary-level educators may be more specialized and only able to provide information relative to a narrow area of achievement (e.g., home economics, civics, algebra, language).

In general, the regular educator may be expected (1) to provide assessment data (possibly anecdotal observations and permanent products) pertaining to the student's performance as referenced to his or her peers, (2) to carry out instructional activities agreed upon by the multidisciplinary team, and (3) to correspond frequently with other members of the multidisciplinary team regarding the student's current achievement level and approaches for enhancing performance.

Administrator

Technically, administrators do not provide direct service; rather, they coordinate and monitor services. Administrators' specific functions vary with their professional assignment. The director of special education (or his or her designate) must attend all IEP staffings in the district. Additional responsibilities include (1) receiving special education referrals; (2) scheduling IEP meetings; (3) monitoring compliance with federal, state, and local regulations; (4) identifying and obtaining nonpublic programs when services within the district are not appropriate; (5) investigating state and federal resources; (6) facilitating intra- and interdistrict transfers; and (7) promoting students' transition to postsecondary settings.

The building administrator or principal has the same responsibilities for the special education student as for other learners. The building administrator may also (1) monitor compliance with federal, state, and local special education regulations; (2) serve as the primary liaison between the educational unit and other agencies and parents; (3) coordinate services among school personnel; (4) evaluate the feasibility and legitimacy of course/curriculum modifications with regard to graduation requirements; and (5) schedule facilities and resources for special services.

Self-Contained Classroom Teacher

■ 5   The special education self-contained classroom teacher is responsible for providing the majority of educational services for 5 to 17 handicapped students with relatively homogeneous characteristics. The number of students served is generally determined by the severity of the handicapping condition and the availability of an instructional aide. The self-contained classroom teacher is responsible for the following activities: (1) attending the IEP meeting and participating in developing students' programs, (2) conducting educational evaluations and reporting findings to other members of the multidisciplinary team, (3) implementing the majority of the educational plan, (4) monitoring students' progress, (5) identifying settings and activities in which the student may be successfully integrated with nonhandicapped students, and (6) maintaining a cooperative relationship with the student's parents and other members of the multidisciplinary team.

More than any other special education service provider, the self-contained classroom teacher often becomes the focal point of the student's educational program. He or she may become the primary advocate for the student in the school program. As such, the self-contained classroom teacher may informally exert a substantial amount of influence on the decisions of other members of the multidisciplinary team. This influence is often justified in view of the amount of time and the range of instructional conditions in which he or she works with the student.

Resource Teacher

Unlike the special education self-contained classroom teacher, the resource teacher provides instruction for the student for a relatively short period of time (often less than an hour). Resource services are typically provided in one or two problem areas. At the elementary level, these may include math, written language, reading, and other basic academic subjects. At the secondary level, resource services may also be directed toward content areas such as history, health, or geography.

Specific responsibilities of the resource teacher include (1) participating in the development of the IEP, (2) collecting and reporting assessment data, (3) implementing instruction as agreed upon by the multidisciplinary team, (4) monitoring the student's progress, (5) maintaining a cooperative relationship with parents and other team members, and (6) consulting with regular classroom teachers who serve the student.

Vocational Personnel

At the secondary level, vocational educators play a significant role in promoting the transition from school to work. These professionals are often aware of available competitive job opportunities that handicapped students might pursue upon graduation. They are also knowledgeable about the competencies required for success in those positions. Finally, they are often responsible for developing basic vocational skills and on-the-job training activities for handicapped students.

The vocational director is responsible for the planning and administration of the school district's vocational education program. He or she maintains cooperative relationships with community employers and postsecondary education programs for the purpose of identifying future training or employment options. The vocational director is also responsible for monitoring the quality of the program as well as its compliance with state and federal regulations. Finally, the vocational director is responsible for organizing and conducting in-service training programs for vocational, special, and regular education personnel. Such staff development activities may be used to promote cooperative planning between the various disciplines.

The vocational educator is responsible for designing and conducting vocational components of the student's IEP. He or she may also serve as a consultant to other teachers to assist in directing curriculum activities toward objectives that promote adult adjustment in vocational, leisure, and independent living settings.

Support Personnel

○ **5**   A range of ancillary personnel may be required to meet the handicapped student's educational needs. The *school psychologist* is responsible for conducting psychological evaluations, interpreting the findings, and making recommendations to the multidisciplinary team. The school psychologist also serves an important role as a consultant in the area of interpersonal skill development and behavior management. Finally, the school psychologist may provide guidance and psychological counseling for the student and his or her parents.

The *speech and language specialist* is primarily responsible for screening and diagnosing students with speech and language problems. This specialist is also responsible for recommending speech and language services for inclusion in the IEP. He or she may also provide therapy identified in the IEP for children with speech production and receptive and expressive language difficulties. Finally, the speech and language specialist may serve as a consultant to the parents and other members of the multidisciplinary team. In this role, he or she may coordinate speech and language training activities across all service providers and parents.

The *social worker* collects the social history required by PL 94-142 as a basis for providing educational services. The social history may result from a review of educational, psychological, and medical records. It also includes information from parent and student interviews. The school social worker may also be responsible for coordinating educational services with other community and social service agencies. This process ensures that the student's domestic and health needs are met in and out of school. Finally, the social worker may serve as a liaison between the school and home. He or she may provide counseling for both the parents and the student.

The *physical and occupational therapists* assist in the development of fine and gross motor skills through exercise, massage, hydrotherapy, and other activities. They also provide or arrange for necessary prosthetic devices, including braces and wheelchairs.

The *school nurse* is primarily responsible for coordinating or providing medical services for handicapped students. The nurse's activities include ensuring that current health, vision, and hearing checkups have been conducted; obtaining pertinent health information from parents; consulting with other team members regarding the effects of specific medications; and consulting with team members regarding physical limitations resulting from the student's disability.

Parents

○ **6** According to the federal mandate, parents are also members of the multidisciplinary team. Although research has indicated that they are seldom influential in planning the educational program (Gilliam, 1979; Gilliam & Coleman, 1981), there is consistent agreement that they should be primary contributors to the decision-making process (Knoff, 1983). In emphasizing this role, PL 94-142 guarantees the following rights for parents:

1. Parents must provide written permission for a placement evaluation to be conducted.
2. The child's placement cannot be changed unless the parents receive written notification about the possible action.
3. Parents must approve the actual change in placement.
4. Parents may request an independent evaluation if they disagree with the results of the school's evaluation.
5. Parents must be permitted to review all of their child's records. They may request that inaccurate, unusual, or misleading information be removed.
6. Parents have the right to be active participants in developing, implementing, and evaluating the educational program.
7. Parents may request a due process hearing if they disagree with the procedures used in developing or implementing their child's educational program. During this hearing, they have the right to legal counsel and the right to examine witnesses, present evidence, and retain a written record of the proceedings and findings.
8. If parents disagree with the results of the hearing, they may appeal to the state board of education and the federal court.

■ 6   The purpose of these legal rights is not to establish an adversarial relationship between parents and schools. Rather, it is to emphasize parents' importance as contributors to the multidisciplinary team's function. Important functions of the parents are as follows:

Identification and Referral
Parents often possess more information about their child than any other person. Consequently, they may be in the best position to identify potential problems and request a referral or more in-depth assessment.

Assessment
When carefully guided by professionals, as suggested by the interview procedures in Action Plan 3.4, parents can contribute a substantial amount of information relevant to the potential disorder. They may select specific behaviors to be monitored, systematically observe the behavior in home and community settings, and report the behavior rates to the multidisciplinary team. They may also provide the team with a complete social history related to the potential problem and complete adaptive behavior scales referenced to the child's or youth's functioning at home.

Planning
The parents may work with the multidisciplinary team in integrating assessment data and arriving at educational goals and strategies. As

ACTION PLAN 3.4   GUIDELINES FOR PARENT INTERVIEWS

Kroth and Simpson (1977) recommend the following procedures for conducting parent interviews:

1. Conduct the interview in a quiet and private environment.
2. Provide a positive outlook while being alert for the parents' underlying agenda/motives.
3. Pay close attention to the parents' nonverbal as well as verbal behavior.
4. Be aware of the nonverbal messages you are sending.
5. Respect the parents' right to privacy by not sharing information with unauthorized persons or agencies.

emphasized earlier, the team should make use of the parents' knowledge of the child when selecting effective educational placements and strategies.

Intervention

A majority of the skills taught in school should be practiced in home and community settings. Reading, writing, and math all have applications in the natural environment (e.g., ordering and paying at a restaurant, sports scoring, using a television guide). Teachers seldom have a means of ensuring that these skills generalize to home and community settings. Therefore, parents' major instructional role may be facilitating the transfer of skills from school to community environments.

Evaluation

The child's or youth's educational program must be reviewed at least once a year. Again, parents may have a substantial amount of information regarding the child's or youth's development over the year.

CASE FOR ACTION 3.2

A young man suspected of having learning disabilities is enrolled in a typical third-grade classroom. Test data indicate that he is normally intelligent (IQ = 106) and that his achievement is at grade level in math, spelling, and written expression. The major problem is that his reading achievement is only slightly above the first-grade level, and he is excessively shy and withdrawn. He seldom interacts with other students and becomes extremely emotional when given corrective feedback. The problems may stem from unfortunate events at home; his father and mother are separated and have been involved in a lengthy custody suit.

You are interested in obtaining complete information about the child. You have initiated a referral for evaluation, leading, if appropriate, to special education services. Who would you suggest to be on the multidisciplinary team? What specific expertise would these team members contribute in studying the problem? How might they contribute in providing an educational program?

THE IEP AS A PLANNING TOOL

■ 7   The preceding sections have identified three major dimensions of the coordination of special education services. Coordination across settings means that a range of educational environments can be made available for handicapped learners and that handicapped students can move freely between settings as indicated by their educational development. Coordination of services over time highlights the importance of an empirical or data-based process of ensuring placement in the least restrictive setting. This process also guides subsequent decisions to move the learner to more or less restrictive environments. Finally, coordination among service providers means that multidisciplinary team members work cooperatively in identifying and promoting educational objectives.

The Individualized Education Program (IEP) required by PL 94-142 is a planning document that is ideally suited to achieving these coordination goals. As discussed in the first chapter, the IEP process emphasizes coordination across settings by requiring that multidisciplinary team members and parents identify services and settings as close to the mainstream environment as appropriate. The IEP document also specifies the amount of time the student will spend in regular education settings. Coordination over time is addressed by the requirements for evaluating and revising the IEP at least annually. The expectation is that the student's performance gains may lead to modifications in instructional services as well as to movement to less restrictive settings. Finally, coordination among service providers results when the multidisciplinary team and parents meet jointly to share evaluation information and prescribe educational interventions. Although one professional may be identified as the primary service provider addressing a goal, there is an expectation for cooperative planning and implementation.

○ 7   PL 94-142 identifies seven major features of the IEP:

1. The inclusion of data that identify the student's *current level of performance*.
2. *Annual goals* targeting general achievement gains anticipated over the year.
3. *Short-term objectives*, which are component skills comprising the annual goals.
4. The identification of *objective criteria, evaluation procedures, and schedules* for assessing performance on the short-term objectives on at least an annual basis.
5. The extent of the student's *participation in the regular education program*.
6. *Special education and related services* addressing the student's objectives as well as special instructional materials, media, and methods.
7. Finally, the *dates projected for beginning and the expected duration of services*.

These features will be discussed separately in the following sections.

Current Performance Levels

Before establishing educational goals and methods, it is important that the multidisciplinary team have a comprehensive view of the student's learning and behavioral characteristics. According to the IEP interpretation guidelines published in the *Federal Register* (1981), current performance levels should include an accurate description of the effects of the handicap on the learner's academic performance (reading, math, communication, etc.) and nonacademic performance (independent living, mobility, vocational, etc.). Exceptionality labels may *not* be used as a substitute for behavioral descriptions. The description should be presented in objective and measurable terms. Test scores may be included, where appropriate, but should be self-explanatory (that is, should not require the use of a test manual for interpretation) or should be accompanied by an explanation. Finally, data presented should be directly related to other components of the IEP. For example, data identifying deficiencies in reading performance should be followed by goals, objectives, and services in the area of reading.

○ **8**   Potential sources of assessment information, discussed in more detail in chapters 5 and 6, include the following:

- The student's cumulative file, including psychological report, medical record, social history, educational history, speech and language evaluation, and reports from other educational specialists.
- Commercially available standardized assessment instruments, including intelligence tests, achievement tests, and formal diagnostic tests.
- Criterion-referenced tests, both teacher-made and commercially produced, which assess the learner's skills against specific educational objectives.
- Informal diagnostic tests prepared by the teacher to analyze the student's response to various teaching methods and materials, specific error patterns, appropriate instructional levels, and the anticipated rate of learning.
- Systematic observation, providing reliable and comprehensive information on the student's behavioral characteristics.

Although individual team members may collect data reflecting current levels of performance, the full multidisciplinary team is responsible for analyzing these data. In general, this process includes integrating data presented by individual team members, determining whether a sufficient amount of information is present to develop the IEP, collecting additional data if necessary, identifying skill deficits for which goals and objectives should be prepared, targeting educational materials and methods suited to the student's identified characteristics, and projecting the duration of services.

Annual Goals

■ 8   Annual goals are written statements identifying general performance gains anticipated through the special education program. The annual goals should be broad enough to reflect expected behavior changes over the period of a year, yet specific enough to suggest component short-term objectives. As emphasized earlier, annual goals should reflect data presented in the IEP section on current level of performance. In general, these data allow for the designation of priority goals, an accurate appraisal of entry behaviors, realistic expectations of performance changes anticipated over the calendar year, and an assessment of the amount and type of instructional time necessary for achieving the goal.

A number of considerations are involved in establishing the final goals once the data are obtained. These considerations, reviewed in detail in the preceding chapter, include the student's learning characteristics, the student's behavioral characteristics, the availability of instruction, the student's chronological age, and the anticipated postsecondary environments in which the learner is expected to reside and work. Since several of these considerations are somewhat subjective, goals selected may differ as a function of various professionals' perspectives. Consequently, the entire multidisciplinary team, including the student's parents, should be involved in the goal selection process.

Short-Term Objectives

Annual goals are broken down into smaller component skills that are defined as short-term objectives. According to the U.S. Department of Education, IEP objectives are "(a) developed based on a logical breakdown of the major components of the annual goals, and (b) can serve as 'milestones' for indicating progress toward meeting the goals" (*Federal Register*, 1981, p. 5470). This new point implies that IEP objectives address the needs of the learner, that they are objective and measurable descriptions of the individual skills that comprise the annual goals, and that they are logically sequenced, building from the student's current abilities to the annual goal.

○ 9   As commonly written, instructional objectives have four principal components (Mager, 1984). The first component is the identification of the student by name. This component establishes the role of the objective in the individual learner's program. Inclusion of the student's name emphasizes to the multidisciplinary team, the student, and the parents that the objective was prepared with reference to the characteristics and goals of the specific learner.

The second component, identifying the target response, provides an objective and measurable statement of the behavior the student is expected to acquire. This component ensures that the multidisciplinary team is in agreement regarding the precise set of behaviors expected to be influenced. In addition, because the target behavior is identified in observable and measurable terms, all members of the team can agree at a later time on the extent to which the objective has been achieved.

The third component, the conditions under which the target response is expected to occur, states the instructional conditions designated to produce the target response. Instructional conditions are antecedents or stimulus events that the professional may use to increase the probability that the student's performance will meet the teacher's expectations. As emphasized in chapter 2, knowledge of these influencing events is particularly important because a student who is able to perform a skill with specific prompts present may not be able to engage in the same behavior with different prompts. Therefore, the statement of relevant instructional conditions ensures that all members of the multidisciplinary team agree on the events expected to support the occurrence of the behavior.

The final component of a complete objective is the performance criteria. This component establishes the minimal level of performance expected of the student upon achieving the objective. The criteria may involve the frequency, latency, magnitude, rate, consistency, or quality of a response, depending on the nature of the response. Problems solved correctly may be identified by a rate (number correct divided by the number attempted), class attendance may be stated as a frequency (number of classes attended), and attending to task may be stated as a duration (amount of time spent working).

Most target responses can be performed with varying levels of proficiency. Acceptable performance in reading from a word list may be defined as identifying 100%, 90%, or 80% of the words accurately, depending on the expectations of the professional. To ensure that all members of the multidisciplinary team agree on the expected performance level, these criteria should be stated explicitly.

Objective Criteria, Evaluation Procedures, and Schedules

■ 9   Goal and objective selection, discussed in the preceding sections, forms the foundation for this IEP component. PL 94-142 requires "appropriate objective criteria and evaluation procedures and schedules for determining on at least an annual basis whether the short term instructional objectives are being achieved" (*Federal Register*, 1977, p. 42491). This requirement ensures that multidisciplinary team members monitor the learner's performance toward the annual goals and short-term objectives. This process facilitates (1) the identification of future objectives, (2) the revision of current objectives, and (3) the selection of efficient and effective teaching strategies.

The performance criteria discussed earlier establish the quality of responses expected of the learner following instruction. Once a criterion is established, the multidisciplinary team must identify an evaluation procedure for testing the extent to which the criterion was met. The major rule to follow in selecting an evaluation procedure is to obtain as direct and reliable a sample of the target behavior as possible, given the available time and resources. Thus, the actual evaluation procedure is closely related to the performance objective.

Responses in the cognitive domain (e.g., computational accuracy in math problems) are best assessed by evaluating permanent products of the cognitive skill (e.g., percentage of problems solved correctly on tests, quizzes, or worksheets). Responses in the motor domain (e.g., endurance during physical activities) are best assessed through direct observation of the learner under the instructional conditions delineated by the objective (e.g., number of meters run over a 20-minute period). Chapters 5 and 6 will provide a more detailed discussion of evaluation procedures suitable for a range of instructional objectives.

Finally, the evaluation schedule ensures that learner progress toward the objectives is assessed on at least an annual basis. As will be emphasized in the evaluation chapters, more frequent evaluation affords the greatest sensitivity to performance changes. When data are collected on a daily basis, the teacher can identify relationships between the student's responses on a given day and the educational procedures used that day. Infrequent evaluations do not allow the educator to isolate specific educational procedures that are effective or ineffective. For example, knowing that a student acquired 200 sight words over a school year does not allow the educator to identify specific lesson formats that produced the greatest gain in sight word acquisition. Daily assessment may reveal that lessons involving high-interest materials and concrete examples consistently produced two or three new sight words, whereas lessons involving drill and repetition on worksheets produced one new sight word at best.

Frequent evaluation also ensures that program modifications are made before a substantial amount of ineffective instructional time is expended. Failure to identify ineffective educational programs quickly may have several detrimental effects that can be avoided by frequent evaluations: (1) the student may be allowed to practice incorrect responses over extended periods of time, rather than being provided corrective feedback as a result of the evaluation; (2) the student may experience repeated frustration and failure, rather than receiving instruction redirected at a lower level or slower pace; and (3) valuable instructional time may be wasted, rather than providing frequent opportunities for the educator to assess potentially more effective instructional strategies.

○ **10**   As stated earlier, PL 94-142 requires that evaluation take place on at least an annual basis. This annual review may be better described as a summative evaluation, in which data that are collected daily and used to modify the instructional program are summarized and reported. Summative data reported at this time may also include annual achievement test scores, results from formal diagnostic tests, skills checklists, and grades. Depending on the objectives, continuous data collected through the school year may include (1) attendance data, (2) data from homework assignments, (3) data from in-class assignments, (4) criterion-referenced test results, (5) data from direct observations, (6) anecdotal and self-report data, and (7) data from permanent products of the student's work.

Participation in the Regular Program

■ **10**   It is important that all handicapped learners spend at least a portion of each day with nonhandicapped individuals. The influence of appropriate peer models may be an important contributor to the learner's adult social adjustment. Therefore, the multidisciplinary team should identify and document the extent of the student's involvement with nonhandicapped peers in the regular education program.

Ideally, regular program involvement should occur in areas in which the student is most able to compete successfully. Special high-interest areas (e.g., science, history, driver education, building trades), areas emphasizing fine or gross motor skills (e.g., physical education, art), or areas in which the environmental structure is such that a high degree of individualization occurs are ideally suited to mainstreaming handicapped learners. These areas should be sought out and utilized whenever possible. Informal school settings—including the lunchroom, school assemblies, the playground, the student lounge, and hallways—are areas in which all handicapped learners can interact with their nonhandicapped peers.

Special Education and Related Services

■ **11**   The designation of programs and services to be provided the learner may be the most critical aspect of IEP documentation. As discussed earlier, the multidisciplinary team is responsible for providing (1) a range of educational environments, (2) free movement into more or less restrictive environments on the basis of student performance, and (3) an emphasis on services in less restrictive settings. PL 94-142 requires formalization and documentation of this planning in the IEP. The initial section of this chapter reviewed available special education services, including regular classes, regular classes plus supplementary services, part-time special class, full-time special class, special stations, homebound services, and hospital, residential, or total care settings. Beyond the actual special education services to be provided, the IEP must also stipulate related services, which are defined as "transportation and such developmental, corrective, and other appropriate supportive services as are required to assist a handicapped child to benefit from special education" (*Federal Register*, 1977, p. 42479). The major related services enumerated in PL 94-142 are the following:

- Speech pathology and audiology
- Psychological services
- Physical and occupational therapy
- Recreation
- Early identification and assessment of disabilities
- Counseling services
- Medical services for diagnostic or evaluation purposes
- School health services
- School social work services
- Parent counseling and training

In addition to specifying related services, the IEP must indicate the extent and precise nature of these services. The extent of services may be recorded by identifying times and days on which the educational resources will be made available to the learner. The nature of services is specified according to qualitative features.

○ **11**   It is important to note that the extent and nature of services provided cannot be limited by the resources available to the school district. If the district does not have the resources necessary to provide the identified services, arrangements must be made to contract for services outside the district. Common interagency arrangements frequently used by school districts include neighboring districts sharing the services of one or more specialists or programs; districts across several counties forming joint agreements whereby low incidence resources and programs are shared; and individual districts contracting for services through private agencies.

Dates Projected for Beginning and the Expected Duration of Services

The final IEP component specifies the date on which IEP services are to be initiated as well as the anticipated period of time over which the IEP is to be in effect. In the majority of cases in which the child or youth is continuing in a special education program, these dates will correspond to the beginning and ending days of the school year. In cases in which the original need for service was identified during the current school year, the date for initiating service will be as soon following the development of the IEP as it is possible to arrange the services. This may be as early as the next day or as late as several weeks later. The duration of services in such cases will generally run through the school year, and the next annual review will serve as the time to formally establish that services are no longer needed or that they should be continued.

SUMMARY

The provision of special education services to exceptional learners is a multidimensional effort. First, services must be coordinated across settings. This ensures that the learner is placed in the least restrictive educational setting appropriate to his or her learning and behavioral features. Second, services must be coordinated over time. This facet emphasizes that the student's progress is continually reflected through increased time in less restrictive educational environments. Finally, services must be coordinated among service providers. Often, several professionals are working on similar goals with the same student. It is therefore important that these professionals work together in providing complementary services.

The Individualized Education Program (IEP) has been described as a planning document that facilitates these coordination efforts. Coordination across settings is enhanced when multidisciplinary team members and parents integrate assessment data to determine the most appropriate instructional settings for the student. Coordination over time is enhanced through the annual revision of the IEP on the basis of changes in the student's performance. Finally, coordination among service providers results from a team of professionals contributing to the development of the educational plan.

Appropriate educational services go well beyond the philosophical and organizational aspects discussed in this and preceding chapters. It is hoped that these discussions have provided a framework within which effective educational strategies may be applied. Subsequent chapters will discuss specific techniques that may be used to achieve objectives for handicapped students.

CASE FOR ACTION 3.3

A local parent group recently asked you to discuss quality indicators of handicapped students' Individualized Education Programs. What would you include in your presentation?

Part II

Educational Approaches

4

Direct Instructional Procedures

■ DID YOU KNOW THAT...

■ **1** . . . direct instructional procedures utilize assessment data to identify instructional goals and strategies?

■ **2** . . . in direct instruction, daily lesson plans are formed from short-term objectives?

■ **3** . . . the direct instruction approach uses instructional materials that provide feedback and reinforcement?

■ **4** . . . replicable procedures are used in direct instruction?

■ **5** . . . identifying what motivates a student to learn is an integral aspect of the direct instructional process?

■ **6** . . . reliable data are the foundation upon which direct instruction is based?

■ **7** . . . instructional goals must meet the learner's educational and social needs?

■ **8** . . . the steps of component objectives and task sequences need to be correctly sized, clearly defined, and in logical order?

■ **9** . . . instructional planning may be used to structure advanced lesson plans or to formulate more flexible classroom decisions?

■ **10** . . . contingency plans should be included in advanced lesson plans?

■ **11** . . . the use of contingency plans by practicing teachers is unfortunately limited?

■ 12   ...instructional procedures, materials, and motivational techniques are highly interrelated?

■ 13   ...instruction should occur in a logical sequence?

■ 14   ...students should be taught in the manner in which they're expected to perform?

■ 15   ...instruction is enhanced through numerous examples and frequent explanations?

■ 16   ...the teacher should plan the prompts used in each lesson?

■ 17   ...a teacher should immediately interrupt behaviors that are not conducive to success?

■ 18   ...drill results in more automatic and permanent performance?

■ 19   ...motivational procedures should be employed to promote the development of new skills and strengthen existing ones?

■ 20   ...teachers should identify a range and a hierarchy of motivating events for each student?

■ 21   ...the continuity and momentum of instruction can increase student attention?

■ 22   ...the use of frequent and random information checks keeps students alert?

■ 23   ...goal statements should be revised only after several attempts to revise instruction?

○ CAN YOU...

○ 1   ...use the results of an assessment battery to develop an instructional plan?

○ 2   ...determine when a learner would benefit more from a developmentally sequenced curriculum or a functional skills curriculum?

○ 3   ...break a goal down into its component objectives and task sequences?

○ 4   ...develop lesson plans, including content, materials, and classroom management strategies?

○ 5   ...develop contingency plans?

○ 6   ...select appropriate commercial instructional materials?

○ **7** . . . incorporate into a lesson plan instructional strategies that are effective with slow learners?

○ **8** . . . determine the appropriate number of explanations and examples that should be given to a student?

○ **9** . . . identify the levels of prompts you would use to teach a skill?

○ **10** . . . plan your prompts to ensure a high rate of success?

○ **11** . . . sequence the levels of prompts to provide the greatest possible degree of independence?

○ **12** . . . effectively utilize independent practice as an instructional strategy?

○ **13** . . . establish a review schedule to ensure that important skills and concepts are not forgotten?

○ **14** . . . develop guidelines for implementing reinforcement procedures?

○ **15** . . . identify procedures that may be used to avoid performance problems?

○ **16** . . . develop a systematic strategy to test for problems in the instructional process?

The preceding chapter emphasized the use of the Individualized Education Program (IEP) as a planning document. In many states, the IEP is developed on two levels. The first—the full service level—includes general assessment data, annual goals, specific services, the extent of participation in the regular program, and a schedule for revising the program. This document is completed by the multidisciplinary team. The second level—the implementation level—includes the development of component objectives of the annual goals, criteria and procedures for monitoring student progress, and specific instructional procedures employed. This document is developed by individual service providers. The present chapter is primarily concerned with the development of instruction on the implementation level. The procedures discussed are the basis for developing individual implementation plans.

THE DIRECT INSTRUCTION APPROACH

The requirements of PL 94–142, as well as recent writing and research, favor the use of direct instructional procedures (Carnine & Silbert, 1979; Haring et al., 1978; Lovitt, 1984; Silbert et al., 1981). Direct instruction—including precision teaching (Lindsley, 1964), task-analytic instruction (Sulzer-Azaroff & Mayer, 1977), diagnostic teaching (G. P. Cartwright & Cartwright, 1972), and applied behavior analysis instruction (Hallahan & Kauffman, 1976)—is characterized by specific instructional procedures. Haring and Schiefelbusch (1976) describe the following components of direct instruction:

1. Assessing learner characteristics
2. Establishing instructional goals
3. Systematic planning of instruction
4. Using instructional materials
5. Using replicable instructional approaches
6. Using motivating consequences
7. Monitoring student success

An assessment of learner characteristics is conducted to establish the entry-level skills of the student. In addition, assessment data are used to identify specific instructional procedures that are likely to be effective. Instructional goals that result from this assessment provide objective descriptions of the expected outcome of instruction.

Teachers who follow a direct instruction orientation use goal statements as a gauge for annual progress. If the student meets or exceeds the goal, that is an indication that the educational program was effective. A rate of progress below the anticipated goal suggests an ineffective educational procedure. In the latter case, the educational approach is likely to be modified.

■ 2   Systematic planning of instruction involves breaking down a goal into component short-term objectives and even smaller task sequences. These task sequences are the backbone of the daily lesson plan. Educators who follow direct instruction principles ensure that each lesson is a sequential building block, leading to the short-term objective and annual goal. The order of task sequences (whether forward-chained or backward-chained) is carefully prescribed according to the nature of the task and the characteristics of the learner.

Direct instruction literature and research has produced a variety of instructional materials, many of which are designed according to direct instruction principles. Such materials may include models designed to promote correct performance. The models are faded as the learner's skills increase (O. R. White & Haring, 1980). Other materials utilize shaping procedures whereby the student is initially reinforced for an approximation of the expected skill.

■ 3   The quality or rate of the students' performance is expected to increase as they progress through the materials. Many materials include systematically applied reinforcement procedures, linking a motivating consequence to desirable performance and corrective feedback to substandard performance.

■ 4   Another hallmark of a direct instructional approach is that the operational aspects of the teaching procedure can be clearly and completely described. Thus, other educators can replicate the instructional procedures with similar effects. Emphasizing this quality, recent applied researchers in education and psychology have addressed the issue of procedural reliability (Peterson, Homer, & Wonderlich, 1982), which pertains to the correspondence between the written or verbal description of an educational method and the teacher's actual practice in using the method. Procedural reliability is important because effective techniques are expected to be passed along with the student from one classroom to another, rather than expecting the teacher's style to match the learner's needs. To make procedures replicable, step-by-step activities or rules are usually listed in a 1, 2, 3 order. The procedures in the lesson plan discussed in the next section (and depicted in figure 4.2) are a good example of how procedures should be stated.

■ 5   Motivational consequences are another important facet of a direct instructional approach. The consequences used may range from intrinsic outcomes, such as pride in achievement and positive self-statements, to more primary rewards, including food items and tokens. Direct instruction principles emphasize the importance of identifying the motivational features of the learner and providing the most natural incentives that are effective.

■ 6   Finally, direct instruction involves the use of precise and continuous measurement of performance. In general, direct instruction educators monitor preinstructional performance as well as performance throughout the duration of instruction. These performance data should produce a reliable estimate of the rate of skill acquisition. Also, continuous monitoring allows the effects of intervening instructional variables (e.g., special materials, teacher presentation formats) to be isolated, so that procedures associated with an increased rate of skill acquisition can be utilized more frequently. In more rigorous applications of measurement procedures, direct instruction educators use applied behavior-analytic designs to produce more confident statements of the effect of instruction on skill acquisition (see, for example, Schloss, Sedlak, Elliott, & Smothers, 1982).

In summary, direct instruction is a student-centered approach that links pupil performance data to systematic teaching procedures. Direct instruction involves a comprehensive set of educational principles that address the structure of the learning environment, the differentiation of teaching practices on the basis of learner characteristics, the effective use of motivating consequences, and the systematic articulation of instructional objectives.

THE SEQUENCE OF INSTRUCTIONAL ACTIVITIES

This section provides a seven-step model for planning instruction and making systematic decisions on the appropriateness of the instruction and on changes that might need to be initiated. The model incorporates the positive features of several authors' work on systematic instruction (G. P. Cartwright & Cartwright, 1972; Gearheart & Willenberg, 1980; C. D. Mercer, 1981; Peter, 1965) It depicts a cyclical process of instruction and decision making (see figure 4.1).

1. Identify Learner Characteristics

○ 1   The first step in the process is the identification of the learner's characteristics. The importance of assessment in the direct instructional process will be stressed throughout this text. It is required both for designing *and* for monitoring instruction. In the initial phase, the teacher is concerned with using assessment data to develop the instructional plan. In this phase, the identification of learner characteristics is conducted not only by the individual teacher, but also by the entire multidisciplinary team. Data provided by these professionals should offer a fairly comprehensive picture of students' learning and behavioral features that might influence instruction.

The multidisciplinary team's assessment should provide sufficient data for making two important decisions. The first decision relates to the starting point of instruction. For this purpose, assessment is necessary to provide sufficient information for selecting initial instructional goals. The second decision relates to the nature of instruction. The multidisciplinary

FIGURE 4.1 The Sequence of Instructional Activities

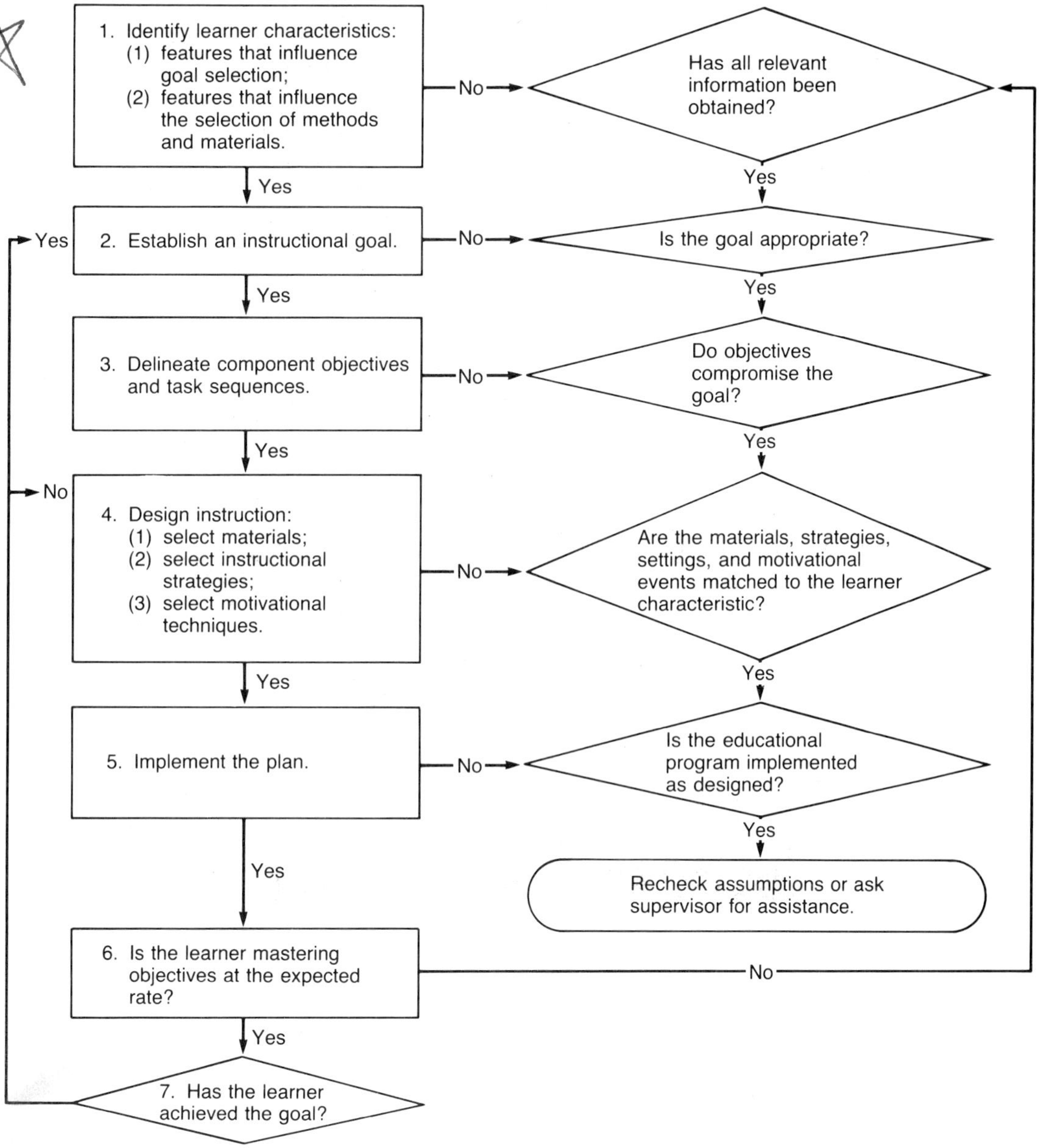

1. Identify learner characteristics:
   (1) features that influence goal selection;
   (2) features that influence the selection of methods and materials.

— No → Has all relevant information been obtained?

↓ Yes

2. Establish an instructional goal. — No → Is the goal appropriate?

↓ Yes

3. Delineate component objectives and task sequences. — No → Do objectives compromise the goal?

↓ Yes

4. Design instruction:
   (1) select materials;
   (2) select instructional strategies;
   (3) select motivational techniques.

— No → Are the materials, strategies, settings, and motivational events matched to the learner characteristic?

↓ Yes

5. Implement the plan. — No → Is the educational program implemented as designed?

↓ Yes

Recheck assumptions or ask supervisor for assistance.

6. Is the learner mastering objectives at the expected rate? — No

↓ Yes

7. Has the learner achieved the goal?

team's assessment should provide the educator with reasonably sound hypotheses regarding the instructional strategies most likely to be effective.

Errors in any phase of the instructional process generally result from either inadequate data or improper interpretation of data. Because many of the standardized instruments in special education are of questionable validity (Salvia & Ysseldyke, 1985), practicing teachers must continually judge the adequacy of these data.

An appropriate reaction to instructional problems is to collect additional data. This reaction may range from reconvening the multidisciplinary team for a more comprehensive evaluation to acting on systematic or anecdotal data obtained during an ineffective instructional process.

2. Establish Instructional Goals

■ 7 ○ 2 The second step in the process requires the specification of an instructional goal. Specific goal selection is determined by the learner characteristics and the curriculum philosophy of the team. Chapter 2 provided a rationale for using the learning and behavioral features of exceptional students to establish goals. It also expressed a specific curriculum philosophy based on the development of functional skills that can be used in current and future environments. A decision about instructional goals requires consideration of the following principles:

1. The efficiency with which a student acquires new information suggests the total amount of information that may be acquired in a school year. Efficient learners are more likely to benefit from larger goals.

2. Students with a large number of acquired skills may benefit from sequential goals based on this foundation. Less adaptive learners are more likely to benefit from specific functional skills.

3. Students who are available for a substantial amount of formal instructional time (young learners, students with high on-task rates, etc.) can be expected to benefit most from developmentally sequenced curricular sequences. Students who are likely to be absent from school often, or students with high off-task rates, are more likely to benefit from goals that address functional skills.

4. Finally, young students are more likely to benefit from developmentally sequenced basic skills instruction. This foundation may then be used to promote specific functional skills as the student progresses through adolescence.

Developmentally sequenced instructional goals are generally obtained from regular curriculum materials, whereas functional skills goals result from the educator's analysis of future environments in which the student is expected to participate.

Errors in goal selection may have two major effects. First, the goal may be excessively large. This error will result in an initial growth pattern below the rate necessary for goal attainment. More modest goals may be required. Second, the goal may not meet the learner's social or educational needs. In this case, the learner may make adequate progress, but once the goal is attained, it will have little effect in promoting the student's adult adjustment. It may be necessary to consider more relevant goals to correct this error.

3. Delineate Component Objectives

○ **3** As discussed earlier, component objectives and task sequences are the sequential building blocks that form the instructional goal. A goal pertaining to the student's ability to use a telephone, for example, may be composed of five objectives: locating a number, dialing a number, initiating and terminating a conversation, answering the telephone, and taking messages. Each of these objectives may be broken down into task sequences. Locating a number, for example, may include selecting the appropriate phone book, obtaining the correctly spelled name and address of the person to be called, locating the person's name and address in the phone book, locating the telephone number, and writing the telephone number on a piece of paper.

■ **8** Three major errors may occur in this facet of the instructional process. First, the objectives and task sequences may be poorly matched to the student's learning or behavioral features. Adaptive learners are able to make larger gains over shorter periods of time. Consequently, their component objectives may be fairly large. Less adaptive learners require smaller steps. Component objectives that are too large will result in frustration and failure, and those that are too small are likely to produce boredom and disinterest. In either case, the student will not make the progress of which he or she is capable.

Second, the objectives and task sequences may not be defined in clear and complete terms. Ambiguity in the statement of objectives leads to inconsistencies in the educational procedures as well as invalid measurement. The ambiguous objective "Johnny will have a deeper understanding of social forces that resulted in the drafting of the Bill of Rights" does not offer a direct target for instruction or measurement, because lessons and experiences could include a wide range of topics. Also, the educator would not be able to measure the achievement of this objective precisely. Consequently, the student is not as likely to make the same progress he or she would make if the objective had identified discrete skills to be developed.

Finally, objectives and task sequences may not be logically arranged components of the goal. Addressing objectives that are related to the goal in random order is not likely to produce the same effects as building sequentially toward the goal. The obvious solution to this, as well as to the previous errors, is to review the objectives and task sequences and consider modifying the objectives to improve their sequence, clarity, and relevance.

4. Design Instruction

■ 9   Instructional planning has been identified as a critical variable supporting the effectiveness of educational interventions (Shavelson, 1983). Careful planning allows educators to formulate and implement decisions in a deliberate and intentional manner. This function is particularly important because of the complexity and variability of typical classroom environments. Instructional planning may be considered from two perspectives. The first includes the planning and organization that occur prior to the work with students. The second involves the contingency planning or "in-flight" decision making that is employed when unforeseen events make the original plan unworkable.

○ 4   Recent research in the general education literature has highlighted the importance of instructional planning. A review of the literature provides the following conclusions:

1. For many educators, the instructional plan serves as a road map for lessons. Once the plan is initiated, teachers are likely not to deviate from it (Shavelson & Stern, 1981; E. L. Smith & Sendelbach, 1979).
2. A teacher's behavior in the classroom can be predicted from his or her instructional plan (Stern & Shavelson, 1981; E. L. Smith & Sendelbach, 1979).
3. Instructional plans often control the content, materials, and social climate of the classroom (Shavelson & Borko, 1979; D. F. Walker & Schaffarzick, 1974).

A similar body of evidence has pointed out how educators develop and use their instructional plans. The following conclusions derive from this literature:

1. Most instructional planning focuses on the content as opposed to the structure of instruction (C. Clark, 1978; Shavelson, 1974, 1981; Shavelson & Stern, 1981).
2. Assessment information describing the student's characteristics often underlies the resulting instructional plan (Borko, 1978; Mintz, 1979; N. A. Russo, 1978; Shavelson, Cadwell, & Izu, 1977).
3. Classroom management, including student grouping and the selection of motivating events, curricular materials, and behavioral control techniques, is often included in teachers' plans (Mintz, 1979; E. L. Smith & Sendelbach, 1979).

Contingency plans include decisions made by the teacher throughout the course of instruction. More than any other form of planning, contingency decisions require the teacher to think on his or her feet. Often, these decisions must be made on only a moment's notice, and the teacher does not have an extended period of time for reflective analysis or additional data gathering. It can be legitimately argued that this pattern of decision making is of equal importance to the preparation of advance lesson plans.

■ 10   The contingency plans a teacher employs are often associated with the advance lesson plan. The advance plan may include a range of possible contingency plans to employ if the original lesson should not proceed as expected. This allows the teacher to anticipate potential problems and solutions in advance. When an anticipated problem occurs, such as a student acting out, the teacher's on-the-spot decisions can be based on solutions conceived through more careful and thoughtful reflection. This anticipatory process changes decision making from a fill-in-the-blank activity, in which all facets of the solution must be developed and implemented at that time, to a multiple choice activity, in which the teacher may select from several preplanned options.

Another relationship between the two forms of planning is that many advance plans direct the teacher into contingency plans. For example, Bellack, Kliebard, Hyman, and Smith (1966) have described a sequence of teaching activities that require immediate contingency plans, including structuring, soliciting, responding, and reacting. Although structuring the lesson and soliciting and obtaining student responses can be planned in advance, the teacher's reactions will be a function of qualitative aspects of the responses.

■ 11   Recent research in the general education literature has provided information on the processes teachers use when implementing contingency plans. A review of the available literature provides the following conclusions:

1. The rate of teachers' minor decisions that cannot be planned in advance ranges from about 10 to 15 per lesson (Morine-Dershimer & Vallance, 1975).
2. Aside from minor adjustments, teachers are not likely to change their preplanned routine (Joyce, 1978).
3. Contingency plans are often used to compensate for and check the progress of low-achieving students (Conners, 1978; Marland, 1977).
4. Teachers who employ contingency plans generally consider only two or three possible solutions (MacKay, 1977; Morine-Dershimer & Vallance, 1975).
5. Highly content-oriented instructors are less likely to employ contingency plans than those who are more concerned with the process of teaching (Zahorik, 1970).

The Instructional Design Process

Although the available literature provides more information on what teachers do than on what is most effective, reasonable hypotheses about teacher effectiveness can be generated. First, it is likely that careful advance planning enhances the instructional process. Advance plans allow the teacher to prescribe instruction on the basis of a thorough analysis of the learner's characteristics. Missing information can be obtained before entering the instructional process. Second, plans that do not encourage the use of contingency decisions may have an adverse influence on student performance and attitudes. Therefore, effective planning should provide sufficient flexibility for the educator to modify the lesson on the basis of learner behavior in the instructional sequence. Third, to maximize the effectiveness of "in-flight" decisions, the educator should be able to anticipate student reactions to the components of each lesson. Prior to instruction, the educator may identify alternative instructional procedures for each potential reaction.

○ **5**   Action Plan 4.1 presents procedures for developing an advance lesson plan. The instructional plan presented in figure 4.2 describes how a lesson is expected to be conducted. This plan contains the elements of contingency

ACTION PLAN 4.1   PREPARING AN INSTRUCTIONAL PLAN

1. Determine the lesson objective and enumerate the subskills.
2. List the materials to be used.
3. Describe the manner in which information will be presented.
4. Describe procedures for checking students' comprehension or skill attainment.
5. Establish procedures to be followed if the presentation is not effective.
6. Describe guided practice and progress-check procedures.
7. Establish procedures to be followed if guided practice is not successful.
8. Describe independent practice and progress-check procedures.
9. Establish procedures to be followed if independent practice is not successful.
10. Establish enrichment activities to be done if the students successfully complete the lesson before the end of the period.

FIGURE 4.2   Lesson Plan for Teaching the Parts of a Carburetor

Objective
Upon completion of the planned activity, the students will be able to match the major parts of a carburetor (e.g., butterfly, needle valve, float) to their written label.

Materials
Working model of a carburetor, worksheet and text. *Possible* use of overhead transparencies.

Procedures
(a) Use the working model to demonstrate the major parts of the carburetor; (b) ask the class to label the parts orally when presented at random; (c) ask the class to complete a worksheet that requires them to match a written label with a pictorial representation of the carburetor; (d) check the worksheets in class; (e_1) if the students' success rate exceeds 80%, proceed with independent reading of the carburetor parts section in the text; (e_2) if the students' success rate is below 80%, use the "small engine parts overhead transparency series" to provide further drill and practice prior to reading.

Evaluation
Students will demonstrate mastery of the objective by tagging a carburetor with written labels.

planning that have just been discussed. The specific performance objective of this lesson involves the learner's ability to identify the major parts of a carburetor. First, the instructor uses a working model to identify the major parts of a carburetor. The students are asked to label the parts orally as a drill activity. Next, the students are provided a brief worksheet and are asked to demonstrate and practice their knowledge of the major parts independently. Then they work together as a class in scoring their worksheets. Finally, they read a section in their text that provides further background on the parts of a carburetor.

The major contingency plan in this lesson relates to the students' performance on the worksheet. Progressing from teacher-directed instruction to the independent reading without being familiar with the major terms will substantially reduce the extent to which the students benefit from material in the text. Consequently, the teacher uses performance on the worksheet as a check to determine (1) whether further teacher-led instruction on the definition of terms is necessary or (2) whether the students are prepared to use their knowledge of the terms to acquire more information from the text. If the first contingency applies, the teacher plans to use overhead transparencies for drill in part recognition. If the second contingency applies, the teacher will proceed with the reading activity.

Components of Instruction

■ 12   The discussion to this point has centered on the planning process, highlighting both advance plans and contingency plans. Equally important to the process is the content of instruction, including the selection of materials, strategies, and motivational techniques. Although we will discuss these procedures separately for the sake of clarity, they are closely intertwined. Decisions regarding the instructional procedures often involve selection of the materials and motivational techniques. Similarly, the selection of materials invariably influences the instructional and motivational techniques.

Materials

The passage of PL 94-142 substantially increased the scope and availability of special education instructional materials. Currently, a wide range of companies specialize in materials suited to the curricular needs of special education programs. The availability of commercially produced materials has substantially reduced the need for educators to design and construct learning aids. The obvious advantage has been that educators now have more time to orchestrate classroom activities. A disadvantage is that the potential exists for teachers to use some materials simply because they exist, rather than because they match the learning and behavioral features of the exceptional student.

○ 6   It is important for special educators to recognize that because materials companies are profit-motivated, they are unable to produce materials directed toward a restricted number of students. Consequently, current materials are suited to the general needs of the average special needs learner, and they are not likely to match the needs of learners whose characteristics deviate from those of the general handicapped population. Thus, it is important that educators be able (1) to select materials on the basis of the characteristics and needs of the learner; (2) to modify existing materials to match learners' needs and abilities more closely; and (3) to construct materials when commercially available products are not appropriate.

Each of these requirements suggests the importance of recognizing the features of materials that make them useful for particular students. Necessary considerations in the evaluation of materials are outlined in Action Plan 4.2.

Instructional Strategies

○ 7   Recent research has sought to identify instructional procedures associated with learner achievement. The Direct Instruction Follow Through Program (Becker, 1977), the Texas School Studies (Evertson, Emmer, Sanford, & Clements, 1982; Emmer, Evertson, Sanford, & Clements, 1982), the Missouri Mathematics Effectiveness Study (Good & Grouws, 1979), and the Texas First Grade Reading Group Study (Anderson, Evertson, & Brophy, 1979, 1982), to name a few of the more notable projects, have

ACTION PLAN 4.2   PROTOCOL FOR EVALUATING INSTRUCTIONAL MATERIALS

Purpose
Is the purpose for which the material is designed directly associated with the learner's goals and objectives?

Ability Level
Is the material designed at a level matched to the learner's ability? For example, is the word difficulty appropriate; are the math skill requirements consistent with the child's or youth's ability; does the learner have the prerequisite vocabulary?

Chronological Level
Is the material presented in a manner consistent with the learner's age level? Is its format and appearance consistent with general educational materials used by the learner's peers?

Evaluation
Does use of the material produce formative data for evaluating the learner's performance? Can these data be used to make ongoing instructional decisions? Does use of the material produce summative data identifying the outcome of the instructional process?

Flexibility
Can the material be adapted to meet specific educational needs? Does the material include contingency options that may be used if the learner does not react as expected?

Correction Procedures
Does the material allow for the immediate correction of errors, or is it possible for errors to be practiced repeatedly prior to correction?

Input Dimensions
Are the processes by which instruction occurs (e.g., written description, pictorial description, physical manipulation, or graphic symbolization) appropriate to the learner's cognitive ability?

(continued)

ACTION PLAN 4.2   (continued)

Output Dimensions
Are the learner's anticipated reactions to the materials (e.g., construction, identification, written statement, oral statement, or graphic symbolization) matched to the performance objective and the evaluation method?

Learning Principles
Does the material make use of empirical learning theory principles, including modeling, presenting an example, providing cues to promote initial performance; pacing, encouraging the learner to work at a steady rate; shaping, expecting increasingly refined approximations of the terminal response; reinforcement, providing motivating consequences for correct responses; and fading, requiring the gradual removal of cues and reinforcers?

Durability
Is the material designed to sustain repeated use?

begun to identify strategies that are associated with teacher effectiveness. Four general instructional strategies are derived from this literature: presenting new information, guided practice, independent practice, and reviewing/reteaching.

PRESENTING NEW INFORMATION   The initial phase of an instructional sequence involves the demonstration of new concepts or skills. Although the importance of this step may seem obvious, it is an often neglected area (Durkin, 1981). Reports by Evertson, Emmer, and Brophy (1980) and Good & Grouws (1979) have demonstrated a significant relationship between educators' time in presenting new information and student achievement. This literature has provided a series of guidelines for presenting new information.

■ 13   First, as has been emphasized repeatedly in this text, skills and concepts should be arranged in a logical sequence. The sequence may be forward-chained, beginning with the first component in the instructional chain and building sequentially to the final element in the chain, or backward-chained, starting with the final element in the chain and building toward the initial component. Whether the instructional sequence is forward- or backward-chained is a function of the material presented. Forward chaining is more appropriate when the students need to possess initial skills before they can benefit from the later concepts. For example, reading instruction progresses more efficiently through a developmental series of word attack skills, beginning with elementary skills and progressing through complex skills. Backward chaining may be more beneficial if skill in the final element of the chain motivates the learner to acquire the preceding elements. For example, a history lesson may begin with the students learning that John Glenn was the first astronaut to circle the globe. (Remember, the others were cosmonauts.) This knowledge may then motivate the students to learn about the events leading up to Glenn's selection as an astronaut.

Whether concepts are forward- or backward-chained, the components should be presented individually. The educator should be careful to avoid digressing to previous concepts when presenting a new concept. Also, presenting information or skills that are to be developed later in the chain should be avoided. In short, material should be presented so that one concept or skill is mastered at a time. Once the target skill or concept is acquired, the next target may be introduced.

■ **14**   The second guideline involves the nature of the presentation. The research literature emphasizes that new concepts and skills should be presented through a format as close as possible to the learner's expected performance (O. R. White & Haring, 1980). Cawley et al. (1976, 1977) have described four potential input or presentation dimensions: construct, present, state, and graphically symbolize. The goal in meeting this second guideline is to match the input or presentation dimension to the expected student performance or output dimension. For example, if the objective of a lesson is for the learners to be able to name the seat of government of the United States (state), the lesson should include a verbal description of the seat of government (state). If an expected outcome of a lesson is for the students to be able to tune a car (construct), the presentation should involve a demonstration of procedures used in tuning a car (construct). Finally, if the objective of a math lesson is for the students to be able to balance a checkbook (graphically symbolize), the presentation should involve actual checkbook balancing procedures (graphically symbolize).

A related point is that when instruction involves a left/right or back/front orientation, the instructor should position himself or herself so that the learners view the same orientation. Presentations involving writing skills, for example, are best conducted by the teacher standing next to the student and facing in the same direction. In this regard, it is best that individual and small-group instruction be physically structured so that the teacher sits alongside or stands behind the student, rather than sitting or standing across a table from the student.

The third guideline suggests providing a discrete cue to indicate that a presentation is about to begin and not initiating the presentation until all students have maintained an attentive posture for several seconds. This guideline increases the likelihood that students will benefit from the presentation. The cue is intended to signal to the students that new information is about to be given. Over time, they will recognize that no other activities will occur until they are attentive.

■ 15   The fourth guideline suggests the use of numerous explanations and examples. As discussed earlier, explanations should focus on one concept at a time. They may be redundant, in that the same ideas are conveyed through slightly different vocabulary and syntax, but they should include only terms and concepts that the students have already mastered. Examples should be relevant to the experiences of the students, and their relationship to the skill or concept being taught should be clear. Finally, the difficulty of a skill or concept is directly related to the frequency with which explanations are given and the number of examples used.

○ 8   A final guideline is that the educator should frequently ask questions to assess the students' progress. As the students demonstrate an understanding of the concept or skill, the number of explanations and examples may be faded. When examples and explanations are no longer required for the learner to demonstrate proficiency, instruction should progress to the guided practice phase. These guidelines for presenting new information are summarized in Action Plan 4.3.

GUIDED PRACTICE Following the presentation phase, the learner is encouraged to practice the new skill under successively less clear or less directive prompts. The hierarchy of frequently used prompts, from most to least intrusive, is as follows:

○ 9   1. *Manual Prompt:* The teacher physically guides the learner through the appropriate movement. In writing, for example, the teacher places his or her hand on the student's hand and provides gentle pressure, forming the learner's fingers around the pencil. For most responses, it is not possible for the student to err under a manual prompt.

ACTION PLAN 4.3 GUIDELINES FOR PRESENTING NEW INFORMATION

When presenting new information, we recommend that the teacher:

1. Arrange the content in a logical sequence.
2. Present concepts and skills in a format that is as close as possible to the students' desired performance.
3. Provide a discrete signal or cue indicating that the presentation is to begin.
4. Begin the presentation only after all students have maintained an attentive posture for several seconds.
5. Use multiple explanations and examples.
6. Ask frequent questions to assess students' progress.

2. *Modeling Prompt:* The teacher performs the target behavior immediately prior to the student's response. For example, the teacher may pronounce a word before the learner pronounces it or grasp a pencil with the proper finger placement before the student grasps it. In content areas, modeling prompts involve supplying the correct answer to the student.

3. *Oral Prompt:* The teacher orally describes qualitative and/or quantitative aspects of the target behavior prior to the learner's performance. In this case, the teacher may describe, without modeling, how the actual sound is made—that is, how to pronounce a word—or how to grasp a pencil.

4. *Graphic Process Prompt:* The teacher provides a graphic representation of the process the student is expected to follow when engaging in the target behavior. For example, the teacher may provide the letter *a* with arrows indicating the direction of pencil strokes. Pronunciation and syllabication guides are graphic process prompts for word attack skills.

5. *Graphic Product Prompt:* The teacher provides a graphic representation of the product of the target behavior. For example, the teacher may present the letter *a* written in the same manner expected from the student or may display an addition problem completed through the same process the student is expected to use.

6. *Cue Prompt:* This is the least intrusive of the prompts. The teacher simply cues the student to perform the target behavior by saying, for example, "Grasp the pencil" or "Read the first word."

■ 16   The most crucial aspect of the guided practice phase is the way in which the educator manages these prompts. Five major principles govern the effective use of prompts. First, the teacher should preplan the specific prompts to be used. For most instructional situations, three or four levels of prompts are sufficient to move the learner into the independent practice phase. For example, spelling instruction for a mildly handicapped youth may be structured along three levels of prompts: (1) a modeling prompt, whereby the teacher spells the word before the youth does; (2) an oral prompt, whereby the teacher provides necessary rules or exceptions for identifying specific letters; and (3) a cue prompt, whereby the teacher simply says, "Spell the word _____." Similarly, instruction in math computation may follow three levels of prompts: (1) a graphic process prompt, whereby the student is provided an outline of the steps involved in completing target word problems; (2) a graphic product prompt, whereby the student is provided a completed word problem; and (3) a cue prompt, whereby the student is simply told to complete the problems.

○ 10   The second principle is that the most intrusive prompt should provide sufficient support to ensure a high success rate. Research by Fisher et al.

(1980), Anderson et al. (1979), and Gersten, Carnine, and Williams (1981) has suggested a strong relationship between the percentage of correct responses during instruction and subsequent achievement gains. Although the ideal rate of success cannot be stated confidently on the basis of existing research, 80% to 95% may be a reasonable estimate.

○ **11**   The third principle is to begin with the least intrusive prompt (self-initiation) and progress sequentially through the most intrusive prompt. This process, exemplified in figure 4.3, ensures that the student always performs the skill with the highest possible degree of independence. As the student becomes more proficient, the level of prompts will reduce until he or she performs consistently at the self-initiation level. The teacher may differentially reinforce students who are not motivated to perform under

FIGURE 4.3   System of Hierarchical Prompts

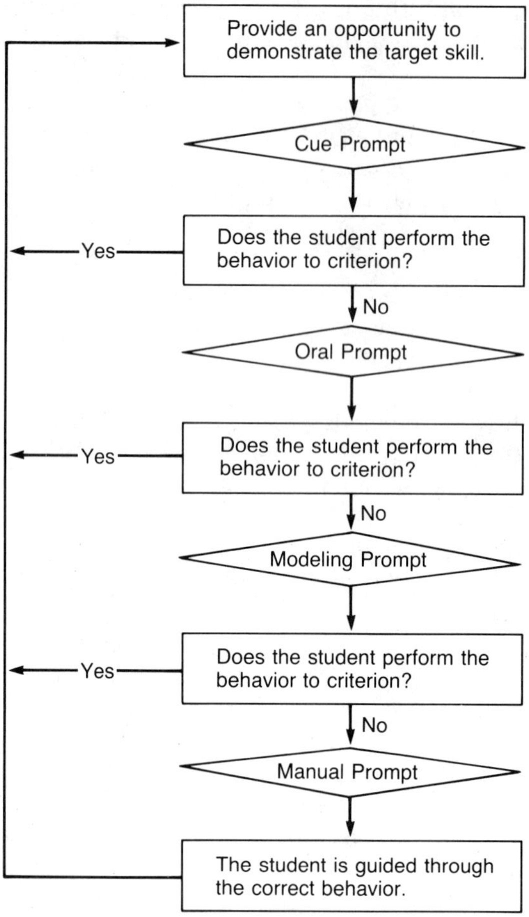

lower prompt levels on the basis of the level of prompt used. For example, a star may be given for each step of a problem that is self-initiated, but no reward is given for steps that require higher prompts.

The fourth principle is that less intrusive prompts should always be paired with more intrusive prompts. For example, even though instruction in using a saw has progressed to the level of a manual prompt (e.g., the instructor holds the saw with the student), less intrusive prompts should be employed simultaneously. This principle allows for the pairing of intrusive prompts with more natural prompts. Pairing is expected to increase the likelihood that the student will benefit from the less restrictive prompts in subsequent trials.

■ 17   The final principle is that nontarget behaviors—including both incorrect and off-task behaviors—should be interrupted as soon as they occur. Such incorrect responses are interrupted so that students do not practice errors. It is reasonable to assume that if practice increases the strength of target behaviors, it may also strengthen nontarget error behaviors. Incorrect responses that are practiced may be more difficult to correct than novel incorrect attempts.

Similarly, off-task behaviors that occur within the prompting hierarchy may become increasingly difficult to remove. The ultimate demonstration of an appropriate response is often reinforced by pride in achievement, associated teacher praise, or other response-contingent rewards. Also, the behavior chain leading up to the target behavior is likely to be reinforced by the final consequence. Both off-task and target responses are strengthened if the final outcome is success and reinforcement. Thus, by interrupting off-task behavior, the teacher can isolate only productive responses in the chain leading to success.

If these principles are followed, the student will eventually be able to perform the target skill independently. Because these procedures are time-consuming, instructional assistants, such as peer tutors, may become involved. Action Plan 4.4 provides a set of procedures for using peer tutors in the guided practice phase of instruction.

■ 18   INDEPENDENT PRACTICE In the independent practice or drill phase, the student is encouraged to apply the newly acquired skill to relevant problems. The importance of independent practice is highlighted by our knowledge that drill activities result in more immediate or "automatic" responding. When basic component skills are performed automatically, a greater portion of the learner's attention in hierarchical skills can be directed to the higher level concepts. For example, automatic recall of addition and multiplication facts allows the learner to focus on conceptual aspects of solving story problems. When basic facts cannot be retrieved automatically, the components of the problem that require student concentration increase substantially.

ACTION PLAN 4.4 PROCEDURES FOR CONDUCTING PEER TUTORING

We recommend the following procedures for conducting peer tutoring in the classroom:

1. The role of the peer tutor should be limited to carrying out the teacher's instructional plan.
2. The teacher should model the guided practice procedure with the peer tutor.
3. The peer tutor should rehearse the procedure with the teacher.
4. If necessary, reinforcement or corrective feedback should be provided to the tutor.
5. When the tutor initially works with the student, the teacher should supervise closely to ensure that the actual instruction is consistent with the instructional plan.
6. As the tutor becomes more competent, the teacher may observe less often.
7. The tutor should make frequent reports on the student's progress to the teacher. Permanent products of the student's work may be the most reliable indicator of this progress.
8. Both the tutor and the student should be liberally reinforced by the teacher for their cooperative efforts.

CASE FOR ACTION 4.1

A new student in your math resource program virtually refuses to work on problems. He typically waits until you supply correct responses or complete steps of problems for him. You speculate that the student is not concentrating on the work. Also, you believe that by waiting, the student ensures that all the problems are completed correctly (by you). How will you ensure that the student completes an increasingly large number of problems with less and less assistance?

Researchers have also suggested that drill to the point of automatic performance increases the likelihood that the skill will be a lasting part of the learner's repertoire (Travers, 1967). This, of course, is a primary goal for any instructional sequence, since there is little point in teaching skills that will be forgotten quickly.

Independent practice typically takes the form of seatwork. Worksheets, workbooks, and chapter exercises are frequently the focal points of seatwork activities. A less frequently employed independent practice activity is teacher-led drill, whereby the educator presents questions (e.g., math facts, sight words, comprehension questions) to an individual student or to a group (see, for example, Becker, 1977). Independent practice may also be orchestrated around instructional media, such as microcomputers, videotapes, audio tapes, word masters, and the like.

○ **12**   The effectiveness of independent practice may be enhanced through several teaching strategies. First, independent seatwork is more likely to produce achievement gains if it is preceded by presentation of the concepts and guided practice (Evertson et al., 1980). These procedures ensure that the students are able to perform the skill with some degree of success during independent practice. Second, the effects of seatwork may be enhanced by matching the independent activity directly to the presentation and guided practice activity. To meet this objective, the final guided practice activity may be the initiation of several of the independent practice problems (Anderson et al., 1979). Third, the teacher may increase seatwork effectiveness by remaining available to provide feedback, correct errors, and restate the initial directions (Good & Grouws, 1979). Fourth, students perform better during several short seatwork periods interspersed with additional presentations and guided practice than during a single long seatwork period (Evertson et al., 1982). Finally, because students often view independent drill activities as tedious or boring, educators may consider using external reinforcers for task completion (O. R. White & Haring, 1980). The foregoing guidelines for implementing independent practice are summarized in Action Plan 4.5.

○ **13**   REVIEW/RETEACHING Mildly handicapped students are often characterized by deficiencies in retaining previously acquired skills. As a result, it is important for the teacher to provide frequent and distributed practice following skill acquisition. It is expected that a consistent schedule for reviewing and reteaching material will ensure that important skills are not lost over time.

The review/reteach function may be carried out over three phases. The first phase, beginning immediately after the skill is acquired, involves daily review. On the day following mastery of the skill, the teacher highlights critical skills or concepts from the previous day. The teacher also informally assesses the extent to which retention has occurred and provides

ACTION PLAN 4.5   PROCEDURES FOR ENHANCING THE EFFECTIVENESS OF INDEPENDENT PRACTICE

We recommend the following procedures to enhance the effectiveness of independent practice:

1. Precede the independent practice session with a presentation of the concepts or skills and guided practice.
2. Match the guided practice procedure directly to the independent practice procedure.
3. Circulate among the students, providing feedback, correcting errors, and restating instructions.
4. Intersperse short seatwork periods with additional presentations and guided practice.
5. If necessary, provide external reinforcement for tedious or repetitive drill activities.

required additional instruction. In the second phase, the teacher reviews a concept on a weekly basis. For example, Friday may be set aside to review concepts or skills developed during the week. Finally, the third phase involves monthly reviews. For example, the last Friday of each month may be designated for extended review.

The review/reteach function is substantially more efficient if the curriculum goals are functional and age-appropriate. Skills that meet this standard (e.g., reading, math, independent living skills) are practiced frequently in natural environments, so the need for artificial review and reteaching is reduced. Disfunctional skills, which are seldom used in natural environments (e.g., historical facts, world geography), may be subject to structured review to enhance maintenance.

Action Plan 4.6 presents nine strategies for implementing instruction with mildly handicapped learners. These strategies are based on a review of the literature by Rosenshine (1983) and are consistent with the foregoing discussion.

Motivational Techniques

■ 19   Chapter 3 emphasized that the performance objectives teachers establish for students should not be limited to the acquisition of skills (e.g., upon completion of _____, the student will be able to _____). It was argued that besides promoting new skills, teachers are also responsible for increasing existing skills (e.g., upon completion of _____, the student will _____ more consistently or more frequently). Many handicapped learners at the secondary level possess sufficient skills to enter and succeed in adult environments. A problem exists, however, in that they are not moti-

ACTION PLAN 4.6   STRATEGIES FOR IMPLEMENTING INSTRUCTION

Rosenshine (1983) suggests the following procedures for working with learners who are "younger, slower, and/or have little background" (p. 366):

1. Utilize structured curricula as opposed to discovery learning.
2. Emphasize small and briskly paced instructional components.
3. Provide detailed and repetitious instructions and explanations.
4. Provide numerous examples.
5. Include frequent questions and opportunities to practice actively.
6. Provide frequent and immediate feedback and correction, especially in the early phases of instruction.
7. Design instruction for high rates of success.
8. Limit the duration of seatwork.
9. Arrange for overlearning to occur through frequent drill and practice.

vated to engage in these skills at an acceptable level. For example, under highly reinforcing conditions, a learner may be able to use proper social amenities when talking with strangers. However, the same youth may have difficulty in a sales position because of abrupt interactions with potential customers. Similarly, a third-grade student may know her basic addition facts but seldom complete assignments.

Both of these examples illustrate cases in which motivational objectives—objectives intended to influence the occurrence of existing skills—would be highly appropriate. As discussed earlier, skill objectives and motivational development objectives are often closely related.

Many handicapped learners acquire an aversion to academic activities early in their school careers. Subsequently, the teacher may expect that academic skills will not be developed without motivating the student to participate in instruction. In such cases, both motivational and skill training objectives and procedures are important.

Current reinforcement principles form the basis of effective motivational procedures. It is generally recognized that, to a large extent, the consequences for performance that teachers structure into classroom activities influence future performance in similar activities. Classroom activities that produce satisfying consequences are likely to recur. Conversely, activities that produce aversive events are likely to diminish. Educators who recognize and use these principles are more effective in sustaining the goal-directed behavior of their students. Educational activities that provide frequent and immediate rewards for task completion and remove rewards for off-task responses are more likely to promote achievement.

■ **20**   The motivating consequences teachers build into instructional activities should be specific to the characteristics of each child or youth. Events that motivate one learner may be aversive or neutral to another. For example, one student may be highly motivated by praise, whereas being singled out by the teacher for any reason may be quite unpleasant for another student. Therefore, the teacher should be aware of specific consequences that influence each student's behavior.

Beyond identifying a range of motivating consequences for each student, the teacher may create a hierarchy of reinforcers from least to most natural to the classroom setting. Reinforcing consequences that are most natural should be adopted in lieu of unnatural incentives. If they are equally effective, praise and good grades should be selected as reinforcing events over special breaks, consumable items, or tokens. If praise and good grades are ineffective, the other reinforcers may be considered, but the unnatural incentives should always be paired with the more common motivating events.

A number of principles described in behavioral texts suggest potentially effective procedures for selecting and applying consequences. These procedures are presented in Action Plan 4.7.

Having assessed the learner's characteristics, having established instructional goals and objectives, and having developed an advance plan for conducting instruction, the teacher is prepared to initiate instruction. The following section reviews teacher behaviors that have been demonstrated to be effective in carrying out instructional plans.

5. Implement Instruction

○ **14**   The preceding section emphasized the importance of teachers' advance plans, stressing both the expected course of action during a lesson and contingency plans. Without diminishing the importance of advance plans, there is little question that the written procedures cannot convey all potential teacher behaviors exhibited during a lesson. Not stated is the actual approach the teacher uses in carrying out the plan, including the pace of instruction, teacher affect, consistency in implementing planned procedures, proximity of the teacher to the students, and so on. Kounin (1970) has described a number of these approaches, and a subsequent review by Brophy (1983) has supported his findings. The following discussion presents techniques covered in this literature that address the ways effective teachers implement instructional plans.

ACTION PLAN 4.7 SELECTING AND USING CONSEQUENCES

We recommend the following procedures for selecting and using consequences:

1. Select the most natural reinforcing consequence available.
2. Use natural reinforcers, such as praise, liberally and in combination with unnatural incentives.
3. Define for the student the behavior to be reinforced, the surrounding conditions, and the exact reinforcers to be used.
4. Use a variety of reinforcers to avoid satiation.
5. Apply the reinforcement procedures consistently.
6. Monitor the effect of the reinforcement procedures on the student, gradually decreasing the rate or delaying the delivery time of the incentives.
7. When possible, allow the student to self-manage the motivating consequences.
8. Do not allow the learner to acquire satisfying consequences by engaging in disruptive responses (Schloss, Selinger, Goldsmith, & Morrow, 1983).

Continuity and Momentum

■ 21   Effective teachers are able to move rapidly through sequential instructional activities. Continuity is established by instructional sequences that build upon one another without the teacher "backing up" to develop missing information or skills. Momentum is enhanced through speedy transitions from one phase of instruction to the next. Both continuity and momentum result from careful advance planning by the educator. Task sequences, materials, and specific instructional procedures must be prepared in advance to ensure uninterrupted and sequential progress through the lesson.

Continuity and momentum enhance student performance by increasing the extent to which the learners attend to instruction. Conversely, interruptions and digressions have been described as removing the "signal" for continued attention (Brophy, 1983). In short, effective delivery of instruction depends, in part, on teachers obtaining student attention at the start of instruction. Once the students' attention has been obtained, the lesson progresses quickly and sequentially so that their attention is not lost.

Overlapping

To maintain continuity and momentum, educators must be able to conduct several activities at the same time. Effective teachers are able to reinforce or punish individual students while maintaining the pace of instruction with others. Teachers who break the momentum of a lesson to reprimand or praise one student run the risk of losing the attention of all the students.

"With-it-ness"

○ **15**   Continuity and momentum are also enhanced through educators' ability to avert potential performance problems and intervene before major disruptions occur. Effective educators are often able to predict behavior chains that might progress toward severe problems. For example, a teacher may recognize that for one student, two-digit multiplication problems frequently produce frustration, which leads to looking out the window and wringing his hands. These behaviors lead to hand or foot tapping, which attracts peer attention. The child is then likely to produce verbally aggressive statements and, finally, to engage in physically aggressive responses. The concept of "with-it-ness" implies that the teacher is able to recognize this potential chain and intervene at an early stage. By averting the problem at the prefrustration stage, the teacher can avoid a major problem that would break lesson continuity and momentum for all the students.

Numerous teacher behaviors are associated with "with-it-ness." First, effective educators recognize the potential impact of various lesson formats, content, and difficulty levels on student behavior. These teachers structure the lessons in advance to promote success. Also, they are able to anticipate problems that result from unforeseen or uncontrollable events (e.g., staying up too late, getting into a fight on the bus). Second, effective educators continually solicit new data from which they can make more accurate predictions of student performance. They may ask frequent questions, so that the learner's frustration level is not reached. They may also check seatwork at frequent intervals to assess the adequacy of previous instruction. Finally, they may circulate in the classroom, rather than remaining behind their desks. This allows them to monitor and provide feedback on student achievement, and it also puts them in a better position to deliver social reinforcement.

Group Alertness and Accountability

■ **22**   Finally, effective presentation of instruction involves the use of techniques that raise the alertness of students. In general, these techniques involve giving students frequent and random opportunities to demonstrate their knowledge or skill. Specific strategies include randomly interspersing group and individual responding and alternating between calling on volunteers and calling on random students. These strategies prevent the students from anticipating when they will be expected to respond, so they must be continually alert to the possibility that they will be expected to provide information.

6. Evaluate Mastery of Objectives

The second to the last step in the flowchart in figure 4.1 raises a crucial evaluation question: "Is the learner mastering objectives at the expected rate?" This question implies, first, that the objectives were stated in clear and complete terms. Second, it implies that an anticipated progress line (e.g., performance change over time) was established against which the learner's progress could be gauged and that criterion-referenced tests or behavioral observations were employed to assess the student's performance reliably. An affirmative response to the question of a student's progress suggests that the instructional procedures are effective. A negative response indicates a breakdown in the instructional process.

○ **16**   Unfortunately, recognition that a student is not progressing at a desirable rate does not pinpoint the specific problems that occurred during instruction. As emphasized in figure 4.1, one or more errors could have occurred anywhere in the process, from identifying learner characteristics to implementing the plan. It is recommended that to isolate and correct instructional problems, the teacher generate a set of hypotheses, as illustrated in figure 4.4. For example, the teacher may hypothesize that the motivational techniques are ineffective, that the materials are not appropriate, or that the task sequences are too broad. The teacher may then order these hypotheses from most to least likely. He or she may subsequently alter the most likely item on the list (e.g., use tangible instead of social reinforcers) while continuing to present instruction and collect data. If this procedure has the desired result, a permanent change will be made and instruction may continue until the objective is achieved. If it does not, the teacher may alter the second item on the list (e.g., utilize high-interest materials). Again, the teacher may test to determine whether the desired effect is obtained. If not, the next item on the list may be addressed, and so on.

It is critical to this approach that instructional procedures hypothesized to be deficient are altered and evaluated separately and sequentially. This strategy allows the teacher to accept or rule out individual hypotheses one at a time. Altering several instructional conditions does not allow the teacher to isolate specific problems. The result may be that the teacher (1) corrects one problem while creating a new one, (2) creates additional problems while not addressing the actual problem, or (3) corrects the actual problem at the cost of focusing increased time and effort on additional areas that were not problematic.

■ **23**   If all reasonable hypotheses have been tested and the learner is still performing below expectations, the final step is to alter the expectations. This, of course, is accomplished by revising the goal statement. A major advantage to this approach is that performance problems are not addressed by an automatic reaction to lower expectations. This practice would (and often does) initiate a self-fulfilling prophecy, in that inappropriate instruc-

FIGURE 4.4   Hypothesis-Testing Procedure for Identifying Instructional Problems

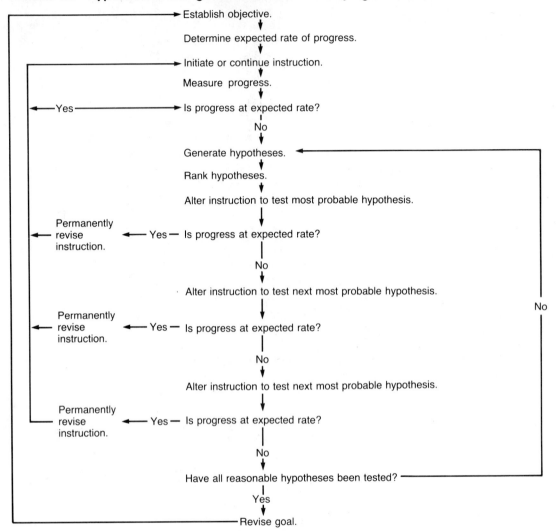

tion is misinterpreted as student failure and attributed to the student's exceptionality. It is recommended, however, that student failure be a signal for evaluation of each component of instruction. When such evaluation has been done, the decision to revise expectations is based on the knowledge that every reasonable effort has been made to test instructional procedures that might be accountable for the suppressed performance.

7. Determine Whether Goals Have Been Achieved

The net result of effective instruction is achievement of socially valid instructional goals. Therefore, the final step in the sequence of instructional activities raises the question, "Has the learner achieved the goal?" The appropriate reaction to an affirmative response to this question is to establish and initiate instruction toward another goal. Negative responses should not occur, as performance problems should have been identified early and should have signaled revision of instructional activities or goals.

Goal achievement has major effects on the student and the teacher. The most direct result is that the learner possesses a skill or information base that he or she did not have prior to instruction. For many handicapped learners, the additional knowledge or skill may make available a range of natural consequences (e.g., community mobility, access and success to recreational or leisure settings, the ability to earn and spend money). A related consequence of goal achievement is that the student experiences success in the school setting. For many students, success motivates future efforts in similar curriculum endeavors (R. W. White, 1960). Also, goal attainment may help the student form a "learning set"; that is, the student's success allows him or her to benefit from future instruction—he or she learns how to learn. Finally, an instructional sequence that leads to goal attainment provides the educator with valuable assessment data indicating effective educational strategies for the learner. Subsequent educational interventions may then employ similar techniques.

SUMMARY

This chapter has outlined a sequence for designing and implementing instruction for mildly handicapped learners. The critical steps include identifying learner characteristics; establishing goals, objectives, and task sequences; designing and implementing instruction; and establishing evaluation procedures for troubleshooting instructional deficiencies.

The procedures for designing and implementing instruction that have been discussed in detail here will be applied to specific content areas in part III of this text. Chapter 12, for example, will review this sequence of instructional activities with special emphasis on specific strategies that are most effective for achieving math goals and objectives.

CASE FOR ACTION 4.2

You are asked by your building administrator to help the third-grade teacher develop an instructional plan for a student in her class. When you talk to the teacher, you find that the major problem with the student is in spelling. Although the learner's other academic skills are above grade level, he spells at the first-grade level. The teacher reports that her primary source of information is his performance on a standardized achievement test administered twice a year. When asked about instructional procedures used during spelling class, the teacher describes the following sequence of activities: She assigns a section in the spelling workbook at the start of each week. She then grades the section in class. Next, she asks the students to correct their errors. Then she gives a quiz covering the words in the section. Finally, she requires that students write words missed on the quiz five times. What elements are missing from her instructional plan? What would you suggest she do to restructure instruction for this learner (and others)?

5

Criterion-Referenced Measurement: Paper-and-Pencil Instruments

■ DID YOU KNOW THAT...

■ 1 ...teachers are able to determine which instructional methods are most effective and efficient by collecting student performance data?

■ 2 ...norm-referenced tests are designed to measure interindividual differences—the differences between one person and other persons in a group?

■ 3 ...criterion-referenced tests are designed to direct the instructional process?

■ 4 ...criterion-referenced tests are designed to measure intraindividual differences—differences within a single student?

■ 5 ...criterion-referenced tests may include direct observation of student performance as well as paper-and-pencil measurements?

■ 6 ...objectives must be stated in clear and complete terms?

■ 7 ...a teacher acquires more information by assessing performance on subskills than by assessing performance on terminal objectives?

■ 8 ...a teacher may be able to identify students' specific skill deficiencies by conducting an analysis?

■ 9   . . . teachers should report test scores as falling within a range that takes into account the extent of error in testing?

■10   . . . even if a test is reliable, it may not be valid?

○ CAN YOU . . .

○ 1   . . . avoid the negative aspects (or limitations) of norm-referenced tests?

○ 2   . . . determine the extent to which students have accomplished objectives by using criterion-referenced tests?

○ 3   . . . develop a criterion-referenced test?

○ 4   . . . write complete behavioral objectives?

○ 5   . . . formulate test specifications that include the objective and subskills to be measured, the stimulus features, and the expected response features?

○ 6   . . . develop binary-choice, multiple-choice, matching, short-answer, and essay items?

○ 7   . . . conduct an error analysis?

○ 8   . . . evaluate the reliability of a test?

○ 9   . . . develop a test that exhibits content, concurrent, and predictive validity?

○ 10   . . . determine the instructional sensitivity of a test?

Two earlier chapters have discussed the importance of instructional evaluation. Chapter 2 linked assessment directly to curriculum development. The curriculum model encourages educators to develop objectives from observations of people in functional settings. Matching curriculum objectives to the behavioral standards established in natural environments is intended to enhance the impact of training on the learner's adult adjustment. This curriculum development process includes features for testing the student's skill acquisition. Once the skills required in the functional settings are identified, the teacher is encouraged to construct a skills checklist, which is intended to assess the learner's level of proficiency on the curriculum objectives prior to instruction. Skills on which the learner fails to demonstrate proficiency become the focus of instruction. The checklist is also recommended for use during and after instruction to evaluate the learner's progress.

Chapter 4, in describing the direct instructional sequence, reemphasized the importance of evaluation. The teacher is encouraged to be continually alert to breakdowns in the learning process. This alertness is operationalized as the continual and precise measurement of student performance. As problems become apparent, the teacher is encouraged to use systematic evaluation procedures to pinpoint deficiencies in instruction. This process involves altering one facet of instruction at a time, while continually measuring the students' performance. Instructional procedures used during peak performance may be identified as the most effective. For example, if the teacher changes the reading group's composition, a comparison of the data generated after this change with the data before the change would indicate whether or not the new reading group composition enhanced learning.

■ 1   In general, the primary reason for collecting pupil performance data is to assess the effectiveness of the educational program. Frequent measurement reduces the time and effort spent in using nonproductive instructional methods. A related function of frequent measurement is identification of the most efficient and most effective instructional methods. Continuous measurement allows the educator to test educational procedures reliably. Procedures that produce the greatest performance gains may then be repeated, and those that fail to produce relatively strong effects may be discontinued. These measurement data also motivate the teacher to carry out systematic instructional programs. Graphic depiction of performance changes encourages many teachers to upgrade and intensify instruction continually. Sharing these data with parents, the student, and the multidisciplinary team can also produce a sense of satisfaction for the teacher. Finally, public posting of behavioral data has been demonstrated to have a positive effect on achievement (Van Houten, Hill, & Parsons, 1975; Van Houten, Morrison, Jarvis, & McDonald, 1974). Simply making evaluative information available to students may, in and of itself, have a positive impact on performance.

ASSESSMENT TECHNIQUES

Up to this point, the terms *evaluation, measurement,* and *assessment* have been used to describe a general process of collecting pupil performance data. The actual procedures to be followed in collecting data have not been discussed. Before we embark on the description of specific assessment techniques, it is important to recognize how various assessment approaches can be used during instruction. The following sections will discuss the assessment strategies that are frequently used in special education programs.

Norm-Referenced Measures

■ 2   Probably the most frequently used distinction in assessment procedures is that between *criterion-referenced measures* and *norm-referenced measures*. Norm-referenced measures report interindividual differences—differences between one person and a group of persons. Scores on a standardized achievement test, for example, compare a student's performance to that of a normative sample. A percentile rank of 74 indicates that of this reference group, 74% obtained scores the same as or lower than the student's score; 26%, of course, had scores higher than that of the student. Similarly, an intelligence test score of 68, or two standard deviations below the average score, indicates that slightly more than 2% of the normative sample scored below that score.

○ 1   Several major problems limit the usefulness of norm-referenced tests for direct instructional purposes. First, norm-referenced tests provide more information on how an individual's skill level compares to the skill level of others than on how his or her skills compare to community standards. Knowing that Billy, a senior in high school, is achieving at the sixth-grade level in math and reading tells us that his performance is comparable to a median score for the sixth-grade students taking the test. It does not, however, provide an indication of the direction Billy's instruction should take. For example, it doesn't tell us the reading level required for Billy to succeed in his chosen career.

A second limitation of norm-referenced tests is that special needs students are often underrepresented or unrepresented in the norm group. For example, the authors of the Illinois Test of Psycholinguistic Abilities, a norm-referenced test frequently used to diagnose learning disabilities, did not include learning disabled or other handicapped persons in the standardization sample (Salvia & Ysseldyke, 1985). Consequently, comparing data obtained from learning disabled students to the norm group is comparable to referencing the temperature in Quebec, Canada, to the average temperature in the United States.

A third limitation is that norm-referenced tests have been determined to discriminate against minority students (Anastasi, 1976). Language, experiential, and competitive aspects of these tests place children and youth from minority cultures at a decided disadvantage. At best, scores obtained from these learners may predict how they will perform in the dominant culture (Sattler, 1974). Unfortunately, they will do little to project the learners' potential for success in their home community.

The fourth limitation involves frequency and ease of administration. The majority of commercially available norm-referenced measures require a substantial amount of administration time. Many standardized tests require specialized training on the part of the psychometrician. In addition, these tests may not be administered with sufficient frequency to be sensitive to performance changes that occur during instruction. Annual or semiannual administrations limit the teacher to making instructional decisions after the fact, because by the time standardized achievement test data are obtained, a good portion of the school year has elapsed.

Finally, many norm-referenced tests have limited diagnostic potential from a skill training perspective. Efforts to use norm-referenced tests to establish modality preferences that enhance learning have not proved successful (Sedlak & Weener, 1973; Tarver & Dawson, 1980; Ysseldyke, 1973). In addition, the standardization procedure or protocol the examiner must follow to ensure that the conditions of the student's performance are comparable to those of the norm group seldom allows the teacher to test instructional hypotheses. For example, it may be meaningful to determine whether the students' reading performance can be enhanced through the use of social praise, but introducing social praise for correct responses on the reading achievement test would violate the standardization procedure. Consequently, the learner's data could not be accurately referenced to the norm group, as it was not tested under the same conditions.

Despite these limitations, norm-referenced measures have two major values. The first is their usefulness as a *placement evaluation*. Unlike criterion-referenced test data, which will be discussed shortly, norm-referenced tests produce a measure of student behavior that is interpretable to professionals across geographic areas and disciplines and over time. Intelligence tests, aptitude tests, college boards, and certain achievement tests, for example, produce scores that have universal meaning to people in education-related professions. Data derived from these tests, when combined with other information, may be used to make decisions about the student's potential in a given curriculum or program. Similarly, as one of several sources of data, achievement test and intelligence test scores may assist the multidisciplinary team in identifying an appropriate educational placement. It should not be overlooked that the majority of special education labels and subsequent placements are tied by law to norm-referenced measures. Adaptive behavior scales and intelligence tests, for example, are used in arriving at the diagnosis of mental retardation (Grossman, 1973), and performance on the Snellen Chart is tied to the classification of visual impairments (Hatfield, 1975).

The second major value of norm-referenced tests lies in their importance as a *summative evaluation* of the student's long-term performance (B. Bloom, Hastings, & Madaus, 1971). The standardization procedure used with these measures allows the teacher to administer the test series annually and to produce directly comparable data. When these data are matched to the classroom curriculum, they can be used as a general measure of the efficacy of the instructional program. As discussed earlier, these data are not sufficient for instructional purposes, but they do provide a fair appraisal of the long-term benefits of instruction.

Criterion-Referenced Measures

■ 3   It should be evident at this point that although norm-referenced measures are recommended for placement and summative purposes, criterion-referenced tests are the backbone of the continuous direct instructional process. Specifically, criterion-referenced tests are used for diagnostic and formative evaluation purposes.

■ 4   *Formative evaluation* refers to the assessment of learner performance during instruction to ensure steady progress toward the instructional objective (B. Bloom et al., 1971). In contrast to norm-referenced measures, criterion-referenced tests are designed by the teacher to evaluate intraindividual—within the student—differences. Whereas norm-referenced measures compare the learner's performance to that of a group of individuals, criterion-referenced tests compare the learner to the instructional objectives. Thus, rather than reporting a student's standing in the standardization group, a criterion-referenced test reports the learner's standing against the objective. For example, a criterion-referenced test may reveal 80% accuracy in math computation, the ability to change a tire, or an assembly rate of six trusses per hour.

○ 2   Criterion-referenced tests used for the purpose of formative evaluation can be administered at regular intervals. For example, a teacher may give a ten-item computation test at the start of each math period, with the items based on the skills introduced or practiced in the previous math period. Data from these daily assessments allow the teacher to identify the extent to which the objectives of the preceding lesson were met.

Formative evaluation data may also be used to gauge the rate at which new information is introduced. The task-analytic process discussed in earlier chapters involves arranging skills in a logical sequence that leads to the terminal objective. The first skill in the sequence (or the last if backward chaining) is taught to proficiency; then the next skill is introduced. Again, this skill is mastered before the third skill is introduced. This process continues until all skills in the sequence are introduced and mastered. The unwritten assumption is that the teacher has a reliable instrument for ensuring the mastery of each skill in the instructional sequence. The failure to accurately assess skill attainment in each step may lead to gaps in the student's knowledge, or, more critical, the student may not possess the prerequisite skills to progress along the task sequence. For example, not learning to grasp a bat properly before receiving instructions on swinging may lead to failure, since the proper grasp is necessary for a good swing.

Diagnostic evaluation involves the use of criterion-referenced tests to uncover learning difficulties and identify effective educational programs. At a gross level, diagnostic evaluation occurs when a criterion-referenced test demonstrates that the student has not mastered the target skill. The recommendation at this level is for some form of instruction to continue before the next skill in the sequence is introduced. This information, though very important, is not sufficient, as it may simply lead to the continuation of faulty instruction. For example, a student may do poorly on her weekly spelling words, only to have the same words presented in the same manner the following week. It may be that all she needed was additional drill and practice to master the words. Additional use of the criterion-referenced test as a diagnostic indicator, however, might have provided additional insights to facilitate learning.

A more refined level of analysis may be the identification of specific deficiencies in the learner's performance through error analysis procedures (to be discussed later). Beyond simply noting that a skill was not acquired, this level encourages the identification of specific errors that occur during the student's attempts to perform the skill. In the previous example of the poor speller, criterion-referenced test data could be studied to identify patterns of errors that have instructional implications. For example, such an analysis might indicate that the learner had difficulty with specific letter configurations or phonetic conventions.

The most precise level of evaluation is to identify the relative effectiveness of various instructional procedures. As has been repeatedly emphasized, criterion-referenced test data, used wisely, can assist the teacher in matching the most efficient and effective instructional procedures to the learner's characteristics. On alternating lessons, for example, a teacher may change the ratio of teacher-directed instruction to seatwork. Data from criterion-referenced measures taken on high teacher-directed instruction/low seatwork days may be compared with those from low teacher-directed instruction/high seatwork days to determine the ratio that is most effective for the learner.

Summary

Four major forms of assessment are used in direct instruction: placement evaluation, formative evaluation, diagnostic evaluation, and summative evaluation. As depicted in figure 5.1, norm-referenced measures are recommended primarily for placement and summative evaluation purposes, whereas criterion-referenced measures are recommended for formative and diagnostic purposes. Used collectively, these measures provide an empirical basis for designing, implementing, evaluating, and modifying special education programs.

FIGURE 5.1   Relationship Between Assessment Techniques

Assessment Technique	Function	Common Procedures
Placement	Establishing the student's current level of proficiency so that decisions can be made regarding classroom or program placement, appropriate curriculum objectives, and effective educational procedures	Standardized or norm-referenced achievement tests, aptitude tests, readiness tests; criterion-referenced tests, self-reports, other's reports, anecdotal records; observational techniques
Formative	Establishing the attainment of objectives and subskills, determining learning rate, providing feedback on instructional progress	Criterion-referenced measures; observational techniques
Diagnostic	Identifying relationships between performance problems and instructional procedures, identifying and correcting performance problems	Criterion-referenced measures, observational techniques
Summative	Determining long-term progress for the purpose of certifying the mastery of objectives, assigning grades, and determining future grade placement	Standardized or norm-referenced achievement tests, skill checklists, records of cumulative performance

CRITERION-REFERENCED TEST DEVELOPMENT

■ **5**   We have defined a criterion-referenced test as any measure that reliably contrasts a person's performance with that of an objective standard. Therefore, criterion-referenced tests are not limited to traditional paper-and-pencil measures. They also include procedures that involve the recording of student performance through direct observations. Because of substantial differences in the way paper-and-pencil measures and observational measures are conducted, the latter will be discussed in a separate chapter. Furthermore, because of broad differences in the design and intent of commercially available norm-referenced tests, they will be reviewed only briefly in the educational competencies section. Beyond this, the reader is encouraged to refer to the comprehensive review of special education-related assessment instruments by Salvia and Ysseldyke (1985). The remainder of this chapter will focus on the design and use of paper-and-pencil criterion-referenced measures.

  It should be no surprise that criterion-referenced tests are an inseparable part of the curriculum process. There is a direct correspondence between the curriculum development procedures described in chapter 2 and criterion-referenced test development procedures. Therefore, a portion of this discussion will overlap the discussion in chapter 2.

○ **3**   Seven basic steps involved in the preparation of a criterion-referenced measurement system are presented in Action Plan 5.1. The following sections will discuss each of these steps.

1. Identify Objectives

■ **6**   The major value of a criterion-referenced test is its ability to detect discrepancies between students' performance and preestablished behavioral standards. Again, the intent of a criterion-referenced test is to compare a student's ability to a precise objective, which is possible only if the behavioral standard or objective is stated in clear and complete terms. Recent interest in the field in general has led commercial publishers to market criterion-referenced instruments. Although several fine instruments have been developed, some publishers have set criterion cutoffs on the total score or subscores of general performance tests. Although this feature gives the appearance of a criterion-referenced measurement, it overlooks the most crucial aspect of such tests—the ability to specify the precise skill level of the individual with reference to his or her individual educational objectives.

  The foundation on which criterion-referenced tests are built is the learner's set of educational objectives. Knowing that a learner has met the criteria for speed and accuracy in typing is useful only if we agree on the precise nature of the objective underlying the criteria. Was the use of a manual, electric, or electronic typewriter specified? Did the rate reflect the words per minute over a 3-minute timed trial or over an average workday?

ACTION PLAN 5.1   PROCEDURES FOR DEVELOPING A CRITERION-REFERENCED TEST

We recommend the following steps for preparing a criterion-referenced test:

1. Identify in clear and complete terms the objective to be developed through instruction.
2. Enumerate the subskills (i.e., task sequences or enabling skills) subsumed by the objectives.
3. Establish test specifications that describe the objectives, subskills, stimulus features, and response features of the test.
4. Develop items that provide multiple opportunities for the learner to demonstrate each subskill.
5. Develop a recording/scoring procedure that reflects the learner's performance on items measuring common subskills.
6. Design a process for evaluating the reliability of the instrument.
7. Design a process for evaluating the validity of assessment.

○ **4**   As discussed in chapter 3, behavioral objectives include four major components: (1) the student's name, (2) the target response, (3) the conditions under which the response is to occur, and (4) the performance criteria. A well-designed criterion-referenced test is a natural extension of the objective. From a test construction standpoint, the target response and the conditions of performance components dictate the stimulus and response dimensions of the test. From an interpretation standpoint, the entire multi-disciplinary team should be able to agree on precisely what is being measured and how it relates to the team's expectations for the student.

2. Enumerate Subskills

Data indicating a student's performance on a typical objective are generally too broad to produce useful formative or diagnostic information. Even short-term objectives often require a week to a month for completion. A criterion-referenced test that measures performance of the objective might not be sensitive to the intermediate skills acquired each instructional period. Therefore, although such a test would be a useful summative measure, it would be of limited value for making "in-flight" decisions about instruction.

■ 7   To overcome this limitation, assessment procedures are often linked to the task sequence or subskill of the objective. For example, a common breakdown of subskills in typing involves locating the home keys on the left hand, the home keys on the right hand, the third row keys on the right hand, the third row keys on the left hand, and so on. Rather than assessing the terminal objective of identifying key locations, the instructor would gain more information by assessing the subskills of locating specific keystrokes. Related examples are depicted in figure 5.2.

It should be apparent that the subskills further delimit the scope of the test. Once the subskills have been stated, there should be little question of precisely what the test is intended to measure. Furthermore, the enumeration of subskills provides a clear reference point for the construction of particular test items. If one subskill is to use a ruler to measure varying lengths from 1 to 12 inches, specific test items should evaluate the learner's ability to exhibit this specific behavior. If using the ruler to draw a straight line is not included as a subskill, items testing this ability should not be included. Once the objective and the subskills have been established, the next logical step is to describe the test specifications. This procedure is a direct offshoot of the previous steps.

3. Establish Test Specifications

Popham (1978) has argued:

> The most important attribute of a criterion-referenced test is that it provides a clear description of the class of behavior that the examinee can or cannot perform. In fact this description of measured behavior constitutes the criterion to which the test is referenced. (p. 114)

FIGURE 5.2   Relationship Between a Short-Term Objective and the Subskills Assessed by a Criterion-Referenced Test

Objective	Subskill Assessed
Identification of letters of the alphabet	Identifying A, B, C, . . . Z
Identification of Roman numerals	Identifying I, II, III, . . . X
Identification of the major components of a standard ignition system	Identifying spark plug, spark plug wire, distributor, points, condenser, rotor, alternator, voltage regulator, battery
Construction of a wooden box	Measuring parts, squaring parts, cutting parts, applying glue, nailing, sanding edges, applying stain, applying lacquer, steel wooling the finish

Teachers can seldom afford the time to prepare a written statement describing the test specifications, even though the importance of this information might warrant it. In lieu of such a written description, the teacher should at least have a conceptual image of the test specifications. Again, it is the test specification that allows the multidisciplinary team, the parents, and the student to interpret the resulting data.

○ **5**   Test specifications include three general components, the first of which is a statement of *the objective and the subskills being measured.* This statement communicates the scope of the test, so that the teacher and others have a clear understanding of precisely what is being assessed. Highly reliable data are of little use for making instructional decisions if they are not accompanied by an accurate description of the skills being measured. Knowledge of the objective and the subskills allow educators and others to place an instructional value on the student's score.

The second component is *the stimulus features*—that is, the procedures and materials used in the test to elicit a student's response. Stimulus attributes should include all of the critical dimensions that indicate how assessment items were designed and presented (Popham, 1978). Also, they should be consistent with the condition statement of the behavioral objective. In other words, the same stimuli should be available to the learner during the test as are included in the condition statement of the objective. For example, if the objective states that "provided a calculator, John will be able to solve division problems with multiple-digit divisors," the stimulus features of the test should include the use of a calculator. Similarly, an objective specifying the ability to drive eightpenny common nails using a 16-ounce hammer should be tested using these materials.

Common conditions of behavioral objectives that should be reflected in criterion-referenced tests include support information available to the student, such as charts, reference books, calculators, maps, word lists; the amount of time the stimuli are present before a response is expected; and competing stimulus features or incidental events that detract from the learner's performance. In addition, the dimension through which information is presented to the learner is a crucial aspect of the test specification. Potential presentation dimensions include the following: (1) *construct* objects to demonstrate important aspects of the instructions or questions; (2) *present* a fixed visual display of instructions or questions; (3) *state* questions or instructions, or (4) *graphically symbolize* questions or instructions in a nonpictoral format (Cawley et al., 1973).

The final component of the test specification is the *response feature*—the format through which the learner is expected to respond to the stimulus features. Response features include the critical dimensions influencing the learner's response. As with the stimulus features, the response features should be consistent with the target response statement of the objective. The same response features described in the objective should be produced in the criterion-referenced test. If the objective states that the student should be able to operate a lawnmower safely, the test should measure his or her ability to actually operate a lawnmower. A test requiring paper-and-pencil responses would be appropriate only if the objective stated that the learner should be able to list or identify safe operating procedures for a lawnmower.

In addition to the dimension or modality of the response, other response features that may be specified include whether or not the amount of time or space provided for a response is limited; the specific format of the response; and behaviors peripheral to the target response that can influence performance, such as spelling, penmanship, and neatness. As with the stimulus features, the dimension through which a response is provided is extremely important. Response dimensions that may be matched to the original instructional objective include the following: (1) construct or manipulate objects in producing a response; (2) select a response from multiple choices; (3) state a response; or (4) graphically symbolize a response. These response dimensions and the stimulus dimensions are summarized in figure 5.3.

CASE FOR ACTION 5.1

You are asked to develop a set of criterion-referenced tests for the school's mathematics curriculum. Before actually selecting or writing items, you will develop the specifications for each test. Write the specifications for a test designed to evaluate a student's mastery of math numeration.

FIGURE 5.3 Stimulus and Response Dimensions of a Criterion-Referenced Test

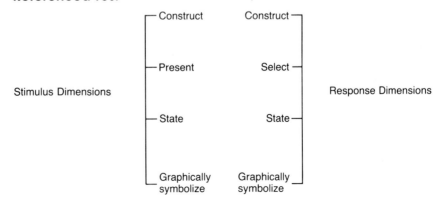

4. Develop Items

Item development is directly governed by the test specifications. The objective and the subskills establish the scope of the test. The stimulus features dictate the nature of the instructions and questions. Finally, the response features indicate the format and modality through which the learner is expected to respond. In general, these three components of the test specification enhance the *validity* of the test (i.e., the extent to which the test measures what it purports to measure), whereas test item construction and scoring procedures enhance the *reliability* or accuracy of the test. Of course, a test that is not a reliable or accurate measure of the student's performance, regardless of the quality of the test specification, will not produce valid information. Therefore, the development of reliable test items is a crucial aspect of criterion-referenced measurement.

Reliable tests can be characterized by six major features. *First, the scope of the test should be limited so that the learner's performance can be easily interpreted.* As emphasized earlier, a good rule of thumb is for the test to measure performance on the subskills of only one objective. Depending on the complexity of the subskills, the expected level of performance for the student, and the amount of instruction preceding the test, only a few or all of the subskills may be measured.

Second, the test should include from 5 to 20 items designed to measure each subskill. The more opportunities a learner has to demonstrate a skill, the more reliable the measure of performance will be. For example, if diving competitions in the Summer Olympics were judged on the basis of one dive, the probability of error in awarding the gold medal would be substantial. Because numerous dives are included in the final tabulations, the likelihood of selecting the best diver on a given day is increased. In the first case, idiosyncratic factors (e.g., wind gusts, nervousness, unfamiliarity with the diving board) could bias the performance. In the second case, these factors are distributed across participants by the number of opportunities to perform.

Third, instructions for completing the test should be clear and complete. All information necessary for responding to the test items should be included in terms that are easily understood by the learner. To ensure the adequacy of the instructions, the test may include one or two sample items, which allow the student to demonstrate his or her understanding of the instructions before being expected to perform.

Fourth, information provided in the question should be unambiguous. Only one reasonable interpretation should be possible for each question, so that the learner's response is a measure of his or her knowledge or skill rather than of the ability to make subtle inferences.

Fifth, the vocabulary and syntax of the questions should be well within the student's ability. For example, complex sentence structure in math word problems may be a major cause of a student's errors, and the test may be performed more as a measure of language skills than math computation.

Finally, embedded clues that provide sufficient information for even an unknowledgeable person to do well should be avoided. Students have been described as "test wise" because of their ability to identify correct responses from the structure of the item. Embedded clues can be obvious, as in the following example:

> What year in recent history did Wall Street set a record for trading volume?
>
> a. 1969 (This is the only date "in recent history.")
> b. 1942
> c. 1913
> d. 1917

Or they may be more subtle, as in this example:

> Who is the well-known comedian known for the theme song, "Thanks for the Memories"?
>
> a. Bill Washington
> b. Bette Davis
> c. Bob Hope (This is the only comedian.)
> d. Howard Cosell

○ **6**   Popham (1978) has defined the most frequently used criterion-referenced test items and has discussed their advantages, their disadvantages, and proposed guidelines for their preparation. The following is a summary of his discussion.

Binary-Choice Items

DEFINITION   Binary-choice items require that the student pick the correct response from two possibilities. The most common form is true/false. Other forms include yes/no, agree/disagree, popular/unpopular, reptile/ mammal, Christian/pagan, and so on.

ADVANTAGES   Binary-choice items are among the easiest to produce and score. They can be used to cover a wide range of content.

DISADVANTAGES   The greatest weakness of binary-choice items is the fact that a correct response can be provided 50 % of the time by chance alone. They are also limited to testing discrete concepts, thereby promoting rote memorization. Similarly, they can be used only to assess objectives specifying that the learner will be able to select from alternatives. Finally, binary-choice tests imply that there are always two extremes (e.g., correct or incorrect). In reality, this is seldom the case; many concepts are partially right or wrong.

SUGGESTIONS   Use binary-choice items sparingly and only when the content naturally breaks down into two categories. Avoid complex and lengthy sentences that are more likely to assess reading ability than content knowledge. Avoid negative statements, and never use double negatives. Include only one concept in each item. In the example, *"Boxers are the most gifted of all atheletes, because they are more able to sustain punishment than others,"* the student must first discern whether one or both concepts are correct, then decide if the relationship between the two is accurate. In scoring the response, the teacher cannot be certain which portion of the information the student had difficulty with. Thus, the diagnostic potential is severely limited. Another important factor is that a relatively equal number of items should be scored with each answer choice. Finally, the length of the items should remain constant. Since true items frequently contain more qualifiers than false items, item length alone can clue the learner to the correct response.

Multiple-Choice Items

DEFINITION   Multiple-choice items include a question or incomplete statement, referred to as a stem, and a set of possible answers. Only one of the answers is correct; the remaining answers or foils are incorrect.

ADVANTAGES   Multiple-choice items can be used to assess a variety of cognitive and affective responses. The large number of foils decreases the probability that students will *guess* answers correctly. Finally, multiple-choice tests are not affected by a student's response set or predisposition to score in a particular manner.

DISADVANTAGES   As with binary-choice items, multiple-choice items are only useful in evaluating objectives that state that the learner will be able to select from alternatives. They do not measure a student's ability to construct, verbally respond, or graphically symbolize. Although the ability to select and the ability to state may be correlated, the teacher cannot be certain that the student would be able to produce a correct response if it were not presented among several alternatives. A related problem is that, as with binary-choice items, the student is encouraged to memorize discrete facts. The test does not measure the student's convergent or divergent capabilities.

SUGGESTIONS   Foremost, the stem should provide sufficient information from which a fill-in-the-blank response could be produced. In other words, students should be able to answer items correctly without benefit of the response alternatives.

Similarly, the response options should be as brief as possible; all repetitive information should be contained in the stem. As with binary-choice items, negatively stated stems should be avoided, and double negatives should not be used in the stem or in the response options. The response alternatives should be unambiguous, and only one should be correct. However, each of the responses should be plausible, as obviously incorrect answers limit the actual number of foils. Each response option should be grammatically consistent with the stem and of a roughly equivalent length. Finally, "all of the above" and "none of the above" alternatives should be avoided. These response options reduce the demand for a student to evaluate each possible option and select the most accurate one.

Matching Items

DEFINITION Matching items require that the student pair words or phrases from two parallel lists.

ADVANTAGES The primary strength of matching items is that a substantial amount of information can be tested in a relatively small space. Also, matching items are fairly easy to construct, as compared to multiple-choice questions. Finally, matching items can be scored objectively.

DISADVANTAGES As with multiple-choice items, matching items can only assess objectives in the "select" dimension. Consequently, objectives requiring a student to construct, verbalize, or graphically symbolize cannot be assessed through this format. Furthermore, many objectives do not rapidly produce homogeneous matching lists. Also, as with the preceding item types, matching questions require simple rote associations.

SUGGESTIONS As with all forms of test questions, information presented in the columns of matching items should be unambiguous. There should be one and only one correct match for each entry. The lists and matching items should be homogeneous (e.g., matching parts of an engine with their function, presidents with their achievements, states with their capitals). More items should be included in the response column than in the premise column so that the learner cannot match the last item by default. The responses should be listed in logical order, providing additional clues. The instructions should specify the basis on which matches are to be formed. Finally, the entire question set should be included on a single page.

Short-Answer Items

DEFINITION Short-answer items require that the student respond to a question or incomplete statement by providing a word or phrase.

ADVANTAGES The major advantage of short-answer items is that they permit the measurement of "construct," "graphically symbolize," and "verbalize" objectives. Thus, they assess higher level convergent and divergent abilities than the preceding forms of items. Also, short-answer items can assess a broad range of concepts and skills in a brief amount of time. Finally, these items may be more easily constructed than any of the preceding forms.

DISADVANTAGES The major limitation of short-answer items is the speed and accuracy of scoring. Short-answer items require that the teacher analyze each response and make subjective judgments. A specific item may have several correct responses, and some responses may be partially correct. With the exception of essay responses, the manner in which short-answer items are scored is more prone to errors than any other type of test.

SUGGESTIONS Short-answer items should be constructed in a manner that limits the student's response to a word or brief phrase. Open-ended questions that are more likely to be answered with an extensive discussion should be avoided. Similarly, each question or statement should be developed with one response in mind. Qualifiers may be included in the question to limit the response to the precise answer. The number of blanks in incomplete statements should be limited to one or two; additional blanks create unnecessary ambiguity and compound potential errors. If a student gets one blank wrong, he or she has less information from which to produce the subsequent answers. Finally, the blanks should be a uniform length. Variable lengths provide embedded clues or distractions.

Essay Items
DEFINITION There are two forms of essay items, both requiring that the student provide a relatively long written response to a question. The *restricted response* item limits the scope or length of the response; the *extended response* item gives the student more flexibility in formulating an answer.

ADVANTAGES As with short-answer items, essay items are able to evaluate objectives outside the "select" dimension. By far, essay responses require the highest level of thought. They are able to assess convergent processes, whereby the student brings together discrete pieces of information to produce a unified response. Also, they can evaluate divergent processes, whereby the student uses his or her restricted information to respond to broad issues. Finally, more than any other test form, a small amount of time in question preparation can produce a substantial amount of student information. A one-sentence question, for example, can produce reasonable information on the breadth and depth of a student's knowledge and his or her ability to organize and integrate the knowledge.

DISADVANTAGES As with short-answer items, the major limitation of essay items is the speed and accuracy of scoring. There is little question that essay items are most prone to reliability errors in scoring. Equally important, the amount of time spent in evaluating one student's test may exceed the time required to grade an entire class's multiple-choice or binary-choice exam. Except in extremely well prescribed restricted items, little advance structure is placed on the response. Thus, the teacher cannot be entirely certain that he or she will sample the appropriate information. Similarly, because of the time required in completing an essay exam, relatively few times can be addressed. Therefore, the text may sample an insufficient number of skills or concepts.

SUGGESTIONS For most objectives, restrictive questions are preferred to open-ended items, because it is possible for reliable preconceived scoring criteria to be developed for the restrictive items. To assist in delimiting items, prepare a set of scoring criteria in advance. Be certain that there is a direct relationship between the qualifiers in the item and the criteria for scoring. If spelling, grammar, and penmanship are part of the objective being evaluated, they should be qualified in the question and reflected in the scoring. Specify, in advance, the amount of time provided for each item. Contrary to common practice, do not allow the student to select from several questions. If a particular skill is important, it should be sampled; if not, it should be deleted. Finally, if possible, the teacher should arrange for another person, possibly a neighboring teacher or aide, to evaluate sample items using the preconceived scoring criteria. Then the teacher can compare his or her scores with those of the independent evaluator. This procedure will provide an informal test of the adequacy of the scoring criteria.

5. Develop Recording/Scoring Procedures

It should again be emphasized that one of the major purposes of criterion-referenced measurement is to provide detailed information about student performance. Simply obtaining percentage-correct data does not make use of the full potential of the test. For example, if two students obtain identical test scores of 90% on a word attack skill test, this information provides a rough estimate of the relative proficiency of the two students on the subskills included in the test. However, it does not indicate differences in proficiency within each subskill. One of the students might have made a majority of his or her errors on decoding the silent k in kn (e.g., knife). Although this information is important for providing subsequent instruction, the percentage-correct data could lull the teacher into believing that a minimum level of proficiency was reached and that entirely new skills could be introduced.

■ 8   Sedlak, Steppe-Jones, and Sedlak (1982) have described a very useful procedure for obtaining diagnostic information from a criterion-referenced test. The procedure, referred to as *error analysis*, involves systematic evaluation of students' responses on a test for the purpose of identifying common mistakes. These mistakes are then hypothesized to indicate specific skill deficiencies that may become the focus of future instruction.

○ 7   The initial planning of a criterion-referenced test can substantially reduce the amount of time spent in conducting an error analysis. As discussed earlier, the test specifications identify the subskills to be measured by the test, and from 5 to 20 test items developed for the test are matched directly to these subskills. By design, the majority of instructional deficiencies may be noted within one or more of the subskills. Error analysis then involves obtaining component scores that reflect performance on the individual subskills. When a subskill score is below criterion, the teacher can study the subskill items to obtain further clues to assist in subsequent instruction. Action Plan 5.2 summarizes the steps involved in conducting an error analysis.

The examples presented in figures 5.4 and 5.5 illustrate the value of error analysis. The first example, in figure 5.4, includes five problems for each of four subskills. The total score for the test is 16 of 20, or 80%. The 80% correct score is rather deceiving in that it suggests a generally high level of competence, whereas error analysis data reveal that the majority of errors occurred in subskill D—product of 2-digit and 1-digit multipliers, no carrying, horizontal format. A study of the student's performance on the incorrect items reveal potential difficulty in sequencing operations in the horizontal format. Specifically, the student may have difficulty with the concept of place value in this format. Further evaluation and instruction could be conducted to confirm this.

ACTION PLAN 5.2   ERROR ANALYSIS PROCEDURES

The initial procedures in test construction involve developing from 5 to 20 items to assess each subskill. When the test has been administered, the following error analysis procedures may be used:

1. Obtain component scores for the items within each subskill.
2. Study incorrect items contributing to low component scores.
3. Develop instruction to overcome subskill deficiencies.

FIGURE 5.4   Error Analysis for Multiplication Problems

Directions: Solve each of the following problems.

Subskill	Problems					Score
A. Product of two 1-digit numbers, vertical format	$\begin{array}{r}6\\ \times 0\\ \hline 0\end{array}$	$\begin{array}{r}4\\ \times 3\\ \hline 12\end{array}$	$\begin{array}{r}8\\ \times 5\\ \hline 40\end{array}$	$\begin{array}{r}7\\ \times 2\\ \hline 14\end{array}$	$\begin{array}{r}5\\ \times 1\\ \hline 5\end{array}$	5/5
B. Product of two 1-digit numbers, horizontal format	$3 \times 3 = 9$ $2 \times 9 = 18$ $5 \times 8 = 40$ $5 \times 7 = 35$ $6 \times 7 = 42$					5/5
C. Product of 2-digit and 1-digit multipliers, no carrying, vertical format	$\begin{array}{r}42\\ \times 4\\ \hline 168\end{array}$	$\begin{array}{r}13\\ \times 2\\ \hline 26\end{array}$	$\boxed{\begin{array}{r}61\\ \times 8\\ \hline 58\end{array}}$	$\begin{array}{r}22\\ \times 3\\ \hline 66\end{array}$	$\begin{array}{r}52\\ \times 4\\ \hline 208\end{array}$	4/5
D. Product of 2-digit and 1-digit multipliers, no carrying, horizontal format	$\boxed{3 \times 12 = 63}$ $5 \times 11 = 55$ $1 \times 97 = 97$ $\boxed{6 \times 21 = 612}$ $\boxed{2 \times 74 \times 814}$					2/5
Total score						16/20

FIGURE 5.5   Error Analysis for Capitalization and Punctuation Problem

Directions: In 100 words or less, identify the president of the United States you believe had the greatest effect on our current standard of living. Identify his three major accomplishments and the results of these accomplishments. Your response will be scored for correct capitalization and punctuation.

> I think president Lincolon was the most important president in history. Do you know about the important things he did. I will write about three of them. First, he freed the slaves. Important black leaders like doctor King said that he was responsible for our civil rights today. Second, president Lincoln helped us through the civil war. If this did not go well we could have ended up being a country like russia. Last, he helped us to understand about the importance of our type of government. A lot of the speeches he made like the one at gettysburg are used today to talk about democracy.

Subskill	Score
A. Capitalize first word of sentence	8/9
B. Capitalize first letter of proper name	3/5
C. Capitalize first letter of a title	0/3
D. Capitalize name of a place	0/2
E. Use period at end of sentence	8/8
F. Use question mark at end of question	0/1
G. Use commas after introductory clauses	3/3
Total score	22/31

A more complex test from an error analysis perspective is presented in figure 5.5. This essay test was designed to evaluate seven subskills relating to capitalization and punctuation. As discussed in the section on essay item development, the subskill scoring criteria were established in advance and included in the instructions. Because of the nature of essay tests, however, the examiner cannot be certain of the frequency with which subskills will be demonstrated. In some cases, a subskill may not be sampled a sufficient number of times to produce reliable information; this is exemplified by subskill F, the use of question marks. Aside from this, the error analysis data reveal reasonable proficiency in all of the subskills, except for capitalizing the first letter of a title and capitalizing the name of a place. As in the preceding example, these data provide a focus for future evaluation and instruction.

6.   Evaluate Reliability

On every test, a difference exists between the score a student obtains and his or her actual level of competence. The discrepancy between an obtained score and the real score is known as *measurement error*. Test developers strive to reduce measurement error through the procedures discussed in this chapter (e.g., clear and complete instructions, unambiguous items, consistent scoring procedures). Despite these efforts, however, students' performance on even the most sophisticated test is described as a function of their *actual skill* level plus the amount of *error* present in the instrument. For example, a marksman's ability to aim a rifle at a target is his or her *actual skill* in shooting accuracy. The impact point of the bullets on the target, however, is influenced not only by that skill but also by *error*. In this case, the error is a function of the quality of the rifle, the weight and composition of the bullet, the wind velocity, and so forth.

CASE FOR ACTION 5.2

You are asked to assist the high school English teacher in providing written composition instruction for a mainstreamed learning disabled student. The teacher reports that the student consistently fails her weekly independent writing exercises by having more than six grammar errors on each exercise. You learn that the teacher conducts no further analysis of the errors. How might you aid the teacher in developing an error analysis procedure? How would this procedure be used to guide future instruction?

■ 9   To reflect the extent of error in testing, measurement experts suggest that scores be reported as falling within a *confidence interval*, which reflects the range of error around the true score. The notion of error being present in any measurement is critical to accurate interpretation. For this reason, teachers should be equipped to informally evaluate the amount of error present in their tests and recognize procedures for reducing this error. Although the formulas for calculating error levels are beyond the scope of this text, teachers should be aware of the factors that contribute to error and should know how to avoid them in testing.

○ 8   *Reliability* is the major factor governing error in a test. A reliable test will produce comparable scores on repeated administrations; test that lacks reliability will produce variable results. Three major procedures are commonly used to evaluate the reliability of an instrument. The first, *test–retest reliability*, reports the stability of the instrument. A number of educational and psychological variables are not expected to fluctuate significantly over time. Although height, weight, intelligence, achievement, sensory acuity, and so on, may change during the course of several months or years, substantial changes should not be evident over the period of several weeks. Therefore, a test measuring these variables should produce comparable scores from one week to the next. Test–retest reliability is a measure of the consistency of an obtained score over a period of time.

The level of consistency accepted by a teacher should be a direct function of the decisions being made. Low consistency may be sufficient if the teacher is deciding whether or not extra drill and practice should be provided. Higher consistency may be warranted for major placement decisions.

The second reliability measure, *alternate forms reliability*, involves providing two equivalent forms of the same test to a group of students. The scores on the two tests are then correlated to produce a reliability coefficient.

The final reliability measure, *internal consistency reliability*, involves creating alternate forms from items within the test. A simple way of accomplishing this is to determine the relationship between students' scores on even and odd items.

As illustrated in Action Plan 5.3, the procedures used to test the reliability of a criterion-referenced test are quite simple. It may be very useful for teachers to evaluate their instruments in this manner.

7. Evaluate Validity

■ 10   As discussed earlier, reliability is the extent to which a test produces equivalent findings over time and across forms or split halves of the same form. Although reliability data ensure the accuracy of measurement, they do not confirm that the test measures what it purports to measure. A scale

ACTION PLAN 5.3   CHECKING THE RELIABILITY OF CRITERION-REFERENCED TESTS

We recommend the following procedures for checking the reliability of criterion-referenced tests:

Test-Retest Reliability
1. Test a number of students using the instrument.
2. From 1 to 30 days later, retest the students using the same instrument.
3. Determine the relationship between the two scores for each student.

Alternate Forms Reliability
1. Develop equivalent forms of an instrument with different items measuring the same skill.
2. Provide the first form to half the students and the second form to the other half.
3. Ask the students who took the first form to take the second and vise versa.
4. Determine the relationship between scores obtained from the two forms.

Internal Consistency Reliability
1. Test a number of students using the instrument.
2. For each student, tabulate the number of even numbered items correct and odd numbered items correct.
3. Determine the relationships between even and odd item scores.

may produce highly consistent or accurate results while measuring a skill or ability other than the one for which it was intended. Therefore, it is necessary to evaluate the *validity* of the test.

Test developers commonly describe three measures of validity. Although not all of them are directly applicable to criterion-referenced tests, an understanding of how they are used may help teachers to produce more sensitive instruments.

Content validity is judged by determining that the items in the test reflect the skill areas being measured. Developers of criterion-referenced tests may consider three separate questions. First, do the items reflect the objective and the subskills being assessed? Second, are all of the subskills sampled adequately? Finally, is performance on the items consistent with the stimulus and response dimensions specified in the domain? The test development procedures discussed early in this chapter were intended to produce affirmative answers to these questions. First, the test specifications require a comprehensive description of the objective and the subskills being assessed. Then, 5 to 20 items should be developed to sample performance in each subskill. Finally, each item should match the behavioral dimensions of the objective; that is, if the objective calls for the learner to select, the test should involve the selection of correct responses; if it calls for the learner to construct, the test items should involve the production of a correct response.

Content validity is the most important measure of validity used with criterion-referenced tests. It is extremely difficult to conceive of a valid criterion-referenced measure with items that do not reflect the objective and the subskills being evaluated. Visual inspection of a test to determine the correspondence between the test specifications and the actual test items may be the most pragmatic test validation method.

Concurrent validity refers to the extent to which performance of the criterion-referenced test corresponds with other measures of the same skills. There is little use in obtaining a measure of basic academic, vocational, independent living, or other skills if that measure does not correspond with actual performance. Thus, a test of interviewing skills should produce data that correlate with employers' judgments about a student on the basis of an actual interview. Similarly, a test of consumer math should correlate with the person's ability to make transactions in a department store or food store.

Predictive validity is very similar to concurrent validity. However, rather than determining the correspondence between the criterion-referenced test score and some immediate variable, predictive validity involves a correspondence between the test and some future variable. The question being asked is whether the criterion-referenced test score predicts performance in some future endeavor. A criterion-referenced test should not only reflect the student's skill level in current functional environments, but it should also predict how the learner will do in future environments. The student who scores well on an interview test should perform well in interviews over a period of time following instruction. Also, the learner who obtains a high score on the consumer math test should be an efficient consumer upon graduation from school.

Predictive validity may also involve determining the extent to which criterion-referenced test scores predict achievement on end-of-year achievement tests. Students who consistently perform well on criterion-referenced tests should perform well on the norm-referenced achievement measures that evaluate the same skill domains. Conversely, students who perform poorly on criterion-referenced tests should not do so well on the achievement tests.

Although content, concurrent, and predictive validity have been discussed as separate forms of validity, it should be clear that they are closely related. To be useful, any test must exhibit all three forms of validity to some extent. That is, it must possess items that reflect the domain of interest; data from the test must correlate with other applied data; and the test results should tell us something about the long-term adaptive skills of the learner.

○ **10**   A final validity measure that is appropriate to criterion-referenced tests is *sensitivity to instruction*. One of the major justifications for using criterion-referenced tests is to demonstrate the effectiveness of instruction. Therefore, one measure of the validity of a criterion-referenced test is its ability to detect performance changes resulting from an educational program. The most sensitive test will identify a 100% change in scored performance (e.g., from a pretest score of 0% to a posttest score of 100%). The least sensitive test will identify no change in scored performance (e.g., a pretest score of 80% and a posttest score of 80%).

Action Plan 5.4 illustrates the procedure for computing an instructional sensitivity coefficient for a ten-item test taken by six students. Analysis of these data indicates that, in general, the test was only modestly sensitive to instruction. A study of the performance on each item reveals that item 10 was the most sensitive (% gain = 100) and item 8 was the least sensitive (% gain = 17). Also, it appears that the high performance of the third student on the pretest reduced the test's instructional sensitivity for the group. Removing the third student's data from the analysis would increase the test instructional sensitivity coefficient to 68%.

SUMMARY

This chapter has presented criterion-referenced paper-and-pencil tests as an approach to evaluation in the direct instructional process, with emphasis on the use of these procedures as a formative and diagnostic measure of student performance. These techniques are intended to assess (1) the skills a student has required, (2) the amount of time it took him or her to acquire the skill, (3) the most effective instructional procedures that influence skill development, (4) specific impediments and solutions to skill development, and (5) the appropriate time to introduce a new skill.

It should again be emphasized that criterion-referenced assessment is not an isolated evaluation procedure. Nor is the sole intention of data collection to specify the student's current level of performance. As articulated by Gronlund (1976):

> Evaluation includes a number of techniques that are indispensable to the teacher. . . . However, evaluation is not merely a collection of techniques —evaluation is a process—it is a continuous process which underlies all good teaching and learning. (p. 3)

Used effectively, then, evaluation involves the identification of a purpose for assessment, the selection of a test on the basis of this purpose, the use of multiple measures when warranted, recognition of the limitations of the measure, and most important, application of the results to improve the educational performance of the learner.

CASE FOR ACTION 5.3

The school nurse reports that on the basis of a criterion-referenced test she developed, your student has "immature ideas about sex." Before you can be confident about this finding, you would like to know more about the test. What questions would you ask to assess the reliability and validity of the test? How may these attributes be evaluated? Why would dimensional inconsistency be a problem with tests designed to evaluate sexual behavior?

The intent of this chapter was to provide a basis for applying these principles to informal test construction and administration. Consistent with this purpose, Popham (1978) has proposed six criteria teachers can apply when selecting commerical instruments; the criteria are also useful for evaluating teacher-made instruments:

1. Does the instrument have a clear descriptive scheme? Can the objective and subskills that the instrument is designed to assess be identified? Are the results easily interpreted with reference to the objective and subskills?
2. Does the instrument contain enough items to provide a reasonable sample of each subskill? Is there a close relationship between the items' characteristics and the subskills?
3. Is the focus of the test limited to, at most, one objective and/or several subskills?
4. Does the test provide reliable data? Do test–retest, alternative forms, and/or split-half reliability estimates support the precision of the measure? Can factors be identified that would contribute to the likely amount of measurement error in each score?
5. Does the test produce valid findings? Do the test items reflect the objective and the subskills being measured? Are the item dimensions consistent with the condition and target skill statements of the objective? Does performance on the test concur with performance on other measures? Does it predict how the learner will perform in similar future endeavors? Is it sensitive to instruction?
6. Has the test been demonstrated to be useful in applied situations?

The next chapter will discuss another approach to criterion-referenced measurement—systematic observational procedures. These two criterion-referenced evaluation approaches are discussed separately because of substantial differences in their design and operation. It should be emphasized, however, that they are both intended to provide formative and diagnostic data regarding a learner's performance in the instructional program.

ACTION PLAN 5.4   INSTRUCTIONAL SENSITIVITY

The following exemplifies the computation of an instructional sensitivity coefficient for six students who took a ten-item pretest and posttest:

Item	Student 1 2 3 4 5 6	Pretest #+	Pretest %+	Student 1 2 3 4 5 6	Posttest #+	Posttest %+	% Gain
1	- + - - - -	1	17	+ + + + + +	6	100	83
2	- - + - + -	2	33	- + + + + +	5	83	50
3	- - + - - -	1	17	+ + + + + -	5	83	66
4	- - + - - -	1	17	- + + - + +	4	67	50
5	- - - - - -	0	0	- - - + + +	3	50	50
6	- + - - - -	1	17	+ + + + - -	4	67	50
7	- - + - - -	1	17	+ + + + + +	6	100	83
8	- + + - + +	4	67	+ + + - + +	5	83	16
9	- - + - - -	1	17	+ + + - + +	5	83	66
10	- - - - - -	0	0	+ + + + + +	6	100	100
						Average Gain:	61%

The instructional sensitivity coefficient is obtained through the following steps:

1. Apply the pretest to a group of students.
2. Record the percentage of students passing each pretest item. In this example, one of six students passed item 1, for a 17% pass rate; two of seven, or 33%, passed item 2; and so on.
3. Provide instruction in the subskills measured by the test.
4. Apply the posttest to the same students.
5. Record the percentage of students passing each posttest item. In this example, six of six students passed item 1, for a 100% pass rate; five of six, or 83%, passed item 2; and so on.
6. Subtract the percentage passing the pretest from the percentage passing the posttest for each item to obtain the percentage gain. In the example, 17% passed item 1 in the pretest and 100% passed it in the posttest, for a gain of 83%. Item 2 had a 50% gain, with a pretest pass rate of 33% and a posttest pass rate of 83%.
7. Add the percentage gain scores and divide by the number of items to produce the average gain. In the example, individual item gain rates ranged from 16% to 100%, with an average gain of 61%. This indicates that the overall sensitivity of the test to instruction was 61%.

6

Criterion-Referenced Measurement: Observational Procedures

■ DID YOU KNOW THAT...

■ 1 ...observational methods should be objective, valid, and reliable?

■ 2 ...a teacher can use frequency recording to determine the number of occurrences of discrete behaviors?

■ 3 ...a teacher may record response rate using the formula Rate = Frequency/Time?

■ 4 ...permanent products are the lasting effects of students' responses?

■ 5 ...task-analytic teaching methodology is most effective when a teacher is able to determine when to introduce each component skill?

■ 6 ...a teacher may use duration recording to assess the amount of time a student engages in a behavior?

■ 7 ...interval data are most representative of students' behavior when the recording periods are picked at random?

■ 8 ...the reliability of an observational system may be judged by comparing two individuals' observations?

■ 9   . . . an observer's expectations may influence the accuracy of measurement?

■ 10   . . . observational data can be evaluated by four criteria: mean, level, trend, and latency?

■ 11   . . . education's primary goal is to enhance students' adjustment to adult environments?

○ **CAN YOU . . .**

○ 1   . . . evaluate behavioral objectives by using dimensionally consistent observation procedures?

○ 2   . . . use frequency recording to monitor students' performance?

○ 3   . . . use instructional aids to collect rate data?

○ 4   . . . evaluate the permanent products of a student's performance?

○ 5   . . . monitor student progress using task-analytic assessment?

○ 6   . . . use duration and latency data to monitor student performance?

○ 7   . . . use whole, partial, and momentary interval recording to monitor student performance?

○ 8   . . . determine the level of interobserver agreement for observational data?

○ 9   . . . graph and analyze observational data?

○ 10 . . . facilitate students' transition to functional adult environments by providing socially significant instruction?

The preceding chapter discussed the use of paper-and-pencil criterion-referenced tests, which allow the teacher to evaluate students by scoring written products. It was emphasized that these measures are appropriate only when they are consistent with the behavioral dimension of the performance objective. Objectives stating that the learner will be able to locate, identify, describe, match, state, or compute in written form may be consistent with paper-and-pencil measures. However, objectives stating that the learner will be able to build, assemble, remove, use, provide, and so on, require actual performance of a skill. To be dimensionally consistent, systematic observation procedure necessary to record the learner's actual performance of the skill. This chapter discusses these procedures.

■ 1   The applied behavior-analytic literature has developed a number of conventions for reliably monitoring and reporting changes in learner behavior. Highlighting these conventions, Sulzer-Azaroff and Mayer (1977) suggest three major elements found in current observational methods. First, observations must be objective. The data should not be biased by the expectations or feelings of the observer, and variability in measured performance should be attributed as much as possible to actual behavior change rather than to observer "drift" or error. Second, observations must be valid. Validity in observational recordings is ensured through direct observation of behavior. Finally, observations must be reliable. Reliability of observational measures is judged by the extent to which observations conducted by independent recorders yield similar results. The following sections will discuss observational procedures that are consistent with these guidelines. A later section will present evaluation designs that isolate the effect of an educational procedure on a learner's performance.

LINKING OBJECTIVES TO OBSERVATION METHODS

○ 1   As with paper-and-pencil measures, systematic observation procedures must be dimensionally consistent with the behavioral objective under evaluation. Dimensional consistency of observational procedures involves three considerations. First, the setting and conditions under which observations are conducted must match the condition statement of the objective. Second, the behavior being observed must match the target response statement of the objective. Finally, the measure of behavior strength must correspond with the criterion statement of the objective.

Objective Statements

Condition Statement
The condition statement of the behavioral objective indicates the stimuli and conditions under which the target behavior is expected to occur. To be dimensionally consistent, behavioral observations should be made under

the same conditions that are specified in the objective. If an objective states that the student will put together a gasoline engine given a schematic and specific tools, observations should be conducted while the learner is using these devices. If an objective indicates that a learner will wash his hands using a washcloth, a bar of soap, and a towel, these same elements should be present during observation.

Target Response Statement

The target response statement is the precise definition of the behavior being developed or eliminated. It indicates the behavior that is being observed and measured. Thus, an objective indicating that the student will remain seated at her desk throughout the class period would be evaluated by recording the portion of time during which the student was seated. Similarly, an objective stating that the learner will engage in silent reading for 20 minutes each day would be evaluated by recording the duration of silent reading activity. Prior to initiating observations, it is important for the teacher, the student, and the entire multidisciplinary team to have a clear understanding of precisely what is being measured. To achieve this understanding, the teacher must define the target response in clear and complete terms.

Clear and complete definition of a target response enhances the learning process in three ways. First, it helps the student identify the anticipated outcome of the educational program. This information may serve as an advanced organizer for the student. Also, it may motivate the learner, particularly if he or she values the skill. Second, the definition of target responses may assist the teacher in carrying out the educational program. Knowledge of the exact target of the educational program helps the teacher use modeling, shaping, and reinforcement procedures more effectively. Finally, a clear response definition enhances the reliability of the observation procedure.

For example, vague statements of a student's characteristics—such as insensitive, unfriendly, or disinterested—do not provide the learner with a clear focus on the objective he or she is expected to attain. Furthermore, the teacher is not likely to obtain an accurate measure of these ambiguously labeled characteristics. Finally, without a precise behavioral description, the teacher's attempts to influence the responses through social learning procedures will be haphazard at best.

The traditional measure of the adequacy of a response definition is the extent to which two independent observers agree on the occurrence or nonoccurrence of the behaviors. Clear and complete definitions will result in a high rate of agreement between observers, whereas ambiguous definitions will often produce a low rate of agreement. Procedures for testing the objectivity of response definitions and observation systems are referred to as *interrater* or *interjudge reliability* techniques. They will be discussed in relation to each measure of behavior strength.

Criterion Statement

The criterion statement of the behavioral objective indicates the level of performance that is expected following intervention. It also implies the measure of behavior strength or specific observational procedure to be employed. This chapter will discuss five general observational measures of behavior strength that correspond to most criterion statements: (1) frequency and rate data, (2) permanent product data, (3) task-analytic data, (4) duration data, and (5) interval data.

Observation Methods

Frequency Recording

■ 2 ○ 2 Frequency or event recording procedures are used to determine the number of occurrences of discrete behaviors. Because these recording techniques involve simply counting the number of episodes of a response, they may be the most practical of all measures discussed here. For example, a teacher may evaluate a student's interpersonal skills by recording the number of social amenities used in a class period. Disruptive responses may be recorded by counting the number of times the learner "talks out" in class. Other examples of commonly recorded frequency measures are the number of between-meal snacks, assignments completed, days absent or tardy, and free throws made.

Frequency recording is appropriate for behaviors that have discrete start and stop times. Responses that are of a relatively constant duration and intensity are also suitable for frequency measurement. It would be inappropriate, however, to measure episodes of positive affect using a frequency measure, because valuable information regarding the length of each episode would not be available. One day a child might have one episode that lasts all day, whereas another day, the child might have six brief periods of positive affect. Also, a frequency record would ignore important aspects of the intensity of the positive affect. In one episode, the child might be moderately pleasant; in another, she or he might be elated. Finally, without a discrete indication of the start and stop of positive affect episodes, little agreement would be reached on whether a day included numerous occurrences or one sustained occurrence. In contrast, the number of swear words vocalized may be accurately measured with frequency techniques. For this response, there is a distinct beginning and end to the vocalization; the intensity with which it is uttered may be relatively constant; and the duration is fixed by the period of time needed to state each word.

Frequency data are often converted to rate data so that the teacher can compare measures from one day to the next. When simple frequencies or counts are kept, the amount of time available for observation may influence the resulting total. For example, one day the teacher may count 23 episodes of pencil tapping; the next day he or she may record 24. One might erroneously conclude that the strength of pencil tapping was comparable on the two days, unless it is known that on the second day, the learner was dismissed from school at lunchtime. Consequently, the day in which 23 episodes were reported represented lower behavior strength than the half-day in which 24 episodes were reported.

■ 3　　To account for this limitation, frequency data obtained over variable periods of time are commonly transformed into rate data. Response rate is computed by dividing the number of occurrences by the period of time over which the student was available for observation (O. R. White & Haring, 1980). For example, a student may leave his seat six times in a 40-minute period, four times in a 30-minute period, and five times in a 50-minute period. The respective rates of out-of-seat behavior computed using the formula Rate = Frequency/Time would be 6/40, or .15; 4/30, or .13; and 5/50, or .10. Action Plan 6.1 provides guidelines and procedures for collecting and using rate data.

A variety of instructional aids may be used to increase the teacher's efficiency in frequency or rate recording. For example, Mahoney (1974) demonstrated the use of an abacus watchband; Lindsley (1968) used a golf counter; and Holman and Baer (1978) piloted the use of a beaded bracelet for young children's self-recording. These devices are particularly appropriate for classroom use because they allow the teacher to overlap data collection procedures with other instructional responsibilities.

ACTION PLAN 6.1　COLLECTING RATE DATA

Rate recording is appropriate in the following circumstances:

1. The teacher is interested in knowing the number of times a behavior occurs over a period of time.
2. Behaviors have discrete start and stop times.
3. Behaviors are of a consistent duration.
4. Behaviors are of a consistent intensity.

Rate data may be collected by the following procedures:

1. Define the target behavior.
2. Determine the times, settings, and conditions under which the student is to be observed.
3. Record the times at which observations are initiated.
4. Tally each occurrence of the target behavior.
5. Record the times at which observations ended.
6. Divide the number of tallies by the amount of time the student was observed.

In addition to the device used to count responses through the day, it is important that a sheet be kept to summarize data from one day to the next. The recording sheet presented in figure 6.1 illustrates a standard format for storing data over extended time periods.

FIGURE 6.1   Format for Recording Rate Data

Student ———————————————   Behavior ———————————————

Teacher ———————————————   Definition ———————————————

Setting(s) ——————————————   ———————————————

——————————————————   ———————————————

Date	Frequency	Observation Period			Rate
		Begin	End	Total	

Permanent Products

■ **4** Many student behaviors that are of interest to educators produce tangible results. For example, on-task behavior results in completed assignments. Math computation produces correct answers. Aggression toward objects results in damage to the objects. These permanent products may be measured in a manner similar to event recording. The major difference is that rather than counting transitory responses, the educator counts the lasting effect of the responses. The primary advantage of this procedure is that permanent products of students' behavior (e.g., seatwork, homework, quiz responses, shop projects) may be collected and analyzed at times that are convenient for the teacher.

Measures of permanent products reported in the professional literature have ranged from highly complex to very simple. On the complex end of the continuum, Helwig, Johns, Norman, and Cooper (1976) have demonstrated an elaborate scoring procedure for measuring the rate of students' correctly formed letters. Their criteria for recording the permanent products of students' writing were as follows:

1. The total stroke must be within the confines of the line of overlay.
2. Each stroke that is not a complete circle must begin and end between the small slash mark and in the line forming the confines of the letter.
3. All circles in the letters a, b, d, g, o, p, q, and the top of the letter e must be closed curves.
4. All strokes must intersect each successive stroke at one point except for the dot above the i and j.
5. The letter must be complete with all strokes present.
6. The horizontal stroke in the t and f must intersect the other stroke within the confines of the ellipse near the center of the vertical stroke. (p. 232)

○ **4** Permanent product data can be compared from one day to the next only if the task demands remain relatively constant. Using problems with varying levels of difficulty, providing varying levels of assistance, or allowing different amounts of time may obscure conclusions that may be drawn from studying permanent product data. As with frequency data, differences in the amount of time available for the student to complete the permanent products (e.g., math problems, sentence composition, light industry assemblies) may be controlled by recording the rate of production. This is accomplished by dividing the number of products completed by the amount of time available. For example, the rate for writing ten sentences in a 20-minute period would be .5 sentence per minute. Action Plan 6.2 provides guidelines and procedures for collecting and using permanent product data.

Task-Analytic Measurement

Chapter 4 included a discussion of task-analytic and prompt-reduction procedures. Task analysis was described as a strategy for breaking down complex behaviors into their component parts or skills. In forward chaining, the teacher develops the first component skill until a success criterion is

ACTION PLAN 6.2   COLLECTING PERMANENT PRODUCT DATA

Permanent product recording is appropriate in the following circumstances:

1. The student's behavior results in a tangible product that the teacher is interested in evaluating.
2. Task demands are somewhat equal from one period to the next.

Permanent product data may be collected by the following procedures:

1. Determine the product that is to be evaluated (e.g., math problems, words spelled, assemblies completed).
2. Establish a criterion for the acceptable completion of each product.
3. Record the time the student begins working on the product.
4. Record the time the student stops working on the product.
5. Determine the number of products completed.
6. Divide the number of products completed by the amount of time worked by the student.

achieved, then initiates instruction on the second skill, linking it to the previously mastered response. Once criterion is again achieved, a third component skill is introduced. This process continues until all of the component skills are mastered and the complex behavior is performed to criterion. In backward chaining, the process is reversed by teaching the last skill in the sequence first, then the second to the last skill, and so on.

■ 5   Clearly, the effectiveness of the task-analytic teaching methodology is closely tied to the teacher's ability to recognize when criterion is achieved on one component skill and a second skill can be introduced. Moving too quickly from instruction in one component skill to the next will result in gaps in the learner's performance of the complex behavior. Moving too slowly is likely to bore the student or make inefficient use of the available instructional time. For this reason, task-analytic assessment is an important part of direct instructional programs.

○ 5   There are four important features of task-analytic assessment, as illustrated on the form in figure 6.2. First, the short-term objective—the complex behavior that is composed of the component skills—is listed at the top of the sheet. Second, the component skills, or tasks, are listed sequentially, from the first skill taught to the last. These skills should be

FIGURE 6.2 Format for Recording Task-Analytic Data

Student _____

Date initiated _____

Teacher _____

Short-term objective _____

_____

_____

Task	Trial									
	1	2	3	4	5	6	7	8	9	10
1										
2										
3										
4										
5										
6										
7										
8										
9										
10										

PROMPT KEY
s = self-initiate
v = verbal
m = modeling
p = physical

stated in clear and complete terms, so that the criteria for their acceptable performance is apparent. Vague descriptions, which are not subject to reliable measurement, should not be used. Third, spaces are provided for recording a series of trials for each skill. Task-analytic assessment is not a static process. Data collected in a given session should represent numerous opportunities for the student to perform. Finally, codes should be used by the teacher to identify the level of prompts he or she used to encourage the student's performance. Recording of prompts allows the teacher to monitor his or her level of involvement in the learning process. When the systematic prompt reduction discussed in chapter 4 is used, the teacher may expect a steady increase in the number of tasks performed under successively less intrusive prompts.

A simplified version of a task-analytic observation system is presented in figure 6.3. On this recording form, component skills performed

FIGURE 6.3 Format for Recording Simple Task-Analytic Data

Student _____

Date initiated _____

Teacher _____

Short-term objective _____

_____

_____

Task	Day				
	Monday	Tuesday	Wednesday	Thursday	Friday
1					
2					
3					
4					
5					
6					
7					
8					
9					
10					

PROMPT KEY

+ = independent

− = with proof

independently are scored with a plus sign (+); all others (e.g., manual prompts, verbal prompts) are scored with a minus sign (−). Although the data recorded on this form are easier to collect, the information provided has substantially less diagnostic value. Although these data tell the educator the component skills the learner has mastered, the level of teacher involvement required on skills below criterion cannot be identified.

Task-analytic data is best summarized by reporting the number of component skills completed independently on the final trial of the instructional period. It must be emphasized that this summary is a gross measure of the student's progress in acquiring component skills over time. It does not indicate performance on the specific skills over time, and it does not indicate the specific skills acquired or the level of prompts used in skills below criterion. These data must be obtained from the individual recording sheets. Action Plan 6.3 provides guidelines and procedures for collecting and using task-analytic data.

ACTION PLAN 6.3   COLLECTING TASK-ANALYTIC DATA

Task-analytic data recording is appropriate in the following circumstances:

1. The teacher is interested in measuring the student's progress in learning a complex skill.
2. Component skills that comprise the complex skill can be organized sequentially, from last to first or from first to last.
3. Mastery of the component skills can be observed and recorded objectively.

Task-analytic data may be collected by the following procedures:

1. Determine the complex skill or objective to be mastered by the student.
2. List the component skills in the order of instruction.
3. Determine the criterion for acceptable performance of each component skill.
4. Establish a scoring procedure for the component skills (e.g., prompt required, can or cannot do).
5. Ask the student to perform the complex skill.
6. Score the student's performance on each component skill.

Duration and Latency Recording

■ **6**   Duration recording is useful for evaluating any objective that relates to the period of time during which a student is engaged in a behavior. Latency recording assesses the period of time that elapses from some cue (e.g., teacher request to sit down) to the time the learner engages in the target behavior (e.g., the student sits down). These recording procedures are used to monitor changes in the amount of time students spend engaging in activities. For example, Whitman, Mercurio, and Caponigri (1970) used duration data to measure the amount of time spent in social interactions by participants in an interpersonal skill training program. E. L. Phillips (1968) used a latency recording technique to evaluate a program designed to reduce tardiness or predelinquent youth.

○ **6**   Figure 6.4 illustrates a form commonly used to collect duration data. The recorder simply enters the time the behavior begins and ends. The difference between the ending time and the beginning time is the duration for one episode. A given observation period (e.g., class period or school day) may include a number of episodes, and the individual durations may be summed to produce the total duration for the period. As with the other observational procedures, duration data may be adversely influenced by the amount of time available for observations. A day in which the student was observed for 3 hours cannot be compared to a day in which he or she was observed for 6 hours. Therefore, these units may be converted into percentage data by dividing the total duration by the time available for observation. For example, a student may have had three episodes of out-of-seat behavior, lasting 2, 6, and 10 minutes, respectively. The period during which she was available for observation was 40 minutes. Therefore, she was reported to be out of seat for 45 percent of the period.

The form may be modified to collect latency data by changing the column indicating the time the behavior began to indicate the time the cue or signal was provided and changing the column indicating the time the behavior ended to indicate the time the response was initiated. Of course, the duration column would be changed to report latency from the cue to the response. Action Plan 6.4 provides guidelines and procedures for collecting and using duration and latency data.

Duration and latency data are somewhat limited for most classroom purposes, because they require a subtantial amount of observation time. Not only must the teacher attend closely to the student's behavior, but he or she must also focus attention on a clock or stopwatch. In addition, many behaviors do not have an obvious beginning or end. Therefore, many educators prefer to use frequency or permanent product data rather than duration or latency data. For example, rather than studying the amount of time a student is on-task (one of the more difficult behaviors to record reliably), the teacher may study the number of academic products completed. Although the two measures record different responses, their outcomes are highly correlated (e.g., as on-task time increases, so do permanent products).

FIGURE 6.4 Format for Recording Duration or Latency Data

Student _____ Behavior _____

Teacher _____ Definition _____

Setting(s) _____ _____

_____ _____

Date	Time		Duration
	Begin	End	

ACTION PLAN 6.4   COLLECTING DURATION OR LATENCY DATA

Duration or latency recording is appropriate in the following circumstances:

1. The teacher is interested in determining the amount of time the student is engaged in an activity (duration) or the amount of time that elapses from a prompt to the initiation of the student's response (latency).
2. The behavior has an obvious beginning and end.

Duration or latency data may be collected by the following procedures:

1. Define the target behavior.
2. Determine the time period, setting, and conditions under which the student is to be observed.
3. *For duration data,* record the time each behavioral episode begins and ends. *For latency data,* record the time of the event expected to prompt the behavior and the time the behavior is initiated.
4. Subtract the first time from the second to obtain individual response durations or latencies.
5. *For duration data,* add the separate durations and divide by the total time the student was observed to produce the percentage of time engaged in the behavior.
6. *For latency data,* add the separate latency times and divide by the total number of times recorded to produce the average latency.

Interval Recording

■ 7   Interval recording is another alternative to duration or latency recording. Unlike duration or latency data, interval data are useful for monitoring behaviors that do not have obvious start or stop times. Also, unlike frequency and rate data, interval data are sensitive to changes in the length of time of a response. Interval data are collected by sampling the student's behavior within a portion of the school day. For example, a 6½-hour day may include two or three time samples of 10 minutes each. These time samples can be divided into shorter intervals (e.g., from 5 to 60 seconds), and the response can then be scored as occurring or not occurring during each interval. The resulting measure is the percentage of intervals sampled in which the target behavior occurred. When the time periods during which interval recording is conducted are picked at random, and when the amount of time sampled is sufficiently long, the resulting data accurately represent the student's behavior throughout the entire day.

○ **7**   To illustrate this procedure, two 5-minute time samples are conducted in a 50-minute instructional period. The times at which data are collected each day are picked at random to avoid bias resulting from time selection. The 5-minute periods are divided into twenty 15-second intervals. The resulting measure of behavior strength would then be the percentage of 15-second intervals in which the target response occurred. In a similar example, Marholin and Steinman (1977) used an interval method to record on-task behaviors of special needs adolescents. They divided 5-minute observation periods into twenty 10-second observation intervals, each followed by 5 seconds for recording. An observation period was scored as on-task if the learner was engaged in the assigned academic task for 9 seconds of the 10-second interval.

Three procedures are described in the literature for scoring interval data. The usefulness of each procedure depends on the instructional conditions or target behaviors. *Whole-interval recording* involves scoring responses only if they occur throughout the total duration of the interval (e.g., 10 seconds of laughing in a 10-second interval). *Partial-interval recording* involves scoring responses if they occur at any time during any interval (e.g., one pencil tap during a 15-second interval). Finally, *momentary-interval recording* involves scoring responses only if they are occurring at the precise time the interval ends (e.g., talking at the time the interval ends). Action Plan 6.5 provides guidelines and procedures for collecting and using interval data.

Interval recording and other recording procedures may be used to assess the responses of a number of students at the same time. For example, Kazdin (1980) described an interval procedure in which one child is observed in the first interval, a second child is observed in the second interval, a third child is observed in the third interval, and so on until all of the children are observed. Then the recorder returns to the first child and repeats the sequence. This process continues until all of the children are observed for a reasonable number of intervals.

A standard sheet for recording interval data is presented in figure 6.5. A plus (+) or minus (−) is used in each square to denote the occurrence or nonoccurrence of the behavior at the end of the interval (if momentary-interval recording is used), throughout the entire interval (if whole-interval recording is used), or at any time during the interval (if partial-interval

ACTION PLAN 6.5   COLLECTING INTERVAL DATA

Interval recording is appropriate in the following circumstances:

1. The teacher is interested in knowing the portion of time a student is engaged in a behavior.
2. The behavior does not have discrete start and stop times.

Interval data may be collected by the following procedures:

1. Define the target behavior.
2. Determine the times, settings, and conditions under which the student is to be observed.
3. Divide the observation periods into 5- to 60-second intervals.
4. Score the behavior as occurring or not occurring throughout each interval (whole interval), as occurring at any time during the interval (partial interval), or as occurring at the end of the interval (momentary interval).
5. Divide the number of intervals scored affirmatively by the total number of intervals.

CASE FOR ACTION 6.1

You are developing an Individualized Education Program for a 13-year-old learning disabled student who has been described as hyperactive. One of the objectives of the program is to increase the amount of time he spends engaged in academic tasks. A second objective is to reduce the amount of time it takes for him to comply with teachers' requests. A final objective is to increase his use of social amenities, such as "please," "thank you," and so on. Describe a data collection system that might be effective in monitoring progress on these objectives.

recording is used). The numbers over the columns indicate the separate intervals. Finally, the data are transformed to report the percentage of intervals in which the behavior occurred by dividing the number of occurrences by the number of intervals.

FIGURE 6.5 Format for Recording Interval Data

Student _____ Behavior _____

Teacher _____ Definition _____

Setting(s) _____ _____

_____ _____

Interval length _____

Date	Time	1	2	3	4	5	6	7	8	9	10	% scored +

KEY
+ = occurrence
− = nonoccurrence

INTEROBSERVER AGREEMENT

■ 8   The requirement for teachers to be accountable is not limited to simply collecting data; it extends to ensuring the accuracy of data. Teachers who are called upon at due process hearings or multidisciplinary team meetings must provide evidence that the student is or is not progressing toward the stated objectives. This evidence should include actual data reporting the students performance as well as a measure of the teachers' confidence in the data. As with paper-and-pencil tests, the most complex and complete observational system is of little value if it produces inaccurate or unreliable estimates of students' performance. Using unreliable data is comparable to using an elastic ruler in constructing a house. Decisions regarding the structural integrity of the house or the students' performance gains are likely to be in error.

Interobserver agreement is the primary method for judging the reliability of an observational system. Interobserver agreement is defined as the extent to which separate persons concur on the occurrence/nonoccurrence or duration of the target behavior. In general, interobserver agreement reports the correspondence between two independent persons' observations. The procedure for collecting interobserver agreement data varies according to the measure of behavior strength being used.

○ 8   To determine interobserver agreement for frequency data, two individuals (e.g., the teacher and his or her aide) independently collect data over the same time period. Following data collection, reliability is determined by dividing the lowest frequency by the highest frequency.

Permanent product data are evaluated in a similar manner. At the end of the performance period, the teacher collects and evaluates the learner's products. He or she then requests that another person use the same procedures to evaluate the products. Reliability is determined by dividing the smaller score by the larger score.

Task-analytic data reliability is somewhat more difficult to compute. As with the other procedures, two independent observers monitor the student's performance over a number of trials through the task sequence. Then the ratio of agreements to the number of trials is computed for each subskill. This produces separate interobserver reliability coefficients for each subskill. The average of these coefficients for the entire task sequence is the overall interobserver reliability coefficient for the task-analytic recording system.

Duration or latency data reliability is computed by simply dividing the shorter time by the longer time reported by independent observers.

Finally, the rate of interobserver agreement for interval data is determined by dividing the number of intervals for which both observers score an occurrence by the number for which either one or both of the observers score an occurrence. Intervals for which both observers score a nonoccur-

ACTION PLAN 6.6   DETERMINING THE RATE OF INTEROBSERVER AGREEMENT

Frequency/Rate Data
Divide the smaller count by the larger count of two independent observers.

Permanent Product Data
Divide the smaller score or count by the larger score or count of two independent observers.

Task-Analytic Data
Divide the number of trials on which two observers agree by the total number of trials. Average this quotient for all of the subskills.

Duration/Latency Data
Divide the shorter time by the longer time reported by two independent observers.

Interval Data
Divide the number of intervals for which two observers scored an occurrence by the number for which one or both of the observers scored an occurrence.

rence are excluded from the analysis. Action Plan 6.6 summarizes procedures for establishing interobserver agreement.

■ 9   Recent researchers have become increasingly concerned about the effect of *observer drift*—that is, a gradual change in the observer's expectations that produces an artificial change in the measure of behavior strength without a corresponding change in actual behavior. For example, a teacher may have high expectations for a novel behavior management approach. Because of these expectations, he or she may believe that a change is occurring in the learner's behavior and may unknowingly reflect this belief in his or her observational data even though an actual change has not occurred. The major safeguard against observer drift is to collect interobserver reliability data prior to baseline, to ensure the initial adequacy of the measurement system during baseline, and every few weeks throughout the program. Any changes in the intervention procedure that may alter the ease of measurement may also be accompanied by a reliability check.

CASE FOR ACTION 6.2

> You have been counting the number of times a behaviorally disordered girl uses profane language for six weeks. Your data indicate that she has become much better over this time period, although your fellow teachers strongly disagree. Develop an interobserver agreement testing procedure that would determine whether you or the other teachers are correct.

The adequacy of a reliability coefficient is a function of the difficulty with which the behavior is measured. Affective behaviors, such as smiles or sad expressions, may produce necessarily lower reliabilities than discrete responses, such as steps taken or balls hit. Also, the reason for which the data were collected suggests the level of acceptable reliability. Program placement decisions should be based on highly reliable data, whereas decisions affecting the use of peripheral instructional materials or free-time activities may be made on the basis of less reliable data. In general, reliability coefficients exceeding .70 may be considered adequate for most instructional decisions. Interobserver agreement coefficients in the lower end of this range should have more frequent reliability checks, because these data are more susceptible to observer drift. Coefficients in the higher end of this range need not be tested as often.

As discussed earlier, low interobserver agreement coefficients suggest that the target response has not been defined in clear and complete terms. Redefining the behavior (e.g., from "makes negative statements about self" to "says, 'I hate myself' or 'I am bad' ") is likely to improve the rate of interobserver agreement. Also, practical or logistic aspects of the measurement system may limit its reliability. A study of responses on which the two observers disagreed may suggest ways of improving the measurement system.

ANALYSIS OF OBSERVATIONAL DATA

○ 9   Data obtained on summary sheets such as those presented in figures 6.1 through 6.5 are most easily interpreted when they are presented in a line graph format. This format, illustrated in figure 6.6, has five major features. First, the horizontal axis of the graph reports the time associated with each measurement. For most educational purposes, this axis will be labeled *Day*, *Class Period*, or *Session*. Second, the vertical axis reports the measure of be-

FIGURE 6.6 Conventional Graph for Displaying Observational Data

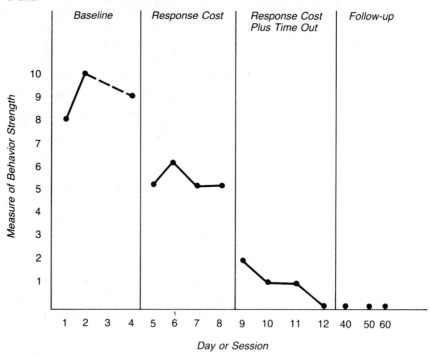

havior strength. As discussed in this chapter, the measure may be frequency, rate, permanent product, subskills performed in a task sequence, duration, latency, or percentage of intervals. Accompanying the measure is an operational description of the target response (e.g., rate of assignments completed). Third, vertical lines in the graph denote the onset of intervention or modifications in the program. Each of these lines should be accompanied by a brief description of the program change (e.g., change in medication, increase response cost, or use high-interest materials). Fourth, missing data points are denoted by connecting points adjacent to them with broken lines. Fifth, follow-up data, used to demonstrate that the program had a lasting effect on the learner's performance, are displayed by adding a vertical line at the end of the formal program and labeling a new phase *Follow-up*. The time line or vertical axis is labeled to reflect the days on which follow-up data are collected. These points are not connected unless they occur on adjacent days or sessions.

The same systematic observation procedure may be applied to more than one behavior in one setting (e.g., simultaneously recording a student's rates of math, spelling, and writing assignment completion), to the same behavior of the student in multiple settings (e.g., simultaneously recording a student's rates of negative self-statements in the gym, hallways, and lunchroom), and to the same behavior of several students in the same setting (e.g., simultaneously recording Billy's, Jim's, and Karen's percentage of problems completed correctly). The format for graphing these data, illustrated in figure 6.7, allows the teacher to make comparisons among the variables selected.

FIGURE 6.7 Conventional Graph for Displaying Observational Data for Multiple Objectives

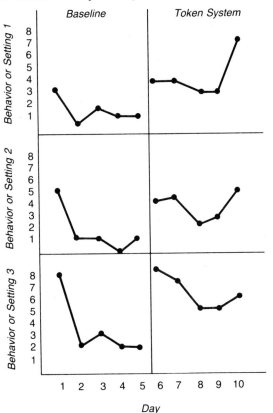

VISUAL INSPECTION OF DATA

■ **10**   Four criteria for analyzing observational data have been discussed in the literature (Kazdin, 1982): mean, level, and latency. These criteria increase the teacher's confidence in the impact of educational procedures on charted behaviors and generally reflect the strength of the intervention procedure in changing the student's behavior. Although they will be discussed separately here for the sake of clarity, it is important to recognize that the four criteria interact with one another to produce a clear representation of program effectiveness.

The *mean* is probably the most frequently applied criterion for analyzing program effectiveness. It refers to the average measure of the behavior during a given program phase. A teacher would expect a mean rate of performance higher than the baseline average following the introduction of a program designed to increase independent sentence composition. Conversely, a teacher might expect a decrease in the mean rate of disruptive social responses following the introduction of a punishment procedure. Figure 6.8 illustrates the importance of means in comparing observational data. Baseline measures indicated that 5, 4, 6, and 5 problems correct on the respective days, and the intervention phase indicated frequencies of 9, 7, 7, 9, 8, and 8. The baseline average, or mean, for problems correct was 5, and the intervention average was 8. The mean increase of 3 illustrates the positive impact of intervention.

FIGURE 6.8   Using Means to Analyze Program Effectiveness

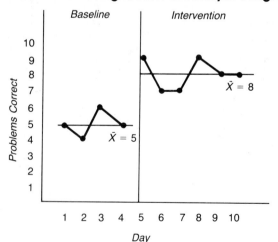

The *level* is another commonly used measure of the differences between program phases. Determining the level involves comparison of data points immediately preceding and following a phase change. As with the mean, one would expect a change in the level of performance immediately following intervention. The larger this change, the stronger the impact of intervention on the target response. Figure 6.8 shows a change in level from 5 at the final baseline data point to 9 at the first treatment data point. This change is substantially greater than what may be expected from random fluctuations in the data. Therefore, it supports the effectiveness of the intervention procedure. Although this analysis involved only the two points adjacent to the phase change, two or three points on either side of the phase change may be used for more variable data.

Trend is the slope of the best fitting straight line between points in the baseline and intervention phases. Besides expecting a change in mean and level, the teacher may anticipate that the person's performance will gradually improve following the introduction of intervention. The stronger the change in trend from baseline to intervention, the more potent the educational procedure. In the most extreme case, the baseline trend may be strongly decelerating, whereas the onset of intervention coincides with a strongly accelerating trend. More subtle trend changes may involve a shift from a gradually accelerating trend to a strongly accelerating trend.

O. R. White and Haring (1980) have described a technique for establishing the trend of data in baseline and intervention phases. Their procedure involves the following steps:

1. Draw a vertical line through the mid-date of data in the phase. If the phase includes an odd number of data points, this line will cross the middle data point. If it includes an even number of points, the line will fall between the two middle data points.
2. Draw a vertical line through the mid-date of each half of the phase. This should separate the phase into four quarters.
3. Draw a horizontal line through the mid-rate of the first half of the phase. If there are an odd number of data points, the mid-rate will cross a point and an equal number of points will fall on either side of the line. If there are an even number of data points, the mid-rate will fall between two points. Data points of equal value should be treated as separate values. In a similar manner, draw a horizontal line through the mid-rate of the second half of the phase using the foregoing procedure. At this point there should be three vertical lines (the overall mid-date for the phase and the first-half and second-half mid-dates) and two horizontal lines (the mid-rate for the first half of the phase and the mid-rate for the second half of the phase). The mid-date and mid-rate lines should be perpendicular to one another.

4. Draw a connecting line through the intersection of the mid-dates and mid-rates of the two half-phases.
5. The *quarter intersect line* (Koening, 1972) just completed provides an accurate appraisal of the trend associated with the learner's progress. As a final step, O. R. White and Haring (1980) suggest relocating the line so that an equal number of points fall above it and below it. This line, parallel to the quarter intersect line, is referred to as a *split middle line*. It not only indicates trends in the data, but it also establishes the entry and exit level of performance for the phase.

Action Plan 6.7 illustrates the construction and use of a split middle line in comparing trends in data between baseline and intervention phases.

Latency—the period of time that elapses from the start of intervention to evidence of a performance change—is the final criterion used in the visual inspection of data. Powerful interventions, such as effective punishment procedures, typically produce a short latency from intervention to behavior change. For example, initiating a procedure whereby the student must remain in the classroom during recess if he or she talks out in class is likely to produce an immediate reduction in the rate of talk-outs. A less powerful procedure, such as simply ignoring the talk-outs, may take substantially more time to produce an initial reduction in the behavior. These two alternatives and the resulting latencies are illustrated in figure 6.9.

One may note from comparison of the data in figure 6.9 that latency results from the combined influence of level and trend. Data with a large shift in level correspond with a brief latency. Conversely, data with a minimal change in level between phases and a gradually accelerating trend correspond with an extended latency. These relationships illustrate the importance of using the four criteria—mean, level, trend, and latency—in combination to analyze observational data. The most convincing demonstration of treatment effects occurs when all four vary simultaneously (e.g., an increase or decrease in mean and level, a strong positive or negative trend, and a brief latency). Changes in only one of the four criteria are less obvious, so the power of the intervention is less apparent. An obvious exception would be data that indicate equal or neutral trends but differ substantially in mean and level. For example, a student fails to complete any assignments for 10 days of baseline. Following application of a token reinforcement system for work completion, his rate immediately increases to 90 percent, where it remains stable. In this case, the trend did not change from baseline to intervention, but changes in mean and level overrode the importance of this criterion.

ACTION PLAN 6.7   SPLIT MIDDLE LINE PROCEDURE FOR ESTABLISHING TRENDS IN OBSERVATIONAL DATA

1. Draw vertical line through mid-date of phase.

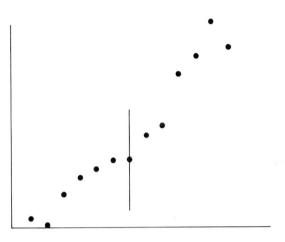

2. Draw vertical lines through mid-dates of half-phases.

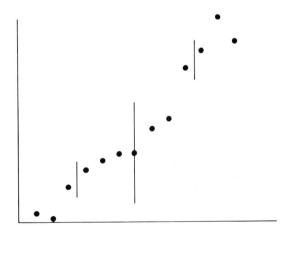

(continued)

ACTION PLAN 6.7   (continued)

3. Draw horizontal lines through mid-rates of half-phases.

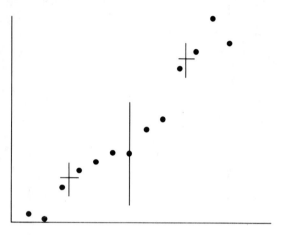

4. Connect intersections of the two mid-dates and mid-rates.

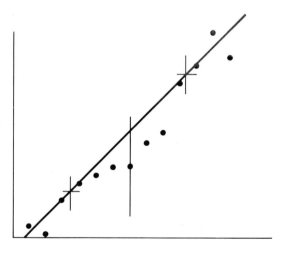

(continued)

ACTION PLAN 6.7   (continued)

5. Draw a parallel line with equal number of points above and below.

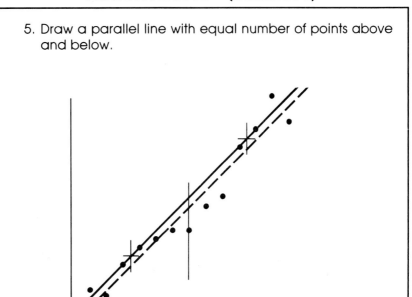

FIGURE 6.9 Data Patterns Expected from Ignoring and Recess Loss Programs

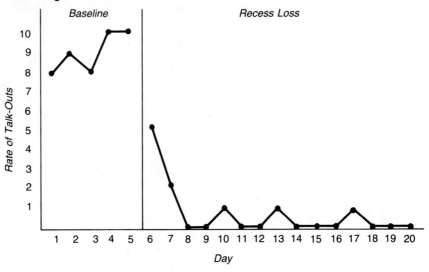

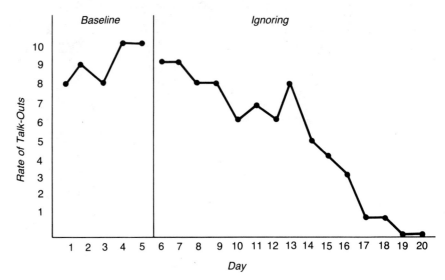

SUMMARY

■ **11** The foregoing discussion of observation procedures and the preceding chapter on paper-and-pencil measures provide strategies for reliably quantifying the effectiveness of educational procedures. The educator should be cautioned, however, that the resulting data leave what may be the most crucial question unanswered—that is, to what extent did the performance change influence the long-term quality of life for the student? The overriding goal of educational programs, as discussed in this volume, is not simply to develop or reduce specific behaviors. Rather, the goal is to enhance the learner's adjustment in functional adult environments.

○ **10** Behavioral researchers have recently discussed criteria by which the social importance of educational or therapeutic strategies may be evaluated (Kazdin & Matson, 1981; Wolf, 1978). These same criteria may be adopted by teachers to evaluate the social significance of classroom-based interventions. The criteria include (1) the significance of the goals, (2) the importance of the effects, and (3) the appropriateness of the procedures.

Significance of the goals and *importance of the effects* refer to the following questions raised by Wolf (1978): "Are the specific behavioral goals really what society (or the individual) wants? Are consumers satisfied with the results?" (p. 237). Kazdin and Matson (1981) suggest two approaches that may be used to answer these questions. The first, *social comparison*, involves observing the performance of functional individuals under environmental conditions similar to those in which the learner is expected to compete after training. These observations are expected to result in the identification of specific skill and performance levels necessary for effective participation in those settings.

The astute reader will quickly recognize that the curriculum development process discussed in chapter 2 is consistent with this criterion. In that discussion, teachers were encouraged to develop functional goals and objectives by analyzing the skills necessary for integration into community work, recreation, consumer, and independent living settings. By doing so, teachers ensure that educational targets produce skills that are valued by society.

The second approach suggested by Kazdin and Matson (1981), *subjective evaluation*, establishes the social importance of goals through feedback from others. Mainstream educators, ancillary personnel, building administrators, parents, and others may be asked to provide information regarding the effect of performance changes on the learner's social adjustment. Again, chapter 2 highlighted the importance of collecting data from the multidisciplinary team for the purpose of arriving at socially enhancing goals. Without these data, teachers' observational or paper-and-pencil assessments may reveal substantial performance changes, but these changes may be of little importance to the learner or others.

Appropriateness of the training procedures suggests that the value of the performance change must be weighted against the cost of the program to the individual, the educational agency, and society. Educational programs operate within limited resources. The cost of one program (e.g., recreational skills development) may detract from resources used by another program (e.g., independent living skills training). Consequently, to be socially valid, educational programs should be worth the allocation of resources that would otherwise be used to achieve other goals. The initial step in evaluating behavior changes against this criterion is to establish the expected cost of the training regimen. Then significant people concerned with the learner's development can determine the relative value of the program.

Cronin and Cuvo (1979) illustrated the initial step of applying this criterion by conducting a cost–benefit analysis for an independent living skills training program. They reported the analysis as follows:

> The value of the materials consumed . . . was $600. Only the thread used was nonrecyclable. Trainer time could be estimated at $4.26 per hour. . . . The average training cost per participant for three skills was $19.94 with a range of $13.28 to $35.28. Testing costs averaged $20.73 with a range of $16.69 to $26.63. (p. 405)

Finally, the training program should involve the most cost-effective strategy available to the teacher. It is generally recognized that a number of educational approaches may be used to achieve the same objective. However, some of the rival procedures may be more cost-effective than others. It is important that the teacher select the least expensive strategy that has the greatest potential benefit. This may be accomplished through the direct instruction hypothesis-generating procedures discussed in chapter 4. In addition, the teacher's familiarity with the professional literature will assist him or her in selecting strategies that have been demonstrated to be cost-effective.

In conclusion, this chapter has discussed the major strategies for collecting observational data, testing their reliability, and producing a graphic display. Strategies for visually inspecting data were highlighted, so that differences in performance resulting from interventions could be readily identified. Finally, emphasis was placed on interpreting measured changes in performance from within the context of its social importance.

CASE FOR ACTION 6.3

You have presented observational data indicating that a preschooler's interactions with others have increased substantially. You thought that this was an important achievement, because the youngster had been described as withdrawn. Unfortunately, the building administrator disagrees with your emphasis on social behaviors and suggests that you concentrate on preacademic skills. How might you use social validation procedures to convince the administrator that your focus on social interactions is justified?

7

Management

■ **DID YOU KNOW THAT...**

■ **1** ...classroom rules should be taught just as any other subject is taught?

■ **2** ...nonacademic procedures should be established at the beginning of the school year to save time?

■ **3** ...action zones in a classroom should be minimized?

■ **4** ...use of time in a school day can be viewed as allocated time, transition time, engaged time, and academic learning time?

■ **5** ...instruction time is a critical element that affects student achievement?

■ **6** ...a teacher can control and plan antecedent events that will prevent behavior problems?

■ **7** ...modeling can incidentally develop negative as well as positive behaviors?

■ **8** ...consequences influence the likelihood that a behavior will reoccur?

■ **9** ...coordinated home–school plans can play an important role in enhancing the skills of a learner?

○ CAN YOU...

○ **1** ...establish a set of rules for a classroom?

○ **2** ...create a physical layout and a seating arrangement for a classroom that are conducive to good management?

○ **3** ...create a schedule that maximizes the time available for basic subjects?

○ **4** ...specify three strategies for enhancing the engaged time of learners?

○ **5** ...specify how to manage seatwork activities effectively?

○ **6** ...use modeling as an effective behavior change strategy in a classroom setting?

○ **7** ...use social reinforcement effectively in classroom situations?

○ **8** ...develop a contingency contract?

○ **9** ...design an effective home–school plan for problem learners?

Management is a critical component of effective instruction. Without an effective management plan in place, valuable time is lost on matters unrelated to instruction. Since instructional time is the most important factor associated with student achievement, any strategies that can increase the amount of instructional time available should enhance achievement. This chapter will provide strategies for increasing instructional time through better management of the classroom and the decisions made regarding instructional practices.

GENERAL COMPONENTS OF EFFECTIVE MANAGEMENT

Effective management of a classroom environment involves (1) teaching rules and procedures, (2) consistently maintaining those rules and procedures, and (3) organizing the physical environment of the classroom.

Teaching Rules and Procedures

■ 1   ○ 1   Teaching students the rules and procedures of the classroom will minimize behavior problems and disruptions in the learning process. Merely posting or reciting the rules is generally not sufficient. In addition, students need to demonstrate that they know the rules and the consequences for violating the rules. During the first few weeks of school, the rules should be taught in the same way as other subject matter. Through the use of examples and modeling, students can be given specific situations to which the rules apply. As students proceed through the school day, the teacher should carefully monitor students' behavior and provide feedback to them on examples of appropriate behavior as they occur. Classroom rules should be kept short, and probably no more than seven rules should comprise the list. Consequences for violations of the rules should also be specified.

■ 2   Procedures for both nonacademic and academic class business should be specified and should be known by the students. Procedures should be established for such nonacademic business as movement in and out of the room, bathroom use, distribution of materials, use of materials (e.g., dictionary, pencil sharpener), and talk among students. Procedures should also be established for academic class business, such as setting up and taking down lessons, obtaining help, using learning centers, and the duties of volunteers. When students know the routines and procedures, time is saved, because students will not waste time asking about the procedures.

CASE FOR ACTION 7.1

> Students in one teacher's class have been shouting and "calling out," rather than raising their hands, when they need assistance, when the teacher is teaching, or when one student wants to talk with another. The noise level is not conducive to learning, and the room management seems to lack structure. What suggestions would you make to the teacher to help her manage her class better?

Maintaining Rules and Procedures

Once the rules and procedures have been established, the teacher must apply them consistently. *Prevention* is the key ingredient in behavior management, so the teacher must be in a position at all times to observe the entire classroom. For example, while working with a small group of students, the teacher must be aware of the behavior of other members of the class and make a conscious effort to scan the classroom periodically. This scanning allows the teacher to detect early signs of disruptive behavior.

Organizing the Classroom

■ 3 ○ 2   The physical arrangement of the classroom contributes significantly to the overall management plan. The arrangement should consider the traffic pattern within the class, minimizing disruptive movement around the classroom and ensuring that the teacher has a clear view of all students at all times. The actual seating of learners in a classroom is crucial. If they are left to seat themselves, students will create "action zones" in the room. Students of like ability will cluster together—the more capable and talkative students clustering toward the front and the less able and less outgoing students clustering in the rear. The teacher should eliminate these action zones by intermingling the students in the seating plan. Otherwise, hand raisers are likely to cluster in one section of the room, and the teacher will begin to direct attention to this section of the room and spend less time interacting with the total group. By spreading the students throughout the room, the teacher's attention is more evenly divided and thus is sensitized to low responders. Research in teacher effectiveness studies has found that the students with the lowest ability level are often seated farther from the teacher, are called on less often to respond to questions, make less eye contact, are smiled at less often, and are given less time to respond to questions than the more able students in a class. Some of these problems can be minimized by the organization of the classroom and the sensitization of the teacher to the problems.

TIME MANAGEMENT

■ **4**   The use of time in the school day can be divided into four categories, each of which can be planned for by the teacher: allocated time, engaged time, transition time, and academic learning time.

Allocated Time

○ **3**   Allocated time is the time during the school day that is scheduled for various activities. In general, it represents the maximum amount of time available for instruction in a subject area. At the elementary level, teachers are generally in control of the amount of time that is allocated for each subject; at the junior high and senior high levels, the time allocations are often prescribed. If time is not scheduled for a subject or if the length of time scheduled is inadequate, students will learn far less in that subject merely because they did not have the time necessary to learn it.

Time is also allocated within a period in regard to the planned activities that take place. Time allocations regarding direct instruction, independent practice, guided practice, and evaluation are all consciously allocated by a teacher. A balance must be struck in the amount of time devoted to each activity. Time allocated to practice without allocation of corresponding instructional time generally results in students' performing poorly on independent work.

Useful strategies for allocating time are summarized in Action Plan 7.1.

Engaged Time

○ **4**   Engaged time is the time during which a student is working on the material that is being presented or the time during which a student is performing the task that was directed. Engaged time is time on-task—the working time. In general, the more time students spend on-task, the better their achievement levels will be. Teachers can influence students' on-task attention by frequent questioning, by scanning the class while teaching, by establishing eye contact, by using nonverbal signals to nonattenders, by teaching in close proximity to the students, by praising students engaged in relevant tasks, and by directing questions to students that they can answer or be cued to answer. Students who are receiving feedback while being instructed have a higher level of engaged time than students who are not receiving such feedback. Frequent teacher questions keep students engaged longer and also influence achievement (Sindelar, Smith, Harriman, Hale, & Wilson, in press).

ACTION PLAN 7.1   GUIDELINES FOR ALLOCATING TIME

We recommend the following procedures for allocating time:

1. Allocate time for independent practice of new skills to a point of mastery in a demonstration–practice–feedback paradigm.
2. Examine the weekly schedule and compute the number of minutes allocated to each subject each week and adjust the schedule accordingly.
3. Build a time allocation into the schedule for each subject area of activity. If time is not assigned, the activity will not be done.
4. Include planning time in your weekly schedule and adhere to it.
5. Consider the time needed for transitions and setups when building the schedule.
6. Pace the instruction as quickly as possible in the allocated period to maximize the use of the time.
7. Plan your use of allocated time in relation to the time spent in actual teaching and time for seatwork or practice.

CASE FOR ACTION 7.2

The school principal has just observed your class and has noted that while you were teaching, the students did not appear to be paying attention. One student was gazing out the window; another was doodling on a sheet of paper; and another didn't even have the right book on her desk. The principal has asked you to correct these problems and to present her with a one-page plan of how you will accomplish this. What will your plan contain?

Transition Time

Time must be controlled or it becomes lost. Therefore, lessons must start and finish on time. If there is "extra" time left in a period, the teacher should have a list of time-filler activities that reinforce or review previously learned material. Punctuality is a virtue that should be practiced by both staff and learners. Students need to know the scheduling of their classes, and they need to be able to anticipate when classes are to begin and end. Orderly movement between activities is an important goal. Practiced procedures for these movements may be necessary, and it might be useful to provide a listing of expectations for students' preparation for each class. Action Plan 7.2 lists procedures for controlling transition time.

ACTION PLAN 7.2   STRATEGIES FOR DECREASING TRANSITION TIME

We recommend the following procedures for controlling the time spent in transition:

1. Post work assignments on the board so that students can begin working immediately after returning from lunch or recess.
2. Establish routines for distributing materials, gathering up materials, and rearranging the classroom for specific classes.
3. Minimize the time spent in explaining workbook and worksheet assignments. If the explanation takes as long as the assignment, perhaps that assignment should not be used.
4. Signal the end of an activity one or two minutes before the end of the period so that students can put materials away and prepare for the next activity.
5. Make your expectations clear to students—that each class is to begin promptly and that they are expected to be ready for class at that time.

Academic Learning Time

■ 5   Academic learning time (ALT) is time in which students are on-task and achieving at a high rate of success. When the material is geared to the level of the students, they will remain on-task and be successful. ALT is highly correlated with student achievement. To maintain a high degree of ALT, classroom material should be presented in small steps, students should be given frequent feedback on their performance, and they should practice materials on which they will be tested.

○ 5   Academic learning time is generally higher during periods of direct instruction than during seatwork activities, because the student's engaged time is greater. During seatwork, a student's mind will wander and he or she will become distracted from the focus of the activity. Early completion of seatwork could also reduce academic learning time if a procedure is not in place for directing the student to a new activity. Specific strategies are identified in Action Plan 7.3 that can be used by a teacher to increase ALT for seatwork activities.

ACTION PLAN 7.3   EFFECTIVE USE OF SEATWORK TIME

We recommend the following guidelines for using seatwork time:

1. Students should practice skills in seatwork only after the skills have been taught.
2. Teachers should monitor seatwork by circulating frequently among the students.
3. Spot-checking seatwork while circulating saves time and provides students with immediate feedback.
4. Provide assistance to students for short periods (30 seconds) when checking their work. If the assistance requires more time, perhaps the assignment should be changed.
5. Check for error patterns in work and reteach as necessary.
6. Require that students correct their errors.

INDIVIDUAL BEHAVIOR MANAGEMENT STRATEGIES

The management procedures that were discussed earlier in this chapter address the total management of a classroom from a time and physical management perspective. This section addresses the components of behavior management strategies that relate to the management of individuals. These components fall into two categories: antecedents (things we do to prevent the occurrence of disruptive behavior or to facilitate appropriate behavior) and consequences (events that follow exhibition of a behavior).

Antecedents

■ 6   Antecedent control is synonymous with prevention. It involves identifying and changing events that are believed to produce disruptive behaviors. High rates of failure, peer influences, repetitive and nonchallenging activities, public reprimands, and unstructured time have been identified as events that are commonly associated with norm-violating behavior (V. F. Jones & Jones, 1981). Consequently, they exemplify antecedent events that may be changed to reduce disruptive responses. Antecedent control involves determining whether these or other events are, in fact, associated with a student's problem behaviors and then eliminating or replacing the provoking events with antecedents that are expected to produce prosocial behaviors (e.g., more challenging work, positive peer influences, novel lesson formats).

Antecedent control usually should not be adopted as an isolated intervention approach. When possible, self-control skills and interpersonal skills should be developed so that the student is able to face provoking antecedents without becoming disruptive. Structuring consequences to motivate appropriate behaviors and to punish inappropriate behaviors may also be used to help the student work through difficult situations.

The use of antecedent control procedures along with teaching and the delivery of appropriate consequences should help students master their own behavioral reactions. For example, simply removing difficult math assignments will not teach the student to remain calm while solving complex problems. However, the teacher may gradually reintroduce difficult assignments while teaching the learner to remain calm, ask for assistance, or engage in other appropriate coping behaviors. Of course, reinforcement should be applied when these coping behaviors occur.

Rate of Success

The frequency of success and reinforcement in public school classrooms has been associated with students' social behaviors (Brophy & Evertson, 1976; Fisher et al., 1980; Gambrell, Wilson, & Gantt, 1981). Students who continuously exceed the teacher's criteria for success are likely to become bored and disinterested in classroom activities. Consequently, they may be more prone to exhibit disruptive behaviors. Conversely, students who continuously fall short of success and reinforcement criteria are likely to become frustrated and aggressive. To avoid such a problem, high rates of success should be a goal of academic programs. *Instruction* should be given on tasks that the student performs 70 to 90 percent correctly. Skills are considered *learned* at the 90 to 99 percent correct level. *Mastery* is achieved with 100 percent correct responding. Finally, below 70 percent achievement is referred to as the *frustration* level. Tasks on which the learner performs in this final range should not be used as independent activities.

Teacher–Student Interactions

Rogers (1969), Swanson and Reinert (1984), Applebaum (1982), and others have emphasized the role of interpersonal interactions in the development of a positive self-regard. Security that results from being understood, respected, and supported enhances positive social responding. These feelings develop as a result of stable interactions characterized by sincere interest in the person's ideas and expectations (Baird, 1973; Costin & Grush, 1973; Elmore & LaPointe, 1975). Several researchers have associated supportive teacher–student interactions with student performance gains (Hefele, 1971; McKeachie & Lin, 1971). In summarizing these data, Conger (1977) has argued:

> Adolescents in our culture tend to prefer and to respond more favorably to teachers who are warm, possessed of a high degree of ego strength, enthusiastic, able to display initiative, creative, reactive to suggestions, poised and adaptable, able to plan, interested in parental and community relations, aware of individual differences in children, and oriented toward individual guidance. In contrast, teachers who are hostile or dominating generally appear to affect pupil adjustment adversely. (p. 375)

Numerous authors have recommended guidelines for enhancing teachers' communication skills with students. The following is a summary of these principles:

1. *Speak in concrete terms*. Talk in present terms. Events that occurred days or weeks ago may not be easily understood by the mildly handicapped learner. Use vocabulary and syntax that reflects the language skills of the student.

2. *Talk directly to the student in an age-appropriate manner*. Avoid trying to influence a student's behavior by talking about or to him or her in

a public forum. Do not talk down to students, particularly adolescents and young adults.

3. *Balance the rate of corrective feedback with socially enhancing interactions.* As a general rule, the teacher should deliver four or five complimentary statements for every critical statement. This guideline requires that the teacher "catch" students behaving appropriately more often than he or she "catches" them behaving disruptively.

4. *Be aware of nonverbal language.* The teacher should consider not only *what* is being said to a student but also *how* it is being said. Voice inflection, posture, gestures, and facial expressions should support the vocal message. Similarly, the teacher's proximity to the student communicates interest. Circulating among students' desks, for example, is preferred to remaining stationed behind a desk in front of the class.

5. *Provide objective feedback.* Frequent and immediate feedback has been repeatedly demonstrated to enhance the performance of handicapped learners. Limit the number of responses for which feedback is provided. Mildly handicapped learners are more likely to benefit from a concentrated focus on three to eight responses than from feedback on a wide range of behaviors. Finally, remain objective. Referring to a learner's "insensitivity to the needs of others" will not have so strong an effect as labeling the precise behaviors that are inappropriate.

6. *Encourage students to identify solutions to their problems.* Ask reflective questions to help the student clarify his or her beliefs and feelings. Statements such as "It seems as if you are saying..." "You believe that..." "You are saying that..." keep the responsibility for arriving at a solution with the learner. Furthermore, such statements assist the student in clarifying or redirecting a line of thought.

7. *When necessary, redirect students to more goal-directed and rational statements.* Many handicapped learners do not have sufficient information to arrive at acceptable solutions to their problems. Similarly, they may not be motivated to arrive at a socially enhancing solution. Consequently, teachers should be prepared to direct students into more rational statements. Ellis (1963) summarizes this process as:

> ...constantly, frequently questioning, challenging, and reindoctrinating [students] until they are ready to give up their dysfunctional behavior patterns and replace them with more functional philosophies and behaviors. (p. 52)

8. *Avoid allowing the student to practice dysfunctional lines of discussion.* The importance of using reflective questions to help students clarify their views has been emphasized. The potential exists, however, for the student to repeat and reinforce dysfunctional views. When this occurs, the teacher should be prepared to intervene and provide more rational statements. This may involve questioning, challenging, and providing alternatives to irrational statements.

Modeling

■ 7 ○ 6   Modeling has been demonstrated to have a substantial influence on the behavior of mildly handicapped learners. The systematic use of modeling involves arranging instructional conditions so that the students' behavior is enhanced by their observations of others. The research literature suggests three possible outcomes of modeling procedures:

1. Modeling can be used to develop new skills that are not currently in the learner's repertoire. For example, when teaching interpersonal skills, a teacher may demonstrate appropriate ways of interacting.

2. Modeling can be used to encourage students to use previously learned skills. A student may be motivated to take a building trades class because, while on a class field trip to a construction site, he or she observed workers performing what he or she viewed as enjoyable work.

3. Finally, modeling can be used to inhibit behaviors. A student may decide to stop smoking as the result of interactions with a professional athlete.

Unfortunately, modeling can inadvertently develop negative behavioral characteristics as well as positive characteristics. Frequent observation of another learner gaining satisfaction by being aggressive may result in the mildly handicapped student's using aggressive behavior. For this reason, the use of modeling as a behavior management strategy involves not only presenting the learner with socially appropriate models but also avoiding occasions in which he or she observes inappropriate social models. This has been a major rationale for the limited use of self-contained classes or special stations for handicapped learners (Bruininks & Rynders, 1971; Csapo, 1972). By excluding adaptive learners, these settings seldom offer appropriate peer models.

Factors influencing the effectiveness of modeling have been identified and described in numerous research reports (Bandura, 1971a, 1971b; Kazdin, 1973; Ross, 1970; Stevenson, 1972; Zinzer, 1966). The following five features support the effectiveness of modeling:

1. Students are more likely to emulate the model's behavior if they are reinforced for engaging in the same behavior.
2. Modeling is more likely to occur if the modeling situation is similar to situations in which students are expected to perform.
3. The way the students feel about themselves will influence the extent to which they model others' behavior.
4. Students are more likely to model behavior that they feel competent to perform.
5. Students are more likely to emulate the behavior of persons whom they view as having high social status.

Action Plan 7.4 provides guidelines for establishing a modeling process in the classroom.

Consequences

■ 8 Consequence control involves procedures to be used *after* a behavior has occurred. Behavior that is followed by a satisfying consequence and subsequently increases in strength may be said to have been *positively reinforced*. For example, answering questions in class is often positively reinforced by praise from the teacher. Behaviors that increase in strength as

ACTION PLAN 7.4   GUIDELINES FOR MODELING IN THE CLASSROOM

We recommend the following procedures for modeling:

1. Identify the behaviors that are expected to be influenced by the modeling process.
2. Structure the learning environment so that the student is frequently able to observe high-status models engaging in the target behaviors.
3. Arrange for the student to be reinforced each time he or she models the target behavior.
4. Ensure that the learner is able to perform the target behaviors.
5. Promote the student's positive view of his or her ability to engage in the modeled behavior.
6. *Eventually* vary the models and settings so that the behavior change generalizes to a range of other conditions.

the result of their function in helping the learner avoid or escape unpleasant events are said to have been *negatively reinforced*. For example, the rate of a student's cheating might increase because it helps him or her avoid bad grades. Similarly, driving within the speed limit may be negatively reinforced because the driver avoids traffic citations. Finally, behaviors that reduce in strength as the result of being followed by unpleasant consequences are said to have been *punished*.

Reinforcement and punishment refer to relationships between behaviors and consequences that can be observed to occur in nature. An event is a reinforcer *only* if it does, in fact, produce in increase in the strength of the student's behavior. Similarly, an event qualifies as a punisher *only* if it is observed to reduce the rate of the behavior being punished. It should be evident that reinforcement and punishment relationships are unique to each student. Consequences that are reinforcing for one student may be punishing to another, and vice versa. The teacher should identify specific reinforcing or punishing events related to the individual student's behavior. In many cases, the behavior can be changed simply by altering the naturally occurring consequences. For example, a teacher may simply refrain from calling on students who wave their hands violently and call only on students who raise their hands in a desirable manner.

Social Reinforcement

○ **7**   Social reinforcement involves the use of interpersonal interactions to influence the future strength of a student's behavior. Social reinforcement may be positive when pleasant interpersonal interactions increase the rate of a student's behavior. For example, complimenting a student on her or his appearance may result in increased attention to his or her personal care. Social reinforcement may also be negative when adverse interactions increase the rate of a student's behavior. Criticizing a student for work that is of poor quality, for example, may improve the quality of future work.

As noted in the discussion of the principles of reinforcement, an event cannot be identified as a social reinforcer unless a relationship is established between the event and the increased frequency with which the behavior occurs. Complimentary statements cannot be labeled as social reinforcers unless it can be demonstrated that compliments increased the rate of the student's desirable behavior. This is an important concept, as the teacher must continuously be alert to identify supportive relationships between his or her interactions and the student's desirable behavior.

An equally important principle is that social reinforcement can motivate both positive and disruptive behaviors. It is widely recognized that the disruptive responses of many learners are motivated by the social interactions of the teacher or other students. Hasazi and Hasazi (1972), for example, demonstrated that number reversals in an 8-year-old boy's math computation were sustained by the teacher's one-to-one attention. Removing one-to-one attention following reversal errors and providing attention only after correct responses corrected the reversal problem. The authors high-lighted the potential negative effect of misdirected social reinforcement on academic performance as follows:

> It is typical practice to give a student individual attention when learning problems develop, and hence, the possibility of [social] reinforcement of inappropriate academic behaviors exists. (p. 160)

Used properly, social reinforcement may motivate a range of positive social behaviors for mildly handicapped learners. Specific features recommending its use include the following: (1) little time, effort, or expense is required to administer social reinforcers; (2) social reinforcement is natural to most educational and community environments; (3) social reinforcement used with one student may have a positive effect on other students; and (4) social reinforcement can be easily used in combination with other behavior management approaches. Action Plan 7.5 summarizes necessary considerations in using social reinforcement.

ACTION PLAN 7.5   USING SOCIAL REINFORCEMENT

The following factors should be considered in using social reinforcement:

1. Be certain that the student is aware of behaviors that will be socially reinforced.
2. Use the person's name in connection with the socially reinforcing statement.
3. Label both the process (e.g., walking slowly) and the product (e.g., arriving at class safely) of the student's behavior.
4. Ensure that the interpersonal interaction is in fact reinforcing.
5. Always pair social interactions with less natural reinforcers when the latter are required.
6. Suggest that parents, peers, and other teachers socially reinforce the student when he or she uses the target behaviors.
7. When the behavior reaches an acceptable level, gradually reduce the rate at which the social reinforcers are applied.

Extinction

Whereas social reinforcement is used to increase the strength of students' positive behaviors, extinction is used to reduce the strength of disruptive behaviors. Extinction is defined as the removal of positive reinforcement that has previously maintained a behavior. It is expected that the removal of these reinforcing consequences will be a disincentive for the student to engage in the behavior in the future. For example, a teacher may begin ignoring a student who waves his or her arm to be called on. It is expected that removing the reinforcing consequence of being called on will reduce the likelihood that the student will wave his or her arm.

The use of extinction has many of the advantages of social reinforcement. It is a highly natural procedure that requires little time, effort, or other resources. It may be used with several students at a time and several students may benefit from observing the teacher using extinction with one student. Finally, extinction can be used in combination with other strategies. Specifically, extinction and social reinforcement are natural counterparts. The teacher may remove attention from disruptive behaviors (extinction) while calling attention to alternative positive responses the learner uses (social reinforcement).

There are two potential problems that are associated with the use of extinction. First, behaviors that are being extinguished often increase before decreasing in strength. Failing to call on a student for waving his or her arm, for example, will initially result in more severe arm waving. If this higher rate response fails to produce satisfying attention from the teacher, the student's arm waving may cease. Calling on the student during the more violent behavior may result in more frequent occurrence of this behavior in place of the less severe arm waving. Consequently, before initiating an extinction procedure, the teacher must be prepared to deny the reinforcement despite initially higher rates of the disruptive behavior.

The second problem in using extinction is that many events that reinforce disruptive behaviors cannot be identified or controlled. For example, it may be difficult to remove peer attention from disruptive classroom or hallway behaviors. Removing only a portion of the available reinforcement (e.g., one or two peers persist in socially reinforcing the student) may result in maintenance of the disruptive behavior by less frequent reinforcement. This may have the undesirable effect of making the behavior more resistant to change.

Because of these potential problems, extinction procedures require considerable advanced planning. Alternative strategies should be considered (1) if all of the reinforcement supporting the behavior cannot be identified and removed or (2) if it is not possible to withhold reinforcement despite initially more severe behavior.

Response Cost

Response cost is the removal of reinforcement as a consequence of the student's engaging in a disruptive behavior. Response cost procedures are fairly common to natural environments. A traffic citation (the removal of money), delivered as the consequence of driving too fast, is a familiar example of a natural response cost. Similarly, a penalty charged by a bank for bouncing a check is another form of response cost. The common element of these examples is that the removal of money is expected to reduce the rate with which the target behavior (speeding or writing bad checks) occurs.

Response costs have several major advantages. First, response cost procedures can be administered easily. For example, simply docking privileges following a disruptive behavior may be considerably less time-consuming than many of the tactics previously discussed. Second, because response cost procedures are commonly used in natural environments, it is possible that behavior changes accomplished in school will generalize to community settings. For example, if a student learns that being late for school results in having his or her allowance docked, he or she may avoid being late for work as an adult, when this might result in a loss of earnings.

Several major limitations are associated with the exclusive use of response cost procedures. First, the contingent removal of reinforcers does not teach or motivate the learner to use socially appropriate behaviors. Recognizing that being argumentative will result in a loss of privileges may result in the student's avoidance of arguments, but it will do little to provide alternative assertiveness skills that serve the same purpose as the argumentative behaviors. To overcome this limitation, response cost procedures may be used in combination with interpersonal skills training approaches (chapter 14), differential reinforcement of incompatible behaviors, or other positive approaches designed to enhance positive social replacement behaviors.

A second limitation is that response cost procedures have been demonstrated to produce negative emotional reactions (Matson & DiLorenzo, 1984). Anyone who has driven along an interstate highway and has seen a state police car approaching in the same lane with red lights flashing can readily attest to this effect. This effect alone may not be bad, because the negative feelings may do as much to deter future occurrences of the behavior as the actual response cost. For some students, however, these negative emotions may lead to higher rates of disruptive behavior, which may be substantially more difficult to manage than the initial problem behavior. For example, denying a recess privilege as a consequence of doodling on the desk may produce verbally and physically aggressive behaviors from the student.

A final concern involves balancing the amount of reinforcement being docked with the amount of reinforcement available to the individual. Withdrawing too much may result in the reinforcer no longer being available to suppress future occurrences of the behavior. For example, a problem may arise if a teacher arranges for a student to lose 10 minutes of the 30-minute recess for each time he or she is noncompliant. Once the student has been noncompliant three times, there is little incentive to be compliant for the remainder of the period. Conversely, withdrawing too little of the reinforcer may not be sufficiently aversive to the student. Docking 1 minute of recess time for each noncompliance episode may not be a disincentive to the student (three episodes of noncompliance would result in losing only one-tenth of the recess). Ideally, the withdrawal should be sufficiently large to have an influence on the student, yet small enough to ensure that the reinforcer is not exhausted in a typical day.

Action Plan 7.6 provides guidelines for constructing a response cost program.

Contingency Contracting

○ **8**   A contingency contract is a written agreement between the student and the teacher that clearly indicates the relationship between specific behaviors and consequences. Included in a contract are a concise description of behaviors expected of the student, a statement of satisfying consequences to be gained by performing the behaviors, a statement of unpleasant consequences that will result from failing to perform the behavior or engaging in

ACTION PLAN 7.6   CONSTRUCTING A RESPONSE COST PROGRAM

We recommend the following procedures for developing a response cost program:

1. Specify the target behavior to be reduced using the response cost procedures.
2. Select the type and amount of reinforcer to be withdrawn each time the target behavior occurs.
3. Establish procedures to ensure that the student is motivated to learn and to use alternative positive social behaviors.
4. Inform the student of the consequence arrangements (e.g., "Each time you violate a classroom rule, you will lose 5 minutes of activity time").
5. Monitor the student's behavior to ensure that the response cost has the desired effect.
6. Establish backup procedures to manage higher rates of disruptive behavior that may initially result from the response cost.

other disruptive behaviors, an indication of the teacher's responsibilities in facilitating the student's success, and a statement of how maintenance of the desired behaviors will be rewarded.

A distinctive feature of contingency contracting is that it involves mutual negotiation between the teacher and the student. The student's involvement in planning, implementing, and evaluating the behavior change program may increase the likelihood that he or she will abide by its guidelines (Gardner, 1977). Equally important, this planning process may help the learner recognize the relationship between his or her behavior and the reactions of the teacher. The negotiation process is an excellent opportunity for the teacher to assist the learner in clarifying personal goals, recognizing the expectations of others, exploring alternative behavior change strategies, and recognizing the long-term benefits of the behavior change goals. Once the contract is formalized, the learner should have a clear understanding of the scope, plan, and purpose of the intervention strategy. Furthermore, he or she should be a cooperative participant in the plan.

Reinforcement and punishment procedures may be included in a contingency contract. A positively reinforcing component would indicate that a pleasant event will result from the performance of a prosocial behavior (e.g., "When your desk is neat at the end of the day, you will be permitted 5 minutes of time in the activity center"). A negatively reinforcing component would indicate how displaying a behavior will result in the avoidance or removal of an unpleasant event (e.g., "When you complete your assignments for the day, you will not have to stay in during recess"). Finally, a punishing component would state how an unpleasant event will result from the student's engaging in a disruptive behavior (e.g., "If you swear in school, you will have to write lines out of the dictionary"). Reinforcing or punishing contingencies may be used separately or in combination, depending on the student's behavioral characteristics and the objectives of the program. Whenever punishment is included, a reinforcing component

CASE FOR ACTION 7.3

An 8-year-old has temper tantrums—screaming, stamping his feet, and occasionally lying down on the ground and kicking his feet. Often, if he is holding something, he will throw it. This behavior occurs both in school and at home. What steps would you follow in designing a plan to manage this behavior, and what antecedent strategies would you use to minimize the likelihood that the tantrums would occur?

should be added so that the student is encouraged to display a positive social behavior to replace the behavior being eliminated. For example, if fighting on the playground results in the loss of tokens, another component of the contract might award tokens for cooperative play. Thus, cooperative play would be reinforced as replacement behavior for fighting.

It is important that the contingency contract be stated in terms that are complete and clear to the teacher and student alike. The behaviors expected of the student, the responsibilities of the teacher, and the consequence arrangements should be articulated so that the chances of subsequent misunderstandings are reduced. Attention to details in the negotiation and planning stages may avoid controversies resulting from vague, poorly worded agreements.

Action Plan 7.7 summarizes the procedures for developing a contingency contract, and figure 7.1 illustrates a typical contingency contract format.

ACTION PLAN 7.7   DEVELOPING A CONTINGENCY CONTRACT

We recommend the following procedures for developing a contingency contract:

1. Meet privately with the student and explain the rationale and procedures for developing the contract.
2. Agree on a clear and complete description of the behaviors to be developed and reduced by the contract procedures.
3. Agree on the responsibilities of others (e.g., teachers, parents) in helping the student achieve the goals of the contract.
4. Agree on the pleasant consequences available to the student for meeting the behavioral criteria indicated in the contract.
5. Agree on the unpleasant consequences, if any, that will result from the student's failure to meet the behavioral criteria of the contract.
6. Agree on a maintenance goal to encourage the learner to sustain his or her progress over an extended period of time.
7. Formalize the contract by writing it in positive terms and having it signed by all persons concerned with its success.

FIGURE 7.1   Sample Contingency Contract Format

I, _____(Student's Name)_____, will do the following:

1. (behavior to be reinforced) _____

   _____

2. (behavior to be reinforced) _____

   _____

3. (behavior to be reinforced) _____

Every time I do these behaviors I will gain (*positively reinforcing conse-quence*) _____

I will no longer do the following:

1. (behavior to be punished) _____
2. (behavior to be punished) _____
3. (behavior to be punished) _____

When I do these behaviors I will lose (*unpleasant consequence*)

_____

I _____(Teacher's Name)_____ will assist in helping to meet the goals

of this contract by

_____

_____

Others, including (*parent, other teachers, etc.*), will help to meet the goals
of the contract by

_____

_____

If the goals of this contract are met for 9 weeks, ____(Student's Name)____

will gain (*long-term reinforcing consequence*) _____

_____

Date _____

Student's Signature _____

Other Participants' Signatures _____

_____

_____

Family Involvement

■9 ○9   Home and school cooperation can play an important role in enhancing a learner's educational program. Conger (1977) has emphasized this point by noting that "an increasing body of empirical data indicates that the single most important external influence...in the accomplishment of developmental tasks...is [the student's] parents" (p. 221). Four factors recommend parental involvement in school behavior management programs: (1) the minimal expense and high availability of parents as change agents; (2) the strong influence parents may have on their child's behavior; (3) the availability of backup reinforcers in the home that are not accessible or appropriate in the school setting; and (4) the potentially positive influence that home–school cooperation may have on parents' behavior management skills.

One basis for initiating a home–school management program is a parent–teacher conference in which specific problems are raised and a strategy is planned for controlling the behavior. The sample reporting format in figure 7.2 can be used by a teacher to serve as a record of the problems raised at the meeting and how they are to be addressed.

FIGURE 7.2   Sample Reporting Format

Student   _____

Parent Present   _____

Date   _____

Issues discussed:

_____

_____

_____

Student behavior expected to resolve the issue:

_____

_____

_____

Ways teacher may assist in resolving the issue:

_____

_____

_____

Several studies over the past decade have suggested useful strategies for involving parents in the school program. In one example, Bailey, Wolfe, and Phillips (1970) involved parents in a program designed to reduce rule violations while improving study behavior. The youths were required to take home each night a report card marked by their teachers. If the report card indicated that the youth had followed the class rules and had studied through each period, all home privileges were awarded. If a rule violation or study deficiency was recorded by any teachers, the privileges were restricted. The study concluded that the daily reporting system was an effective and practical behavior management technique.

Effective techniques for developing home–school coordination are summarized in Action Plan 7.8.

ACTION PLAN 7.8   EFFECTIVE HOME-SCHOOL COORDINATION TECHNIQUES

We recommend the following techniques for developing home–school coordination:

1. Meet with parents early in the school year at a mutually convenient time and place. DO NOT WAIT FOR A PROBLEM TO ARISE BEFORE MEETING.
2. Discuss the scope, plan, and purpose of the meeting with the parents.
3. Discuss general classroom expectations and the student's specific goals and objectives. These may have been established in advance by the multidisciplinary team.
4. Describe behavior management procedures that are used in the classroom. Present data supporting their effectiveness.
5. Determine whether a modified version of the classroom approach would be beneficial if carried out at home.
6. Identify the school's responsibility in helping the parents meet behavior management objectives.
7. Identify the parents' responsibility in helping the school meet the same objectives.
8. Establish a communication system between the school and the home (e.g., daily or weekly reports, periodic phone calls) to review progress or problems or to modify the plan.

CASE FOR ACTION 7.4

At a student's IEP conference, his mother has requested that more coordination be established between the school and the home. The mother has been pleased with the boy's progress at school but would like to see even more if that is possible. Another concern is that she has been having problems with her son at home, but the school is not experiencing such problems. You are the boy's teacher. What steps would you follow in establishing a home–school coordination plan?

SUMMARY

Management of the physical environment of the class, the time management aspects of instruction, and individual behavior management strategies all play roles in the development of a total management plan for a classroom. This chapter has provided specific strategies regarding each of these aspects of management that can be put into operation immediately and has also provided the rationale for the use of each strategy.

8

Technology and Instruction

■ **DID YOU KNOW THAT...**

■ **1** ...achievement levels may be higher when teachers systematically use new and old technology?

■ **2** ...any individual who is unable to read print is eligible for services from the American Printing House for the Blind, including the Talking Books Program?

■ **3** ...some educators believe that taping lectures makes it unnecessary for the students to take notes and often reduces their attention in class?

■ **4** ...public television offers a wide variety of programming, which can be integrated into the curriculum by subscribing to the local educational network?

■ **5** ...conventional and talking calculators are accepted as alternatives to arithmetic computation and are motivational for special needs learners?

■ **6** ...self-correcting materials can benefit students who have a history of failure, because confidentiality of mistakes is improved and immediate corrected feedback is offered to avoid the practice of errors?

■ **7** ...microcomputers represent a significant advance in education and are particularly useful with special needs students?

■ **8** ...although several criteria should be considered when selecting a microcomputer system, the two most important factors are the availability of a reliable service dealer and the availability of applicable software?

■ **9**   . . . there is a vast array of software in the public domain, which means less cost and easy accessibility, but that such programs should be reviewed carefully?

○ CAN YOU . . .

○ **1**   . . . identify the most frequently used type of instructional equipment and cite several examples of its use?

○ **2**   . . . identify the basic principles relevant to the design of all programmed instruction (PI) materials?

○ **3**   . . . identify several audio devices and describe how each may be used in the classroom?

○ **4**   . . . cite some applications and advantages of cassette tape recorders?

○ **5**   . . . enhance comprehension of class lectures by tape recording appropriate information at appropriate times?

○ **6**   . . . use calculators as an effective motivational device and as an alternative to hand computation in arithmetic?

○ **7**   . . . identify several formats used for constructing self-correcting materials and cite examples of how each might be applied?

○ **8**   . . . describe several factors that should be given thorough consideration when evaluating computer software?

■ 1   With the increased emphasis on microcomputer robotics applications, some of the "older" technologies are having a resurgence of acceptability. One aspect of this resurgence is the increased use of these technologies in school programs. Various machines and media have been implemented with the handicapped quite successfully in the past for circumventing, accommodating, or compensating for the disabling condition. The systematic use of new and old technologies can advance the achievement levels of the learners and maximize the use of instructional time. To use technology successfully, the teacher needs to know what technologies are available, what types of support devices or programs are needed to use them, and how to plan to use them systematically in a classroom setting. This chapter will describe both old and new technologies and will offer some suggestions on their use for instruction. Among the old technologies to be discussed are the chalkboard, overhead and opaque projectors, programmed instruction, audio cassette recorders, the Language Master®, instructional television, and filmstrips, films, and slides. Both conventional and nonconventional uses of these technologies will be discussed. The new technologies described will include calculators, Speak and Spell/Math/Read®, videotape recorders and cameras, self-correctional materials, and microcomputers.

THE OLD TECHNOLOGIES

Chalkboard

○ 1   The chalkboard remains the most frequently used type of instructional equipment, and it holds high motivational promise. Students like to write and draw on a chalkboard, using white, yellow, or colored chalk.

A student who is stuck on a math problem at his or her desk can be brought to the chalkboard for a brief math lesson. The change from seatwork to boardwork often gets the student back on track. Drill and practice, games, quick examples, and individual work assignments may all take advantage of the availability of the chalkboard. Notices to students about coming events, changes in the daily schedule, and behavior problems may also be written on the chalkboard to remind the teacher as well as the students of fluctuating situations. Root words or prefixes for spelling words or new reading vocabulary can be highlighted using colored chalk. Teachers should not overlook the chalkboard in their mastery of media.

Overhead and Opaque Projectors

Overhead and opaque projectors are valuable and versatile pieces of equipment. They have both instructional and motivational value in teaching the mildly handicapped.

An overhead projector can be used to project an image from a transparency onto a screen, wall, or chalkboard. Transparencies can be made ahead of time by the teacher (or purchased from a commercial publisher). When a lesson is taught, the teacher can put each transparency on the overhead as needed. The pace of a lesson can be regulated by blocking out segments of the transparency and then gradually revealing each section. Instructional time is maximized in the presentation of the lesson, because the teacher can be giving additional information, rather than spending time writing the information on the chalkboard. Transparencies can be prepared in a variety of background and print colors. Specific segments of information on the transparency can be highlighted by preparing them in different colors. Using the projector allows the teacher to face the students while teaching (unlike teaching from a chalkboard) and to monitor continuously for lapses of attention. Students enjoy writing on transparencies or directly on the glass top of the overhead projector.

Paper-based teaching materials can easily be transformed into transparencies with the aid of a thermogram machine. Menus, employment forms, checks, or job announcements can be easily duplicated onto transparencies, projected with the overhead, and then completed by students or by the teacher. In our opinion, next to the chalkboard, the overhead projector is probably one of the most valuable pieces of instructional equipment in a classroom.

An opaque projector can be used to project printed material or three-dimensional objects on a screen or wall. It is not as convenient to use as an overhead, but it has the advantage that almost any type of material can be projected with no advance preparation. One enjoyable activity with an opaque is to project images onto the chalkboard or large sheets of paper (or bulletin boards) and then trace them. If the teacher is not gifted as an artist, the opaque projector can help tremendously when a complex figure is needed for a chart or bulletin board. Students can operate and use the machine without much teacher guidance.

Programmed Instruction Materials

○ **2**   A variety of programmed instruction (PI) materials are available for the special education student. Some of these materials are in textbook formats; others are machine operated. The design of all PI materials relies heavily on five basic principles:

1. Careful analysis of the task
2. Sequencing of the components
3. Presentation of information in small increments
4. Overt responding by the learner
5. Feedback to the learner

Some programs have branching capabilities, although most that are not machine operated are basically linear. Some PI programs can be extremely tedious and slow-paced. They are best for short periods of time (e.g., 10 minutes) to maintain student interest.

Audio Cassette Tape Recorders

○ **3**   The use of cassette tape recorders may represent a reasonable alternative to reading as the primary means of acquiring information in content subject areas, such as social studies, science, and health. Recorders are inexpensive and can be used in a wide variety of ways. One major drawback to their use is the time required to prepare the tapes. The teacher needs to be organized and creative. Putting printed material on tape need not be the job of the teacher, however; it can be done by the classroom aide, volunteers, room mother, student council members, or other members of the class.

■ **2**   Talking Books for the Blind is also a source of taped materials that might be usable with the mildly handicapped learner. In 1978, Congress changed the definition of eligibility for services from the American Printing House for the Blind, in terms of its Talking Books Program, to include anyone who is unable to read print. Such a change in definition made dyslexic, learning disabled, and mentally handicapped learners eligible for the program. The services include the permanent loan of variable-speed cassette tape recorders and adapters and access to a cassette tape library at no cost. Further information about the program can be secured by writing to the American Printing House for the Blind or Physically Handicapped, Lexington, KY 40504, or by contacting a local public library.

Variable-speed tape recorders offer one major advantage over conventional recorders—the playback speed feature. The speed of playback can be varied up to 250 words per minute without excessive distortion of the voice. Since the typical reading speed of most adults is about 250 words per minute, it is possible for a student to listen to material at about the same rate as most people could read that material. Speeding up the playback on a conventional machine results in a garbled or "Donald Duck" effect, but the variable-speed machines minimize this distortion. This speeded-up playback is referred to in the literature as "compressed speech."

Again, the key here is the emphasis on teaching. Students must be trained to use the machine and to increase their listening comprehension skills to make maximum use of the machine's capabilities. A shaping procedure would be used to assist in such teaching, and the students would be carefully positioned so that there would be limited visual and other auditory interference. Earphones are recommended when using this procedure to cut down on distracting background noise.

○ **4**   Advantages and suggested uses of conventional or variable-speed cassette tape recorders include the following:

1. They allow the student to replay all or a segment of a tape for review.
2. They allow the student to play a tape at a slow or accelerated rate.
3. They can be used at a learning station.
4. Instructions can be individualized for each student.
5. Students can record their reading or spelling lessons and self-monitor mistakes.
6. Teachers can record large group lectures for individual student review.
7. Students can record stories that can be transcribed later for reading lessons.
8. They can be used for room background music.
9. They can record radio news broadcasts.
10. They can record TV and radio commercials for discussion.

Cassette tapes can be erased and reused. Sometimes, however, they can be erased by accident. To avoid this, the teacher can punch out the plastic squares on the edge of the cassette tape so that it cannot be accidentally erased by a student. Snap-in plugs can be purchased to fill in these squares later if the teacher wishes to record over the tape, or the punch-out can be covered with tape.

■ 3   A tape recorder can be used as a compensatory device for handicapped students. The four major uses are taped lectures, lecture summaries, taped textbooks, and paraphrased material. Some educators believe that if their students simply tape lectures, they will not need to take notes and that this often reduces the learners' attention in class because of their total reliance on the machine. Studying with tapes is a time-consuming activity, with the possibility of 20 to 25 hours of taped instruction available each week. Students who have difficulty listening in class in the first place are not likely to benefit much from sitting through the class again. Here again, technology does not provide an easy answer to a problem but requires creativity by the teacher in using the technology. The following are some guidelines for taping lectures:

1. Do it when a student will be absent from class.
2. Do it when a student believes that relistening to a specific lecture will help.
3. Try it out in a resource room setting first to see whether the student benefits.
4. Selectively tape lectures on the most difficult topics; confer with the content teacher to arrive at these topics.

○ **5**   Another option for audio tapes is the lecture summary. Such summaries should be brief—15 to 25 minutes long—and should emphasize the major points or concepts of a lecture. An outline of the major topics also might be attached. The tapes should be recorded in outline format, with references to specific figures or charts in a text or handouts. The assistance of the content teacher is very helpful if these tapes are to be produced and reused.

Textbooks or other reading assignments also can be placed on audio tapes. As a general rule, each unit or chapter should be put on a separate tape and labeled to facilitate the management of the tapes. The reader should have a pleasant reading voice that provides appropriate inflection. The printed material should be available so that the listener can follow along.

Taped paraphrased materials are used like lecture summaries except that they are based on printed material. The paraphrased materials should include directly quoted sections that are central to understanding the material. Examples of dialect and style are often important if the taped material is based on a literature assignment.

Action Plans 8.1 and 8.2 summarize the procedures for taping lecture summaries and textbooks.

ACTION PLAN 8.1   PROCEDURES FOR TAPING LECTURE OR TEXTBOOK SUMMARIES

We recommend the following procedures for taping summaries:

1. Prepare an outline of key points before recording.
2. For a lecture summary, have the instructor assist with the outline and recording.
3. Record in an outline format, with brief explanations.
4. Refer to figures, charts, or tables in text material.
5. Limit tape length to 15 to 20 minutes.
6. Clearly label the tape and store it carefully.

ACTION PLAN 8.2   PROCEDURES FOR TAPING TEXTBOOKS

We recommend the following procedures for taping textbooks:

1. Record each chapter or unit on a separate tape.
2. The reader's voice should be pleasant, with appropriate inflection.
3. Printed material should be made available to accompany the tape.
4. Use volunteers (e.g., parents, other students, aides) to record materials.
5. Record in an area devoid of background noise.
6. Be selective in determining which materials should be recorded in total and which would suffice with a summary.
7. Clearly label each tape and store it carefully.

Of the many strategies for accommodating the handicapped learner, the simple audiotape recorder is probably one of the easiest to sell to content teachers and can produce immediate results.

CASE FOR ACTION 8.1

A good student who participates eagerly in class discussions and who appears to be quite knowledgeable about the topics discussed if they are based on assigned readings generally does poorly during quizzes and tests on those topics that are based on the teacher's lectures, because she apparently has difficulty simultaneously taking meaningful notes and listening to what the teacher is saying. What recommendations might be appropriate for this student to assist her in retaining more information from the teacher lectures?

Language Master

The Language Master® is an adaptation of a tape recorder with a magnetic tape fastened to the bottom of a card. Several companies produce these audio card readers under different names. When the card is inserted in the machine, whatever is recorded on the tape at the bottom is played back to the learner. Figure 8.1 illustrates a Language Master and card. The top portion of the card might contain a picture or words. Commercially prepared cards are available in language arts, speech, math, and science. Blank cards can also be purchased, and lessons can be created by the teacher. Since the student can record, erase, or play back information on the cards, the teacher should not assume that what is printed on the card is the same information that is recorded. It is good practice to spot-check the cards before giving them to the students.

Such machines can be used in teaching sight words, alphabet recognition, spelling, numerals, and a variety of other skills. They are often used with non-English speaking students as a means of developing a speaking and listening English vocabulary. They have also been used in conjunction with microcomputer programs as an inexpensive way to add audio instructions to simple programs. For spelling programs, the words can be printed on the opposite side of the card so that the student can practice the word and then check it by flipping over the card.

FIGURE 8.1 Language Master

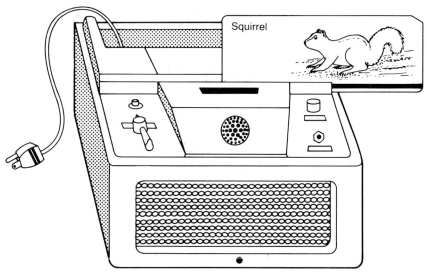

Instructional Television

One technological innovation that has declined in popularity in recent years is instructional television. We believe, however, that instructional television offers a viable option to regular classroom instruction in certain subject areas for mildly handicapped learners.

■ 4   Public television stations and some commercial stations broadcast an excellent array of programs in social studies, health, science, mental health, and language arts. Regular and judicious use of these programs can be a highly beneficial component of the curriculum. The typical program is only 15 minutes long and is well developed and highly organized. Schools that subscribe to the local educational network can obtain study guides and program listings to help teachers plan and guide instruction.

Instructional television is stimulating for the student and provides a change of pace from seatwork and regular classroom activities. It is also an activity that emphasizes listening skills. Brief programs prevent or reduce attention span difficulties, as do the fast-paced presentations. Most teachers would have difficulty delivering as much content in so brief a span of time or as dramatically as these instructional programs.

The amount of time it would take a teacher in a classroom to set up an experiment, prepare the students for what is to take place, carry it out, explain the results, and clean up would far exceed the amount of time it would take to view such a lesson on educational TV. A TV show's direction permits several camera angles and close-ups of important parts of an experiment. Used on a regularly planned basis, educational television programs can make a significant contribution to the total curriculum. Scheduling conflicts can now be resolved by recording the programs on videotape machines and then arranging to replay them at convenient times in the schedule. Action Plan 8.3 summarizes procedures for using instructional television.

Filmstrips, Films, and Slides

Filmstrips, films, and slides are versatile media that can be used to illustrate concepts. Locating and scheduling films and filmstrips generally require advanced planning on the part of the teacher. Slides offer an advantage over filmstrips in that the order of presentation can be modified. Slides also provide a means to personalize the instruction and draw upon local examples and events when teaching. They can be used to help students remember events and to illustrate occupations in the community and the variety of jobs performed by workers in certain occupations.

ACTION PLAN 8.3   USING INSTRUCTIONAL TELEVISION

We recommend the following procedures for using instructional television:

1. Prepare students for what they are to view.
2. Establish a rhythm, and make the television series a regular part of the weekly schedule.
3. Follow each program with a brief review session or quiz.
4. Videotape programs that are not scheduled at convenient times.
5. Monitor the class as a program is aired to maintain on-task behavior.

THE NEW TECHNOLOGIES

Calculators

■ 5 ○ 6   The use of calculators can provide an alternative to the task of hand calculation and can also decrease the amount of time spent on activities that are strictly computational in nature. The use of calculators can increase the amount of time available for the student to learn about the problem-solving aspects of math, not just the computational aspects. Learners initially need to be taught how to operate calculators. Merely giving them calculators to work problems will not result in their getting more problems correct, primarily because the sequences of skills in manual computation and calculator use are different. Talking calculators can be purchased for students with vision problems or for students who may need an auditory rather than a visual check of their computation. Sample task analyses for using a calculator are found in the mathematics instruction chapter of this book (chapter 12).

Speak and Spell/Read/Math

Texas Instruments has produced a series of machines called Speak and Spell®, Speak and Read®, and Speak and Math®. These machines use a touch-sensitive keyboard for responses. Each machine has several major programs and expansion modules. Before attempting to use these machines with students, the teacher must become thoroughly familiar with the machine features.

One feature of the Speak and Spell machine is a drill-and-practice program in which words are organized into ten-item sets. Ten words are displayed on the machine, one at a time, and each word is pronounced. The student is then quizzed on the spelling of each word. In a second version, a quiz is given without the practice session. In each case, the student is given two opportunities to spell the word and is told whether his or her spelling is wrong. After two errors on the same word, the machine spells the word on the visual display and in an audio message. The machine keeps score of students' success and reports with a visual display and an audio message at the end of ten words. Speak and Spell also contains a version of "Hangman" and has a secret code feature for fun activities. Letter recognition is another feature of the machine that makes it usable with youngsters in this readiness stage.

Speak and Math has math problems at varying difficulty levels in the four basic operations. Practice is also provided in number patterns and in trying to guess what number comes next.

Speak and Read has features similar to the other machines and has similar operating requirements. Additional plug-in modules are available to expand the offerings, and earphones can be used so that others are not disturbed.

Earphones and Headphones

Most audio devices have jacks that can accommodate earphones, headphones, or external speakers. Headphones and earphones offer two advantages over the use of a speaker system:

1. Earphones eliminate background noise and help the student direct his or her attention to the audio output.
2. The audio is not distracting to other students in the room.

Unfortunately, many different sized jacks and plugs are needed for different audio devices. The most common diameter size for earphone jacks is 1/8 inch; that for headphone jacks is 1/4 inch. Fortunately, most electronics stores carry adapters that allow a teacher to convert any size plug on an earphone or headphone to be compatible with the plug on the audio device. Adapters are relatively inexpensive and should be part of the hardware available in a classroom. These adapters slip directly on the shank of a headphone or earphone plug and allow the same earphones to be used with a wide variety of audio devices, including the following:

1. Radios
2. Variable-speed tape recorders
3. Language Master®
4. Cassette and reel-to-reel tape recorders
5. Slide/tape machines
6. Educational electronic games
7. Televisions

CASE FOR ACTION 8.2

A student has difficulty comprehending what he reads. He wears glasses and frequently complains of eyestrain during lengthy independent reading assignments. The school psychologist has suggested that he is primarily an "auditory learner"—one who retains information more effectively if it is read to him. You find that diagnosis to be inconsistent with your observations. Considering these factors, what interventions or adjustments might be made in the classroom to help this student benefit more from assigned readings?

Videotape Recorders and Cameras

Video cassette recorders and cameras have a variety of applications in a classroom for the mildly handicapped. Many schools use such systems to tape evening television programs for viewing the next day, requesting special permission to be allowed the privilege to tape these shows for one-time-only use. The school or district librarian would be best informed on the copyright fair use laws in regard to the duplication and use of commercially broadcast programs. The types of shows that might be useful in a class for the mildly handicapped include documentaries and news broadcasts.

Another use for a videotape system is in the areas of social skills development and oral communication. Videotaping simulated job interviews and job activities provides a feedback mechanism for the teacher and the student to critique. The system can also be used by the teacher to improve his or her teaching skills or those of the classroom aide by taping and then replaying and reviewing segments of the school days.

School-oriented programs in science, social studies, and so on, that are broadcast on public television can be taped and replayed at convenient times in the school schedule. We believe that some of the reduced use of educational television has resulted from time conflicts; with the advances and price reductions in video recorders, however, the use of educational television will once again increase.

The videotape machine can freeze frames, move fast forward, and replay segments. It is another valuable tool in the special educator's arsenal of strategies.

CASE FOR ACTION 8.3

A student is going to be placed on home-bound instruction for 5 weeks following an upcoming operation. His assignments will be sent to his home, where he will be expected to complete them. Given the extended amount of time that the student will be out of school, what are some measures the school can take to improve the educational quality of his 5-week recovery period?

Self-Correcting Materials

■ 6 ○ 7 Instructional materials that have a self-correcting feature are available from commercial publishers or can be constructed easily by the classroom teacher, aide, volunteer, or even students. C. D. Mercer and Mercer (1978) have indicated that self-correcting materials are useful for learners who have a history of failure, because they minimize the public occurrence of a mistake when the learner is practicing. The learner also receives immediate corrected feedback so that he or she does not practice errors. Mercer and Mercer (1978) have identified nine formats that can be used for the construction of self-correcting materials: flap, slot, matching card, puzzles, balance scales, tab, pocket, electrical, device, and magnet (see figure 8.2). With such devices, students approach a task as if it were a game.

Microcomputers

■ 7 There is little doubt that microcomputers are making their presence felt in programs for the handicapped. These machines, with the appropriate peripherals and added features, can synthesize speech, play back prerecorded messages from a tape or chips, and respond to spoken commands. Although many things are possible, the base model microcomputer does not usually have these features; they must be purchased as add-ons. Even on machines that are properly equipped with these features, the user must know how to access the features to make them work for the intended purpose. Such an undertaking is usually not accomplished in a brief training session; rather, it requires an ongoing commitment by the teacher to learn and properly use the machine and the accompanying software. This training can be accomplished through formal coursework, in-service training, computer clubs, or self-study. Some selected microcomputer terms with which you should be familiar are defined in figure 8.3.

FIGURE 8.2 Self-Correctional Devices

Balance Scales

Directions: Different numbers of cards are glued to the backs of the answer and corresponding question cards such that each question and corresponding answer weighs the same. Be sure that no two answer cards weigh the same. Envelopes and paper clips could also be used for this activity.

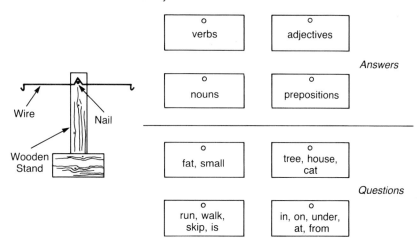

Pocket

Directions: An envelope with the answer key is glued or stapled to the back of a question sheet.

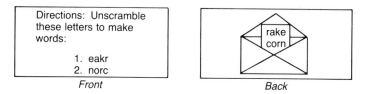

Flap

Directions: An oaktag sheet is placed on top of a stack of cards, with the flap closed. After the learner responds, he or she checks the answer by raising the flap.

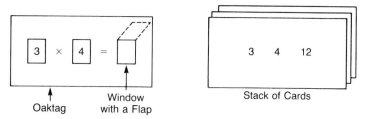

(continued)

FIGURE 8.2 Continued

Magnet

Directions: A paper clip is hidden behind a piece of paper following each equation. The answer card will stick to each equation for which 8 is the answer.

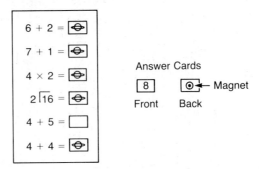

Answer Cards

Puzzles

Directions: Cut materials from oaktag. Make each cut an original—that is, nonduplicative of other cuts.

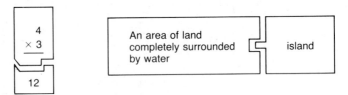

Electricity

Directions: This is a matching task. The learner connects one wire to the metal tabs on the left and the other to the metal tab on the right that represents the correct answer. Activation of the light buzzer or bell signifies the correct answer.

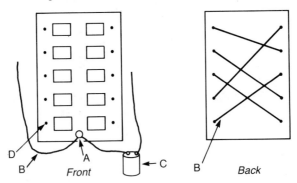

A. Light, Buzzer, or Bell

B. Wire

C. Dry Cell

D. Metal Tab

(continued)

FIGURE 8.2 Continued

Matching Cards

Directions: Cards have a question or problem on the front and an answer on the back.

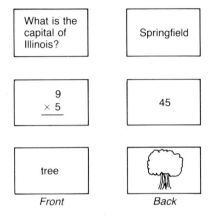

What is the capital of Illinois?	Springfield

9
× 5

45

tree

Front   *Back*

Tab

Directions: An oaktag strip with answers is fastened to the back of the question card so that it can slide up or down.

	Pull up		Pull up
1. The opposite of go is	_____		1. stop
2. The opposite of front is	_____		2. back
3. The opposite of up is	_____		3. down
4. The opposite of run is	_____		4. walk
5. The opposite of win is	_____		5. lose

Slot

Directions: A slot is cut into a box or jar lid. Only cards of "correct" size will fit through the slot. Be sure not to give learner cards that are too small, because they will incorrectly fall through the slot and defeat the purpose of the activity.

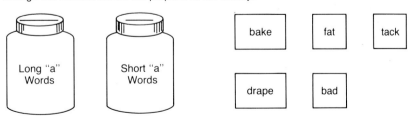

Long "a" Words   Short "a" Words

bake	fat	tack
drape	bad	

FIGURE 8.3   Selected Microcomputer Terms

Hardware   The physical equipment of a computer system.

Software   Generic term for computer programs that are stored in and control the operation of hardware.

Special Net   A telecommunications service that is dedicated primarily to the interests of special educators; the system operates through the GTE Telenet Service and on a subscription basis.

BASIC   Beginners All-Purpose Symbolic Instruction Code—a computer language developed in 1964; all microcomputers can be programmed in this language.

PILOT   A computer language created to develop courseware for computer-assisted instruction.

Modem   An acronym for MOdulator-DEModulator—a device that allows a computer to be linked to other computers over telephone lines.

Light pen   A peripheral that allows the student to respond without typing; when the light pen is touched to a particular spot on the screen, the response is recorded.

Speech synthesizer   An optional peripheral that provides auditory output for text presented on the screen.

Drill and practice   A mode of instruction in which a learner is presented with problems or exercises and is given feedback after each response regarding correctness.

Tutorial   A mode of instruction in which a learner is presented with information and then is tested on acquisition of that information.

Simulation   A mode of instruction in which the real world is simulated in a game format; the learner makes decisions and is then given feedback on the consequences of that decision.

Basic System

The basic microcomputer system usually contains a microprocessor, a typewriter-style keyboard, a monitor or television screen, and a disk drive or cassette tape recorder. In some models, all of these features are built into one piece of equipment; others have them as separate components. Features beyond these must be purchased separately. The user should be cautioned that there may be hidden costs for interfacing peripheral devices with the microcomputer. The interfacing may require the purchase of cables, chips, or boards to make the peripheral operable. In some cases, the interfacing can be as costly as the peripheral. Newer models of microcomputers are making the interfacing easier and less costly because the base models of microcomputers are incorporating more of these interfacing features.

Selection of a System

■ 8   The problem of system selection is becoming more complex as newer models appear and as school systems learn more about how microcomputers can be used. The following criteria should be considered when purchasing a system:

1. Cost
2. Primary use (e.g., instruction, administrative, or word processing)
3. Availability of software
4. Ease and cost of expandability
5. Availability of peripherals
6. Availability of a reliable service dealer
7. Compatibility with other machines in the district

Service and software are probably the two major criteria to consider after a decision is reached on how the system will be used. A computer is only as good as the software that runs on it. It is also useful only if it is in operational condition. In our experience, the components most often in need of service are the disk drives and printers, rather than the basic machine. Components with moving parts have the greatest need for service.

Selection of Software

○ 8   Software is now widely available for most microcomputers, although newer models may have less software available than older models. Compatibility is a major concern regarding software. Software is written for a specific microcomputer system and is not generally interchangeable among machines from different manufacturers. That means that software written for Apples will not run on IBM PC's, and vice versa. Even within the same company, software may not be compatible with all models of the company's microcomputers. When purchasing software, it is crucial to know the machine for which it was written and the amount of memory needed to use the program. Memory is expressed in a unit of measure called a "K"—such as 48K, 64K, 128K. Larger numbers mean that more memory is available in the machine and that it can handle larger and more complex programs. A program labeled for use on an Apple II+ with 48K will run an Apple program that requires 32K but will not run an Apple program that requires 64K.

Locating programs can be a time-consuming process. Information on programs is available from the following sources:

1. Commercial publishers
2. Microcomputer manufacturers
3. Microcomputer journals and magazines
4. Computer clubs
5. Other schools

FIGURE 8.4 Questions to Ask When Evaluating Software

---

1. Are there audible responses to student errors?
2. Is failure rewarded, such as in a game like Hangman?
3. Are there uncontrollable sounds?
4. Are there technical problems in operating the software?
5. Are there uncontrollable screen advances?
6. Are the operating instructions inadequate?
7. Are there errors in grammar, spelling, or content?
8. Are there insults, sarcasm, or derogatory remarks in the feedback?
9. Is the documentation poor?
10. Is a back-up copy denied?

If any of these questions are answered yes, the product could be rejected.

Figure 8.4 contains a list of questions that Lathrop (1982) has indicated should be asked when selecting software. Software available in the public domain may not pass the scrutiny of the Lathrop list, but these programs often can be modified easily by someone with only a rudimentary understanding of BASIC.

Modes of Instruction

Instructional software that can be used directly by students is generally written in one of three formats: drill-and-practice programs, tutorials, and simulations.

DRILL-AND-PRACTICE PROGRAMS Drill-and-practice programs should be used with previously taught concepts in which the learner needs practice to reach a reasonable level of mastery. Short drill-and-practice programs are easy to integrate into an ongoing curriculum. Commercially available and public domain drill-and-practice courseware is widely available for basic math facts, spelling, fraction/decimal equivalencies, states and their capitals, and parts of speech. The computer operates as a flashcard system in the drill-and-practice mode. Recently, drill-and-practice programs have been developed that place the activity within the context of a game. The ARC-ED courseware (Chaffin, Maxwell, & Thompson, 1982) has combined the features of videogames with educationally relevant content. Drill-and-practice programs using this format are available under the tradename Academic Skillbuilders and are marketed commercially by DML, Inc. One of us has used two of these programs with elementary-aged behaviorally disordered students in conjunction with 1-minute timed tests. Continued use of the microcomputer and the Academic Skillbuilder (AS) materials was contingent upon improved performance on the 1-minute tests. Students' performance on both timed tests and the AS materials improved over a baseline condition. The advantages of using micros for drill and practice include the following:

1. Immediacy of feedback to the learners
2. The novelty effect of using the machine
3. Time savings for the teacher
4. The variety of rewards
5. Active (overt) responding by the learner
6. The endless patience of the machine

TUTORIALS   In the tutorial mode, new concepts are presented to the learner, and the learner is then tested by a series of questions. The program evaluates the learner's responses, provides feedback, and then continues the instruction, recycles the student through the material, or takes the student to a remedial branch of the program. If the learner is having trouble, the branching may be to a subprogram that explains the concept in a more simplified fashion. Students who make few errors move rapidly through the program. These tutorial programs can be brief supplements to classroom instruction or lengthy in-depth courses.

SIMULATIONS   In the simulation mode, the learner is presented with situations that require decision making. The chain of events in the simulation is based on these decisions. Simulations imitate real problems. For example, a simulation on comparison shopping would require that a student make decisions regarding the "best" buys. The student would be told that he or she has a certain amount of money with which to purchase items on a shopping list. Poor choices would result in the student's not being able to purchase all items. If the student made all the "best" choices, he or she might end up with money to buy a treat or to put into savings. Simulations can be fun and they can be excellent learning experiences, particularly because they require students to make decisions and then suffer consequences. Having students work on simulations in small groups is recommended so that they can learn from other students' thinking. Mildly handicapped learners have difficulty making appropriate decisions and selecting the best alternatives. Simulations can help in this regard.

Copyright and Software

■ 9   Much software, like other commercially available media, is protected under copyright laws. There are programs available for free use; they are called *public domain programs*. Such programs can be readily copied without legal entanglements. Schools and clubs often make this software available to the public for duplication and use. These programs can also be legally bought and sold by vendors who advertise in magazines. Copyrighted software, however, cannot usually be duplicated legally. Three issues surface regularly regarding copyright and software: back-up copies, multiple loading of one disk into multiple machines at the same time, and networking (Finkel, 1985). Violations can involve not only the physical duplication of a disk, but also the issue of simultaneous use. The issue of violating a copyright of software is based on the test of whether a practice inhibits the sale of the software. Simultaneous usage of the same software by multiple users is a violation of copyright. Back-up copies are allowable so long as they are used only as a back-up and are not used simultaneously (or could be used simultaneously) by several users.

Computer Use in Classrooms

Sedlak and Sedlak (1985) have provided a list of dos and don'ts in regard to microcomputer use in the classroom:

1. *Do* keep work sessions at the microcomputer relatively short.
2. *Do* look for software variations that allow the students to practice the same set of skills.
3. *Do* make a contract with students regarding proper behavior when using the microcomputer—and be consistent in delivering the consequences.
4. *Do* have students chart or record performance data after each session.
5. *Do* review student performance data regularly and change the level of program if necessary.
6. *Do* teach the students the proper care of the equipment, the names for the devices, and how to handle disks properly.
7. *Do* use the computer with pairs or small groups of students in cooperative team activities, not for one-on-one instruction only.
8. *Don't* use the computer exclusively for playing videogames.
9. *Don't* use the computer as a substitute for direct instruction.
10. *Don't* use the computer as "busy work," just to keep students occupied.

Uses in Addition to Instruction

In addition to its use in instruction, the microcomputer can be used for word processing, data management, test scoring and analysis, IEP writing, and the creation of new software through the use of authoring languages or BASIC. Chapter 9 provides some information on word processing uses with students. Authoring systems such as PILOT or E-Z PILOT can be used by teachers to develop new programs, but they require a considerable amount of work on the part of the teacher. Figure 8.5 provides a recommended list of programs and utilities that special education teachers may find useful.

FIGURE 8.5   A Basic Software Set for Classroom Use

For Teachers
1. Word processing program (e.g., Apple Writer, Magic Window)
2. Disk command editor—a set of programs that allows a teacher to change the DOS commands so that students cannot delete programs from the disk or modify them
3. Teacher utility programs (e.g., Teachers Aids, which allows the teacher to create drill-and-practice lessons with teacher-supplied content, or a computer-assisted instruction program such as E-Z PILOT)
4. Graphics print program (e.g., Print Shop, which allows the teacher to create designs on a printer for awards, booklets, advertisements, etc.)

For Students
1. Word processing program (e.g., Bank Street Writer)
2. Spelling dictionary program (e.g., Bank Street Speller) to identify and correct spelling errors
3. Drill-and-practice programs in math and spelling
4. Simulation programs (e.g., Oregon Trail) for decision making

CASE FOR ACTION 8.4

Your school has recently been notified that there are funds available for the purchase of a microcomputer to be used for administrative and instructional purposes in your school. However, before the purchase can be made, the district administration is requesting that each school submit a list of the needed equipment and software as well as a rationale for their purchase. You have been selected to gather the requested information. How will you approach this task, and what steps will you take to ensure the selection of appropriate materials?

SUMMARY

The technology options described in this chapter were presented to stimulate thinking on options for presenting information to students. They were also presented to allow a teacher to consider how their use could circumvent or accommodate a disabling condition within the learner. None of these devices will be effective unless they are used in a planned manner by the teacher. Action Plan 8.4 provides a summary of factors that should be considered in using technology in the classroom.

The options presented here do not constitute a universal set of available technologies for use by the teacher and the learner. Each year, new options become available, and the special education teacher should be alert to nontraditional uses for these new products.

ACTION PLAN 8.4   CAUTIONS IN THE USE OF TECHNOLOGY

The following factors should be considered in using technology:

1. Do not assume that the technology will automatically solve the problem.
2. Use of the technology (equipment and software) must be taught to the learner in the same way as other material.
3. Set rules for when and how equipment will be used.
4. Consider the disadvantages of using technology for a problem (e.g., absence of software, training of students in equipment use) and how they can be overcome.
5. Be sure the technology matches the problem; the older technologies may address a problem better than the newer technologies.
6. Build time into schedules to accommodate the use of technology when necessary.

Part III

Educational Competencies

9

Listening and Speaking Instruction

■ DID YOU KNOW THAT...

■ 1 ...tasks related to hearing and listening represent a major portion of each learner's waking hours?

■ 2 ...teachers affect how much students listen by the cues they give students?

■ 3 ...almost all parts of speech are present in students' language by age 4?

■ 4 ...pragmatics is the use of language in a social context?

■ 5 ...the terms *social skill training* and *pragmatics training* refer to the same sets of skills but are used by two different professions?

■ 6 ...variant-English speakers may not use standard English but do speak a dialect that is rule-governed?

■ 7 ...style switching is a teachable skill that is important for the variant-English speaker to learn?

■ 8 ...there is no cure for stuttering, but structuring the classroom environment into predictable events may minimize stuttering episodes?

■ 9 ...communication between the speech therapist and the teacher is important to maintain the continuity of a speech correction program for learners?

○ CAN YOU...

○ **1** ...specify the major components of language?

○ **2** ...specify the principles for teaching variant-English speakers?

○ **3** ...specify two strategies for improving speech?

○ **4** ...construct a language web with students?

○ **5** ...specify some of the subareas of pragmatics training?

○ **6** ...teach "wh" questions?

○ **7** ...teach sentence-combining skills?

○ **8** ...use several strategies to improve listening skills?

■ 1   Children spend a large percentage of their time engaged in listening activities—listening to the radio, watching and listening to television, listening to the teacher explain directions or assignments, and conversing with friends and acquaintances. Flanders (1970) has estimated that as much as 66 percent of a child's day is spent in listening-related tasks. Burns and Broman (1975) have reported research indicating that adults spend about 42 percent of their waking hours in listening activities, 32 percent in conversations, 11 percent in writing, and 15 percent in reading. Rankin (1954) found that adults spent 45 percent of their waking hours listening and 30 percent talking. These statistics reflect the importance of listening and speaking skills both in the classroom setting and in daily living. The development of listening skills is crucial if the learning opportunities available to the mildly handicapped are to be maximized.

■ 2   Lundsteen (1964) has demonstrated that listening skills can be improved and that being able to hear and being able to listen are not identical skills. Teachers give students subtle cues that can either increase or decrease listening skills. The development of speaking skills is equally important. Research has demonstrated that people make judgments and form positive or negative impressions regarding the competence of a speaker on the basis of his or her oral language skills (Labov, 1966). Because of these diverse communications factors, the development of listening and speaking skills is an important area of any academic curriculum. The problem for the teacher is how best to integrate these crucial skills into the school day.

COMPONENTS OF LANGUAGE

○ 1   Language is a rule-governed system of behavior that results in communication. Language is composed of five identifiable elements, which can be taught and assessed separately but must be blended for the act of communication to take place:

1. Phonology
2. Morphology
3. Semantics
4. Syntax
5. Pragmatics

Phonology refers to the individual speech sounds (phonemes) and the rules that govern the sequence of those sounds. Although the English alphabet contains 26 letters, the phonological system contains 43 sound patterns, of which 19 are vowels and 24 are consonants in the oral language system. Vowels appear in a child's oral communication before age 2 and outnumber the use of consonants up through that age. Parents often imitate and reinforce these sounds when interacting with their babies. Even children who are born deaf make these sounds spontaneously early in their development. Failure to provide feedback to the child will delay the development and regular usage of speech sounds. By 30 months of age, most children use about 27 of the phonemes common in adult speech. By 36 months of age, a child's use of phonemes is still developing, but speech is characterized by substitutions and omissions of middle and final consonants. The acquisition of speech sounds peaks for most individuals by age 8.

Morphology involves the smallest individual meaningful sound elements in the language (morphemes) and the rules for combining these morphemes into words. Morphemes include root words, prefixes, and suffixes. The word *boys*, for example, contains two morphemes: *s*, which indicates plurality, and *boy*, which is a root word. Figure 9.1 lists the types of morphemes in order of acquisition.

Semantics involves the meanings of words of a language. We commonly refer to this aspect of language as *vocabulary development*. Learners acquire new words through interactions with their environment and by having someone label a previously unknown object or the relationship of a previously unmet event (e.g., on seeing a car drive by, a mother will label

FIGURE 9.1   Morphemes in Order of Acquisition

Morphemes	*Examples*
1. Present progressive form of verb	*is* eating
2–3. Prepositions *in, on*	*in* chair, *on* table
4. Plural (regular)	cats, dogs, witch*es*
5. Past irregular tense verbs	*went, came, fell*
6. Possessives	*boy* coat, *Daddy* hat
7. Uncontractible copula	Here I *am;* there it *is;* here we *are;* I *be* good.
8. Articles	*a* ball, *the* doggie
9. Past regular tense verbs	*jumped, poured, waded*
10. Third-person regular verbs	Daddy *drives.*
11. Third-person irregular verbs	Debbie *does;* Mommy *has.*
12. Uncontractible auxiliary verb	I *am* working; boy *is* running; girls *are* jumping; they *be* working.
13. Contractible copula (contraction form of a copula verb)	*He's* boy; *we're* happy; *she's* a mommy; *I'm* good boy.
14. Contractible auxiliary (contraction form of an auxiliary verb)	*I'm* working; *he's* running; *she's* sewing; *we're* playing.

Source: Adapted from Cole, M. L., Cole, J. T. (1981). *Effective intervention with the language impaired child.* Rockville, MD: Aspen Systems. Reprinted with permission of Aspen Systems Corporation.

what her child is seeing by saying, "That is a car; car go bye-bye" or some similar labeling statement). The development of vocabulary, therefore, is highly related to experiences. Failure to provide these early types of stimulation may limit the development of semantics in children. The different types of words are broken into groupings called *form classes* (e.g., nouns, verbs, articles or function words, adjectives, adverbs). Receptive (the listener's) vocabularies develop far faster than expressive (the speaker's) vocabularies. The normal development of vocabulary shows that word acquisition follows this sequence: nouns, verbs, adjectives, pronouns, adverbs, prepositions, articles (function words), conjunctions, and interjections (Weiss & Lillywhite, 1976). All form classes are present in the speech of most children by age 3½ to 4.

■ 3

Syntax involves the use of the rules of the language in combining words into sentences—that is, the placement of different types of words into the proper order to create meaningful sentences. Syntax is developed through experience with the language and repeated exposure. There is a progressive sequence of sentence development that occurs naturally as learners get older. This sequence normally shows development from one-word utterances (e.g., "ball," "go") to two-word utterances (e.g., "shoe on," "daddy go") and telegraphic speech (e.g., "eat cookie now," "Johnny dog run car"). The first "formal sentences" are referred to as *kernel* sentences; they differ from telegraphic speech in that they contain function words (e.g., *a, the, and*). An example of a kernel sentence is "The boy is hitting the ball."

Following the development of kernel sentences, the learner uses sentences that show transformations (the combination of two or more simple sentences into a compound sentence). Transformations reflect greater linguistic maturity than simple sentences do. For example, the kernel sentences "The dog is brown," "The dog is chasing the ball," and "The ball is red" can be combined into the sentence "The brown dog is chasing the red ball" (adjective transformation) or into the sentence "The dog that is brown is chasing the ball that is red" (double-base transformation). Using either of these transformations would indicate a more mature use of the language than is indicated by the preceding short sentences. Sentence combining is a teachable skill and one that the special education teacher may need to add to the language arts curriculum.

■ 4

Pragmatics is the ability to use the language code in the proper social context (L. Bloom & Lahey, 1978; McLean & Snyder-McLean, 1978). Turn-taking, shifts in style, and nonverbal actions are some of the aspects of communication that are covered in the area of pragmatics. Social dialects (e.g., nonstandard English) are also studied in the area of pragmatics.

In 1983, the American Speech and Hearing Association (ASHA) adopted a position on social dialects. This position paper states that "no dialectical variety of English is a disorder or a pathological form of speech or language. Each...is adequate as a functional and effective variety of

English. Each serves a communication function as well as a social solidarity function" (p. 23). According to the ASHA view, speech therapy is not appropriate for dialectical variations in speech. Recognizing the difference between a dialectical variation and a speech pathology is not always easy; when the teacher has a concern, a referral should be made. In lieu of a referral, the teacher should at least consult with the speech therapist on the nature of the concern.

Another area of pragmatics involves the subtle social cues that are a part of the communication process. Learning disabled students may have language problems because the cues to which they must respond are quite subtle. Training to make these students aware of the cues must be specific and systematic. Problems in the area of pragmatics can often be overlooked because they are not so "visible" as the more traditional types of problems that are treated, such as stuttering and articulation disorders.

■ 5   It is interesting to note that pragmatics is an area of study that is known by different names in different disciplines. In special education, problems in this area are generally viewed as *social skills deficits*, whereas speech and language therapists would use the term *pragmatics*. The chapter on social skills development (chapter 14) provides some specific suggestions on curriculum and strategies to foster these skills.

ASSESSMENT OF AURAL/ORAL LANGUAGE SKILLS

The assessment of aural/oral language skills should be based on the five components of language: phonology, morphology, semantics, syntax, and pragmatics. These components of language development can be assessed informally by the teacher through observation and recording or through teacher-constructed activities. These components can also be assessed through formal measures. Figure 9.2 presents a listing and description of standardized expressive and receptive language scales. Standardized measures give some perspective to the degree of a problem a student is experiencing and also focus attention on specific aspects of aural/oral language development. They lighten the burden of the evaluator by giving a prearranged format for administration and providing the stimulus materials needed for the assessment. However, these tests do not totally describe the child's language system. The procedures allow for little flexibility in the administration of the test and yield scores based on item pass/fail but do not necessarily provide an analysis of errors by type of error. It is the *pattern* of errors that can provide the teacher with valuable information for future instruction.

Evaluating the *functional use* of language (use of language to communicate ideas) is the most important aspect of language assessment. Determining functional use of language includes an analysis of the words and syntax used, the ideas expressed, and the organization of these ideas. The speaker's posture is noted as well as the physical distance between the speaker and the listener. Taking turns and staying with the flow of the conversation are also features of functional language use that need to be observed. The teacher should watch for these features of functional language use and make note of deviations in the learner's use of language in social situations. Specifically, the teacher should note whether the student is standing too close to a listener, is not properly projecting his or her voice, is not attending to the appropriate social cues in the conversation (pragmatics), or is failing to follow the logical sequence of ideas being exchanged in the conversation. Once a problem is identified, it can be targeted for correction.

ASSESSMENT OF PRAGMATICS

Until recently, the assessment of pragmatics was usually performed using nonstandardized situations and materials. Prinz and Weiner (in press) developed the first standardized test to assess pragmatics, the Pragmatics Screening Test, which consists of four separate tasks used at three levels. The authors cite the following examples of ineffective pragmatic skills in children:

1. Utterances that lack adequate referential clarity, resulting in listener confusion or misunderstanding
2. Regular failure to initiate requests and waiting to be told what to do or to be supplied with toys, food, books, and so forth
3. Difficulty in initiating topics, maintaining topical relevance, switching and returning to the main issue or topic, and terminating a conversation
4. Frequently impolite interrupting at inappropriate points in the conversation

Observations of student behavior in regular classroom interactions can determine the need for attention to pragmatics instruction. Action Plan 9.1 provides some specific situations that can be created to judge a learner's adequacy in regard to pragmatics.

FIGURE 9.2 Expressive and Receptive Language Scales

Test/Publisher	Purpose	Age Range	Stimulus/Response	Scoring
		Receptive Language Tests		
Peabody Picture Vocabulary Test (PPVT), American Guidance Service, 1965	The test is designed to provide an estimate of a subject's verbal intelligence by measuring his hearing vocabulary; it may more validly represent a child's vocabulary density.	2.0 to 18.0	Given four pictorially represented choices, the tester reads the single-word verbal stimulus with the carrier phrase "Show me" or "Point to." Ex.: "Point to *table*" Ex.: "Point to *edifice*"	Basal and ceiling scores are established; a raw score of number of correct responses is computed and converted into a mental-age score, intelligence quotient, or percentile equivalent. Administration time: 10–15 minutes.
Assessment of Children's Language Comprehension (ACLC), Consulting Psychologist Press, 1973	The test is designed to determine the level at which a child is unable to decode and remember lexical items presented in increasing syntactical length and complexity. The nature of the test helps to isolate areas of difficulty. Complexity: one to four critical elements	Normative data from 3.0 to 5.5 years	When presented with spiral-bound line-drawn picture plates, the testee is to look at each of the pictorial stimuli presented on the plate while the examiner reads the verbal stimulus from the test form using a carrier phrase such as "Point to" or "Show me." Ex.: "Show me the *lady sitting*." Ex.: "Point to *dog eating and cat sitting*."	Part A (one critical element) is scored by adding the number of correct responses. Parts B, C, and D are scored by computing a percentage correct as well as narrative description of error patterns. Administration time: Untimed test, 15–20 minutes for administration and scoring.

Test	Description	Age Range	Procedure	Scoring
Test for Auditory Comprehension of Language (TACL), 5th ed., Teaching Resources Corp., 1973	The test is designed to determine the child's developmental level of auditory comprehension of vocabulary and linguistic structure. Information obtained can lead to guidelines for therapeutic intervention. Language categories measured are (1) form class and function words, (2) morphological categories, (3) grammatical categories, (4) syntactic structure. A screening form is available.	3.0 to 6.0	Given pictorially represented stimulus choices, the tester reads the stimulus items aloud and the child responds by pointing to the appropriate picture.	Responses are scored as correct or incorrect, converting total raw score into an age-equivalent score and percentile rank. The entire test must be administered to utilize the normative data. Administration time: 20 minutes.
Vocabulary Comprehension Scale, Teaching Resources Corp., 1975	The test is designed to assess comprehension of basic concepts, such as pronouns, words of position (e.g., *in, on*), size (e.g., *small, fat*), quantity (e.g., *all, less*), and quality (e.g., *hard, same*).	Preschool to 6.0	Given toy objects (e.g., playhouse, cars, dolls, tea set), the examiner requests testee manipulation of specific object to appropriately represent the verbal command. *Ex.:* "Make the doll go up the ladder." *Ex.:* "Give me the big block."	Each item is scored pass/fail. The items within each category are ranked according to developmental age. The testee's performance level is compared to sample population, yielding a rough index of developmental performance level. Administration time: 45 minutes.

ACTION PLAN 9.1 SITUATIONS FOR JUDGING APPROPRIATE RESPONSES IN PRAGMATICS

Situation	Description	Examples
Directives		
Requests for information (general or specific	Yes/no questions or "Wh" questions, seeking true/false judgments about propositions	"Is he buying it?" "Which one should I pick?"
Requests for action	A request that the addressee perform some action (or stop doing something)	"Get a blue block." "Don't take that one."
Requests for object	A request for the addressee to find and hand over a specific object	"Find the purse." "Give me the block."
Requests for clarification	A question or request to disambiguate or qualify the content or form of a previous utterance	"Huh?" "What?"
Responses to Directives		
Compliances	Verbal or nonverbal acceptance of a prior action or permission request	"Okay." Nod head.
Clarification responses	Supplying the relevant verbal repetition or qualification	"I said not that one."
Denials	Refusal to satisfy a request; assertion that something alleged is false	"No. He is not there."
Acknowledgments	Recognize and evaluate responses and nonrequests	"Right." "Really?" "Mmmm." "Yes."

LANGUAGE AND THE VARIANT-ENGLISH SPEAKER

A high percentage of students in special classes are from ethnic minority groups (Dunn, 1968; J. R. Mercer, 1973). Many of these students use variant or nonstandard English in their oral communication. Writers disagreed on whether these differences should be viewed as *deficiencies* or as *differences*. In fact, such arguments have resulted in lawsuits and court cases (Monteith, 1980; P. C. Robinson, 1980–81; Smitherman, 1981).

■ 6   The *deficiency* argument states that variant or nonstandard usage is associated with a cognitive limitation. Bereiter and Engelmann (1966) have illustrated this view by their conclusions that nonstandard-English speakers are unable to use "causal logic" because of an absence of an "if-then" structure, an absence of specified plurality forms, and the use of double negatives. The deficiency model does not recognize the rule structure of the variant form of a language. The deficiency argument also considers the vocabulary diversity of nonstandard English to be limited.

In contrast, the *difference* arguments (Baratz & Shuy, 1969) state that the variant-English form is rule-based and systematic. Rather than viewing speakers of the variant-language form as deficient, the difference model views them as speaking a language with a different set of rules. The Pennsylvania Dutch have a charming and unique means of expressing ideas that illustrates a difference perspective. An example is the expression, "Throw the horse over the fence some hay." Because the order of the words is not what is expected, the listener must rearrange them mentally to get the appropriate meaning.

■ 7   Depending on the social environment and the purpose of a communication exchange, most speakers will shift to a level of language that is most appropriate for the setting. The range of this shift can fall along a continuum from formal or standard English to the level of jargon, slang, or street language (informal English). Style shifting is a natural and expected aspect of linguistic competence. For example, talking to friends after school is a social situation that calls for informal language usage, whereas a job interview or communication with authority figures (e.g., teacher, police, principal) calls for a different style of language, usually a formal style.

Teaching students to shift among styles according to the social circumstances they encounter is a goal of an oral language program for the mildly handicapped variant-English speaker. Before learning to shift styles, however, the learner must be taught that different language styles exist and must receive training in formal English. Our society categorizes individuals on the basis of how they talk. Therefore, a person's use of variant-English forms in social situations that require the use of formal English will call undue attention to that individual and will shape the perceptions and impressions of others toward him or her. A major problem facing mildly handicapped learners is the "visibility" of their disability through their behavior. One goal of oral language training should be to minimize the differences between the speaker and the expectations of the listeners in the social setting.

Labov (1966) has listed a sequence of eight communication instruction goals for variant-English speakers:

1. Understand spoken English to learn from the teacher
2. Read and comprehend printed materials
3. Communicate to others in spoken English
4. Express themselves in writing
5. Use standard English for written communication
6. Spell correctly
7. Use standard English in oral communication
8. Use appropriate pronunciation to avoid stigmatization

○ **2**   Cohen and Plaskon (1980) have provided eight principles to guide teachers who are instructing mildly handicapped variant-English speakers:

1. The "perfect" English speech form does not exist. A wide range of speech patterns is considered acceptable.
2. The language standards of the child's environment/community are important.
3. If the language style of the child's community differs from the standard form, "the child should be taught to recognize the difference and the parallel forms of the standard and variant forms" (p. 447).
4. Formal grammar should not be taught. Instruction should focus on *how* language is used, not *why* it is used.
6. Opportunities for spontaneous dialogue and structural drills should be balanced.
7. Expect students to make the transition through regular usage of the standard form after they have had sufficient opportunity to learn it.
8. The plan to develop a continuum of styles should start in the early years, but probably will not be fully attained until secondary school.

The following set of dos and don'ts, taken from Sedlak and Sedlak (1985), should help teachers develop appropriate oral language objectives and intervention strategies for teaching variant-English speakers:

1. *Do* model appropriate use of English.
2. *Do* provide sufficient practice on standard forms.
3. *Do* have planned activities for students to practice standard speech forms.
4. *Do* be aware of parallel variant-language and standard-language patterns.
5. *Do* stress the communication aspect of language.

6. *Don't* correct random errors in oral language.
7. *Don't* start at the very beginning of language development.
8. *Don't* constantly correct language and speech "errors."

Action Plan 9.2 provides other guidelines for teaching learners who speak nonstandard English.

TECHNIQUES FOR IMPROVING SPEECH

Speech and *oral language* are not terms that should be used interchangeably. Speech involves the sounds of the language and the intelligibility of those sounds, whereas oral language deals with the structure and content of the language. Problems with speech may interfere with the communication process in the same way that poor handwriting will interfere with the written communication of a message.

The most common types of speech problems are (1) articulation disorders, (2) voice disorders, and (3) stuttering. Articulation disorders are usu-

ACTION PLAN 9.2   GUIDELINES FOR TEACHING VARIANT-ENGLISH-SPEAKING LEARNERS

The following guidelines are suggested for teaching learners who speak nonstandard English:

1. Accept the nonstandard English form, especially in the elementary grades, and build linguistic competence on into high school.
2. Restate a nonstandard English phrase in standard English, but do not call attention to the nonstandard form. That is, if a student responds with a phrase such as "John be goin' to the store," the teacher should follow with "That's right. John is going to the store."
3. Teach styles and have students discriminate among different situations in which each style is appropriate.
4. After the student is able to discriminate style, teach the standard and the variant forms and the appropriate situations for each.
5. Be a good speech model.

ally assessed by means of standardized instruments, such as the Templin-Darley Tests of Articulation or the Goldman-Fristoe Test of Articulation. Voice disorders and stuttering are usually measured on a more informal basis by the speech therapist. When the teacher has a question regarding the quality of a learner's speech, the speech therapist should be consulted for an opinion. Voice disorders include problems related to volume (talking too loudly or too softly), pitch (a mix of high and low tones rather than a monotone or a high pitch), and resonance (degree of nasality).

Stuttering is a communication disorder that is easily identified by teachers and parents. It is characterized by behavior such as repetitions and prolongations that interfere with forward-moving speech.

○ 3   Gearhart and Weishahn (1976) have suggested that students with articulation problems should receive "ear training," which involves specific instruction to the learner to discriminate between the error and the correct articulation. The error and the correction are presented sequentially so that the student can hear the difference. As part of this training, the student needs good speech models in the classroom. Close cooperation with the speech therapist is also essential.

For voice disorders, teachers should confer with the speech therapist for specific treatment strategies. As a general rule, however, reinforcing the child for appropriate voice usage—for example, "I like the way you used your indoor voice," "It pleases me that you are talking in a soft tone"—and using a simple cueing system—for example, "Please use your indoor voice"—are generally accepted practices. A nonverbal signal as a reminder to the student can also curb instances of voice abuse.

■ 8   To our knowledge, no one has solved the problem of stuttering. Therefore, the teacher should not expect a "cure" but rather should seek a reduction of stuttering occurrences. Stuttering seems to occur most frequently in stressful situations. Thus, reducing a learner's level of anxiety by carefully planning and structuring events and responses in the classroom is one means of reducing stuttering instances. By planning a predictable classroom environment, a teacher can do much to minimize stressful situations in which stuttering most likely will occur.

CASE FOR ACTION 9.1

A student's speech is quite garbled and difficult to understand. It is painful for the other students to listen to her, and you really don't know what you can do to help her. Where would you go for help?

The following are some suggested dos and don'ts that the teacher can follow to help students with stuttering problems:

1. *Don't* interrupt the learner when he or she is speaking.
2. *Don't* finish the learner's words or sentences.
3. *Don't* betray your discomfort with the stuttering by shifting positions, losing eye contact, or clearing your throat.
4. *Don't* change the subject of the conversation abruptly.
5. *Do* keep track of the kinds of activities in which the learner is most dysfluent.
6. *Do* reduce speaking demands on the learner.
7. *Do* maintain expectations for the learner's verbal participation in class.
8. *Do* modify the circumstances in which the learner is expected to speak and build up the learner's ability to cope with stressful situations.

■ 9   Although the development of the speech therapy program is primarily the responsibility of the speech therapist, the teacher becomes the extension of the therapist in the classroom. To maximize the effectiveness of the therapy, it is important that consistent corrections and models be available to the learner throughout the school day. The teacher and staff thus remain the primary delivery agents for services. The teacher should feel comfortable discussing the proposed speech program with the therapist and should seek advice on how to respond in different situations. The following rules suggested by Sedlak and Sedlak (1985) should guide the behavior of the teacher in a classroom with students who exhibit speech problems:

CASE FOR ACTION 9.2

A student stutters, and his stuttering becomes particularly severe in science class when he is called upon to answer questions. The speech therapist has recommended that you make science class more predictable and minimize anxiety-producing situations. What two specific strategies could you follow when planning activities in which this student will be asked to respond that will minimize his anxiety?

1. Do not embarrass or reprimand the learner for speaking poorly, because such negative behavior could be modeled by classmates. Do establish an atmosphere in which students feel free to experiment with speech.
2. Do become a good speech model, but do not overarticulate, because such behavior will call undue attention to the speech problems of the handicapped learner.
3. Do set aside time in the schedule for specific practice in speech development. Tape recorders, the Language Master, telephones, TalkBack, and similar types of materials and devices can be used for these periods.

GENERAL PRINCIPLES OF LANGUAGE INSTRUCTION

Lamberts (1978) has delineated the following principles for teaching language skills:

1. The behavior desired from the student must be *directly* derived from the objective.
2. The activities must be planned in a logical, easy-to-hard progression. Presentation of the *stimuli* must be sequenced, and the *type of response* required from the learner must be sequenced.
3. The activities should allow for different types of responses from the learner (e.g., pointing, carrying out an action, imitating a model).
4. Different activities and different materials must be used for the same objective to promote generalization.

Oral Language Activities

The development of good oral language behavior by students is not possible unless the teacher gives the students a chance to talk. Something more than merely a question-and-answer exchange is required. The teacher's role is to provide opportunities for interaction and to structure a theme or topic for spoken interchange. Cohen and Plaskon (1980) have noted the following fairly common topics and strategies used in stimulating oral communication skills:

Storytelling	Explanations
Oral reporting	Telephone use
Announcements	Interviews
Memory games	Debates
Panel discussions	Drama

Each of these activities can be integrated into a content area of the curriculum and used in a natural fashion. In general, we do not recommend scheduling a regular oral language time as a part of the school day; rather we recommend locating opportunities to use these activities in conjunction with established classroom subjects.

One strategy that can be used for involving students in an oral language activity is called *webbing*. Webbing is an oral language stimulation strategy suggested by Cohen and Plaskon (1980) that can be used across a variety of subject areas. The class or teacher selects a common theme and then students generate related points, themes, or terms that can be tied to this central theme. The teacher writes the central theme on the board and then adds the related themes and topics. As ideas are presented, they are connected by lines. The web acts as an organizational tool for students and adds some structure to a brainstorming session. Such an exercise serves the following functions:

1. Vocabulary builder
2. Organizer for subsequent theme writing
3. Graphic form of showing ideational relationships
4. Idea builder
5. Reinforcement and feedback system for student participation

There are almost no wrong answers in such an exercise. It is a device that encourages participation from students, and it is risk-free in terms of failure. A sample web from a discussion on marriage is shown in figure 9.3. Action Plan 9.3 provides additional activities and procedures for enhancing speaking skills.

Pragmatics Training

○ **5** To teach pragmatics skills, the teacher must know what to observe in the oral language of the students. Two areas that are commonly addressed in the pragmatics literature are the *pragmatics of conversation* and the *pragmatics of narrative*. The pragmatics of conversation include:

1. Taking turns in a conversation
2. Initiating conversations
3. Clarifying a point made in a conversation
4. Following the sequential organization of a conversation
5. Making coherent contributions to a conversation
6. Maintaining a reasonable social distance

FIGURE 9.3   Sample Web on Theme of Marriage

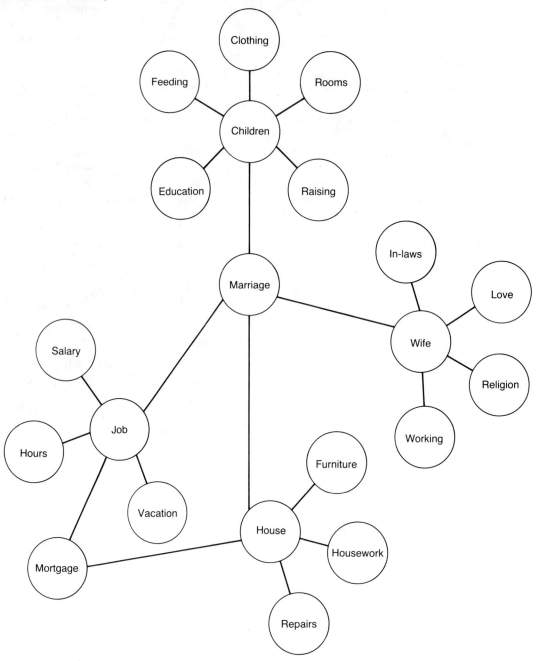

ACTION PLAN 9.3 STRATEGIES TO ENHANCE SPEAKING SKILLS

We recommend the following procedures for enhancing students' speaking skills:

1. Encourage active student participation in classroom discussions.
2. Allow students opportunities for verbal rehearsal of oral or written directions.
3. Encourage students' use of questioning strategy:
   a. Who?
   b. What?
   c. Where?
   d. When?
   e. Why?
4. Provide a structured format for teaching functional vocabulary:
   a. Model positive/negative examples.
   b. Afford opportunities for the student to repeat.
   c. Present positive/negative examples for the student to compare and contrast.
   d. Present descriptions of terms for the student to identify.
   e. Present terms for the student to describe.
5. Provide opportunities for expanded vocabulary via shaping or modeling procedures:
   a. Encourage students' use of synonyms.
   b. Encourage students' use of antonyms.
   c. Encourage students' use of homonyms.
6. Encourage the use of expanded phrases via shaping or modeling procedures.
7. Encourage the use of complex sentences via shaping or modeling procedures.
8. Allow flexibility from written expression to oral expression (and vice versa) in class assignments.
9. Use an individual oral-responding format.
10. Use a unison oral-responding format.

The pragmatics of narrative include:

1. The ability to use inference in interpreting meaning in stories
2. The ability to tell stories or jokes following conventional types of narrative organization

The situations for training pragmatics occur throughout the school day. The skillful teacher will use these opportunities to model appropriate conversational skills. In retelling stories, the teacher should use an outline as a cue to help the students relate the facts in the proper order. The teacher should also provide feedback to the students when they have performed satisfactorily.

Vocabulary Training

The careful selection of words is of the utmost importance when the objective is to increase the expressive or receptive vocabulary of the learner. When working with the young learner, words that refer to objects (*ball, table*), common actions (*stop, go*), and object characteristics (*hot, broken*) should be taught before abstract entities (*yesterday, next week*) or relationships (*tallest, in the middle of*). Words that deal with immediate needs should be emphasized. For both expressive and receptive vocabulary training, it is important that not only nouns but also verbs, prepositions, adjectives, and adverbs be taught. There is often a tendency to rely heavily on teaching nouns, to the exclusion of other speech forms. Such a focus could delay the development of advanced syntactic forms, such as phrases or transformations. The words selected should also be high-frequency use words, so that the learner can have opportunities to practice them.

With older students, the vocabulary taught should consist of vocationally related terms. Instruction should focus on the precise meaning of these words. Students should be required to use these words spontaneously as well as to respond to them receptively.

"Wh" Questions

○ **6**   A "Wh" question is an interrogative sentence that usually begins with the letters *wh*. Learning to ask and respond to "Wh" questions is an important process in the development of language. The normal developmental sequence of "Wh" questions is as follows:

1. Yes/no-answered questions
2. Who?
3. What?
4. Where?
5. How many?
6. How much?
7. When?
8. How?
9. Why?

The ability to ask and respond to the yes/no-answered question is generally assessed by showing a picture or an object and then asking a question that can be answered yes or no. For example, the teacher might show the child a red ball, make the statement "This ball is red," and then ask the question "Is this ball red?" and expect the child to respond "Yes." The teacher might then hold up a doll, say "This is a doll," and then ask "Is this a cookie?" and expect the response "No." A similar pattern of assessment can be followed for each of the "Wh" questions. When these "Wh" questions are presented, the verbal model in the form of a statement is given first and is followed by the question. The student should be provided with feedback and should be given an explanation of the correctness of the response.

Use of Conjunctions

The proper use of conjunctions —such as *and*, *but*, and *because*—enables a student to increase the complexity of sentences. The teacher should instruct in the use of conjunctions by appropriate modeling of their use and by directed practice. To practice the use of *and*, the students could be given two kernel sentences and be asked to restate the idea in a single sentence. For example, the sentences "I like carrots" and "I like peas" can be combined into the sentence "I like carrots and peas." The purposeful teaching of increasingly complex constructions will improve the verbal communication skills of students.

Role Playing and Oral Communication

Role playing is an excellent strategy for practicing aural/oral communication skills, because the student must be not only the transmitter of information but also the receiver of information. Role playing is also good because it is such an open activity and can focus on a variety of topics in different subject areas. While the activity is taking place, the teacher has the opportunity to observe not only the aural/oral skills of the learners but also their problem-solving, comprehension, and planning skills.

Auditory Skills

In any communication exchange, there must be a speaker and a listener. Each party has a role in the exchange of information. Among the skills and competencies needed by the listener are the following:

1. Attention to the speaker
2. Nonverbal signs of attention (e.g., head nod, eye contact)

3. Verbal signs of attention (e.g., "uh-huh," "yeah," "OK")
4. An understanding of the pragmatics (e.g., slang versus formal discourse)
5. Knowledge that the topic has shifted in focus or orientation

To enchance students' listening skills, the teacher must remind them of the need to listen. The teacher must stress good listening behavior throughout the day. This can be done through the following activities or procedures:

1. Establishing situations in which students are required to listen during specific times of the day (e.g., morning announcements, attendance taking, lunch counts, opening classroom exercises)
2. Eliminating distractions and distractive noise in the room
3. Having a planned listening time each day when an interesting story or article is read and then questions are asked about it
4. Reinforcing good listening through the use of rewards
5. Establishing a listening center in an area of the room where earphones and a tape recorder, a Language Master, a radio or a record player are provided for structured (but fun) listening activities.
6. Having students remain silent and then describe what they heard when they were silent.
7. Having learners make up a question after the teacher gives an answer.
8. Having students repeat the questions the teacher asks.

Action Plan 9.4 provides additional activities to enhance listening skills.

SUMMARY

Listening and speaking activities represent a large portion of a child's school day. Therefore, proper instruction in these areas is extremely important. With the mildly handicapped learner, the teacher should not assume that information received aurally is actually retained. Listening skills must be taught and developed in the same planned manner as spelling, reading, or arithmetic.

The way a person talks affects the attitudes of individuals with whom the speaker comes into contact. One of the goals for the handicapped learner is greater integration into society, and behavioral deficits such as an inability to switch language styles will work against the realization of such a goal. Therefore, a planned program for developing and practicing aural and oral skills throughout the school day is required to achieve some of the subtle behaviors necessary in successful aural/oral communication.

ACTION PLAN 9.4   STRATEGIES TO ENHANCE AUDITORY LANGUAGE SKILLS

We recommend the following procedures for enhancing auditory language skills:

1. Use visual and picture aids to enhance auditory skills:
   a. Charts
   b. Graphs
   c. Outlines
   d. Overheads
   e. Posters
2. Use examples to enhance main points; use concrete examples when necessary.
3. Repeat oral directions for class assignments.
4. Cue students to attend to class discussions via prompts:
   a. Written directions
   b. Hand prompts
   c. Touch/manual signals
5. Fade prompts gradually as students' auditory skills increase.
6. Use voice to stress key words in lectures, questions, or verbal directions.
7. Allow students adequate time to process and follow oral directions (e.g., slow down for important points).
8. Use questioning strategy at regular intervals:
   a. Who?
   b. What?
   c. Where?
   d. When?
   e. Why?
9. Reduce distracting visual/auditory stimuli in the class environment.
10. Use auditory aids at regular intervals:
    a. Cassettes/recorders
    b. Language Master
    c. Filmstrips
    d. Movies
    e. Other

CASE FOR ACTION 9.3

A student always seems to be on the wrong page, on the wrong line, or responding to the wrong question. She is constantly "lost" in terms of what is going on in the classroom. Her hearing has tested out in the normal range. Thus, she can hear, but she really doesn't listen. What are some things that you could do to help this student learn to listen?

10

Written Communication

■ 1   ...most skills needed in written expression are not practiced in oral language?

■ 2   ...many written expression deficiencies of the handicapped are skill deficits rather than conceptual deficits and can be corrected by determining the specific problem and focusing on the written expression objectives?

■ 3   ...the teaching of handwriting has been task-analyzed into 97 steps?

■ 4   ...some of the most widely applied techniques for teaching spelling are considered to be the least effective?

■ 5   ...spelling is generally "tested" but rarely taught?

■ 6   ...the acquisition of spelling skills follows a predictable developmental sequence?

■ 7   ...self-correction in spelling practice facilitates the acquisition of unknown words while maintaining a consistent level of retention?

■ 8   ...teaching word processing with microcomputers to mildly handicapped students can improve their written communication skills?

■ 9   ...the use of computer-assisted instruction tutorials is not recommended, but reading the manual and trying the commands hands-on have been found to be more effective?

○ CAN YOU. . .

○ **1**   . . . analyze a writing sample for syntax and mechanical errors?

○ **2**   . . . list functional written communication activities?

○ **3**   . . . differentiate between dialectical errors and mechanical errors in written language?

○ **4**   . . . identify the basic strokes and movements in handwriting?

○ **5**   . . . identify the type or developmental stage of a spelling error?

○ **6**   . . . specify a variety of effective strategies for teaching spelling?

○ **7**   . . . specify a sequence to follow in teaching written composition?

○ **8**   . . . specify a rationale for teaching typing and word processing to mildly handicapped learners?

The opportunity to communicate in writing occurs almost daily for most adults. The communication could be simply writing down a telephone number or writing a shopping list, or it could involve writing a short note to a teacher, spouse, or relative or taking minutes of meetings. Writing checks, copying recipes, or writing an announcement of a garage sale are other forms of written communication we might be required to practice on any given day.

■ 1   The skill of communicating in writing is the highest level of the language arts skills and generally the last to be mastered by the mildly handicapped learner. Like oral language, written language is governed by rules. However, not all the same rules apply, and some new ones are added. Written expression comprises the skills of handwriting, spelling, vocabulary, sentence composition, syntax, and punctuation. Only syntax and vocabulary are common also to oral expression. By this analysis, it should be obvious that written expression is not merely the graphic reflection of oral language. Oral language is characterized by numerous stops, hesitations, and incomplete and run-on sentences. Although such weaknesses are allowable in spoken language, they are considered serious errors when committed to paper (Sedlak & Sedlak, 1985).

ANALYSIS OF WRITING SAMPLES

Figure 10.1 displays facsimiles of written language examples produced by handicapped students in a junior high school. The two students show marked differences in their abilities to express their thoughts in written form. Therefore, different sets of objectives must be set for written language programs for these individuals. Joe's program should focus on the development of spelling skills, punctuation (primarily capitalization), sentence construction, and sentence combining skills. His printing is neat and even shows some innovation (note the circles over the *i*'s). He also appears to show good sequencing in his story. Joe's functional writing exercises should be made up of the types of activities that he needs to practice.

Cathy's story is difficult to read and comprehend. Cathy needs exercises in writing short sentences that express a single thought. These exercises should stress spelling and punctuation. A controlled set of functional vocabulary words should be made available to Cathy for reference. She probably should dictate each sentence into a tape recorder before attempting to write it. Since she is in junior high and has not mastered many of the skills that even primary grade learners have developed, the focus of Cathy's program should be on functional words and writing in functional activities. Manuscript printing might be considered rather than cursive writing in her written communication, reserving cursive writing only for her signature.

FIGURE 10.1 Samples of Two Students' Stories About a Picture

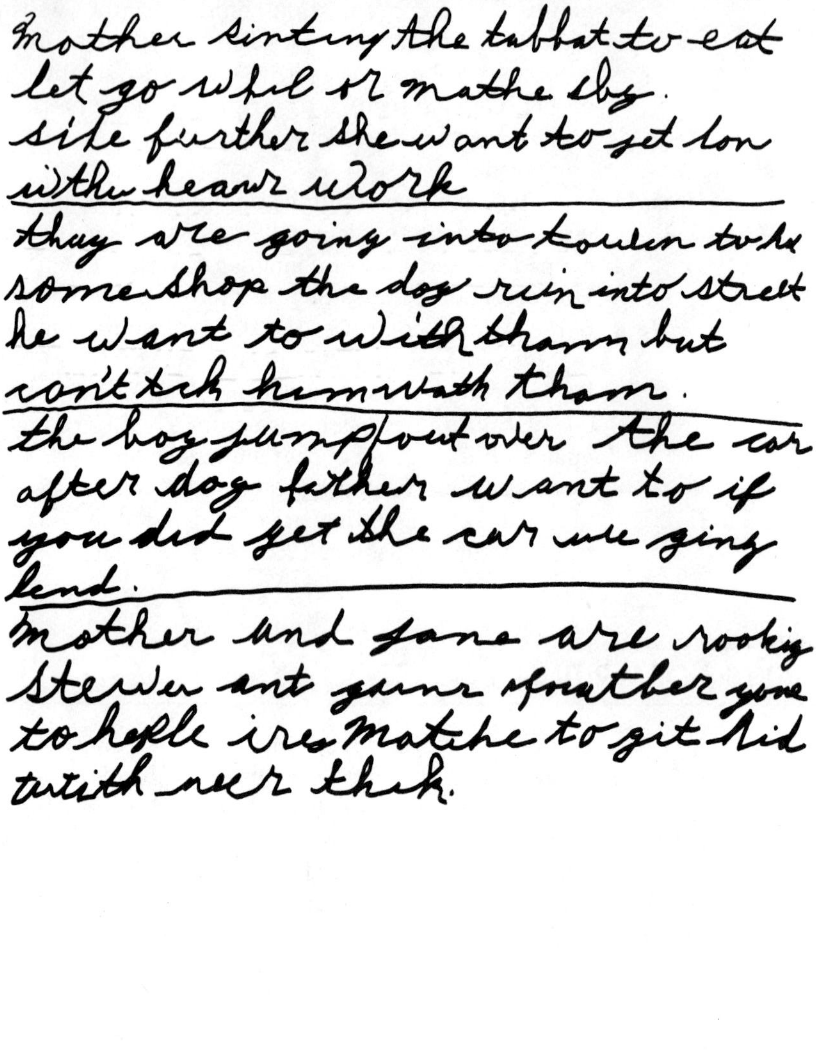

mother sinting the tabbat to eat
let go whil or mathe thy.
site further she want to get lon
with deawr work

thay are going into touen tobe
some shop the dog rin into strett
he want to with tham but
con't tch him wath tham.

the bog jumpf out over the car
after dog father want to if
you did get the car we ging
lend.

mother and jane are rooky
stewer ant gune sfnather you
to hefle ires matche to git hid
wtith nerr thik.

(continued)

FIGURE 10.1   continued

(1) It Looks Like the family is getting Ready for a picket. the mother is picting the basket the little girl is giveing the dog Something to get   and the farther and boy are getting the base ball thivgs together.

(2) It looks Like the family is on it's way but they foR/ got there pet dog.

(3) the family stops and the boy gets out and the dog jumps up on Him and the boy and the dog gets back in the ear.

(4) the mother is cooking the little girl is getting the food out the further and boy and dog are playing baseball.

Reprinted from Teaching the Educable Mentally Retarded by R. A. Sedlak and D. M. Sedlak by permission of the State University of New York Press (Albany, 1985).

■ 2   Many of the deficiencies in the written expression of the handicapped are skill deficits rather than conceptual deficits. These can be corrected by isolating the principal problems and then targeting the written expression objectives. (Brigham, Graubard, & Stans, 1972; Hansen & Lovitt, 1973).

○ 1   An error analysis chart is one means of systematically pinpointing written language deficits (G. P. Cartwright, 1969). Such analyses of a student's errors allows specific objectives to be written that address the deficit areas. Cartwright has suggested the following areas of error analysis:

Verbs: form, agreement, tense
Pronouns: antecedent, usage
Words: omissions, additions, substitutions, substandard
Sentences: incomplete, run-on
Punctuation: periods, commas, apostrophe, other
Capitals: sentence, proper nouns, overuse
Modifiers
Plurals

Action Plan 10.1 lists procedures for analyzing students' written communications.

ACTION PLAN 10.1   PROCEDURES FOR ANALYZING WRITTEN COMMUNICATIONS

We recommend the following procedures for analyzing students' written communications:

1. Examine a sample of writing according to the following mechanical components: handwriting, spelling, vocabulary, syntax, sentence composition, and punctuation.
2. Examine a writing sample for content according to order and clarity of ideas expressed.
3. Use an error analysis chart to count mechanical errors.
4. Use a rating scale to evaluate clarity and order of ideas expressed.
5. Identify one or two priorities from the analysis and target them for intervention.

○ **2**   The goal of a written language program is not to produce novelists but to develop functional communication skills. Functional writing skills include making lists (shopping, chores, phone numbers, etc.); writing a signature; writing a check; completing application forms; writing a note to a teacher, postman, repairman, and so forth; addressing an envelope; writing a letter; and writing directions. Figure 10.2 illustrates the relationship between specific writing skills and community demands.

FIGURE 10.2   Community Environments and Writing Skills

Settings	Community Services				Independent Living				Work					Recreation Leisure				
Writing Skills / *Areas*	Health	Banking	Legal/Government	Business	Transportation	Goods/Services	Home Survival	Insurance	Job Referrals/ Applications	On the Job	Longevity in a Job	School/Vocational Training		Food	Theater	Travel	Indoor Recreation	Outdoor Recreation
Sentences, paragraphs, and themes																		
Vocabulary																		
Grammar																		
Letters																		
Mechanics																		

FIGURE 10.3 Mechanical and Dialectical Errors in Written Expression

1. He be trying to get home.
2. (ef) you wants to go, you can,
3. I never had no trouble with nobody,
4. Him shoes (ar) od,

Note: Errors attributable to speech differences are circled; those attributable to skill deficits are underlined.

ERROR ANALYSIS AND VARIANT-ENGLISH SPEAKERS

○ **3**   In the written expression of the variant-English speaker, not only the presence of an error but also the cause of the error must be determined. Errors in written expression could be the result of structural language differences in the dialect or variant-English speech differences. Many phonological features of words are not accurately represented in standard written form, particularly for the variant-English speaker. Examples of this error source are the spelling of *pin* for *pen*, *sin* for *sing*, *pud* for *put*, *goin* for *going*, and *foe* for *four*. Differences in syntax could account for the omission of the suffix *-ed*, use of *a* rather than *an*, and reordering or omission of words in sentences. Errors attributable to the variant-English dialect must be differentiated from errors that represent deficiencies in spelling skills or skills in mechanics. The sentences shown in figure 10.3 are analyzed according to the types of errors we have discussed. In the figure, spelling or grammatical/mechanical errors that are attributable to speech differences have been circled; spelling or grammatical/mechanical errors that are attributable to skill deficits have been underlined.

HANDWRITING

Decent handwriting is a skill that can have many far-reaching consequences. In school, good penmanship means that a student's work is neat and legible; in mainstreamed classes, such work will enhance the image of the handicapped student, consequently correcting certain misconceptions regarding the student's talent. In the work environment, good handwriting means that an individual can fill out applications and forms, take notes, or deliver messages with success.

Handwriting must be taught directly to the students; it is not a skill that will simply develop by regular use. Proper letter formation must be practiced. The ultimate objective of handwriting instruction is legibility, not perfect calligraphy. The student must understand that the teacher believes that legible handwriting is a very important skill.

Handwriting Skills

■ **3** ○ **4**   Faas (1980) has task-analyzed the writing process into 97 steps for both manuscript and cursive writing. The prewriting process includes the following steps:

1. Hold and manipulate the pen or pencil.
2. Produce random scribbles.
3. Produce vertical lines and scribbles.
4. Produce horizontal lines and scribbles.
5. Draw a circle.
6. Position the paper in relationship to the body and the writing hand.
7. Draw a single-line cross.
8. Draw a square.
9. Draw a rectangle.
10. Draw lines that slant to the left.
11. Draw lines that slant to the right.
12. Draw an X.
13. Join lines that slant to the left and right.
14. Draw an equilateral triangle.
15. Draw vertical and horizontal lines on lined paper.
16. Draw large and small circles on lined paper.
17. Draw full, three-quarter, and half circles.
18. Draw lines that slant to the right and left of the vertical axis on lined paper.
19. Draw squares, rectangles, and triangles on lined paper.

These prewriting skills include all of the essential elements of all letters and numbers.

Following the prewriting steps, manuscript letters and numerals are printed. As the letters are taught, in groups of two or three, the student pronounces the name of each letter as it is printed. Uppercase and lowercase letter forms with tails (e.g., j, p, y) are introduced at Step 29. Two-, three-, and four-letter words with letters of varying heights and tails are written at Step 41.

The transition point from manuscript to cursive occurs at Steps 49 and 50 and requires tracing over letters in words that are topographically similar in manuscript and cursive (e.g., *it, it*) and using lines to connect printed letters while tracing the entire word.

As a general rule, cursive writing is taught following mastery of manuscript writing. If manuscript mastery has not occurred by age 9, however, cursive instruction should begin because the peer group will be involved at this time. The teacher should also be aware that the transition point from manuscript to cursive may interfere with the students' spelling performance, particularly if the spelling words are expected to be written in cursive.

The following procedures are suggested as a general strategy for teaching handwriting:

1. Task-analyze the component features of the letters to be taught and sequence the skills.
2. Model the correct formation of a limited set of letters or movements for the learners.
3. Observe the learner as she or he practices imitation of the movement.
4. Correct errors in the imitation and remodel.
5. Provide sufficient practice for mastery.
6. Provide opportunities for the learner to differentiate between good and poor work.
7. Proceed to the next set of skills in the task analysis and reteach.

Procedures for handwriting instruction are summarized in Action Plan 10.2.

Both manuscript and cursive letters are constructed from the basic strokes identified in the skill sequence. These basic strokes are relatively easy to learn and, once mastered, enable the student to complete letters and words. Students' illegible handwriting can be improved by training them in

ACTION PLAN 10.2   HANDWRITING LESSONS

We recommend the following procedures for handwriting instruction:

1. Schedule daily lessons for 15-minute periods.
2. Provide additional instruction as needed at intervals during the school day.
3. Check for proper posture, position of pencil, and position of paper.
4. Use good quality paper with clear lines.
5. Accommodate the left-handed student.
6. Stress legibility, not perfection.
7. After the student has mastered letter formation into words, use material from the major subject areas as a source of handwriting assignments.
8. Set criteria for legibility for all assignments throughout the day.

letter formation through mastery of these basic strokes. The goal of handwriting lessons should be legibility, not perfection.

When students' skills have advanced beyond practicing basic strokes and simple words, handwriting lessons can begin to make use of more interesting materials and assignments, such as material from the areas of science, history, biography, and geography. Short, informative paragraphs will keep the students alert and can spark interest in unfamiliar subject matter. Writing on specific topics (e.g., "My Career Goals"), writing thank-you or get-well notes when appropriate, and defining words from the dictionary can all be part of the handwriting curricula. Using such activities and materials minimizes students' dependence on the "copy-from-a-model" approach and helps them understand that the skill of handwriting goes beyond the handwriting lesson itself. We further recommend that every teacher set criteria for the legibility of handwriting in all written assignments. Such a criteria facilitates generalization of handwriting skills across subjects.

Surrounding students with examples of good handwriting, praising students who are achieving the goals of good penmanship, and allowing learners the opportunity to evaluate their own writing are powerful reinforcing agents for legible handwriting.

CASE FOR ACTION 10.1

A student wrote the following letter to a friend as part of a class assignment. Analyze the writing sample and identify the areas you would target for intervention.

SPELLING

■ 4   Spelling is a major problem for many schoolchildren, particularly the mildly handicapped (Graham, 1985). There is no consensus, however, regarding what makes words difficult to spell. Part of the problem, of course, is the irregularity of words—the lack of conformance to commonly accepted rules. There seem to be more exceptions to the rules than words that follow the rules. In addition, research has found that some of the most commonly used methods for teaching spelling are also the least effective (Haring et al., 1978). Traditional spelling workbooks present spelling and related language arts skills simultaneously. Although the related skills (e.g., dictionary usage, word building, word meaning) are valuable, they may cause confusion and difficulties for the handicapped learner and detract from the primary purpose of the lesson, which is learning to spell a specified set of words. Studies by Cohen (1969) and Graves (1976) found that spelling texts often contain a large proportion of inappropriate activities.

■ 5   Research on the teaching of spelling has provided a number of findings, including (1) that spelling is generally "tested" but not "taught," (2) that insufficient time is allowed for students to learn to spell words, and (3) that teachers do not know which strategies are effective and often use ineffective ones. Existing spelling myths are also barriers to effective instruction. Among these myths are (1) that children "grow out" of their errors, (2) that spelling errors are generally random or illogical, (3) that teaching spelling rules is effective, and (4) that the activities in the spelling book actually teach the student the words. Although it is true that there are developmental stages of spelling, mere maturity will not correct the problems. In fact, many of these problems persist into adulthood (Gerber, 1984).

Assessment of Spelling Skills

There are a number of norm-referenced spelling tests, some of which have diagnostic properties. Most of these tests, however, provide the teacher with grade-level-equivalent information and little else. In the area of spelling, an assessment should be based on an analysis of a student's error patterns in written work, an analysis of error patterns found on the norm-referenced tests, or an analysis of error patterns found in a teacher-constructed spelling test based on specific spelling rules.

■ 6   ○ 5   According to Lydiatt (1984), five levels of spelling development are critical in a diagnostic approach to the teaching of spelling. At the *precommunicative level,* when asked by the teacher how to spell a word, students offer random strings of letters of the alphabet without letter/sound correspondence; they often include the initials from their names. At the *semiphonetic level*, students give some letters, which represent only some of the sounds in the word. At the *phonetic level*, words are spelled as they sound; it is common for students to miss silent letters and vowels. At the *transitional level*, the visual configuration of the word (ascending/descending letters and word length) is evident. The final level is the correct spelling. Some examples of the same words written at the five levels are as follows:

Precommunicative:	P T
	R S B
	C T S
Semiphonetic:	M T R
	E
	W K K
Phonetic:	M N S T R
	E G L L
	K W K
Transitional:	M O N S T U R
	E G U L
	Q W C K
Correct:	M O N S T E R
	E A G L E
	Q U I C K

The transitional level is the one at which most students become stuck and for which the solution offered is usually practice, practice, and more practice. Although practice is a crucial part of the process of learning to spell, one of the best ways to move students from the transitional level is to teach them to self-monitor their writing for errors. A recommended strategy for teaching this self-monitoring is to have the students underline or circle potential errors—that is, words that the students are unsure they spelled correctly. Although some of the words they circle may be correct, the purpose of the strategy is to teach the students to self-monitor. If they circle correct words, the check that takes place immediately afterward merely verifies that those words are spelled correctly and strengthens the correct spelling (Gentry, 1984).

A more refined analysis of errors made at the transitional level could be undertaken at this point, including the following areas:

1. Omission of a silent letter (e.g., *tak* for *take*)
2. Omission of a sounded letter (e.g., *personl* for *personal*)
3. Omission of a doubled letter (e.g., *fil* for *fill*)
4. Doubling (e.g., *untill* for *until*)
5. Addition of a single letter (e.g., *backe* for *bake*)

6. Transposition or partial reversal (e.g., *pickel* for *pickle*)
7. Phonetic substitution for a vowel (e.g., *injoy* for *enjoy*)
8. Phonetic substitution for a consonant (e.g., *prizon* for *prison*)
9. Phonetic substitution for a syllable (e.g., *stopt* for *stopped*)
10. Phonetic substitution for a word (e.g., *weary* for *very*)
11. Nonphonetic substitution for a letter (e.g., *reword* for *reward*)
12. Nonphonetic substitution for a consonant (e.g., *importent* for *important*)
13. Phonetic spelling of nonphonetic words (e.g., *kwik* for *quick*)

The self-monitoring procedure should correct most transitional errors; additional analysis should be necessary only in specific cases.

Deno, Mirkin, Lowry, and Kuehnle (1980) have found that the correlation between standardized test performance and number of correctly spelled *letter sequences* is as high as the correlation between standardized test performance and number of correctly spelled *words*. The advantage in using letter sequences rather than the total word as the measure of spelling competence is that letter sequences are more sensitive to the effects of instruction. Deno, Mirkin, and Wesson (1984) recommend the following procedure as a generic measure of spelling performance that can be used throughout the school year:

1. The teacher selects a set of words from a spelling series in use.
2. The teacher dictates words for two minutes.
3. The teacher then records the number of letter sequences correctly written or the number of words correctly written.

These authors have defined a letter sequence as "every pair of letters that is written in correct order in the word being spelled, with blank spaces before

CASE FOR ACTION 10.2

A student took a spelling test and performed as follows:

Word	Spelling
street	srteet
city	siti
state	state
building	bilding
name	name

Analyze this student's performance and suggest remedial action.

ACTION PLAN 10.3 WAYS TO COUNT SPELLING ERRORS

Targeted Words:	race	house	town	store	road
Spelling:	rase	huse	twon	stor	rood
Possible letter sequences	5	6	5	6	5
Correct letter sequences	3	3	2	4	3

Summary
A. % of words spelled correctly: 0/5 = 0%
B. % of correct letter sequences: 15/27 = 55%
C. Transitional stage

and after the word" (p. 101). For example, the word *dog* spelled correctly would count as four letter sequences—(space) D, DO, OG, G (space). The spelling "DAWG" would be recorded as two correct letter sequences —(space) D, G (space). Action Plan 10. 3 illustrates ways to count spelling errors.

Selection of Words

The words used in a student's spelling program can be compiled from a variety of sources:

Standard spelling books
Basal readers
Basic "survival" word lists
Word lists based on word frequency (Carroll, Davies, & Richman, 1971)
"Demon" spelling lists
Words from other textbooks used in class
Words the student wishes to learn
Words misspelled or used frequently in written work

There are advantages and disadvantages to each of these sources. For example, many words chosen for inclusion in spelling texts are infrequently practiced in everyday writing tasks; however, these words are generally grouped by some common properties, involve specified activities, require less work for the teacher, and make mainstreaming easier if the student is using a graded spelling book that is used by the rest of the school. The teacher's decision regarding which sources to use must be guided by an understanding of the overall spelling goals for the student and the prognosis for achieving those goals.

In the first two to three weeks of school, we recommend that the words listed in figure 10.4 be assessed and taught by the teacher before beginning the regular spelling program. The list contains word formats frequently used in students' writing and provides a baseline for the teacher in spelling instruction (Hillerich, 1978). Often, even though students are presented with and correctly spell such words as *shepherd, knickers,* and *animal* on their weekly tests, they repeatedly misspell *why* ("whay"), *they* ("thay"), *who* ("how"), *was* ("wus"), and similar high-frequency words.

For primary-age students, spelling words should be words that the students encounter in their reading. These words can be gathered from the basal reading series, from the Dolch Word List, or from experience stories. For secondary-age students, the core of words must be functional; it can be derived from the environments in which the student lives, from words related to employment, from words related to social situations (which should have a high priority), and words needed in mainstream classes in which the student is enrolled. Selection of these content subject words should be made in cooperation with the regular class teacher (Stevens, 1984). We suggest that, initially, five words a week be taught from each content subject area; the number of words to be added or deleted from the list can be determined as the students' needs indicate.

Presentation of Words

A fixed word list is the most commonly used arrangement for teaching spelling. The procedure involves presenting a set of words to be learned as a unit. Graded spelling texts follow this format. Different sets of words are assigned each week, and a review or retention test is given every 6 weeks. The set of words presented in any given week may be partially or totally unknown to the students, and the students are expected to learn to spell the words within a 5-day period. Words that are missed on an end-of-the-week test are generally ignored or added to a missed-word list that the student can practice and review. This procedure works well for *most* students, but it does not ensure spelling mastery for *all* students. It also does not make the most efficient use of a student's time, since in some cases a large percentage of the words presented might already be known to the learner. An alterna-

FIGURE 10.4   The 100 Words Used Most Frequently by Children in Their Writing

The words are listed in order of frequency of use. The first three words account for 11.8% of 380,342 running words. The first five words account for 18.2%; the first ten, 26.1%. The 100 words make up 60% of words used by children in writing.

I	went	know
and	them	your
the	she	home
a	out	house
to	at	an
was	are	around
in	just	see
it	because	think
of	what	down
my	if	over
he	day	by
is	his	did
you	this	mother
that	not	our
we	very	don't
when	go	school
they	do	little
on	about	into
would	some	who
me	her	after
for	him	no
but	could	am
have	as	well
up	get	two
had	got	put
there	came	man
with	time	didn't
one	back	us
be	will	things
so	can	too
all	people	
said	from	
were	saw	
then	now	
like	or	

Source: R. L. Hillerich (1978), *A Writing Vocabulary of Elementary Children* (Springfield, IL: Charles C Thomas). Used with permission.

tive and perhaps more efficient procedure is for each student to practice the words on the list until he or she is able to spell all the words correctly for two or three perfect tests and then proceed to the next list of words. Words for practice or tests can be presented orally by tape recording the word list on a cassette or on Language Master cards. The students can self-correct practice papers, and the teacher can correct tests.

McGuigan (1975) has suggested a procedure whereby individual words are dropped from a pupil's daily study lists and test word lists when he or she learns them to a specified criterion. As old words are deleted from the list, new words are added from a master word list. The criterion commonly followed for moving words off the list is successful spelling of the same word on two consecutive days. This criterion can be modified for the entire class or for individual learners. Some students need more practice than others to retain the skill over time. With this method, each student in the room is operating with a different group of words each day, which might present some management problems for the teacher. Each student should maintain a record of his or her words, either in a notebook or on a set of flash cards. The teacher must determine the number of words to be included on each student's daily list according to how much material an individual learner can tolerate at one time. Some students' lists may have five words while others have ten or twenty words. Two general rules apply in operating this system:

1. The student should master at least one word per day; if the rate is below this level, reduce the words in the student's list.
2. Administer a retention test every one to two weeks by selecting mastered words at random; if the student misses a word, add it back to his or her list.

With this add-a-word method, students learn to spell new words faster and with greater retention than they do with fixed word lists (Hansen, 1978), since the focus is clearly on mastery.

Strategies for Teaching Spelling

○ **6**   Such strategies as peer teaching, home-based tutoring, imitation plus modeling, self-correction, and the cover–copy–compare method have all been found to be effective in teaching spelling.

Peer Teaching
Acting as tutor or as learner in a peer teaching arrangement has been found to result in similarly successful acquisition levels of new spelling words and to be superior to independent study (V. W. Harris, 1973). When using peer tutoring, it is important that a specific set of procedures be followed by the

learners. Merely telling students to arrange themselves into pairs and practice their spelling words is *not* peer tutoring. The following procedures are recommended for peer tutoring in spelling:

1. The tutor should dictate each word to the learner from a flash card or list.
2. The tutor should give feedback if a word is spelled correctly and show the correct spelling if a word is spelled incorrectly.
3. If flash cards are used, each word should be deposited in a mastery or nonmastery stack; if a list is used, correctly spelled words should be marked.
4. Nonmastered words should be recycled.

Students should reverse roles after 10 minutes of practice. In each practice session, the learner should write the words, not merely spell them aloud.

Home-Based Tutoring

Parents can carry out a tutoring program similar to peer tutoring with highly effective results (Broden, Beasley, & Hall, 1978). The teacher should have the student put spelling words on cards or make a list on Monday and take them home, along with a written, step-by-step procedure for the parents to use in tutoring the child on the words. The procedures given for peer tutoring would provide sufficient detail for a parent to carry out the tutoring. The teacher can also send home words that need to be learned for each unit.

Imitation Plus Modeling

For students with spelling problems and attention deficits, imitation plus modeling may be an effective strategy. It involves the following steps:

1. Read a word to the student.
2. Have the student write the word.
3. If the word is spelled correctly, praise the student.
4. If the word is misspelled, write an exact imitation of the misspelled word and say, "This is how you spelled the word"; then show a correctly written model for the misspelled word. Finally, have the student recopy the word from the model.

Research by Kauffman, Hallahan, Hass, Brame, and Boren (1978) has substantiated the use of this procedure.

Self-Correction

■ 7 Students should practice writing their spelling words from memory or dictation and then correct their own papers. This procedure is more effective than having the teacher correct the practice tests. Self-correction allows students to identify their own mistakes and pinpoint the exact source of the error. Hansen and Lovitt (1973) found that self-correction facilitated acquisition of unknown words without a loss in retention. When using self-correction as a strategy, students should practice their words daily until they get all words correct on two out of three trials. Two advantages of the self-correction procedure include the immediacy of feedback and the possible comparison of misspellings to the model to identify specific letter-order errors. If "cheating" is a problem in carrying out such a procedure, we recommend that the self-correction be conducted in view of the teacher, with the students using colored pens.

Cover-Copy-Compare

Hansen (1978) has suggested the cover–copy–compare method for teaching spelling. The student examines each word and identifies the distinctive features (e.g., length, prefix, suffix, configuration). Next, the student writes the word with the model present, silently saying each letter of the word as it is formed. Then the student covers the word and writes it from memory and, finally, compares the written word to the model. This process is repeated until mastery is achieved.

Less Effective Strategies

If spelling rules are to be part of a spelling program, the students must be provided with specific instructions on how and when to use the rules *and* their exceptions. Lovitt (1973) found that students could be taught spelling rules readily but that they had difficulty generalizing these rules to new words and determining the *exceptions* to the rules. In the absence of specific instruction and examples of these exceptions, rule learning is not a highly effective technique for training efficient spellers.

Other Suggestions for Spelling Instruction

Besides the specific procedures described in the preceding sections, several warnings or hints should be noted and followed in the spelling instruction process:

1. Be certain that the student can pronounce each word correctly.
2. Require that the student define each word or use it in a sentence.
3. Point out similarities between words.
4. Note differences in highly similar words.
5. Differentiate between homonyms.
6. Teach the spelling of difficult words in syllables.
7. Color-code prefixes, suffixes, or root words.
8. Change the initial consonant in root words or change prefixes/suffixes for word building.

ACTION PLAN 10.4   STRATEGIES FOR TEACHING SPELLING

We recommend the following strategies for spelling instruction:

1. Use peer tutors or home-based tutoring, providing an explicit set of directions on the teaching method.
2. Teach students to use the cover–copy–compare method of practice to learn new words.
3. On practice trials, have learners self-correct papers, noting errors and making corrections.
4. Provide ample opportunity for students to practice writing words.
5. Be sure learners can pronounce words correctly.
6. Set expectations for correctly spelled words in written work.

Action Plan 10.4 summarizes the recommended strategies for teaching spelling.

WRITTEN COMPOSITION

○ 7   The end product of writing instruction is the student's ability to compose and produce written prose independently. In a frequently recommended language experience approach (Galloway & Gray, 1976; M. Hall, 1977), students receive varying amounts and types of prompting and feedback. Reports of successful interventions with the general population have focused almost exclusively on the use of reinforcement procedures (Campbell & Willis, 1979; Maloney & Hopkins, 1973) and feedback (Hansen & Lovitt, 1973; Van Houten & MacLellan, 1981). A written instruction package that combines these strategies for use with mildly handicapped learners has been described by Schloss, Harriman, and Pfiefer (in press). Their procedure, described as a sequential prompt reduction technique because it systematically fades teacher involvement, involves the following steps:

1. Present (or elicit from the student) a topic for the student to write about.
2. Encourage the student to vocalize each sentence before writing.
3. Tell the student that assistance in spelling will be provided if requested.

4. Wait 20 seconds after announcing the topic. If the student provides a sentence, record SI on a tally sheet because the student *self-initiated* the sentence.

5. If a sentence is not vocalized and written after 20 seconds, provide a motivational prompt, urging the student to begin writing (e.g., "Go ahead and do your best"). If the student provides a sentence, record M because the student developed the sentence using a *motivational prompt*.

6. If a sentence is not vocalized and written after another 20 seconds, provide a content prompt, giving the general content of an appropriate sentence (e.g., "Write about what the dog did to the cat"). If the student provides a sentence, record C because a *content prompt* helped the learner write the sentence.

7. If a sentence is not produced after a third 20-second period, provide a *literal prompt* and record L. In effect, the literal prompt tells the student precisely what to write (e.g., "Write 'the dog chased the cat up the tree' ").

8. As soon as the learner writes a sentence, return to the self-initiated prompt level and repeat the sequence as needed until the composition is complete.

9. Upon completion of the composition, tell the student the number of sentences that were self-initiated and the number that were produced under each prompt level.

10. The student may be reinforced for producing larger numbers of sentences under less intrusive prompt levels.

Deno et al. (1983) have suggested a generic method for evaluating growth in written expression that is time-consuming but easy to use. The procedure involves giving a student a story starter (e.g., "One night last summer I . . .") and then having the student write for 3 minutes. At the end of that time, the total number of words written is charted. Spelling errors are ignored, as are grammar and punctuation errors. As with the generic spelling measure described earlier, this measure of written expression is also sensitive to growth as the result of instruction.

EXPERIENCE STORIES AND CHARTS

People are comfortable talking about things they know or have done. Therefore, experience stories are an excellent technique for early writing instruction. One purpose of an experience story is to teach the student to organize ideas. Using experience stories for writing instruction parallels the language experience approach for instruction in reading. The teacher leads the learner through a logical presentation by a series of questions.

When using experience charts and stories, sentences should be short, and vocabulary should be kept simple. A small number of sentences should be used, but each should contribute significantly to the story. Words should be repeated throughout the story to familiarize the learner with their spelling. The following steps are recommended for creating and using an experience chart:

1. Select a topic (i.e., planning a trip, a picture, summer activities).
2. Discuss the topic with the students.
3. Elicit a title for the story through a series of questions.
4. Print or write the title on a chart or board large enough for all to see.
5. In early stories, each sentence should be only one line long.
6. Have students contribute sentences to the story through the use of questions.
7. Read the story aloud after it is completed.
8. Have the students read the story aloud and copy it.

Since the goal of writing is communication, sharing notes, letters, or directions among students is one means of providing them with feedback on their style and organization. It also helps them determine whether they are communicating. When reading someone else's writing, the learner usually becomes attuned to omitted words, spelling, legible (or illegible) handwriting, phrasing, and organization and realizes the value others put on these aspects of writing.

WRITTEN LANGUAGE AND MICROCOMPUTERS

○ **8**   Writing is a difficult task for most mildly handicapped learners. The reasons vary, but the results are often similar. Finished papers contain numerous misspellings, incomplete or run-on sentences, smudged or crossed-out words, illegible handwriting, and a total absence of spacing or margins. The final product is not particularly satisfactory to either the teacher or the student. When the student is asked to redo the paper, the exercise becomes highly aversive.

■ **8**   Inclusion of a microcomputer equipped with word processing and spelling programs into the special education class can make significant differences in the final products and in students' attitudes toward the task of writing. Word processing software provides the learner with the ability to substitute, add, or delete words; rearrange sentences; correct spelling; and change punctuation without imposing the laborious task of recopying the entire written assignment by hand. Even with a conventional typewriter, such manipulations are not possible, and a written document would have to be totally redone (Hagen, 1984).

As a teaching tool, word processing software is a necessity for teachers who are using microcomputers for instruction. The word processing program not only improves the possibility of expressive written language but also gives the learner a source of pride when the finished product is perfect and neat.

Necessary Equipment

To use microcomputers for instruction in written language, the following equipment and software would be needed:

1. A microcomputer and monitor
2. A cassette or disk drive for data storage
3. A printer
4. Word processing software
5. Typing instruction software

Typing skills are crucial for effective word processing. Students can use a hunt-and-peck method initially, but to keep the situation from becoming unpleasant, it is recommended that students be taught to type in the elementary grades.

Software is currently available that teaches the keyboard to preschool-age youngsters and helps them with letter identification. We recommend that regular typing skills be introduced as early as students' fingers can reasonably fit the keyboard (about age 8). The typing instruction programs are referred to as *typing tutors*. Each of the popular microcomputer brands has a version of such a program. The tutors are self-paced drills that include drill on individual letters as well as practice on paragraphs. Generally, each drill is timed with a word-per-minute readout after each lesson. These typing tutors also come in game formats, which make them entertaining and motivating. Microtyping II is such a program.

Word processing software is the second important system ingredient for use in written language instruction. The Bank Street Writer is a commonly used word processing program that was designed for children as young as age 8. Applewriter, Magic Window, and WordStar are some other popular word processing programs. These programs allow insertion, deletion, and correction of text that has been entered and stored. A program such as WordStar also has a grammar and punctuation checking feature, which checks for capitalization errors, sexist language, double word errors, and some punctuation errors.

Spelling programs can also be used with many of these word processing programs to check for misspelled words. Perfect Speller, Proofreader, and Bank Street Speller are three popular spelling check programs. These spelling check programs must be compatible with the word processing program being used. After the text is entered, it is scanned by the spelling program, which identifies any words that are not currently located in its dictionary. Special-use words, proper nouns, and technical terms are not generally part of these dictionaries, but they can be added. The program points out the words it locates that are not part of its dictionary. The learner can then decide whether it is a real error and make any necessary changes. The spelling program also locates the misspelled word in the text and allows the learner to replace it.

Other features of spelling programs that teachers find useful are a summary of the total number of words in a piece of writing and a summary of the total number of different words used. Both of these are measures of writing fluency and have been used effectively in the assessment of language growth.

Getting Started

■ 9   A teacher who is familiar with general microcomputer operations will need about two to three hours to understand and use the various functions in word processing programs and supporting software. The manual or documentation that accompanies the software is quite important and helps answer many questions. Usually, someone who is already familiar with the software can teach the critical commands for using the program far more easily than locating the information in a manual. However, if a new microcomputer user is not fortunate enough to have someone's help, the manual must be used. Some of the word processing software has computer assisted instruction (CAI) tutorial programs, which explain how to use the system. We have found that these tutorials are generally tedious and

CASE FOR ACTION 10.3

A 16-year-old student does not write in complete sentences. Her spelling is generally in a transitional stage. Her mother would like the IEP to focus on functional writing skills that the student will need to use in the community, on jobs, and at home. Write a set of short-term objectives that would focus on functional writing skills for this student.

confusing, and we do not recommend their use. Reading the manual and trying the commands on the computer has worked best for us and our students. In working with adult learners, we find that Mooer's Law of Information Parsimony prevails: "Users will spend as little energy as possible to get enough information to satisfy their needs." To this end, we recommend that the teacher scan the manual or examine the software to locate the commands that allow the learner to do some basic functions, including:

1. Entering text
2. Saving text
3. Getting back to the menu
4. Printing a hard copy of the text
5. Loading text saved on disks or cassettes back into the program
6. Totally clearing the memory

The procedures for the last step are particularly important; we have seen students add text to a blank screen, then print out the document and, with a great deal of surprise, find much more in the document than they thought was there. Clearing the memory is an important function to learn early.

The second set of commands or procedures that should be learned explains how to change the format of the text appearing on the printer:

1. Centering text
2. Left and right justifying of margins
3. Skipping lines

These procedures are generally easy to learn and provide a great deal of entertainment as the student sees the same set of text in different formats.

The most difficult sets of commands or procedures to learn are those that deal with the editing of text. The most difficult aspect of these procedures or commands is recognizing whether you are in a *writing* mode or in an *editing* mode. We recommend trial-and-error practice and frequent reference to the manual for learning these commands. The basic commands/procedures that we believe should be mastered are as follows:

1. Control of cursor movement up, down, left, and right
2. Addition or deletion of text in the middle of a paragraph
3. Movement of sentences or paragraphs from one place to another

Additional commands and functions of the particular system being used can then be addressed. It is very important that the teacher be thoroughly familiar with all aspects of the word processing system being used before using it with students. If students make mistakes, they need a teacher who can help them correct their errors quickly and efficiently without totally destroying the work they have done. Erasing everything and starting over is not a positive reinforcement when introducing word processing use.

Other Microcomputer Applications

Besides word processing, the microcomputer also offers the option of tutorial and drill/practice instruction in language arts related areas. Developmental Learning Materials has available Language Arts Skill Builders, a set of six disks that offers drill and practice in a game format for word building, subject/verb agreement, and sight word recognition. Dormac, Incorporated, has Lessons in Syntax, a set of eight disks in a tutorial format that teaches negation, yes/no questions, "Wh" questions, "because and so," relative clauses, participles, indirect discourse, and passive voice. A workbook accompanies the disks.

New programs become available weekly. The special education teacher can learn about these new programs from other teachers, from monthly microcomputer magazines, at conferences, or at local educational materials centers. Software does not have to be labeled "handicapped" for it to be useful in special education. If at all possible, the teacher should review the software before purchasing it.

SUMMARY

The overall goal of written expression is communication. To ensure this communication, handwriting must be legible and words must be spelled in a reasonably accurate manner. The written language programs for many mildly handicapped learners are highly individualized. The introduction of the microcomputer for word processing is a major change in the way written language programs will be taught in the future. Therefore, the special education teacher must be competent in teaching its use for word processing. Analysis of errors in writing samples should consider not only the mechanical errors attributable to skill deficits but also the grammatical errors that might be the result of differences in dialect used by variant-English speakers. When they are learning to spell, students will not learn the words incidentally but must be taught directly and must be given repeated opportunities to achieve mastery and overlearning.

Action Plan 10.5 summarizes the strategies that are recommended for enhancing students' writing skills.

ACTION PLAN 10.5   STRATEGIES TO ENHANCE WRITING SKILLS

We recommend the following strategies for enhancing students' writing skills:

1. Encourage a positive student attitude toward writing.
2. Use direct instruction for students to structure paragraphs and themes by shaping or modeling procedures.
3. Encourage the students' vocabulary development.
4. Use direct instruction of note-taking skills by shaping or modeling procedures.
5. Provide opportunities for developing the mechanical skills of writing:
   a. Capitalization
   b. Punctuation
   c. Grammar
   d. Word usage
   e. Neatness
   f. Spelling
   g. Typing
6. Monitor the students' writing skills:
   a. Check continually for strengths and weaknesses.
   b. Provide formative evaluations.
   c. Provide summative evaluations.

11

Reading Instruction

▪ DID YOU KNOW THAT...

▪ **1** . . . reading instruction is a highly individual process, and no single approach is appropriate for all individual learning differences?

▪ **2** . . . part of the sight word vocabulary of secondary-age students should include functional words found in the home and work environments?

▪ **3** . . . both known and unknown words should be included in lists when teaching sight words?

▪ **4** . . . when teaching sight words using flash cards, it may be more effective to pronounce the word for the student than to have the student pronounce the word?

▪ **5** . . . students learn more words faster without the aid of pictures?

▪ **6** . . . reading comprehension may be considered the most important but least understood skill in the reading process?

▪ **7** . . . reading comprehension is a skill that is assessed far more often than it is taught?

▪ **8** . . . less than 1 percent of the time spent in reading instruction is focused on teaching comprehension?

▪ **9** . . . slower students are given less time to respond to teachers' questions than brighter students are?

○ CAN YOU. . .

○ **1**   . . . identify and describe the components of the test–teach–test approach to identifying individualized teaching strategies?

○ **2**   . . . identify some of the functional reading needs of educable mentally retarded learners and other mentally handicapped students?

○ **3**   . . . identify and describe the three major components of the reading process?

○ **4**   . . . identify and describe the two basic approaches to teaching phonics?

○ **5**   . . . define *contextual clues* and describe how they are used in reading?

○ **6**   . . . describe the cloze procedure used in assessing the use of context clues and in teaching the use of context?

○ **7**   . . . describe the use of and associated difficulties with configuration clues?

○ **8**   . . . identify the five corrective feedback statements that Hansen and Eaton (1978) used in teaching expansion of word attack strategies?

○ **9**   . . . define *sight word vocabulary* and describe the flash card method that has been found effective in teaching it?

○ **10**   . . . identify the four strategies for increasing reading rate suggested by Harris and Sipay (1975)?

○ **11**   . . . identify the factors teachers should consider when assessing reading comprehension problems?

○ **12**   . . . identify and describe the three categories of reading comprehension?

■ 1   Extracting meaning from printed words and the sequence of those words is the ultimate goal of reading instruction. In the most comprehensive study ever undertaken on methods of teaching reading, the final conclusion was that no single approach to the teaching of reading can accommodate all individual differences (Bond & Dykstra, 1967; Stauffer, 1967). The teacher and the learning situation (including the characteristics of the learner), rather than a specific approach or specific materials, were found to be the critical variable that determines success. Therefore, the teacher must possess a knowledge of the reading process, a philosophy of teaching reading that is flexible in regard to methods, skill in matching learner characteristics to methods, and a knowledge of the component skills that comprise the reading process.

○ 1   Although standardized reading tests will not provide the full answer for the teacher, a strategy of test–teach–test, including systematic analysis of student performance, will allow the teacher to find an effective strategy or combination of strategies for teaching each learner. Knowing what to test, how to test, and how to interpret the results of the testing are three critical components of the test part of the model. Standardized tests provide a starting point for instruction, but the teacher must examine the specific items that a student responded to correctly and incorrectly on the test. Both content and format of the items are critical variables in determining why a student responded correctly or incorrectly to those items (Sedlak, Steppe-Jones, & Sedlak, 1982). In the *teach* component of this model, the teacher should try specific approaches with each learner and then analyze the student's subsequent performance. The teacher should not be caught in the readiness trap—accepting inadequate readiness as the reason for a learner's nonprogress in reading. The reading process is recognized as comprising several individual skills, all of which are teachable. Thus, the teacher's dilemma is to initiate the best strategy or combination of strategies for teaching them.

FUNCTIONAL READING GOALS

○ 2   The goals of the reading program should focus on the fundamental use of the skill. The function, of course, will be determined by situations that are specific to the needs of each learner. For youngsters who are in classes for the educable mentally retarded, functional reading activities would include newspapers, street signs, telephone directories, signs, public notices, job applications, and labels in clothing and on food products (Gillespie & Johnson, 1974). For the learning disabled student, the same skills are functional and necessary, as are the reading skills needed to successfully handle textbook material they will encounter in regular classes.

The teaching of specialized vocabulary encountered in science, social studies, and health texts may have to become a part of the regularly scheduled reading program. Environmentally specific vocabulary may also have to be taught. We encounter a wide array of traffic and business signs, directional signs, warnings, emergency assistance signs, and vocational signs on a daily basis. These types of words and phrases do not normally appear in basal reading series and must be taught as specific examples.

READING SKILLS

○ **3** Most reading systems divide the reading process into three major components: word-attack skills, sight word vocabulary, and comprehension. These three areas constitute the basic core of questions which a teacher should ask when assessing a new student:

1. What kinds of word-attack skills does the student possess, and on which ones does he or she rely most heavily?
2. What is the extent of the student's sight word vocabulary?
3. What is the extent of the student's comprehension skills?

Word-Attack Skills

Word-attack skills include the set of techniques that enables a learner to decode an unknown word so that he or she can pronounce it and understand it in the proper context (Gillespie & Johnson, 1974). The skills are normally categorized under the headings of phonics, structural analysis, contextual clues, and configuration clues.

Phonics

○ **4** Phonics instruction is designed to help the child develop the ability to work out the pronunciation (or approximate pronunciation) of printed word symbols that, at the moment, he or she does not know as sight words (Heilman, 1972). There are two basic approaches to teaching phonics— analytic and synthetic (Bagford, 1972). The *analytic* approach starts with a pool of 75 to 100 sight words from which the letter sounds are taught. The *synthetic* approach emphasizes sound blending and teaching sounds for certain letters. Research appears to favor the synthetic approach. Research also supports the efficacy of phonics instruction with mildly handicapped learners (French, 1950; Hegge, 1934; Warner, 1967). However, phonics should not be the sole strategy for reading instruction. As noted earlier, the goal of reading is to extract meaning from the printed word. Although phonics helps the student pronounce the printed words, the student must become familiar with the content of the printed material to derive meaning from the text.

Structural Analysis

Structural analysis deals with the structure of the word rather than the elements of sound. Structural analysis involves the following components:

1. Prefixes and suffixes
2. Compound words
3. Root words
4. Contractions
5. Syllables

Since prefixes and suffixes change the meanings of root words, the teaching emphasis should be on the meanings of the prefixes and suffixes as clues the learner can use to identify unknown words. Compound words should be taught from the pool of currently known words. The teacher should be aware, however, that combining two known words will not always result in the student's being able to articulate the meaning of the newly formed compound word.

ACTION PLAN 11.1   PREFIXES

Learning the meanings of prefixes can increase students' comprehension and vocabulary skills. The following are some common prefixes and their meanings:

circum-	around, about
equi-	equal, equally
inter-	between
extra-	beyond, on the outside
intra-	within, during, between layers of
intro-	in, inward, within
mal-	bad, abnormal
mis-	bad, wrong, opposite of, not
non-	not, absence of
pre-	before (in time and space)
re-	again/anew, back/backward

Contextual Clues

○ **5**   When using contextual clues, the student is using information in the text to identify unknown words. The student is taught to look for certain clues, such as synonyms, comparisons, or contrasts, and then to guess the unknown word on the basis of context and perhaps the initial letter of the unknown word.

○ **6**   The cloze procedure is a commonly used technique for assessing the extent to which a student uses contextual clues. It is also a procedure used to *teach* students to use context. In this procedure, every fifth word from a 250–300-word passage is deleted. The student is to fill in the blank with the word that would best suit the context of the passage. So long as the word that is put into the blank maintains the meaning of the passage, the teacher should not penalize the student. Some scoring procedures for this technique recommend scoring only exact matches, but in our judgment, such a rigorous criterion is usually unnecessary. The use of the procedure forces a student to play a guessing game and actively process information as it is read. Generally, the procedure is not suited for students below the fourth-grade reading level.

Configuration Clues

○ **7**   A student who misreads a word that has the same general shape as another word may be relying on configuration clues to help with word identification. Configuration involves the distinctive features of the word, including its length and the position of ascending and descending characters. The shape of the word provides clues that help a learner identify the word and distinguish it from other words. The shape of the word can also intefere with the student's ability to interpret the word, because its shape may be similar to that of many other new words that he or she is learning. For example, making a distinction among the words *pat, pet,* and *pot* may be difficult because they have the same shape. A student would have an easier time discriminating among (and possibly learning) *pot, ranch,* and *fight,* because their distinctive features are dissimilar.

Word-Attack Strategies

The deficient reader may rely heavily on a single word-attack strategy when decoding words and may give up in frustration when the strategy fails to "unlock" the pronunciation of the word. Hansen and Eaton (1978) used a series of corrective feedback statements to teach five mildly handicapped boys to expand their word-attack strategies. The corrective sequence they used was as follows:

○ **8**
1. Tell the student he has misread a word and that he should try another way.
2. Tell the student to finish reading the sentence and guess the word.
3. Tell the student to break the word into parts and pronounce each part.
4. Cover parts of the word and ask the student to decode each part.
5. Locate sounds in the word the student is misreading. Isolate this letter or combination and ask, "What sound does _____ make?"
6. Provide the correct word to the student.

Sight Word Vocabulary

○ **9** Sight words are printed words that are identified automatically by the learner; the learner does not exhibit delay in identifying those words but reads them immediately when they are flashed. Hesitation or even immediate correction should not be accepted as a demonstration of mastery of sight words. Sight words should be presented on flash cards to the student at a rate of one word per 3-second interval. The teacher should put the flash cards into two piles (mastery and nonmastery) as they are read by the learner. A record should then be maintained, including a tally of the number of sight words identified and a listing of the mastered and nonmastered words. The words should be printed on the flash cards in primary type or clear manuscript print.

■ **2** Selecting the words to be used for assessing the extent of a student's sight word vocabulary can be done in a variety of ways. The selection of these words will be guided to some extent by the age of the student. A portion of the sight word vocabulary of the secondary-age student should be based on functional words found in the environment and vocational placements. For the primary-age learner, lists such as the 200 Dolch Word List are an excellent starting point for sight words. Sight word lists can also be taken from basal reading texts as a part of an informal reading inventory (IRI) or from the spelling series in use in the program.

■ **3** Neef, Iwata, and Page (1977) have found that the presence of known items in a list of unknown items facilitates the acquisition of the unknown sight words. The presence of the known items appears to act as a reinforcing agent and is not so frustrating to the learner as when all sight words on the list are unknown. Therefore, they have recommended that both known and unknown words should be presented in lists when sight words are being taught.

■ **4** ■ **5** Hendricksen, Roberts, and Shores (1978) were able to increase the sight word vocabulary of two primary-age disabled readers by modeling basic sight words. The two-step procedure they followed was (1) to show the learner a sight word on a flash card and say, "This word is _____"; and

ACTION PLAN 11.2   STRATEGIES FOR INCREASING READING RATE

We recommend the following strategies for increasing students' reading rate:

1. Provide sufficient practice of the most commonly used words.
2. Use reinforcement and continuous charting of progress during timed reading of selections.
3. Gradually reduce exposure time when flashing words and phrases.
4. Provide controlled reading through presentation devices such as a Language Master.

then (2) to ask the learner, "What word is this?" They found this procedure superior to the procedure of asking the student to name the word first and then telling him or her the word.

Rose and Fur (1984) have found that students learn new words when they are presented both with and then without illustrations but that they learn more words faster without the aid of pictures. It appears that without illustrations, students are able to concentrate on the critical features of the new words.

○ **10**   A basic instructional principle is to stress accuracy first, then speed. Speed becomes important in reading, as in most skills, so that the student can complete an assignment in a reasonable period of time. Harris and Sipay (1975) suggest four strategies for increasing reading rate:

1. Abundant practice of the most commonly used words
2. Timed reading of selections, using reinforcement and continuous charting of progress
3. Flashing of words and phrases with a gradual reduction in exposure time
4. Controlled reading through presentations, such as a Language Master

Action Plan 11.3 summarizes suggested procedures for teaching sight word vocabulary.

ACTION PLAN 11.3   TEACHING SIGHT WORD VOCABULARY

We recommend the following procedures for teaching sight word vocabulary:

1. Intersperse known and unknown words.
2. Show and pronounce each word *first;* then have the student pronounce the word.
3. Stress accuracy, *then* speed.
4. Be sure that the words are in the students' listening vocabulary and speaking vocabulary.
5. Keep a list of the mastered and nonmastered words.
6. Present words at the rate of one per 3-second interval or faster.
7. Point out the critical features of new words to help in recall.

Comprehension Skills

■ 6   Reading comprehension is probably one of the most important, yet least understood skills in the reading process. All authorities would agree that the ultimate goal of a reading program is the development of comprehension skills, but there is disagreement regarding the procedure for achieving this end. Some authorities favor an emphasis on comprehension in the early stages of reading instruction, whereas others emphasize sound/symbol readerships. Most would agree that comprehension is related to language and that a problem in reading comprehension may be as much a thinking problem as it is a reading problem (Moffett, 1968). The teacher must differentiate reading comprehension problems from oral language comprehension problems. Inherent in such an analysis are the following factors that the teacher must consider:

○ 11
1. The past experiences of the reader
2. The content of the written passage
3. The syntax of the written passage
4. The vocabulary of the written passage
5. The oral language comprehension of the learner
6. The questions being asked to assess comprehension

Any one of these or a combination could be a factor in a reading comprehension problem (see Action Plan 11.4).

ACTION PLAN 11.4   ANALYZING READING COMPREHENSION PROBLEMS

The teacher should consider the following factors when analyzing a student's reading comprehension:

1. The past experiences of the reader
2. The content of the written passage
3. The syntax of the written passage
4. The vocabulary used in the written passage
5. The oral language comprehension of the student
6. The questions being asked to assess comprehension

Categories of Comprehension

○ 12   There are three categories of reading comprehension: literal, inferential, and critical. Edgar Dale (1965) referred to these three categories as "reading the lines. . . reading between the lines. . . and reading beyond the lines." *Literal* comprehension involves understanding or answering questions about what an author said. *Inferential* comprehension involves understanding what an author meant by what was said. *Critical* comprehension involves making judgments about what an author said (Hillerich, 1983).

In terms of the levels of difficulty of these three types of comprehension, a literal comprehension of a passage is generally a necessary prerequisite for the other two. To illustrate these three levels of comprehension, consider the following passage:

> The mayor is generally helpful and concerned for the health, safety, and protection of citizens. City council members are interested only in what the service costs and not how necessary it might be.

On the literal level, we might ask, "What did the author say about the mayor?" or "What did the author say about city council members?" Inferential questions might be, "Whom do you believe the author prefers or favors?" or "Whom do you think the author would vote for in the next election?" Critical reading questions would be, "What is there in the author's background that might be influencing the statement?" or "What words did the author use to make clear his position on who is favored?"

■ 7 ■ 8   Research on instruction in comprehension has revealed that it is a skill that is assessed far more often than it is taught. The most common procedure used by teachers to teach comprehension is (1) to have students read passages and then (2) to ask questions to determine what they comprehended. Less than 1 percent of the time spent in teaching reading is actually spent on teaching comprehension skills (Durkin, 1978). Even the types of questions that are generally asked pose problems. Evidence from a variety of studies indicates that 75 to 95 percent of the questions teachers ask are literal questions. This finding is supported at both the elementary and the secondary levels.

■ 9   Research also has shown that teachers do not allow enough time for students to respond. Lucking (1975) reported that adults allow an average of 14 seconds to begin responding to a question, but that teachers working with children allow less than 6 seconds. Slower students are given even less time to respond than brighter students.

Literal Reading Comprehension Skills

The way questions are asked and the manner in which they are responded to influence the degree of literal comprehension. Teachers must be careful not to phrase questions in the same word patterns as were used in the written passage. For example, if there is a passage such as "The young boy and the girl walked down the hill," it is better to ask "Where did the children walk?" than to ask "Where did the boy and girl walk?"

Inferential Reading Comprehension Skills

Inferential comprehension requires more thinking than mere recall. Inferential comprehension includes the following skills (Hillerich, 1983):

1. Drawing general conclusions
2. Inferring the main idea
3. Inferring sequence
4. Inferring comparisons
5. Inferring cause/effect relationships
6. Making judgments
7. Identifying character traits and motives
8. Predicting outcomes
9. Interpreting figures of speech

Questions that begin with "Why" or "How did you know" are generally inferential in nature. Regular verbal feedback to students and expanded explanations are the principal ways of teaching inferential comprehension. The teacher must confirm the learner's response and also must identify the components of the response that made it correct.

Critical Reading Comprehension Skills

Critical reading skills and critical thinking skills are synonymous, except that the former is related to print. The following elements comprise critical reading skills:

1. Identifying the central issue or main idea
2. Distinguishing fact from fiction
3. Identifying particular language styles

Advertisements are particularly useful in developing critical reading skills. In advertisements, students must learn to identify the words and phrases that show slant or bias. They also must read the selection to determine what is *not* said. For example, although "No peanut butter is more nutritious than Skippy" means that many other brands—even those that are cheaper—are just as nutritious as Skippy, an uncritical reading of the advertisement would lead someone to believe that Skippy is *more* nutritious. The sports page of the local newspaper is also an excellent source of biased writing samples (Kimmel, 1973) and is thus an interesting source of materials for teaching critical reading skills. Sports headlines can often be used to show bias in writing. For example, a headline in New York might read "Mets kill Pirates 10–2," while in Pittsburgh the headline for the same game might be "Pirates lose to Mets."

THE READING LESSON

The first step in the preparation of the reading lesson is for the teacher to become familiar with the selection to be read (that means reading it *before* teaching the lesson) and with the related worksheets or workbook pages. At this point, the teacher should determine the appropriateness of the worksheets and the manner in which the reading selection should be taught.

Although the number of components might differ somewhat, most reading professionals agree that a good reading lesson is generally composed of the following elements:

1. An introduction
2. Reading and discussion
3. Skill instruction
4. Follow-up activities

A lesson is not necessarily one fixed period of time but may extend over several days. It is also possible and appropriate to incorporate all four lesson elements into a single time period.

The Introduction

The introduction to a new lesson should include an introduction to new words and to the reading selection itself. In this introduction, the students usually read the title, look at the pictures, and discuss, in general, what the story will be about. The teacher should point out to the students how the reading selection is organized and how that organization is similar to or different from the organization of other selections they have read. If side headings are used, they should be noted, and when charts or graphs are part of the selection, students should be reminded to examine them when they are described in the text.

The introduction is given insufficient attention by most teachers (Hansen & Pearson, 1983). Since the focus of reading is on comprehension, it is crucial that the content of the reading selection not be beyond the experiential background of the students. The introductory portion of the lesson allows the teacher to build the background information the students need to benefit from the selection. Building such background knowledge prior to reading not only facilitates comprehension of the upcoming story or article, it also helps the students develop a mental set of expectations for learning and evaluating the new material in terms of what they already know (Hansen & Pearson, 1983).

When new vocabulary words are introduced, the students should be given the opportunity to pronounce and define the words. Definitions should not be limited to the usages of the words in the reading selection but should encompass variations in meaning. For example, the word *strike* has no fewer than 39 different meanings. Students should discuss the different meanings of each word with the teacher and the group. Since some words will not be readily defined by the group, part of the directed silent reading may be to locate the word in the selection and use the context to determine its meaning. This procedure can also be used to determine which particular meaning was used for a word in the reading selection.

Sufficient time must be spent to prepare the students for the selection they are to read. Hansen and Pearson (1983) have found that when little or no time is spent on the introduction, comprehension of the written passage decreases dramatically.

Reading and Discussion

The initial reading of a story should always be done silently by the learners. The selection can be broken into smaller sections and treated as short instructional units if the teacher finds that necessary. Students should be given a specific purpose for their silent reading—such as a list of questions that they must answer. Both general and specific questions should be included. For low-ability students, general and specific questions are necessary for them to recall both the main ideas and the details. The level of recall from the students is determined by the kinds of questions that are asked (Wilhite, 1984). The teacher should watch as the students are reading silently to see how each student approaches the task. Some students scan the text and search for answers to the questions without really reading the story; such a practice should be avoided.

The discussion that follows the students' silent reading of the reading selection should not be a quiz on their responses to the initial general/

specific questions; rather, it should be a discussion of the selection (Hillerich, 1983): Did they like it? What can they learn from it? Why did the author write it? Do they like the way the author writes? Have they ever read anything similar? The purpose of the discussion is to increase the learners' enjoyment of the story and relate it to other experiences; the session should not be strictly a question-and-answer period based upon the comprehension questions.

Guided oral reading of selected passages can be used as part of the discussion period. Among the benefits of oral reading sessions are that they allow the teacher to observe appropriate word stress, check students' word-attack skills, check reading growth (Deno et al., 1984), help clarify a point of disagreement, and check phrasing, pronunciation, breath control, and eye contact (Hillerich, 1983).

Skill Instruction

The skill portion of the lesson may involve a refresher of old skills or the teaching of new skills, including specific instruction in comprehension as well as word-attack skills. Having the students read the story, discuss it, and do the workbook/worksheet exercises is not teaching reading. The teaching act requires *explanation*, *demonstration*, and *clarification*. Merely assigning work is not teaching, and having students practice skills that they have not been taught is foolhardy. Unfortunately, however, these are all-too-common practices in our schools.

One strategy for teaching comprehension skills is for the teacher to read a passage aloud, stop and "think aloud" the kinds of questions the students should be asking about the passage (e.g., "Who is the leading character?" "What is being accomplished?" "What did I just learn?" "Is this really true?"), and then answer the questions (Grabe & Mann, 1984). The students should then practice this strategy themselves. The development of such self-monitoring skills has produced sizable gains in comprehension performance (Palincsar & Brown, 1984). Words that are used in selections to describe emotion should be highlighted and discussed in terms of how the use of a synonym might totally change the meaning of a passage. Modeling, feedback, explanation, and discussion must be practiced if comprehension is to be improved.

Another strategy for enhancing comprehension is to ask questions that integrate story parts rather than addressing inconsequential details (Tharp, 1982). For example, the teacher should not ask for the color of the girl's sweater or coat if it has nothing to do with the story line. It might be better to ask about the season, temperature, or weather, which can be inferred from the fact that she was wearing a sweater or coat. Discussions that are guided by such questions help students see the integration of all the pieces of information and thus enhance comprehension performance (Gallagher & Pearson, 1983).

Oral reading is another skill that must be developed. Having students read material silently (previewing) before they are asked to read aloud is a commonly used instructional strategy. Lovitt, Eaton, Kirkwood, and Pelander (1971) have found that this strategy results in decreased oral reading errors. Rose (1984) and Rose and Sherry (1984) have found that if the teacher reads this selection aloud while the students follow along in their books, students can then read the selection aloud with few oral reading errors. This strategy was found superior even to silent prereading.

The teacher should measure a learner's reading progress regularly, by unit tests, weekly quizzes, or daily recitations. Deno et al. (1984) have found that findings from a 1-minute oral reading test correlate well with standardized achievement measures. For such a test, the teacher selects a section of the current reading material and the student reads aloud for one minute. The teacher then counts and graphs the number of words read correctly and incorrectly. This method of measurement has been found to be sensitive to the effects of instruction. As the student's reading skills increase, his or her hesitations decrease, words are read more automatically, more words are read correctly per minute, and fewer errors are noted.

Follow-Up Activities

The most frequently used type of follow-up activity is completing worksheets and workbooks. Teachers should judge the appropriateness of the prescribed worksheets and workbooks. One way to judge appropriateness is to examine the exercise from the learners' perspective by asking such questions as "If I were the learner, what would I be expected to learn from this worksheet?" If the response is one of uncertainty, then perhaps the exercise is inappropriate or poorly designed. Another question that should be asked is "Could I correct this worksheet *without* an answer key?" After asking such questions, the teacher may discard or redesign many worksheets or use some as group activities rather than as independent seatwork.

Students learn best with instruction, and achievement scores tend to be lower when they work independently without direct supervision (Stallings, 1975). For seatwork to be beneficial, the teacher must first teach the skills and then have the students do the seatwork, and the teacher must monitor their performance actively while the seatwork is being done. This monitoring involves spot-checking students' work as it is being done and responding to questions. Assigning students seatwork so that the teacher can catch up on paperwork is not a responsible use of instructional time. When teachers or other adults spend more time on academic instruction, students' achievement scores tend to be higher (Medley, 1977; Rosenshine, 1979). It is also quite appropriate to do small- or large-group instruction within the follow-up activities. The immediate feedback that is derived from follow-up activities is an important contributing factor in improved student performance.

SUMMARY OF TEACHING STRATEGIES

Preceding sections of this chapter have described the components of a reading program and specific strategies that can be used to enhance reading skills. The following strategies are suggested for increasing reading comprehension:

1. Build background knowledge before students read a story.
2. Model questioning behaviors.
3. Organize and ask discussion questions that integrate story parts.
4. Develop self-monitoring skills in learners.
5. Ask inferential as well as literal questions.

The following strategies can be used to decrease errors in oral reading:

1. Silent previewing of the selection by the students.
2. Oral reading by the teacher.

Suggested strategies for teaching sight word vocabulary include the following:

1. Intersperse known words with unknown words.
2. Present the words without illustrations so that the learners attend to the distinctive features of each word to be learned.

The responsible teacher will use such strategies when teaching lessons in reading. The current journals are a source of even newer procedures and should be read periodically.

INFORMAL READING ASSESSMENT

The Informal Reading Inventory

The informal reading inventory (IRI) is probably the most common method used by teachers to establish a student's reading level for placement in a basal reading series. In many ways, it is superior to standardized testing for placement in a reading program because it is based on the actual curriculum materials. With an IRI, the teacher can determine the learner's independent, instructional, and frustrational levels in reading. The IRI consists of a series of paragraphs taken from a basal reading series and arranged in increasing order of difficulty. A science or social studies series might also be a reasonable alternative as the content base for the IRI. For the teacher working with students who are mainstreamed, using these curriculum materials as the basis for reading assessment can be quite useful. One obvious use is that the teacher can better determine the appropriateness of the mainstreaming decision.

Sedlak and Sedlak (1985) recommend the following procedures in constructing an IRI:

1. Select two 60- to 120-word passages from each level of a series. For students beyond grade 3, the passages should contain up to 200 words.
2. Retype the passages onto separate sheets of paper.
3. Construct five comprehension questions for each passage, including questions dealing with factual information, main ideas, vocabulary, inferences, and sequencing. Avoid the use of yes–no questions.
4. Compile a list of vocabulary words from each level, selecting every fifth new word (or choose every fifth word from the reading passages and eliminate duplicates).
5. Type vocabulary words on a sheet of paper.
6. Construct a scoring sheet. (It can be merely a copy of the passages and vocabulary words on which the teacher can code errors.)

Administering and Scoring the IRI

Administering and scoring an IRI is not a mechanical process. The results will be useful only if the evaluator understands the reading process and the analysis of errors. The following steps are involved in administering an IRI (Sedlak & Sedlak, 1985):

1. Have the student read the vocabulary words first (words in isolation).
2. Record all errors, such as substitutions, hesitations, omissions.
3. Stop when the student has missed 25% of the words on one level. (Note that self-corrections are not errors.)
4. Have student read the first passage silently at the highest level for which vocabulary recognition was 100%.
5. Record beginning and ending times for the passage.
6. Ask comprehension questions and record responses.
7. Have the student read the passage aloud, and record errors.
8. Use the second passage as a reliability check if needed.
9. If comprehension is less than 50% and oral reading shows a lack of rhythm, meaningless word substitutions, and word recognition difficulties, the learner should stop oral reading.
10. Teacher should then read aloud the parallel passage for the last level and ask comprehension questions. The teacher should continue until the comprehension question errors drop below 75%.

Guidelines for establishing a student's independent, instructional, frustrational, and listening levels are as follows:

1. *Independent:* The student reads in a rhythmical, natural, conversational tone that is free from tension with few oral recognition errors. Comprehension is 90% or better.

2. *Instructional:* The student reads with no more than one word recognition error per twenty words (after silent reading). The student comprehends at least 75% of the questions and reads with good phrasing.

3. *Frustrational:* The student shows extreme difficulty in reading, reads with a lack of rhythm, and makes meaningless word substitutions. Fingerpointing and use of a high-pitched voice may also be signs that the frustrational level has been reached. Comprehension is less than 60%, and word recognition is less than 90%.

4. *Listening:* The student responds correctly to at least 60% to 75% of the comprehension questions asked. This level indicates that the vocabulary and syntactic structure is understood by the learner.

Analysis of Errors

Analysis of a student's reading errors should be based on the *nature* of the errors, rather than solely on the *number* of the errors (Goodman, 1965). Substitution and omission miscues may be acceptable linguistically and conceptually. For example, substituting the word *pet* for *dog* or *football team* for *Pittsburgh Steelers* may be both conceptually and linguistically correct in a passage and may not be counted as an error, since the meaning of the passage was not obliterated by the substitution. The student who reads the sentence "I am going" as "I be going" is demonstrating not a reading problem but only a linguistic difference. In traditional error analyses, self-corrections and repetitions are generally coded as errors, but they could also be viewed as an opportunity for the learner to gain subsequent meaning in a passage (V. Brown, 1975). The types of errors (or miscues) should be analyzed by category to determine whether the error is linguistic, cognitive, or graphic (Hammill & Bartel, 1978).

Listening Comprehension

The relationship between listening comprehension and reading comprehension is a correlation in the range between .40 and .60. Appraisal of a learner's listening comprehension should be part of an assessment of reading comprehension. The test of listening comprehension can be a parallel version of the informal reading inventory, except that all written material is presented orally, including the comprehension questions. In general, the listening comprehension level represents the outer limit possible for reading comprehension.

The Cloze Procedure

The cloze procedure is both an instructional strategy and an assessment strategy. Graded passages are used, just as in the IRI, but the passages are somewhat longer—250 to 300 words. Every fifth word is deleted from the passage and substituted with blank lines of uniform length. The student reads the passage, either orally or silently, and supplies the missing words for the blanks. When the reading is done silently, the student normally supplies the missing word in writing. Ekwall (1976) suggests the following guidelines for determining a student's reading level according to the cloze procedure:

> Independent: 57% or more of the deleted words correct
> Instructional: 44% to 56% of the deleted words correct
> Frustrational: 43% or less of the deleted words correct

There is some disagreement regarding whether the student must substitute the exact word for a blank or whether a synonym is acceptable. We believe that, linguistically and conceptually, correct substitutions should be acceptable.

The cloze procedure can be modified and used by the teacher in other ways as well, including the following:

1. Delete only a specific part of speech from passages to determine whether student error is sensitive to this dimension.
2. Insert the first letter of each deleted word as an added clue.
3. Have the length of the blank line approximate the length of the deleted word.
4. Supply the correct answer and two or three foils from which the learner must select the correct word.
5. Delete words from verbal problems in mathematics and require verbal rather than numerical answers (Sedlak, 1974).
6. Use in subject areas, such as science and social studies, to assess comprehension (Gilliland, 1978).
7. Delete words in passages the teacher reads orally.

CASE FOR ACTION 11.1

You have no records as yet for a new student in your class and have been informed that his IEP and other materials will arrive in a week or so. What steps would you take to assess this student's reading skills and place him in a reading program?

VARIANT-ENGLISH SPEAKERS

The variant-English speaker poses a special problem for the teacher of the mildly handicapped. The basic question regarding the variant-English speaker and reading is whether the language differences interfere with the learner's ability to learn to read. In general, the answer is no. There is some empirical support, however, that indicates that the teacher's reaction to a dialect may result in reading problems (Cunningham, 1976; Rigg, 1978). If the teacher views the dialect pronunciation as a reading error and treats it as such, a problem will probably emerge. The learner will be less responsive in class and will develop a negative affect toward the reading task. A cycle of expectancy then develops, with the learner trying to avoid failure and retreating from the academic program and the possibility of criticism. Teachers who realize that the difference is one of dialect, not a reading problem, will accept the pronunciation and sentence structure and contin-ue the lesson. The primary question for the teacher is "Does the student comprehend the textual material?" The extraction of meaning from the text is the goal of reading.

Following this rule, the teacher should accept the oral reading of the passage "He is going to the game" as "He be goin' to the game". Rearranging the syntax is a complex task, and the learner should not be penalized for that level of sophistication. Somervill (1975) has suggested that such style switching should be viewed as a positive feature, revealing a learner's growth in reading competence. In the same light, Goodman (1965) has discussed the need to recognize phonological miscues and not al-ways label them as errors.

GENERAL INSTRUCTIONAL PROCEDURES IN READING

Although there are specific strategies that teachers can use to enhance the performance of students in different skill areas in reading, two general find-ings have evolved that transcend the specific skills and result in enhanced achievement for learners. The first finding is that students who receive most

CASE FOR ACTION 11.2

A fourth-grade student who has just arrived at your school has been placed in the fourth-grade reading book. Each day an assignment is written on the board: "Read the story and answer the following questions and do the exercises on page _____." This student has been getting about 50 to 60 percent of the assignment wrong and often does not answer the questions. He turns in his papers at the end of the period and gets them back the next day with the comments "Be more careful," "Work faster," and "Try harder." As the days progress, the student is completing fewer and fewer questions and missing more. He is also misbehaving a great deal in class. What do you think is the nature of this student's problem, and what would you do to resolve it?

of their instruction from the teacher achieve more than those who are in self-directed (worksheet-dominated) systems. The second conclusion is that students learn most efficiently when teachers use systematic instruction, monitor student responses, and give students feedback on their performance (Rosenshine & Stevens, 1984).

The first conclusion is based on the body of literature that deals with the relationship of time on-task to academic achievement. Students show higher engagement rates for teacher-led activities than for seatwork-based activities. Instruction in small groups or even in large groups is generally preferable to one-to-one instruction as the regular instructional method of choice. Part of the explanation for this finding is that time is the critical variable that affects learning. In a 60-minute period in a class with 12 students, if each student were to receive an equal amount of one-to-one instruction, each student would receive 5 minutes of teacher instruction and 55 minutes of self-instruction. If the teacher works with groups, the amount of instruction received by each student increases significantly. Seatwork can be effective but must be closely monitored and not relied on to introduce new content.

The second conclusion regarding effective teaching of reading is based on the demonstration–practice–feedback approach. For students to learn new skills, they must be shown the skills in operation with examples and they must be given instructions on how to use the skills. This demonstration phase of the model deals with the way the information or skill is taught. Once teaching has occurred, the student must be given the opportunity to practice the skill. This practice must be frequent, must require active responding on the part of the learner, and must use a variety of examples and question types/formats; it can use group and/or individual responding. The final step of the model is feedback. Without explicit feedback, learners assume that their responses are correct. Therefore, it is crucial to correct errors.

APPROACHES TO READING INSTRUCTION

Thus far, we have described the basic skill components of the reading process, some strategies for teaching those skills, and some strategies for assessing student performance in reading. This section will describe five programmatic approaches to teaching reading. These approaches may share some common instructional elements, but they differ in their philosophical bases, materials, and appropriateness for group versus individual delivery. There is no singularly superior method for teaching reading to the handicapped (Kirk, Kliebhan, & Lerner, 1978). As Heilman (1972) has noted, virtually every method and procedure has been successful with some children and unsuccessful with others. Therefore, it is recommended that no single approach be used with all learners in a class. Successful reading instruction is based on the teacher's versatility in selecting materials and techniques for helping children who are experiencing specific reading difficulties. The skill of the teacher is regarded by many as more important than the efficacy of a specific approach. Special education teachers must be aware of these various approaches so that they can judiciously select an appropriate program for each learner.

Basal Readers

Basal readers are the foundation of most primary and intermediate grade reading programs in the United States. The basal reader approach offers a sequential and interrelated set of books and materials, ranging from reading readiness up to sixth- or eighth-grade levels. Basal series also include teacher's manuals, which present detailed lesson plans for the development of each story. Unfortunately, many of the stories found in these series are devoid of meaningful content. Recently, however, the settings of stories have included apartments, trailer parks, and inner city areas, and characters have been changed to minimize racism and sexism (Gillespie-Silver, 1979).

Instructional time is a precious commodity. Therefore, a reading series that includes stories laden with the meaningful content of science, social studies, careers, and true-to-life situations allows the teacher to teach reading while increasing the overall knowledge base of the learners. Unfortunately, such content may be scarce. Another significant change in basal series noted by G. Wallace (1981) is the addition of word analysis approaches, as opposed to sole reliance on sight word approaches. According to Wilson and Hall (1972), basal reading programs have the following advantages:

1. Controlled vocabulary
2. Sequentially developed skills
3. Emphasis on decoding and comprehension
4. Colorful, attractive materials
5. Teacher's guides with step-by-step outlines for each lesson
6. Supplemental workbooks and related materials

Disadvantages of this approach, noted by a number of writers (Gillespie-Silver, 1979; Heilman, 1972; Kaluger & Kolson, 1978; Niemeyer, 1965; Wilson & Hall, 1972), include the following:

1. There is a lack of variety in sentence structure.
2. The material tends to be dull and repetitive.
3. Language patterns are more simple than the oral language patterns of the learner.
4. The teacher's manuals present a very structured program and don't allow for flexibility or adaptability.
5. Themes of stories draw heavily from middle-class themes and situations.
6. No provision is made for individual differences beyond the traditional three-group structure.
7. Special education students frequently remain in the same basal reader year after year, with little growth and greater resistance to reading.
8. The stories are devoid of content from such areas as science, social studies, health, or vocational options.

To use the basal reading approach successfully, the teacher must adequately prepare for each reading lesson by becoming thoroughly familiar with the instructions in the teacher's edition.

The Linguistic Approach

The linguistic approach, first advocated by Bloomfield in 1933, is based on a whole-word approach to the teaching of reading. The lessons are structured with carefully sequenced presentations of words that follow regular patterns. These regular word patterns are learned first, and new words are learned on the basis of what the student learned from the preceding lesson. The principle of minimal change is emphasized, and initial instruction

CASE FOR ACTION 11.3

A first-grader has been taught to memorize the words *map, sat, rat,* and *can.* When she encounters the new word *Pam,* she misidentifies it as *map.* She is also considered somewhat clumsy by her teacher. What do you think is the nature of this student's problem, and what would you do to resolve it?

consists of three-letter words that have a consonant–vowel–consonant pattern with short vowels (e.g., *ran, fan, pan, can*).

There is little emphasis on word meaning. The focus of instruction is to develop the ability to extract the sound of the words from the printed page. Most linguistic readers have no pictures or illustrations. The phonetic regularity of the words, rather than the frequency of the usage, is the mechanism that is used to control vocabulary (Myers & Hammill, 1976). Rhyming words and stories that use these words are the bases from which students acquire familiarity with printed words.

The Language Experience Approach

The language experience approach integrates reading, listening, speaking, and writing skills. The skills are taught as they are needed for the student to write a story. The age range for the approach is generally considered to be from the first grade through junior high school. Student-generated stories are the basis for the instruction. Each lesson begins with a discussion or picture stimulus to provide a topic for the written part of the lesson. The subject of the discussion could be in a content-related area, such as science or social studies.

The student first produces the story orally, while the teacher writes it on the board or on a sheet of paper. The story can be composed by a single student or by a small group. For older students, dictating a story into a tape recorder may be appropriate. After the story is dictated, it is transcribed. The transcription may be done by the student with the assistance of the teacher or may be typed or printed by the teacher. If the story is produced by a small group or with the teacher, it is helpful to discuss word choices and alternative sentence structures. Copies of each day's stories are kept on file and are reviewed each day. From these stories, a sight word vocabulary is developed and kept on flash cards. Related activities for these stories must be developed by the teacher. Because the student has already created the story orally, reading it from the printed material is greatly facilitated. Familiarity with the content greatly reduces a student's anxiety when asked to read the story aloud.

This approach can be used with variant-English speakers. In transcribing or writing the stories, the teacher should translate the pronunciations and syntax into a standard English form. The student's reading of the passage in a variant-English form should be accepted by the teacher, but the teacher could reread the passage in the standard form. The rereading by the teacher provides the learner with an appropriate model and also with feedback. Miscues made by the student that are of a nondialectical nature should be corrected by the teacher.

The strengths of this approach are as follows:

1. The content is based on the experiences of the student.
2. The vocabulary is within the student's conceptual level.
3. The focus of the instruction is comprehension.

The disadvantages of the approach, cited by Heilman (1972), include the following:

1. There is uncontrolled vocabulary.
2. The method places a heavy demand on the teacher's time.
3. Basic sight words may not be repeated often.

The Direct Instruction Approach

The direct instruction approach to reading instruction requires development of essential reading skills through the most effective and efficient means. The basic information on the direct instruction approach is provided by Carnine and Silbert (1979). The approach can be described in relationship to each of three components:

1. Organization of instruction
2. Program design
3. Presentation techniques

Organization of instruction involves the efficient use of time in the teaching process, including scheduling time and arranging materials. Teachers must schedule sufficient time for activities and must follow the schedule to ensure that possible instructional time is not wasted. Materials used in teaching must be arranged and organized to make efficient use of time. The arrangement of both teacher materials and student materials is critical. Brophy and Evertson (1976) found that students made significant academic gain in classrooms if (1) each student knew his or her assignment; (2) when the student needed help, he or she could get it from the teacher or from some designated person; (3) the student was made accountable for completing the assignment appropriately by having the work checked.

Independent work should be placed in folders on students' desks. Teachers should use colored clips or other markers to indicate where reading level groups are on different pages in the teacher's guides. Greater efficiency in the use of materials and the scheduling of activities results in more engaged time in learning.

Program design involves writing behavioral objectives for essential skills, devising problem-solving strategies, developing teaching procedures, selecting appropriate examples, providing sufficient and appropriate practice, and sequencing skills properly. The scope of reading skills is evaluated, and nonessential skills are eliminated. Objectives are written in relation to skills, not to global functioning levels. Strategies are taught that a learner can use to pronounce new words or derive meaning from a passage. In teaching procedures, a format is followed that specifies what to say, what words to emphasize, what to ask, how to signal, how to correct appropriately, and so forth (Carnine & Silbert, 1979). Student failure is considered teacher failure. Careful selection of examples is important, as is providing sufficient and appropriate practice of a skill. Guidelines for the sequencing of skills (Carnine & Silbert, 1979) are as follows:

1. Preskills of a strategy are taught before the strategy itself is presented.
2. Instances that are consistent with a strategy are introduced before exceptions.
3. High-utility skills are introduced before less useful ones.
4. Easy skills are taught before more difficult ones.
5. Strategies and information that are likely to be confused are not introduced at the same time.

Presentation techniques include small-group instruction, unison oral responding, signaling, pacing, monitoring, diagnosis and correction, and motivation. For small-group instruction, groups of five to ten students are taught for a half-hour each day; the students are seated in a semicircle within 2 feet of the teacher. Unison oral responding requires that all students actively respond to questions, which are asked frequently throughout the lesson. Signals are cues given by the teacher to students to indicate that they should make a response; the signal can be a clap, hand drop, or change in voice inflection. Pacing refers to the rate of presentations; we recommend fast-paced, short presentations. Monitoring involves far more than simply noting correct and incorrect responses; the teacher must also watch students' eyes and mouths to be sure that they are focusing on the proper stimuli and responding appropriately. Attention to the proper seating of high-responding and low-responding youngsters is also critical. Students are questioned individually as well as in groups, but only after adequate group practice. Close monitoring is essential to avoid student confusion and problems. The correction procedure involves praise, modeling, response to a parallel task, and a delay test. The final component of presentation is motivation, such as frequent pats, handshakes, and physical contact for successful reading. If lessons are well planned and structured, students are more likely to be successful.

The direct instruction approach places high demands on a teacher and emphasizes accepted teaching practices. It is a highly effective system that has been demonstrated to increase achievement in learners from low-income families and in variant-English speakers (McDonald, 1976; Tickunoff, Berliner, & Rist, 1975).

The Fernald Approach

The Fernald (1943) approach is also referred to as the multisensory approach. It is used primarily with students who have encountered repeated failure in learning to read. It is an individual approach, not used with groups of learners. The system is also referred to as the VATK system—visual, auditory, tactile, and kinesthetic. Beginning instruction revolves around words the learner wishes to learn. As the student learns to write these words, a story using the words is composed by the student. The teacher spells any of the words the learner cannot spell. All new words are practiced by the VATK procedure. The story is typed and is used for subsequent reading instruction. The four stages of the VATK procedure are as follows:

Stage 1. The learner selects a word, and the teacher writes it in cursive or manuscript large enough to be traced with a finger. The student then looks at the word (visual), says the word (auditory), traces the word (tactile), and copies the word (kinesthetic). The learner continues until the word can be read correctly without prompts or cues. The student may also trace the word in the air for practice. The word is then included in a story and in an alphabet box of new words.

Stage 2. The learner no longer traces the word. The learner looks at the word, pronounces it, and writes it from memory. The word box is maintained, but words are discarded as they are mastered.

Stage 3. The word is no longer written for the learner. The learner merely locates a word on the page, says it, and writes it. Words are no longer self-selected at this stage. Reading from books rather than self-made stories is emphasized.

Stage 4. New words are learned from context cues or by building upon the sight words that the student has mastered. Supplemental reading materials are books that are of interest to the learner.

The VATK method has been found effective with retarded learners and with the learning disabled (McCarthy & Oliver, 1965). Authorities are unsure about why the method works, but it has been hypothesized that it is because of the attention and concentration given to each word, rather than the tracing or writing of the word (G. O. Johnson, 1963; Morris, 1958). Several researchers have modified the VATK procedure, also with beneficial results (Cawley, Goodstein, & Burrow, 1972; M. S. Johnson, 1966; Monroe, 1932).

SUMMARY

The following rules summarize the major points addressed in this chapter relating to general strategies for teaching reading. These rules are based on "general" characteristics of the mildly handicapped in reading, but neither all characteristics nor all rules apply to all learners.

1. When students work independently without direct teacher supervision, they tend to have lower achievement.
2. The more time teachers spend in the act of teaching, the higher the achievement scores.
3. When teachers do more ongoing assessment and use the information to modify the instruction, the achievement scores tend to be higher.
4. Providing feedback to students (particularly corrective feedback for errors) results in higher achievement.
5. Breaking the learning task into small, attainable steps minimizes the learner's expectancy to fail.
6. Providing the learner with sight words in different type styles and locations will maximize the generalization and transfer of the skill.
7. If seatwork is assigned, it should be supervised while the activity is taking place.
8. Comprehension is a skill that needs to be taught, just as word attack or vocabulary.

12

Mathematics Instruction

■ DID YOU KNOW THAT...

■ **1** ...most special education teachers do not teach functional math skills but teach only the four basic operations?

■ **2** ...mathematics instruction should actively involve the student in an applied format?

■ **3** ...eight areas of math are needed by adults to function in today's society?

■ **4** ...solving word problems requires a higher level of information processing than solving simple arithmetic operations?

■ **5** ...there are 16 different ways to teach any math concept systematically?

■ **6** ...students' errors usually follow a logical rule and form patterns that can be identified by the teacher?

■ **7** ...there are at least two types of addition, four types of subtraction, three types of multiplication, and three types of division?

■ **8** ...recognition of both relevant and irrelevant information is an essential skill in solving word problems?

■ **9** ...extraneous information in word problems greatly increases the difficulty level?

■ **10** ...calculator-aided computation requires instruction in processes that are different from those used in traditional computation?

○ **CAN YOU . . .**

○ **1**   . . . use the skill sequences of a developmental math curriculum to plan for the subskills necessary in a functional math curriculum?

○ **2**   . . . apply an error analysis procedure to diagnose a student's learning problems in math?

○ **3**   . . . implement an instructional unit to identify a student's error patterns?

○ **4**   . . . develop a curriculum that incorporates instruction in all four of the basic mathematical operations?

○ **5**   . . . use modeling or verbal mediation as an instructional strategy to teach computation problems?

○ **6**   . . . write word problems that have either cued or uncued questions?

○ **7**   . . . use pictures and manipulatives as instructional aids to develop problem-solving skills?

○ **8**   . . . list a sequence of corrective interventions that would be responsive to the varying levels of student performance with word problems?

○ **9**   . . . develop an instructional sequence for a unit on calculator usage?

○ **10**   . . . use a task analysis format to assess a student's competency in making change or counting money?

Our world is filled with mathematical relationships, and our independent living skills depend heavily on our competent use of mathematics. We learn many mathematical applications through our daily experiences, while others have to be taught formally. For example, estimating is a practice that we use throughout the day—estimating the amount of salt to put on food, the amount of time it will take to get from point A to point B, how much a food bill will be, how much food needs to be prepared for a meal, and so on. Time and distance are also concepts that we use daily and often interchangeably. The correct and appropriate use of money is an indispensable skill. All of these concepts are found within a mathematics program for the handicapped.

■ 1   One concept we have tried to stress throughout this book has been functional skill development. Probably no area of the curriculum has a more applied focus of this concept than mathematics. It is a shame, therefore, that most special education teachers view teaching mathematics as teaching only the four basic operations: addition, subtraction, multiplication, and division. An examination of the amount of time and the types of instructional materials used in classrooms shows an overwhelming focus on these aspects of math, almost to the exclusion of such areas as geometry, problem solving, measurement, or probability.

■ 2   Mathematics of the "real world" has some characteristics that differentiate it from mathematicians' concepts of "pure" mathematics. Sharma (1984) has illustrated this distinction nicely with this problem: "Given a 10-inch long piece of wood, show how many pieces of 2-inch width can be cut from this piece" (p. 223). The pure mathematical answer is 5, but the real-world answer is 4 because, in the cutting process, wood is lost as sawdust and the fifth piece will be less than 2 inches wide. The mathematics curriculum for the handicapped learner must address both the pure and the real world aspects of mathematics.

THE CONTENT OF MATHEMATICS INSTRUCTION

Rapid technological changes in society require instruction that facilitates generalization and transfer of knowledge. Thus, instruction in mathematics must embrace many topics; on the next pages, we will attempt to outline as many of these topics as possible.

■ 3   Sharma (1984, pp. 224–225) has identified eight areas of mathematics that adults need to participate in contemporary society. We have modified this list slightly so that it is more applicable to the majority of mildly handicapped learners:

1. Numbers and numerals
   a. Express a rational number using a decimal notation.
   b. List the first ten multiples of 2 through 12.
   c. Use the whole numbers (four basic operations) in problem solving.
   d. Recognize the digit, its place value, and the number represented through billions.
   e. Describe a given positive rational number using decimal, percentage, or fractional notation.

2. Operations and properties
   a. Write equivalent fractions for given fractions such as 1/2, 2/3, 3/4, and 7/8.
   b. Use the standard algorithms for the arithmetic operations of positive rational numbers.
   c. Solve addition, subtraction, multiplication, and division problems involving fractions.
   d. Solve problems involving percentages.
   e. Perform arithmetic operations with measures.
   f. Estimate results.
   g. Judge the reasonableness of answers to computation problems.

3. Mathematical sentences
   a. Construct a mathematical sentence from a given verbal problem.
   b. Solve simple equations.

4. Geometry and measurement
   a. Recognize horizontal lines, vertical lines, parallel lines, perpendicular lines, and intersecting lines.
   b. Recognize different shapes.
   c. Compute areas, surfaces, volumes, densities.
   d. Understand similarities and congruence.
   e. Use measurement devices.

5. Relations and functions
   a. Interpret information from a graphic representation.
   b. Understand and apply ratio and proportion.
   c. Construct scales.

6. Probability and statistics
   a. Determine mean, average, mode, median.
   b. Understand simple probability.

7. Mathematical reasoning
   a. Produce counterexamples to test the invalidity of a statement.
   b. Detect and describe flaws and fallacies in advertising and propaganda.
   c. Gather and present data to support an inference or argument.

8. General skills
   a. Maintain personal bank records.
   b. Plan a budget and keep personal records.
   c. Apply a simple interest formula to calculate interest.
   d. Estimate the real cost of an item.
   e. Compute taxes and investment returns.
   f. Appraise insurance and retirement benefits.

○ 1   In keeping with our suggested practices for curriculum development (discussed in chapter 2), the focus of the curriculum may have to change at the junior high school level to begin developing functional skills. Until then, it may be quite appropriate to follow a developmental curriculum. The foregoing organization of a mathematics program for the mildly handicapped might best be addressed beginning at the junior high school level and continuing through senior high school. A more developmental approach to mathematics instruction that might be followed for elementary school students would cover curricular strands, including sets, patterns, geometry, measurement, numbers and operations, fractions, and problem solving. The development of skill sequences in these strands might be used to plan the order of necessary subskill development in the functional math curriculum.

Sets

A set is a group in which all members have a common quality other than the fact that they belong to the same group. For example, the set of whole numbers includes odd and even numbers, and the set of even numbers includes numbers evenly divisible by 2. Thus, instruction in sets involves joining classes, breaking down classes, and noting qualities that belong to the same member of two different classes. When working with sets, a heavy emphasis is placed on properties (e.g., color, size, shape, category). Such material should be taught from prekindergarten through third grade.

Patterns

A pattern is a repeating sequence of elements (AA2AA2AA2). Patterns can be copied or extended. Instructional materials used for patterns should have varying dimensions (e.g., shape, size, number, color, category, name), just as those in the sets portion of the curriculum. Patterns can also be taught with pictures or manipulative materials.

    Mildly handicapped learners need to develop a sense of pattern, or of what comes next. Pattern recognition is an early problem-solving experience which the successful student learns how to predict the unknown from information that is known. The following are examples of patterns from which learners can predict what would come next:

red, blue, red, blue, . . .
dog, dog, cat, dog, dog, cat, . . .
2, 4, 6, 8, . . .
square, circle, circle, square, circle, circle, . . .

Patterns should be taught from kindergarten through sixth grade. Sternberg (1975) has described a comprehensive set of activities associated with patterns.

Geometry

Geometry is concerned with concepts of position or location in space. Some basic concepts that must be acquired are open/closed; inside/outside; on, under, over, between; left/right; and so forth. A knowledge of two-dimensional shapes (square, triangle, rectangle) and three-dimensional shapes (sphere, cube, cone, pyramid) provides the learner with an awareness of these shapes in the environment and a means of communicating about them. These concepts should be taught from kindergarten through sixth grade.

Measurement

Measurement topics to be covered include time, temperature, weight, linear measure, volume, and distance. These topics should be taught using real-life examples of their application, such as in cooking, sewing, or woodworking. Coverage of nonstandard measures is also a critical part of the measurement curriculum. These concepts should be taught from kindergarten through sixth grade.

Numbers and Operations

Learners must be given a concrete understanding of what a number is and of the relationships between numbers. Major emphasis should be on basic mathematical facts and on the development of computational skills. Content in this area should include reading and writing number names, addition (with regrouping), subtraction (with regrouping), multiplication, division, and even/odd numbers.

We believe that learners should do minimal work in operations until second grade. We realize that such a statement sounds like heresy, but we believe that teachers often begin to teach 1 + 1 too early, creating problems for the learner later in his or her schooling. Many other mathematical concepts can be taught (and can be assimilated by the learner) in the early primary grades.

Fractions

Fractions are numbers that represent parts of a group or parts of a whole. Basic to the understanding of fractions is an understanding of parts, wholes, and the part/whole relationship. The relationship of the size of the part to the size of the whole should be taught as well as the concept of equivalence—that is, what fraction of the same whole equals the same amount. Third grade is a reasonable time to begin formal instruction in fractions; informal work can begin earlier.

Problem Solving

■ 4   Problem solving promotes language usage, reading comprehension, reasoning skills, and evaluation skills. As mentioned earlier, pattern recognition is an early problem-solving activity. Several variables should be considered in a problem-solving program: the types of numbers used, the types of computations to be performed, the reading level of the learners, the format of instructional materials, extraneous information, and grammatical constructions. Students must be taught to recognize significant information and also to recognize situations in which insufficient information has been supplied. Application of problem solving should begin early in the student's mathematical program and proceed throughout his or her schooling.

THE TECHNOLOGY OF INSTRUCTION

We believe two procedures are critical if instruction in mathematics is to be delivered competently: (1) systematic variation of behaviors performed by the teacher and systematic variation of the behaviors required of the learner—an instruction model referred to as the interactive unit; and (2) systematic application of error analysis.

The Interactive Unit

■ 5   When teaching mathematics to disabled learners, problems emerge in providing meaningful instruction and circumventing the behavioral deficits that are unique to these learners. The interactive unit (IU)—a systematic instructional model designed to accommodate the behavioral needs of the disabled learner (Cawley et al., 1976)—is composed of eight cells; four identify teacher behaviors, and four identify learner responses. Thus, there are 16 possible behavioral interactions. The model allows either the teaching or the assessment of a concept through one or all of the behavioral combinations. Definitions of the IU cells are provided in figure 12.1.

Sedlak and Fitzmaurice (1981) have delineated the advantages of the IU. According to these authors, the IU allows a teacher to:

1. Teach around a disability
2. Provide repeated practice of a skill or concept with varied interactions to minimize boredom
3. Systematically hold constant a learner's response mode while varying the output
4. Systematically hold constant the input while varying the type of response to be made by the learner
5. Use manipulatives in a meaningful way and follow a logical sequence of behaviors up to the graphic symbolic mode
6. Diagnostically look at a learner's understanding of skills and concepts in a way other than with a pencil and paper test. (p. 485)

The IU is an excellent instructional system for teasing out error patterns in students' mathematics work.

FIGURE 12.1   The Interactive Unit

Teacher	Construct (C)	Present (P)	State (S)	Graphically Symbolize (GS)
Learner	Construct (C)	Identify (I)	State (S)	Graphically Symbolize (GS)

Construct (C): The teacher manipulates or uses objects to demonstrate a math concept; the learner uses objects to demonstrate understanding.
Present (P): The teacher presents the learner with a fixed visual display composed of pictures or prearranged objects.
Identify (I): The teacher asks the learner multiple-choice questions using pictures.
State (S): The teacher and the learner use spoken instructions, questions, and/or responses.
Graphically Symbolize (GS): The teacher provides written or drawn symbolic sets of materials, nonpictorial worksheets, and computational worksheets; the learner responds by writing.

Error Analysis

○ **2** A number of authors have proposed diagnostic models based on the analysis of students' errors (Ashlock, 1976; Buswell & John, 1925; Cawley, 1978). These systems have a number of characteristics or principles in common:

○ **3**
1. *How* a student solves a problem is more important than whether the answer is right or wrong.
2. In constructing problems, teachers must be aware of problem dimensions and must know how to control for these dimensions when constructing the problems.
3. The patterns of errors displayed by learners are often conceptual in nature, not a result of carelessness or insufficient drill.
4. Drill in the absence of a corrective instructional sequence is ineffective and possibly harmful.

■ **6** Wallace and McLoughlin (1975) have noted that a lack of readiness for learning certain arithmetic skills might be a basis for future problems. Because of the lack of readiness, the learner uses a rote rule to obtain the correct answer. Wallace and Kauffman (1978) have noted that learning problems may occur because the teacher failed to teach or did not allow for adequate practice of the skill. Ashlock (1976) believes that the error patterns students develop are the result of incomplete concept formation. Essentially, students overgeneralize a rule that works some of the time, especially with more elementary forms of problems. As the problems become more complicated or the dimensions of the problems change, the rule is no longer totally effective, but the students continue to work problems using the rule because they know no alternative. Figure 12.2 provides analyses of two students' error patterns.

FIGURE 12.2 Error Patterns of Two Students

Student 1:

$$
\begin{array}{cccc}
\overset{8\,1}{6\cancel{9}3} & \overset{2\,1}{\cancel{3}25} & \overset{5\,1\,1}{\cancel{7}26} & \overset{2\,1\,1}{\cancel{4}34} \\
-248 & -151 & -349 & -276 \\
\hline
445 & 174 & 287\ (X) & 68\ (X)
\end{array}
$$

1. Works from left to right.
2. Borrows from hundreds place if number in tens position is too small.

Student 2:

$$
\begin{array}{cccc}
 & \overset{1}{} & \overset{4}{} & \overset{0\,0}{} \\
432 & 74 & 385 & 563 \\
+265 & +43 & +667 & +545 \\
\hline
697 & 18\ (X) & 9116\ (X) & 118\ (X)
\end{array}
$$

1. Adds from left to right.
2. Carries the number in units position.

A teacher who examines error patterns only may understand what the student is doing wrong but not why the student is doing it wrong. Also, the teacher may not be able to see an error pattern. When analyzing an error pattern, it may be necessary for the teacher to have the student do the problem aloud. For example, the following problems were done by the second-grade daughter of one of the authors:

(A)	14	(B)	23	(C)	42	(D)	59	(E)	55
	25		32		37		19		19
	19		48		49		28		18
	58		103		128		916(X)		812(X)

The child's father could not figure out the error pattern for the last two problems, and the child was asked to explain how she arrived at these answers. She explained problem D as follows: "9 and 9 are 18 and 8 more are 26. I put down the 1 and carry the 1. Then, 5 and 1 are 6 and 2 are 8 and 1 is 9." When asked why she carried only 1 when the ones column added up to 26—why didn't she carry the 2?—she said, "You can't carry 2's, you can only carry 1's."

In problems A, B, and C only ones were carried. In all the problems they had been practicing at school, none of the examples had carried a number larger than 1. She had generalized a rule that only ones could be carried because it fit all the examples up to that time. To deal with the other half of the 2 in problems D and E, she merely put a 1 in the answer. It took about six more examples and the use of a calculator to demonstrate for her that numbers other than ones could be carried.

Students often have exotic explanations for their responses, even when they are wrong. The teacher's task is to help the students overcome this incorrect logic. Action Plan 12.1 contains a five-step procedure for identifying a student's math problems.

TEACHING SPECIFIC SKILLS IN MATHEMATICS

○ **4** It is beyond the scope of this chapter to provide detailed strategies for teaching concepts in each of the mathematics curriculur strands. Rather, we will address selected areas—arithmetic operations, word problem solving, calculator usage, money, and time—and discuss the critical components of the teaching process for these areas. The reader is referred to Cawley (1984, 1985) for a comprehensive set of strategies and activities for teaching mathematics to the learning disabled.

ACTION PLAN 12.1   DIAGNOSING A STUDENT'S MATHEMATICS PROBLEMS

We recommend the following strategies for diagnosing problems:

1. Use a general achievement test to establish a global picture of the student's functioning.
2. Examine error patterns present on the test.
3. Create small criterion-referenced tests on suspected skill problems.
4. Use a system such as the interactive unit to vary the stimulus and response features of the task.
5. Have the student do problems aloud and ask why he or she is doing certain things.

Arithmetic Operations

■ 7   Operations and problem solving are closely related—not in the computation aspects but in the conceptual aspects. The four basic arithmetic operations are often taught incorrectly to the mildly handicapped because they are presented as facts to be learned by rote. Students are usually *not* taught that there are at least two types of addition, four types of subtraction, three types of multiplication, and three types of division. They are taught incorrectly that subtraction is either a "take away" or "remainder" problem. They learn that in solving a subtraction problem, they start with more but end up with less. Then, when confronted with a problem such as "John has 5 apples and Bill has 2 apples. How many more apples does John have than Bill?" a student cannot conceptualize it as a subtraction problem because nothing is "taken away"—at the end of the problem, both boys still have apples. The problem is asking for a comparison for which the student is unprepared to solve.

Figure 12.3 lists the different types of addition, subtraction, division, and multiplication problems and gives examples of each type. It is recommended that these operations be taught using pictures and manipulatives. The Project MATH lessons (Cawley et al., 1976, 1977) teach these concepts using manipulatives. We have found that small cards (approximately 2″ by 2″) depicting familiar objects are useful for this purpose. Sets of these cards can be made by the teacher. Each set of cards probably need not contain more than ten examples of each object. The objects should be based on different categories. The following are some sample categories and object sets we have found useful:

FIGURE 12.3 Types of Addition, Subtraction, Multiplication, and Division Problems

Operations	Sample Problems
Addition Types	
1. Direct	Three bananas were growing on a tree. Overnight, two more bananas grew on the tree. How many are on the tree now?
2. Indirect	There are five apples left on the tree after Bill picked two. How many were on the tree (originally) before Bill picked some?
Subtraction Types	
1. Remainder	There were five apples on the tree. Bill picked one. How many are there now? (neutral question) How many are left? (cued question)
2. Negation	There are four pieces of fruit on the tree. Three are apples. How many are not apples?
3. Comparative	I have two baskets of strawberries. This basket has five strawberries. That basket has three strawberries. How many more does this have than that? How many less does this have than that? Which has more? How many more do I have to put in this basket so it will have as much as that basket has?
	I have six pieces of fruit (e.g., apples and bananas mixed) in this basket and four pieces of fruit in this basket. How many more do I have in basket 1 than in basket 2? How many more/fewer in basket 2? How many more apples in basket 1 than in basket 2? How many more apples in basket 2 than there are pieces of fruit in basket 1?
4. Indirect	I have five apples. I picked three from this tree and the rest from this tree. How many did I pick from the second tree?
Multiplication Types	
1. Equal units addition	I have three trees. Each of them has three oranges on it. How many oranges do I have?
2. Cartesian	John has three Hawaiian shirts and five pairs of pants each of a different color. How many outfits can John have?
3. Array/matrix	There were six chairs in each of three rows. How many chairs are there?

(continued)

FIGURE 12.3   continued

Operations	Sample Problems
Division Types	
1. Partitioning	Tim has 15 bananas. He wants to put an equal number of bananas in each basket. How many will be put in each basket?
2. Measurement	Bill has 15 bananas. He wants to put 5 bananas in each basket. How many baskets does he need?
3. Matrix/array	There are 48 chairs to be placed in the auditorium in eight rows. How many chairs will be placed per row?

Reprinted from Teaching the Educable Mentally Retarded by R. A. Sedlak and D. M. Sedlak by permission of the State University of New York Press (Albany, 1985).

Category	Objects
tools	pliers, hammer, saw, screwdriver
fruit	apple, banana, pear, orange
clothes	shirt, dress, pants, shoes
furniture	chair, table, desk, couch
drinks	coffee, iced tea, soda, milk

Smith and Lovitt (1975) have demonstrated that modeling (showing or telling the learner how to solve a given problem type) is a successful strategy with learning disabled children in the initial acquisition stage of learning computation problems. With the modeling procedure, the teacher computes the solution to a sample problem on a learner's worksheet and verbalizes all of the steps in the process. The learner then responds to 25 similar problems on the sheet, being permitted to refer back to the sample problem. This strategy has proved successful, as judged by both maintenance data and follow-up data gathered after the model problem was removed.

○ 5   Lovitt and Curtiss (1968) used verbal mediation as the strategy to improve a learner's correct response rates for problems of the type _____ $- 3 = 6$. For the intervention, the learner is required to verbalize each problem and its answer before writing the answer. For example, the student can say, "What number minus (or take away) three equals six?" Several verbalizations may be necessary before the correct response is given. Action Plan 12.2 provides a general sequence of activities that could be used to teach different types of division.

ACTION PLAN 12.2 TEACHING THREE TYPES OF DIVISION

We recommend the following procedures for teaching division:

1. Explain that there are three types of division; they sound different, but they are computationally the same.
2. Use manipulatives and pictures to illustrate each type of division.
3. Have the learner create problems of each type using the manipulatives.
4. Change the materials and create more problems; have the learner do likewise.
5. Introduce number sentences *after* the concepts are established.

Solving Word Problems

■ 8 Just as comprehension is considered the ultimate outcome of reading instruction, the development of problem-solving skills is considered the ultimate outcome of a mathematics program. Computation is generally incidental to problem solving; the type of information processing required in any problem situation is of far greater importance. Sifting out from a set of information those bits that are needed in a given situation is a necessary skill. Much of the literature in verbal problem solving suggests that students do not always apply that skill. To recognize that some of the information is irrelevant to the question being posed is one skill; to recognize that not enough information is provided to answer a question is yet another essential skill. Both of these recognition skills must be developed.

Problem-solving activities should focus on relevant situations. Some limited research has indicated that having students find solutions to real classroom and home problems—rather than solving simulated problems—is highly effective in developing their recognition skills (Lydra & Church, 1964). Problem solving, especially at the secondary level, should cover a wide range of topics and problem types. To this end, problems and topics such as estimating the cost of a date, planning a budget, or comparison shopping for clothes or food can be used with the secondary-age handicapped learners. The areas addressed by Sharma (1984) at the beginning of this chapter are another source of ideas for problems.

Goodstein (1981) has analyzed the process to be followed in solving word problems. In general, it is a four-step process for the learner:

1. Identify the required arithmetic operation.
2. Identify the relevant sets of information.
3. Appropriately and accurately display the computation. (This step is often unnecessary for simple computations; it would be replaced by "Accurately enter the computational factors" if a calculator were being used.)
4. Accurately compute the answer. (This step would automatically follow successful completion of Steps 1–3 if a calculator were being used.)

A teacher who is following an error analysis model would have to be aware of the step at which an error was made and then take appropriate corrective action.

Parameters Of Word Problems

Many factors enter into the process of determining the difficulty level of a word problem. For a teacher to approach the process of instruction in word problems, therefore, he or she must be familiar with some of the more salient parameters and how they influence performance. Goodstein (1981) has identified the following parameters from the research literature:

1. Vocabulary difficulty
2. Presence of cue words
3. Syntactic complexity
4. Presence of extraneous information
5. Superordinate and subordinate set language

VOCABULARY DIFFICULTY   Vocabulary can be a variable that affects the performance of learners in solving word problems. However, research has found that EMR youngsters can solve problems they cannot read (Devard, 1972)—even problems composed of nonsense words (Bessant, 1972). Students who are successful in solving problems despite the vocabulary are apparently using other cues to arrive at the solution. If this is the case, they are using strategies that will be successful some of the time but not all of the time. Such habits are hard to break and difficult to spot unless a teacher is looking for possible problems. The teacher can avoid this pitfall by checking periodically to see that students can actually read the problems.

○ **6**   PRESENCE OF CUE WORDS   One common strategy students adopt is to use cue words to determine the operation in a problem. Students will look for a word such as *left, altogether, added, divided, times,* and *more* and then follow the operation that is commonly associated with the word. In most cases, this strategy works; but it does not work when the task is an indirect problem, such as the following:

A boy had four apples left after he had given three away. How many did he start with?

Students who follow a cue word strategy are not actually processing the information, and they should be discouraged from using this strategy. Repeated examples of indirect problems help students realize why the strategy is not efficacious.

SYNTACTIC COMPLEXITY The complexity of the wording of a problem definitely affects the students' performance. When the question portion of a problem is written as a complex interrogative sentence, the performance of learning disabled students is severely impaired (Larsen, Parker, & Trenholme, 1978). Cawley (personal communication, 1985) has provided an example of the role of syntax in the construction and solution of word problems. This example further illustrates the processing component of problem solving, in which the student is required to organize information in different ways. The example was stated in a complex sentence in which a relative clause modifies an object. Students were to respond to a series of questions (statements) by "true," "false," or "unable to tell."

Situation
The three cars hit the tree which the men were cutting; another two cars hit a pole which the men were fixing.

Questions
1. The men were cutting the tree that was hit.
2. The men were cutting the cars.
3. More cars hit the tree than hit the pole.
4. There were five smashed cars.
5. The men were fixing five poles.

CASE FOR ACTION 12.1

A student can usually solve direct addition and subtraction word problems, but he generally does not solve indirect problems correctly. His third-grade teacher had told him to look for the clue words in a problem and to use those words to decide what operation to use. He is still following this strategy 4 years later. What would you do to break this habit? Would you use neutral questions as part of your strategy?

■ 9   PRESENCE OF EXTRANEOUS INFORMATION   Extraneous information is probably one of the major components of word problems that affects their difficulty. The strategy used by most students with such problems is to sum all of the numbers. The following is an example of a problem with extraneous information:

> Three apples are in the first basket. Four pears are in the second basket. Five apples are in the third basket. How many apples are in the baskets?

The response often given by mildly handicapped students is 12. This strategy of adding all the numbers is referred to as a *rote computational habit*.

One factor in a learner's recognition of extraneous information is the proximity of the irrelevant information to the numbers in the problems. If the extraneous information is located in the (grammatical) object of the sentence structure, the problems are more difficult than if the extraneous information is in the subject of the sentence structure.

SUPERORDINATE AND SUBORDINATE SET LANGUAGE   The use of superordinate and subordinate set language is illustrated by the following problem:

> Four boys are on the playground. Three girls are on the playground. How many children are on the playground?

The use of the word *children* in the question statement is a superordinate set reference to "boys" and "girls." This particular problem would not affect the performance of most learners, largely because it does not contain extraneous information. When extraneous information is added to such a problem, the result is a tremendous increase in problem difficulty.

CASE FOR ACTION 12.2

> A student can solve problems that do not contain extraneous information, but as soon as a problem contains too much information, she becomes lost. She has recently been encountering problems with insufficient information, but she can't figure out what is needed. Could you create problems of each type for this student and suggest some strategies for correcting her problem?

Instructional Strategies In Teaching Word Problems

Thibodeau (1974) has observed that rote computational habits and rigid problem-solving strategies are easier to correct in their earlier stages than in their later stages. The use of pictures and manipulatives has been found an effective means to prevent the development of such negative strategies or to break such habits when they have been developed (Goodstein, Bessant, Thibodeau, Vitello, & Vlahakos, 1972; Helfgott & Voris, 1972; Schenck, 1973).

○ **7**   The materials and approach used in the verbal problem-solving component of Project Math (Cawley et al., 1976, 1977) rely heavily on pictures and manipulatives in the development of the problem-solving skills. Mats that depict a scene or subject of one of the statements of a problem are used in conjunction with small (2″ by 2″) object cards, such as those depicted in figure 12.4. The teacher and learners arrange and rearrange the cards as the problem evolves. These aids help the learners focus attention on the critical attributes of the problems-solving task, not solely on the numbers.

Fafard (1976) and Cohen and Stover (1981) have found that using direct instruction for problems that contain extraneous information alerts students to the presence of irrelevant information and helps the students break their rote computational habits within a relatively short period of time.

○ **8**   Blankenship and Lovitt (1976) were able to teach 12 different types of word problems by the following procedures: One of three levels of intervention was initiated if the learner failed to reach the criterion level of three consecutive 100% scores on three worksheets within 6 days. If the criterion was reached, the learner was given a different class of problems. The three levels of intervention were as follows:

> *Technique 1:* Orally read each incorrectly answered problem and state the correct answer.
> *Technique 2:* Write out each incorrectly answered problem and furnish the correct answer.
> *Technique 3:* Orally read each incorrectly answered problem, explain how the solution was arrived at, and provide the correct answer.

If the learner failed to reach the criterion within 6 days while Technique 1 was being implemented, Technique 2 was initiated. Technique 2 was also given a 6-day period for success before Technique 3 was initiated. If Technique 3 failed, the learner was recycled through Technique 1.

Action Plan 12.3 provides a set of procedures for teaching problem solving that is based upon the preceding set of information.

FIGURE 12.4   Sample Problem Mat Used in Project MATH

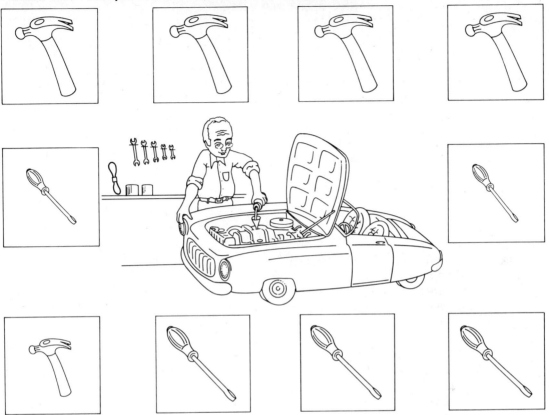

Note: This material is now in the public domain.

ACTION PLAN 12.3   TEACHING VERBAL PROBLEM SOLVING

We recommend the following procedures for instruction in problem solving:

1. Start teaching word problems in the primary grades.
2. Start with pictures and manipulatives to create the problems.
3. Focus on the process of solving a problem, not on the mechanics. (There is more than one correct approach for solving a problem.)
4. Keep both the language and the math simple initially; then gradually increase the complexity of the language, but keep the math aspect simple.
5. Create problems that contain insufficient information and problems that contain extraneous information.
6. Gradually withdraw the pictures and manipulatives.

Using Calculators

Shoppers in grocery stores use calculators to estimate food costs; college students use them to do basic (and advanced) mathematics and statistics; schoolteachers use them for balancing their checkbooks. In short, calculators are an accepted alternative to traditional computation in our society. Wrong answers are considered far more stigmatizing than reliance on a calculator for correct computation.

■ 10 ○ 9   Initial instruction in using a calculator should focus on the meaning and use of each symbol on the calculator. The second step in instruction in using a calculator is for the teacher and the students to realize that the process of computation on a calculator differs from the process followed in traditional computation. When performing traditional computation, the student generally performs work from right to left (e.g., adding ones, then tens, then hundreds); with a calculator, these intermediate steps are done by machine. Therefore, the process of calculator usage must be taught differently from traditional computational skills. Students do need to be *taught* to use calculators; untrained students will try to use them to do problems in the conventional manner, following all of the intermediate steps. We therefore recommend a task analysis approach for assessing and instructing in calculator usage.

To perform a task analysis for assessment purposes, the teacher gives each student a calculator and a problem and tells him or her to solve the problem. The teacher observes the student at work and puts a plus or minus sign next to each step of the task analysis to indicate a correct or incorrect response. Each step of the task analysis is written as an observable behavior. Action Plan 12.4 provides two task analyses for using a calculator. The procedure thus can pinpoint the step at which a problem occurs. In some cases, a step in a task analysis may have to be broken down into smaller segments—especially if a student has difficulty within the step. In all cases, the

ACTION PLAN 12.4   TASK ANALYSIS OF CALCULATOR USAGE

Problem

$$\begin{array}{r} 45 \\ + 38 \end{array}$$

Task Analysis
1. Clear calculator by pressing C.
2. Press key for numeral in tens place (4).
3. Press key for numeral in units place (5).
4. Press + .
5. Press key for numeral in tens place (3).
6. Press key for numeral in units place (8).
7. Press = .
8. Write or state numeral on display (83).

Problem

$$\begin{array}{r} \$4.53 \\ + \quad .62 \end{array}$$

Task Analysis
1. Clear calculator by pressing C.
2. Press key for numeral in dollar position (4).
3. Press . (decimal point).
4. Press key for numeral in tens place (5).
5. Press key for numeral in cents place (3).
6. Press + .
7. Press . (decimal point).
8. Press key for numeral in tens place (6).
9. Press key for numeral in cents place (2).
10. Press = .
11. Write or state numeral on display (5.15).

steps in a task analysis should be observable behaviors. *Caution:* When students are taught to use calculators, the skills of estimation and rounding must also be taught so that calculator usage does not become a rote process. If the calculator is used in the elementary grades, it is recommended that students use it only to check their work, not as the first step in solving computation problems.

Money

○ **10**   Making change and counting money are necessary and functional skills in society. These skills should be taught and practiced with real money, not as a paper-and-pencil exercise; that is, the students should actually handle bills and coins. Being able to count by 1, 5, 10, 25, and 50 is a major prerequisite for making change. Another prerequisite is knowledge of coinage equivalencies (e.g., 5 pennies = 1 nickel, 5 nickels = 1 quarter). As with calculator usage, the process of counting money or making change can be assessed using a task analysis format.

Time

Digital watches and clocks have changed the way students learn to tell time and the way they write time notation. With traditional timepieces, students "translated" the position of the clock hands into time notation. There was also a tendency to use such phrasings as "a quarter after," "a quarter to," and "half past the hour" in telling time, since the segments of the clock were perceived as a pie graph. With digital clocks, there is a greater tendency to state the time according to hours and minutes—for example, 4:15, 4:45. Digital clocks thus eliminate the translation step in writing time notation. It probably is still necessary for secondary students to be able to use and understand the traditional language of telling time, but digital timepieces present an alternative.

CASE FOR ACTION 12.3

A 16-year-old student has had a traditional mathematics program until now. He can add, subtract, and multiply, but his long division is poor. He can do word problems occasionally, but he has had little experience with them because the focus of his program has been on the four basic operations. What are some suggested IEP goals for this student in mathematics?

SUMMARY

Teaching mathematics to older handicapped learners is partly an exercise in correcting poor earlier instruction. For younger handicapped learners, the teacher's primary task is to get the students off to the right start. Mathematics is a very concrete subject area; almost all of mathematical concepts can be demonstrated with physical materials. It is important that the teacher not spend a large amount of the available time for math instruction assigning seatwork activities in which the learner works alone; rather, the teacher should spend the time actively engaging the learner in the study of mathematics and all of its applied features. The single most important contributing variable to student achievement is instructional time. The more time the teacher spends in the art of teaching mathematics, the higher the expected level of student performance should be. Teachers should not fear deviating from textbook sequences or exercises in favor of more functional and relevant materials and examples.

13

Vocational Skills Training

■ DID YOU KNOW THAT...

■ **1** ...career and vocational development experiences increase the employment potential of handicapped students?

■ **2** ...vocational evaluation should occur before, during, and after instruction?

■ **3** ...vocational interest inventories do not measure a student's aptitude?

■ **4** ...the response requirements of a vocational aptitude inventory may prevent a handicapped student from demonstrating his or her actual abilities?

■ **5** ...the results of a vocational aptitude test are a function of the learner's previous exposure and motivation, the test's response requirements, and the specific work demands?

■ **6** ...vocational goals and objectives should be included at all grade levels?

■ **7** ...instruction in basic skills should become more vocationally oriented as a student approaches graduation?

○ CAN YOU...

○ **1**   . . . use vocational evaluation data to assess a student's vocational aptitude, interests, progress toward objectives, and attainment of goals?

○ **2**   . . . select an interest inventory that would be appropriate for mildly handicapped populations?

○ **3**   . . . select an aptitude inventory that assesses a student's vocational potential?

○ **4**   . . . identify appropriate vocational goals at various grade levels?

○ **5**   . . . integrate basic skills math or reading curricula with vocational competencies?

○ **6**   . . . develop curricular sequences to teach social, personal, and motor skills in a vocational context?

In what may be the most comprehensive review to date, McAfee and Mann (1982) have identified prognoses for mildly handicapped students across a number of functional dimensions. With reference to career outcomes, they have drawn the following conclusions:

1. The employment rates of mildly handicapped persons leaving secondary schools range from 30% to 92%.
2. A majority of handicapped people are likely to change jobs more than three times in the 2-year period following graduation.
3. Interpersonal problems are the most common cause for dismissals.
4. The longer handicapped young adults are in the work force, the more likely it is that they will obtain stable employment.
5. A small percentage of handicapped youths enter skilled occupations upon leaving school.
6. When a handicapped young adult has been in the work force for a period of time, the probability of obtaining a skilled position increases.
7. Employed handicapped workers are generally satisfied with their jobs; the major source of dissatisfaction is the lack of opportunity for advancement.
8. The modal earning level of handicapped workers is estimated at only slightly more than minimum wage.

It should be emphasized that the majority of the data in this review were collected from young adults who had graduated from high school before or shortly after full implementation of the Education for All Handicapped Children Act (PL 94-142) in 1975. Therefore, one cannot be certain that the data present accurate prognoses for today's youth. However, recent comments by Madeline Will (1984), Assistant Secretary of Special Education and Rehabilitation Services, are not optimistic:

> Youth with disabilities face an uncertain future when they leave the nation's public schools. Qualification for employment is an implied promise of American education, but between 50 and 80 percent of working age adults who report a disability are jobless (U.S. Commission on Civil Rights, 1983; U.S. Bureau of the Census, 1982). Without employment, many individuals turn to community services only to find long waiting lists. Those adults with disabilities who do gain entry into publicly-supported day and vocational services often experience low wages, slow movement to employment and segregation from their nondisabled peers (U.S. Department of Labor, 1979). (p. 2)

■ 1   Despite this pessimistic view, career and vocational development activities may enhance handicapped students' transition into community life. For example, in a follow-up study of 160 mentally retarded, learning disabled, and emotionally disturbed vocational school students, Parker et al. (1976) reported an employment rate of 80%. Similarly, Redding (1979) reported that 70% of the mildly handicapped graduates of a work-study program were employed shortly after graduation. On a more optimistic note, Titus and Travis (1973) reported that over 95% of the graduates of a comprehensive vocational education program were employed within 3 years of graduation.

It is uncertain whether these relatively high employment rates are attributable to the youths' educational experiences or to other factors. It is reasonable to assume, however, that vocational preparation may be responsible for at least a portion of their vocational success. The ability of students to appraise their own vocational interests and aptitudes, to identify and apply for compatible positions, and to meet employer expectations on the job may be a primary determinant of their economic independence.

Therefore, this chapter describes methods for (1) assessing vocational interests, aptitudes, and achievement; (2) selecting vocational goals and objectives; (3) promoting students' career awareness; and (4) teaching general and specific vocational skills.

VOCATIONAL EVALUATION

■ 2 ○ 1 Vocational evaluation is not a single, discrete activity that occurs at specific intervals during the school year. Rather, it is an ongoing process that results in continual accumulation of information. Information obtained through the vocational evaluation process may be described as *preinstructional* when it comes from the evaluation of vocational aptitudes and interests, *instructional* when it derives from the formative evaluation of progress toward short-term objectives, and *postinstructional* when it is part of the summative evaluation of vocational goal attainment and potential for competitive work success. Figure 13.1 illustrates the relationship of these assessment procedures to the vocational instructional program.

FIGURE 13.1 Sequence of Vocational Evaluation Activities Throughout the Instructional Program

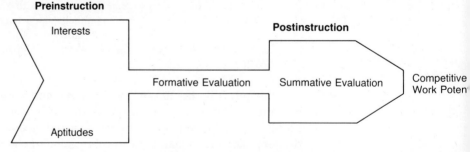

Vocational Interests

○ **2**   It has long been assumed that placing students in high-interest career tracks will enhance their potential for vocational success. Working within these career clusters is expected to be intrinsically motivating for the learner. Also, educational activities that are aligned with a high-interest career are considered likely to pay off when the student actually enters the career upon graduation.

Unfortunately, the most popular interest inventories, including the Strong-Campbell Interest Inventory (SCII) and the Kuder Occupational Interest Inventory are minimally useful for mildly handicapped populations. These inventories require reasonably well-developed vocabulary and reading abilities (e.g., sixth grade or higher). In addition, they assume that the respondent has a fairly rich experiential background. Consequently, they are poorly matched to the psychoeducational features of many mildly handicapped youngsters.

Several other interest inventories have been developed that require little or no reading ability. The AAMD-Becker Reading-Free Vocational Interest Inventory, for example, requires that respondents circle enjoyable pictured activities. These activities are keyed to 11 occupational areas for men and women alike—ranging from automotive to materials handling and including laundry service through housekeeping. Another pictorial inventory, the Wide Range Interest Opinion Test (WRIOT) is structured in a similar manner. In this inventory, however, students are presented with triads of pictures arranged in various combinations. Separate occupational interest and vocational aptitude scores are obtained from the pattern of high-preference pictures selected from each triad. Appendix 13A (at the end of this chapter) presents the major features of these and other vocational interest inventories.

■ **3**   These inventories are intended to evaluate the aspirations and interests of students. They do not, however, purport to determine the viability of those interests. A student may be highly motivated to be a civil engineer but lack basic and advanced math skills. Similarly, a youth may desire to be a truck driver even though a physical impairment would virtually eliminate any potential for hin to load, unload, and maneuver a large truck. To obtain a more balanced view of a student's preinstructional features, it is important to evaluate aptitudes as well as interests.

Vocational Aptitudes

Aptitude tests are used to determine the extent to which a student is likely to succeed in a future activity. Thus, vocational aptitude tests are designed to predict future performance in various careers. A high aptitude score in a building trades occupation, for example, suggests that the student has the ability to learn the skills necessary to succeed as a carpenter, electrician, plumber, and so on.

The major goal of vocational education is to improve the student's ability to succeed in the workplace. To meet this goal, it is important to recognize the student's vocational potential. Preparing a highly capable youth for an unskilled position can be as detrimental as attempting to prepare a learner for a career in which he or she has little chance to be successful. Ideally, a student should be prepared to enter a high-interest career for which he or she has a reasonable aptitude for success.

■ 4 ○ 3   Several tests have been developed to appraise vocational aptitudes. Unfortunately, since no special-needs individuals were included in the standardization samples for these instruments, their validity for use with handicapped populations may be questioned. As with the interest inventories, because of the reading and written response requirements of some of the tests, handicapped students' scores may not reflect their actual performance aptitude (i.e., students' reading and writing deficiencies may limit their ability to demonstrate their vocational abilities). Even when actual performance items are used, there is some question of whether a student's behavior under standardized assessment conditions accurately reflects actual work performance. Finally, aptitude tests use current behavior to predict future behavior, so instruction or other environmental variables that occur after the initial assessment may invalidate the prediction. For example, although a test may reveal that a student has little mechanical aptitude, the student's aptitude may change after he or she takes an extensive course in automative re-

ACTION PLAN 13.1   INTERPRETING VOCATIONAL APTITUDE TESTS

We recommend that the teacher consider the following factors when interpreting the results of a vocational aptitude test:

1. Has the student previously been exposed to the tasks presented in the test?
2. Is the student motivated to perform well on the test?
3. Does the student possess necessary test-taking behaviors (e.g., reading and writing)?
4. Does the test format, as well as the desired student response, accurately reflect work demands in the actual vocational setting?
5. Are the results corroborated by informal data about the student's basic skills and learning characteristics?

CASE FOR ACTION 13.1

On the basis of a standardized vocational aptitude test, the school's career counselor suggests that a student in your class would not be able to succeed as an electrician. You are aware that the youth has worked for the last two summers as an "apprentice" to an electrician. The person he has worked for speaks very highly of his competence and believes that it might be an attainable career for the youth. What questions might you ask the career counselor to test the validity of his conclusions? How might you collect more information to support or refute his findings?

pair. Thus, it would have been inaccurate to advise, on the basis of the initial test, that the student not enter a mechanical trade.

■ 5   Because of these limitations, vocational aptitude test results should be viewed cautiously. Action Plan 13.1 suggests factors teachers should consider before drawing conclusions on the basis of a student's performance on these tests. Appendix 13B describes several of the commonly used vocational aptitude tests.

SELECTING VOCATIONAL GOALS AND OBJECTIVES

■ 6 ○ 4   Goals and objectives leading to vocational competence should be developed throughout the school program. Vocationally oriented goals may be developed from preschool to postsecondary levels within both academic and technical curricular areas. A major criterion for selecting goals throughout this span is the extent to which they will enhance the learner's entry into less restrictive settings. The final, least restrictive environments for which special education programs typically prepare handicapped learners are community-based leisure, living, consumer, and vocational settings. Consequently, the skills and abilities necessary for a person to be gainfully employed are a constant focus of all educational programs. Several authors, including Brolin (1976), Miller and Schloss (1982), Phelps and Lutz (1977), Schloss (1984), and Weisgerber, Dahl, and Appleby (1980) recommend that training settings fall on a continuum from classroom to industry environments. In addition, the instructional strategies employed in each setting should approximate the actual practices used in business and industry. The position taken in this book is that as a student progresses through school, his or her educational experiences should become successive approximations of the applied-skill/community-based end of the continuum. In the student's early school years, basic academic skills that are needed in vocational settings should be developed through regular classroom activities. Later, school-based simulations of vocational settings should be used to develop specific vocational competencies. Training may then occur at work stations in business and industry. Finally, the student may compete in business and industry under the regular supervision of an employer. The components of this sequence will be discussed in subsequent sections.

Basic Skills Training in School

Academic Skills

■ 7 ○ 5   Though often overlooked, academic skills, including written and spoken expression, math numeration and computation, and reading, are basic to the development of vocational competence. In the primary grades, these basic skills are developed outside a vocational context. Math problems are typically presented through workbook and worksheet exercises that have little relevance to vocational or other functional contexts. Reading activities are typically presented through basal reading series—again, with little reference to community events. Of course, teachers can construct materials that are vocationally oriented.

As students reach the intermediate grades, high-interest and low-vocabulary materials should begin to focus on vocational themes. Math problems should become more applied, reflecting the academic skill demands of business and industry. Finally, in the secondary grades, reading activities should be directed at repair manuals, work shedules, menus, directories, letters, and other work-related materials. Similarly, math problems should have specific vocational contexts. For example, students should be required to weigh, measure, and count materials and to compute expenses, profits, interest rates, and so on.

Social Skills

○ 6   As is emphasized in chapter 14, social skills may be the most important predictor of work success. Consequently, they are essential basic vocational skills. As with basic academic skills, they may be developed in the primary grades without direct reference to vocational contexts. Skills in using social amenities, communicating basic needs, negotiating when disagreements occur, and responding to criticism all can be enhanced in the early school years. Later, these abilities may be applied to vocational demands through behavior rehearsal and role-play activities. Finally, at the secondary level, actual work placements should provide opportunities for guided practice of interpersonal skills on the job.

Personal Skills

Personal care skills—including grooming, dress, and hygiene—result from training both at school and at home. These skills are also crucial to vocational success, particularly in consumer and service-related positions. Again, personal care skills should be developed early in life. At the preschool and elementary level, students should learn to put on their clothing, manipulate fasteners, and store clothing on hooks. They should also begin to brush their teeth, wash their hands and faces, and select nutritious food. In intermediate grades, students should begin to select clothing, prepare basic foods, and wash and bathe independently. Finally, at the secondary level, students should become able to plan and prepare entire meals, launder, press, and store clothing, and the like.

Motor Skills

As with the foregoing basic skills, motor performance becomes increasingly refined with age. Strength, speed, dexterity, coordination, and balance underlie the most basic vocational behaviors, such as locomotion and posture. They also contribute to highly developed vocational competencies, such as completing small parts assemblies, handling large materials, or using tools.

A number of activities can be included in the elementary and intermediate curriculum to strengthen fine and gross motor skills. For example, students may use crayons, pencils, puzzles, building blocks, beads, or paint brushes to develop their fine motor skills. Playground apparatus, gym equipment, basic calisthenics, and team sports may be used to develop gross motor skills. At the secondary level, motor skill development turns more directly to vocational competencies. For example, students may learn to use specific tools, such as hammers, nails, clamps, wrenches, and screw drivers. They may learn to operate typewriter keyboards, data processors, calculators, cash registers, and word processors. Finally, they may learn to manipulate large objects, using hand trucks, dollies, jacks, winches, and other devices.

Action Plan 13.2 summarizes the integration of vocational objectives with the general curriculum.

Specific Goal Selection

Rusch, Schutz, Mithang, Stewart, and Mar (1982) have developed an empirically based assessment and curriculum guide for mildly handicapped learners. His instrument, the Vocational Assessment and Curriculum Guide (VACG), was produced from surveys of employers in light industry, food service, janitorial service, and maid service occupations. The four primary functions of the VACG, as cited by Rusch et al. (1982), are as follows

ACTION PLAN 13.2   INTEGRATION OF VOCATIONAL OBJECTIVES WITH THE GENERAL CURRICULUM

Integrated objectives include the following areas:

Academic
Academic objectives involve the basic expressive, receptive, and quantitative skills needed to succeed on a majority of jobs, including reading orders, reading technical manuals, writing invoices, writing employment applications, computing fees, and determining profits.

Social
Social objectives involve the interpersonal skills necessary for establishing and maintaining supportive relationships in the workplace, including interactions with employers, co-workers, customers, and representatives of other businesses.

Personal
Personal objectives involve health care, grooming, hygiene, and dress skills that are conducive to success on a job. Selecting and wearing appropriate clothing, bathing, using deodorant, brushing teeth, maintaining a nutritious diet, and the like, are related objectives.

Motor
Motor objectives include the development of the strength, speed, quickness, dexterity, coordination, and balance necessary to meet the physical requirements of a job.

1. To assess and identify the vocational training needs of handicapped persons.
2. To analyze behavior and skill deficits in terms of competitive employment expectations.
3. To prescribe training goals designed to reduce identified deficits, and
4. To evaluate student/worker performance by administering the instrument at the beginning of training in order to define appropriate goal areas and then to periodically assess progress toward identified goals by reassessing the student/worker after he/she has been trained. (p. 1)

The VACG includes eight performance categories: attendance/endurance, independence, production, learning, behavior, communication skills, social skills, and grooming/eating. Questions within each category reflect the priorities identified by the surveyed employers.

Student data are interpreted as falling at or below employer expectations. Items scored below employer expectations are suggested to be included as objectives in the student's IEP. To facilitate this process, the VACG includes objectives that are matched to each of the scale items. For example, objectives that correspond to the production items include the ability to work alone and increase productivity on own and the ability to complete repetitive tasks previously learned to a proficiency within 25–50% of industry standards. Objectives corresponding to the attendance/endurance performance category include the ability to decrease the number of absences to one per month, to increase work participation to 5–6 hours per day, and to increase continuous work to 1–2 periods.

This assessment and curriculum model is highly consistent with the curriculum approach described in chapter 2 in that it focuses on behaviors necessary for successful functioning in a postsecondary school job setting. We recommend that teachers go beyond the VACG objectives when the goal is training for a specific job. When specific job training is the intended outcome, a detailed job analysis must be conducted, including observing regular employees engaged in the work and developing skill sequences. More details on conducting job analyses as part of a training program will be described later in this chapter.

CAREER INFORMATION AND EXPLORATION

As the preceding section emphasized, the development of basic vocational skills is a process that begins in the early grades and may or may not be referenced to a specific occupation. Similarly, the development of career knowledge is a lifelong process that may be general or specific in nature. Experiences that enhance one's general understanding of the world of work occur throughout one's life. Television series that focus on characters in various occupations (e.g., emergency medical technicians, truck drivers, car drivers, salespersons, etc.) may be an early source of general career information. More specific career information may also be obtained early in life by listening to relatives and parents discussing their own jobs.

Unfortunately, handicapped students are less likely to obtain accurate career information as an incidental part of watching television or talking to relatives. They may be unable to sort out facts from fiction in television shows, and they may be overly susceptible to sex-role stereotypes and glamorized career images in many serials. Therefore, it is especially important that special educators make a direct effort to enhance students' knowledge of available careers. Methods particularly appropriate for this effort are discussed in the following paragraphs.

Field Trips

Class visits to businesses and industries may be a valuable source of career information. In preparation, students may be asked to research the target occupations, using encyclopedia, newspaper and magazine articles. This research may help students focus the questions to be asked during the visits. Action Plan 13.3 suggests procedures for conducting field trips. Note the emphasis on student involvement in planning the trip.

Guest Speakers

Students may select and invite representatives of various businesses and industries to address the class. These guests may be asked to bring tools, apparel, or products associated with their jobs. When appropriate, guest speakers may demonstrate actual work tasks for the class. For example, a barber may give a haircut, a policeman may take fingerprints, or a cook may prepare a salad. As with the field trip procedures, students may study

ACTION PLAN 13.3   CONDUCTING FIELD TRIPS

We recommend the following steps when arranging a field trip:

1. Determine the students' general vocational interests.
2. Survey the community to identify businesses and industries that are compatible with those interests.
3. Appoint student committees to arrange individual field trips. These committees may be responsible for contacting representatives of the business or industry, establishing a time for the visit, arranging transportation, sending a follow-up letter to the business or industry representative to confirm the arrangements, and sending a thank-you letter.
4. Prior to the trip, have students use the library to obtain basic information about the business or industry and its products.
5. Based on the students' library research, ask them to prepare several questions to have answered during the field trip.
6. After the field trip, use the prepared questions as a basis for discussion about the business or industry.

in advance the business or industry that the guest speaker represents and use their research to generate discussion questions.

Information Center

Students may work together to develop a center that provides information on various occupations. Depending on the students' reading abilities, literature may be obtained from business magazines, from the business section of the newspaper, and from trade publications. In addition, students may write to companies for brochures on career opportunities. Major utilities, food service chains, and other corporations generally have well-developed personnel departments that can provide useful materials for the career information center.

Perhaps the most comprehensive item in a students' career information center is the *Dictionary of Occupational Titles* (U.S. Department of Labor, U.S. Employment Service, 1965), known as the DOT. The DOT is a two-volume taxonomy of the American job market. For a given job, the DOT describes required general education levels and specific vocational preparation, aptitudes, interests, temperaments, physical demands, working conditions, and relationships among the job and people, data, and things. Entries in the DOT are cross-referenced with other jobs with similar elements. Action Plan 13.4 lists items that may be included in a career information center.

Community Job Survey

The students and the teacher may work together to conduct a survey of local jobs. First, they should develop a survey instrument for determining the characteristics of jobs in the community. The entries in this instrument may parallel entries in the DOT or reflect the class's particular concerns.

ACTION PLAN 13.4 ITEMS TO INCLUDE IN A CAREER INFORMATION CENTER

We recommend that the following items be included in a career information center:

1. Magazine and newspaper articles
2. Photocopies of encyclopedia articles
3. The *Dictionary of Occupational Titles*
4. Literature from specific businesses and industries
5. Photographs and reports obtained through field trips and guest speakers

For example, the sample survey instrument in figure 13.2 assesses a business's requirements for general education levels, specific training, aptitudes, interests, physical demands, and working conditions. Such job surveys are best administered through interviews between students and employers, either over the phone or in person. In either case, it is probably best for the teacher to prearrange the interviews. Data resulting from the surveys may be filed in the career information center. Individual students who collect the data may also deliver oral reports to other students.

Job Tryouts

Probably the most valid and complete source of information about a career is obtained through an actual job tryout. A tryout involves actually working on a job long enough to determine its advantages and disadvantages. For many students, a job tryout is the acid test. Other sources of career informa-

FIGURE 13.2   Student Survey of Community Employment Opportunities

Name of Business/Industry: _____

Name of Contact Person: _____

Address of Business: _____

_____

_____

Positions Available	General Education Level Required	Specific Training Required	Special Skills Needed	Likes and Dislikes Related to the Job	Strength and Endurance Required	Working Conditions

CASE FOR ACTION 13.2

A student in your learning disabilities resource room seems to have extremely unrealistic career interests. The youth would like to be a county agricultural agent, but you know that such a position requires reasonably well developed reading, math, and social skills. Further, it typically requires a college degree in agriculture. Although the youth's math skills are at grade level, his reading achievement is below third-grade level. Moreover, he is extremely introverted and would find it extremely difficult to meet and talk with the number of people encountered by an agricultural agent. Finally, talking in front of small groups of people, as frequently required of an agent, would be very threatening for the youth.

You suspect that if the youth knew more about the professional responsibilities of an agricultural agent, he would opt for a more suitable career. How would you guide this student in establishing a career choice that is better matched to his abilities?

tion may make a job sound extremely challenging and exciting, whereas once the student is on the job, he or she may learn that the challenge and excitement are often interspersed with periods of boredom.

INSTRUCTIONAL STRATEGIES

This section describes instructional strategies for four aspects of vocational programming. These strategies are supported by empirical evidence and therefore can be used with some confidence by the practicing teacher. The areas addressed are job analysis, job seeking, work station simulations, and work stations in business and industry.

Job Setting Analysis and Training

An eight-step model defines the stages of constructing a program for specific job training:

1. Identify current or future work environments.
2. Observe others on the job.
3. Develop a skills checklist.
4. Pretest.
5. Prescribe prosthetics or modifications.
6. Delineate task sequences.
7. Conduct training.
8. Posttest (reassess).

To identify current or future work environments, career information and guidance programs should be used to assist the learner in identifying high-preference jobs. These programs may involve helping the learner match his or her interests and abilities to available jobs in the community. Work station simulations and tryouts may also be conducted to confirm the student's choice. Once potential jobs have been selected, the teacher (and the student, if appropriate) should observe successful workers in the specific job settings. It is best if these observations occur throughout the workday so that all facets of successful job performance, from preparing for work to departing from work, are studied. The teacher should then develop a skills checklist based on the actual competencies exhibited by the employee. This checklist may be comparable to the checklist included in the VACG. Also, the teacher and the student should discuss the entries on the checklist with the employer. At this time, the employer should target items on the checklist that are priorities for successful performance. Those that are less crucial may also be indicated.

The student should then be pretested, using the checklist. To this end, the teacher may arrange for a job tryout during which the checklist data can be collected from actual performance on the job. A more economical approach is to interview persons who have observed or supervised the student in a similar work setting. A final alternative is to use a work station simulation in the classroom.

Prescribing prosthetics or modifications may be a necessity for skills in the work sequence that the learner cannot perform. Prosthetics (e.g., pictorial cues, calculators, work station modifications) can help a learner perform some of the skills. Before establishing a final set of objectives, the teacher and others should determine essential skills to be developed through training and those to be dealt with through the use of compensatory aids. Clearly delineated task sequences must be written. Skill deficiencies that are not compensated by the use of prosthetics become the objectives of the vocational program. Skills that are developed to overcome these deficiencies should be written in objective form—stating the student's name, the conditions for performance, the skill to be acquired, and the criterion for success. These objectives should be organized in a logical sequence. For example, skills should be sequenced as first to last skill performed on the job, last to first performed on the job, easiest to most difficult, or most to least important for job success.

As the next step in the curriculum sequence, the teacher conducts training. As this book emphasizes, instruction should make use of concrete materials, multiple modalities, distributed drill and practice, and frequent feedback and reinforcement. We recommend that the most effective way to meet these guidelines for vocational competencies is to make use of work station simulations and work stations in business and industry. Work station experiences ensure that instruction focuses directly on the skills necessary for occupational success. Furthermore, the on-the-job materials, feedback, and incentives are likely to be more direct and more concrete than those used in classroom-based presentations, drills, and practice exercises.

The final activity in the vocational curriculum sequence is to reassess the student according to the original checklist. Posttest data may be contrasted with pretest data to determine the effectiveness of instruction.

Teaching Job-Seeking Skills

The career information activities described earlier should help handicapped learners align their interests with available jobs. Once potential positions have been identified, students may wish to apply for one or more of them. The two major components of the job application process are completing the application form and participating in an employment interview. A good deal hinges on the impression the handicapped learner initially makes on a personnel officer. The basic academic skills used in completing the application form and the interpersonal skills displayed during the interview may determine whether or not the youth is hired (R. M. Smith, 1968). Unfortunately, these are the areas in which many handicapped students are deficient (Jones, McCormick, & Heward, 1980).

Most training programs presented in the literature are consistent with the direct instruction procedures discussed in chapter 4. In one study, Clark, Boyd, and Macrae (1975) used modeling, feedback, and token reinforcement to teach mildly handicapped and disadvantaged youths to complete application forms. The training program enhanced the participants' abilities to provide their telephone number, date of birth, address, name, signature, reference name, reference occupation, and reference address.

In a related study, Hall, Sheldon-Wildgen, and Sherman (1980) taught application and interview skills to mentally retarded young adults. The skills included introducing oneself, filling out a standard application form, answering questions, and asking questions. The training program used instruction, modeling, role playing, feedback, and token reinforcement.

In another study, Kelly, Wildman, and Berler (1980) conducted a series of interview skill training sessions with mentally retarded adolescents. As in the preceding example, the trainers used instruction, modeling, and behavior rehearsal. The training was effective in enhancing the youths' abilities to disclose positive information about their experiences and background. It also helped the youths learn to convey interest in the position and

ACTION PLAN 13.5   TEACHING APPLICATION FORM COMPLETION

We recommend the following procedures for teaching students how to complete application forms:

1. Obtain from six to ten application forms that are good representations of those typically used in your community. Order them from most common to those found in the community to least common.
2. Quiz the students to determine whether they know the general information requested on the forms (e.g., birthdate, place of birth, social security number, address).
3. If necessary, have the students make a personal data card that contains information likely to be asked on an application form. This card can be carried in the student's wallet and used when applying for a job.
4. Demonstrate correct completion of one of the sample forms. Establish and emphasize criteria for legibility and completeness.
5. Ask the students to complete the same form using their own personal information.
6. Provide assistance, feedback, and reinforcement as necessary.
7. If the students do well, ask them to complete another form.
8. Again, provide support as needed. Demonstrate the completion of new items with which the students have difficulty. Reteach responses to items the students forget.
9. Continue to introduce new forms until it appears likely that the students are able to handle almost any form they might encounter in the workplace.

ACTION 13.6 TEACHING INTERVIEWING SKILLS

We recommend the following procedures for teaching students how to participate in an employment interview:

1. Develop a list of questions that are likely to be asked in an employment interview.
2. Discuss each question, and acceptable responses, with the students.
3. Identify and demonstrate appropriate interpersonal behaviors that should be used during an interview (e.g., smiling, using social amenities, shaking hands).
4. Use another teacher or an aide to "act out" an effective interview.
5. Ask students to comment on the quality of the applicant's answers to specific questions and on his or her interpersonal skills.
6. Ask each student to engage in a practice interview, with the teacher taking the employer's role.
7. Ask the other students to provide feedback.
8. Review or reteach as necessary.
9. Arrange for students to be interviewed by an actual employer.
10. Ask the employer to give the students feedback on their performance.

ask relevant questions about the position. Action Plans 13.5 and 13.6 summarize the procedures used in these studies.

To assist educators in teaching application form completion skills, Schloss, Schloss, and Misra (1985) conducted a comprehensive review of application forms encountered by handicapped youths. The authors identified the most frequently occurring words and questions on a sample of 200 applications obtained in several communities. Appendixes 13C and 13D present the questions and the words respectively. One can expect that students who are taught to identify these words and answer these questions will be able to respond effectively to most application forms.

The foregoing teaching activities are intended to prepare students for entry into the world of work. Programs that develop basic skills, career information, and job-seeking skills provide a foundation on which specific employment skills may be developed. The following sections discuss two strategies for developing specific vocational skills.

Work Station Simulation

One of the major obstacles to the vocational development of handicapped youths involves the transfer of training from academic to applied situations. Many handicapped youths readily learn the basic math, expressive and receptive language, and reading and writing skills necessary to compete in the work force. Unfortunately, these youths often have difficulty applying these skills to actual work situations. Therefore, school programs must bridge the gap between basic skills learned in the academic setting and actual work demands.

One of the more promising strategies for promoting the transfer of training is the use of work station simulations in the classroom. Work station simulations are centers in the classroom, shop, or other school facilities that contain a majority of the critical features of particular jobs. A simulated grocery checkout station, for example, might include a cash register, merchandise, a conveyor, bags, shopping carts, and a produce scale. A simulated small parts assembly station might include a work table, a swivel chair, parts bins, parts, and appropriate tools. A simulated clerical/receptionist station might be composed of a desk, a swivel chair, a typewriter, a multiple-line telephone, an intercom, and an appointment schedule.

Work station simulations may be highly complex or quite simple, depending on the nature of the actual job site. The expense of work stations may be well beyond the resources of the typical classroom budget, so the teacher may have to settle for developing the best simulation possible with available resources. For example, a "conveyer" may be a 36″ × 72″ conference table; merchandise may be empty boxes, and a multi-line telephone may be replaced by the single-line instructional phones available for use at many phone centers.

A valuable source of components for work station simulations may be the actual work site being copied. Many businesses and industries store surplus, obsolete, or damaged equipment, and they may make necessary items available to the school on loan or permanently. Although such equipment may not be identical to the equipment actually in use, it may be satisfactory for instructional purposes.

Once a work station simulation is developed, the teacher may follow the four-step instructional sequence discussed in chapter 4. First, the teacher *presents and demonstrates the new concepts or skills* necessary to perform in the work station. As emphasized earlier, the skills and concepts should be arranged in a logical sequence—often one that parallels the order in which the skills are performed on the actual job. Also, discrete cues, redundant explanations, and frequent questions that test the learner's comprehension may be used.

The second instructional phase in a work station simulation is *guided practice.* Guided practice should be organized around a hierarchy of prompts, ranging from least to most intrusive. As discussed in chapter 4, the teacher may provide 3 seconds for the student to self-initiate, then use a more intrusive prompt (an oral prompt). If the learner then fails to complete the task in 3 seconds, the teacher may use a more intrusive prompt (a modeling prompt). Finally, if the student is unable to demonstrate the skill in the 3 seconds following the modeling prompt, the teacher may use a physical prompt. This process may continue through each step in the task sequence. After a number of trials, the student may be able to self-initiate all steps in the task sequence. At that time, the next phase of instruction may begin.

In the third phase, *independent practice*, the student works at the station with minimal assistance. This phase should parallel the actual requirements of the job, so the teacher's involvement should resemble that of an employer or supervisor. The teacher may check the student's work periodically and provide encouragement or corrective feedback.

Once the student performs well under these conditions, instruction may enter the fourth phase, *reviewing/reteaching*. At this time, the student may leave the mastered work station and begin working at a new station. Then, at intervals throughout the week or month, the student may return to the initial work station to review and practice previously mastered skills. This procedure is intended to enhance the extent to which these skills are maintained.

Although the standard instructional sequence discussed in this book ends in reviewing/reteaching, a preferred conclusion to the sequence, when resources permit, is *a transfer to actual community settings.* The following section on work stations in business and industry considers this option.

Work Stations in Business and Industry

Classroom-based instruction, whether basic skills training or work station simulations, focuses on the skills necessary for effective participation in the community. Thus, the ultimate test of the effectiveness of this instruction is how well the learner actually performs in the community setting. The use of work stations in business and industry permits educators to apply this test.

Cooperative work experience programs are the major vehicle through which special education and vocational education personnel establish work stations in the community by entering into training agreements with employers. In such an agreement, the school guarantees (1) that the student will meet a minimum standard for social and occupational behavior, (2) that a portion of class time will address work-related competencies, (3) that school personnel will periodically visit the student on the job to troubleshoot performance problems and coordinate class activities, and (4) that the student's performance will be evaluated on a regular basis to ensure the continued value of the program in his or her vocational development. In return, the employer guarantees (1) that the student will be given a position comparable to those held by permanent employees, (2) that work condi-

FIGURE 13.3 Cooperative Training/Placement Agreement

This agreement has been initiated for the purpose of providing vocational training and placement for _____.

The teacher agrees to:
1. ensure that all assigned work is completed during the daily employment period (whether done by the staff or the student),
2. assume initial responsibility for training the student to perform assigned work to the employer's specifications and satisfaction,
3. ensure that minimum standards for social and personal behavior are met by the student,
4. remain on the job with the student until the employer agrees that less frequent assistance may be appropriate,
5. provide follow-up services as needed, once the student is able to perform the job independently.

The student agrees to:
1. arrive at and depart from the job at the scheduled time,
2. dress and groom properly for the job,
3. demonstrate positive social behaviors during work,
4. perform assigned work independently, following training.

The employer agrees to:
1. provide a minimum wage to the student,
2. provide space, materials, and tools necessary for the student to perform work responsibilities adequately,
3. complete weekly checklist evaluations on the student and offer comments regarding work performance,
4. assume direct supervision responsibilities once the student's performance matches that of a typical worker.

_____
Teacher Signature

_____
Student Signature

_____
Employer Signature

tions will not jeopardize the learner's health and safety, (3) that the youth will be provided necessary tools and equipment to perform adequately, (4) that supervision will be provided at a level consistent with that received by other entry-level workers, and (5) that progress reports will be provided on a weekly basis. A sample agreement is presented in figure 13.3.

As suggested by the agreement, the student is expected to possess a majority of the skills necessary for success in the community-based work station before placement. However, the student's performance is likely to fall short in some areas, so on-the-job training may be required.

The work skills checklist developed for the work station simulation may serve as a guide for on-the-job training. The employer and teacher may initially use the checklist to evaluate the youth. At this time, they may agree that the deficiencies are sufficiently small to warrant on-the-job training rather than classroom-based prework training. Next, the teacher may work with the employer and youth to prioritize the skill deficits and delineate sequential short-term objectives expected to be accomplished through on-the-job training. Each week, the employer may be asked to focus the training effort on one or two high-priority short-term objectives. He or she may also be asked to reevaluate the student each week to determine when additional work skills (short-term objectives) should be targeted. Upon completion of a successful on-the-job training experience, the student will have developed all skills necessary for successful employment.

CASE FOR ACTION 13.3

An 18-year-old student in your self-contained class for mentally retarded youths appears to have lost all interest in school. He seldom completes his math worksheets, is often tardy after lunch, and recently has become verbally aggressive when he receives bad grades on assignments. You speculate that his lack of motivation and negative behavior are occurring because the academic curriculum is not relevant to things he values. One thing that he frequently mentions is his strong interest in having a job and making money. To take advantage of this interest, you have decided to center the curriculum around his desire to be employed. How would you develop this curriculum? How would you ensure that it is considered relevant by the youth?

SUMMARY

This chapter has suggested a life-span approach to the vocational education of handicapped children and youth. This approach begins with the selection of developmental and functional curriculum objectives. The manner in which vocational competencies evolve from the preschool stage through the postsecondary school stage has been described from a developmental perspective. From a functional perspective, worker characteristics that employers consider important for success in entry-level jobs have been translated into curriculum objectives through a norm-referenced measure (the VACG) and through the functional curriculum sequence discussed in chapter 2.

Vocational evaluation has been described in this chapter as a focal point of the life-span approach to vocational education. Vocational interest inventories have been described as important in matching the curriculum objectives to the interests of the learner. Aptitude measures have been described as useful for identifying vocational goals that are attainable for the learner.

We have suggested that interest and aptitude data be used jointly in identifying high-interest/high-attainment vocational goals. Formative evaluation techniques discussed in chapters 5 and 6 have been suggested for use in monitoring students' short-term progress toward vocational objectives, and summative measures have been suggested to measure long-term student progress.

Finally, the chapter has reviewed a number of instructional strategies. Basic skill training strategies have been stressed because of the importance of basic skills as a foundation for entry into a career. Career information and exploration activities have been suggested to enhance students' knowledge of the world of work. A related subsection on job-seeking skills has described methods and materials for developing interviewing and application form completion skills, and the final subsections have described the development of classroom and community-based work stations.

A primary tenet emphasized throughout this volume is that special education services should prepare learners to enter functional community settings. As adults, a majority of our waking hours are spent in work-related pursuits. Even the time not spent at work is often influenced by our work. Our social contacts, life style, and leisure pursuits are often determined by our careers. Consequently, the vocational curriculum must go beyond the traditional technical training at the secondary level and must influence all levels and domains of the special education curriculum.

Appendix 13A
Selected Vocational
Interest Inventories

INVENTORY AAMD-Becker Reading-Free Vocational Interest Inventory

TARGET STUDENTS Secondary-level students with limited reading proficiency.

FORMAT Students are asked to circle pictures of activities they enjoy performing. The pictured activities represent occupations in which mildly handicapped persons have been successful.

SUBSCALES Interest scores are provided in 11 professions.

INVENTORY Career Awareness Inventory

TARGET STUDENTS General student population at the late elementary and intermediate level.

FORMAT Multiple-choice items emphasizing career information, social attitudes and personal experiences. Items may be completed independently or read to the student if reading ability detracts from test performance.

SUBSCALES The inventory includes nine sections: careers, workers, job occupations, awareness of educational requirements, personal acquaintance with workers, familiarity with occupations, high prestige jobs, common clustering jobs, and job requirements.

INVENTORY Career Maturity Inventory (CMI)

TARGET STUDENTS General student population.

FORMAT Composed of an attitude scale and a competency test. Whether administered to a group or an individual, the time needed to complete the attitude scale is 30 minutes, and each part of the competency test takes 20 minutes. Oral directions may be given to subjects who have less than a sixth-grade reading level.

SUBSCALES The attitude scale includes orientation to work, independence in decision making, preference for career choice factors, and concepts of the career choice process. The competency test consists of five parts: self-appraisal, occupational information, goal selection, planning, and problem solving.

INVENTORY The Geist Picture Inventory Revised

TARGET STUDENTS Secondary-level students with limited verbal skills or experimental backgrounds.

FORMAT Self-administered picture triads; students are required to respond "most liked" and "least liked."

SUBSCALES Assesses 11 male and 12 female areas of general interest.

INVENTORY Kuder Occupational Interest Inventory

TARGET STUDENTS General student population.

FORMAT Students respond to occupational triads by choosing most preferred to least preferred. The inventory requires a sixth-grade reading level. It may be group administered in 30–40 minutes.

SUBSCALES Includes 114 occupational scales.

INVENTORY Minnesota Importance Questionnaire (MIQ)

TARGET STUDENTS General student population.

FORMAT Questionnaire consisting of 210 items. The student indicates degree of importance in paired statements. The questionnaire is self-administered but may be orally administered if the student has less than a fifth-grade reading ability. Administration time is about 40 minutes.

SUBSCALES Measures 20 vocational needs related to job satisfaction—for example, activity, advancement, and social status.

INVENTORY   Minnesota Vocational Interest Inventory

TARGET STUDENTS   Secondary-level male students.

FORMAT   Contains 158 triads representing nonprofessional occupations. The student indicates most and least preferred.

SUBSCALES   Consists of 29 occupational scales (e.g., baker, printer) and 9 area scales (e.g., mechanical, food service).

INVENTORY   Ohio Vocational Interest Survey (OVIS)

TARGET STUDENTS   General student population at the secondary level.

FORMAT   Students are asked to respond to items using a 5-point Likert scale ("likes very much" to "dislikes very much"). The scale is useful for students with limited reading and is machine-scored.

SUBSCALES   The inventory contains 24 interest scales, including machine work, personal service, and clerical work.

INVENTORY   Strong-Campbell Interest Inventory

TARGET STUDENTS   General student population at late secondary and postsecondary levels.

FORMAT   Consists of a 325-item inventory, most presented in a "like–indifferent–dislike" format. It may be administered individually or in a group. Completion of the inventory requires a sixth-grade reading ability. The administration time is about 30 minutes, and it is machine-scored.

SUBSCALES   The inventory is arranged in seven sections: (1) occupations, (2) school subjects, (3) activities, (4) amusements, (5) types of people, (6) preference between two people, and (7) personal characteristics.

INVENTORY   Super's Work Values Inventory (WVI)

TARGET STUDENTS   General student population at intermediate and secondary levels.

FORMAT   Subjects respond to 45 value statements on a 5-point scale ranging from "very important" to "unimportant."

SUBSCALES Measures occupational choice and job satisfaction through 15 value scales, such as creativity, achievement, and security.

INVENTORY Vocational Interest and Sophistication Assessment (VISA)

TARGET STUDENTS Mentally retarded students at secondary and postsecondary levels.

FORMAT An individually administered pictorial inventory that uses verbal responses. Separate forms are used for males and females.

SUBSCALES The inventory assesses levels of knowledge about job information, understanding of relations between workers and supervisors, and interests.

INVENTORY Wide Range Interest Opinion Test (WRIOT)

TARGET STUDENTS General student population.

FORMAT Includes triads of pictures arranged in 150 combinations. Students are asked to select the most liked and least liked photographs. It may be individually or group administered in about 40–60 minutes. The test is appropriate for students with limited reading and verbal abilities.

SUBSCALES Scores are grouped into 18 occupational interests—such as art, sales, social services—and 7 vocational attitudes—such as risk and ambition.

Appendix 13B
Selected Aptitude
Assessment Tests

APTITUDE TEST Bennett Hard Tool Dexterity Test

TARGET STUDENTS General student population.

FORMAT The student is timed while removing and fastening nuts, bolts, and washers of three sizes, using three wrenches and a screwdriver.

SUBSCALES Measures functional proficiency in using standard tools.

APTITUDE TEST Bennet Mechanical Comprehension Test (BMCT)

TARGET STUDENTS General student population.

FORMAT The student is given 68 questions pertaining to illustrations of pulleys, gears, and levers. The test is group administered.

SUBSCALES Assesses perception and knowledge of mechanical principles.

APTITUDE TEST Crawford Small Parts Dexterity Test

TARGET STUDENTS General student population.

FORMAT Part I: the student uses tweezers to place pins in 42 holes in a board and to place a collar over the pins. Part II: the student uses a small screwdriver to place 30 screws into a plate.

SUBSCALES Assesses eye–hand coordination.

APTITUDE TEST Differential Aptitude Test

TARGET STUDENTS General student population.

FORMAT A written test that may be administered in two to six sessions.

SUBSCALES The test includes seven scales: verbal reasoning, numerical ability, abstract reasoning, clerical speed and accuracy, mechanical reasoning, space relations, and spelling and language usage.

APTITUDE TEST Flanagan Aptitude Classification Tests

TARGET STUDENTS General student population.

FORMAT The students record responses to multiple-choice questions.

SUBSCALES Measures potential for occupational success and vocational program planning, including inspection, coding, memory, and other scales.

APTITUDE TEST General Aptitude Test Battery (GATB)

TARGET STUDENTS Severely handicapped students (mentally retarded, deaf, emotionally disturbed).

FORMAT This instrument is used for training, job selection, and job placement. It is a timed test that is group administered in approximately 2 1/4 hours.

SUBSCALES Measures nine aptitudes, including general learning, verbal aptitude, numerical aptitude, and special aptitude.

APTITUDE TEST Minnesota Clerical Test

TARGET STUDENTS General student population.

FORMAT This is a timed test of students' abilities to match identical figures.

SUBSCALES Measures speed and accuracy in clerical-related tasks, including letter, number, and symbol differentiation.

APTITUDE TEST Non-Reading Aptitude Test Battery (NATB)

TARGET STUDENTS Students with limited verbal and reading skills, including the disadvantaged and the mentally retarded.

FORMAT   Similar to the GATB but does not require reading.

SUBSCALES   Measures the same nine aptitudes as the GATB, including picture–word matching, oral vocabulary, coin matching, and design completion.

APTITUDE TEST   Purdue Pegboard

TARGET STUDENTS   General student population.

FORMAT   This test is timed and assesses gross motor movements of hands, arms, and fingers and specific finger manipulations. Reading is not necessary.

SUBSCALES   The individual must place 25 pins into pegholes using his or her right hand, left hand, and both hands simultaneously. In the final subtest, the student assembles pins, washers, and collars in 1 minute.

APTITUDE TEST   Revised Minnesota Paper Form Board Test

TARGET STUDENTS   General student population.

FORMAT   The test includes 64 items, consisting of two-dimensional diagrams separated into parts. The student chooses a figure that includes the exact parts needed to construct the original diagram.

SUBSCALES   Assesses mechanical skills; provides a nonverbal measure of intellectual performance.

APTITUDE TEST   SRA Mechanical Aptitudes

TARGET STUDENTS   General student population.

FORMAT   The student identifies 45 common tools and their uses, constructs 40 figures cut into two or three pieces, and completes 124 arithmetic problems. The reading level required is estimated at the fifth-grade level.

SUBSCALES   Measures mechanical aptitude, including mechanical knowledge, spatial relations, and shop arithmetic.

APTITUDE TEST　SRA Typing Skills Test

TARGET STUDENTS　General student population.

FORMAT　The student types a 225-word, four-paragraph business letter from a clear copy.

SUBSCALES　Measures students' ability to use either mechanical or electrical typewriters; measures speed and accuracy.

APTITUDE TEST　Stromberg Dexterity Test (SDT)

TARGET STUDENTS　General student population.

FORMAT　Consists of a collapsible board with 54 discs on one side. The student is timed while transferring set patterns of colored discs from the form board to the open board, using only one hand.

SUBSCALES　Measures speed and accuracy of students' arm and hand movements.

Appendix 13C
Questions Asked
Frequently on 200
Sample Application
Forms

Personal Information

Name
Social Security Number
Phone Number
Date
Handicap (illness, injury)
Address
Marital Status
In Emergency Notify (address, phone)
Citizen of U.S.
Criminal Record
Rank in Military
Weight
Height
Extracurricular Activities
Branch in Military
Foreign Language
Skills
Dependents
Dates of Military Service
Permanent Address

Educational Background

High School Name
College Name
High School Address

College Address
Other School's Name
College, Major Courses
Other School's Address
High School, Major Courses
High School, Dates Attended
College, Dates Attended
Other Schools, Dates Attended
Did You Graduate
Grammar School Address
Grammar School Name
Grammar School, Dates Attended
Grammar School, Major Courses
College, Degrees, Diplomas
High School, Degrees, Diplomas
Other Schools, Degrees, Diplomas
Subject of Special Study/Research
Highest Grade Completed

Employment History

Reason for Leaving
Salary
Dates Worked
Position Held Previously
Employer's Address
Employer's Name
May We Contact Previous Employer
Supervisor's Name and Title
Relative or Friend in Company
Previously Applied to Company
Previously Employed by Company
Company Name
Nature of Duties
Full-Time—Part-Time
Employed Now
Hours Available
Phone Number
Referred By
Company Address

References

Address
Name
Occupation
Unrelated Persons Known at Least 1 Year
Years Acquainted
Phone Number
Unrelated Persons

Appendix 13D
Words That Appear
Frequently on 200
Sample Application
Forms

Name
Social Security Number
Date
Address
Signature
Leaving
State
Employment
Last
Position
Years
High School
Zip Code
School
Apply/Applied
College
Middle
Educational
Phone
City
Graduated
Number
Business
Salary
Employed
Other
Company
Employer
References
Physical

Street
Information
Presently
Military
Month
Desired
Application
Job
Reason
Perform/-ing/-ance
Service/Served
Related/Relationship
Permanent/-ly
Attended
Special
Convicted
Age
Notified
Completed/Completing
Relatives
Record
Study/-ing
Subjects
Former
Activities
Supervisor
Personal
Trade
Citizen of U.S.
Emergency

Weight
Birth
Below
List
Height
Degree
Available
Person/-s
Referred/Referral
Telephone
Grammar School
Previously
Time
Type
Separated
Line
Continued
Experience
Duties
Rank
Explain/Explanation
Branch
Received
Member/-ship
Skills
Correspondence
Location
Describe/Description
Major
Course
Contact
Language
Required/Requirement
In Case
Part
Defects
Sex
Occupational
Foreign
Indicate/Indicating
Acquaintances/Acquainted
Least
Married
Circle
Consider

Hours
Check/-ed
Print
Fluently
Crime/Criminal
Answered
Training
Highest/Higher
U.S. Citizen
Dependents
Area
Details
Days
Hearing
Color
Grade
Ability
Applicant
Recent
Injury/Injured
Wages
History
Include/Including
National
Guard

14

Interpersonal Skills Development

■ DID YOU KNOW THAT...

■ **1** ...interpersonal skills deficits are the leading factor associated with the employment difficulties of handicapped adults?

■ **2** ...interpersonal skills training may have a positive effect on handicapped learners?

■ **3** ...interpersonal skills are social behaviors that are mutually satisfying for the student and his or her friends?

■ **4** ...it is best that social skills be specifically defined?

■ **5** ...functional and developmental aspects should be considered when establishing interpersonal skills goals?

■ **6** ...a behavior must be valued by people in the student's immediate environment to be "applied"?

■ **7** ...the term *behavioral* suggests that the response can be reliably measured?

■ **8** ...a teacher can demonstrate the effectiveness of a treatment by using single-subject designs?

■ **9** ...assessment is necessary to determine whether an interpersonal skill deficit is severe enough to warrant intervention?

■ **10** ...self-reports are used to identify potential intervention targets?

■ **11** ...in vivo observations involve observing student behavior in natural settings, and analogue observations occur in a structured testing setting?

○ **CAN YOU...**

  ○ **1** ...select developmentally appropriate interpersonal skills training objectives?

  ○ **2** ...select functional interpersonal skills training objectives?

  ○ **3** ...use self-reports to identify possible intervention targets?

  ○ **4** ...design and implement a self-monitoring system?

  ○ **5** ...obtain ratings of a student's interpersonal skills from others?

  ○ **6** ...conduct behavioral observations of a student's interpersonal skills?

  ○ **7** ...select a commercial instrument to evaluate a student's interpersonal skills?

  ○ **8** ...facilitate instruction by providing adequate attention to students engaged in an interpersonal skills training program?

  ○ **9** ...use social reinforcement to motivate students engaged in an interpersonal skills training program?

  ○ **10** ...arrange conditions that enable students to model appropriate social behaviors?

  ○ **11** ...provide opportunities for students to practice social competency behaviors in natural settings?

  ○ **12** ...provide feedback to students engaged in an interpersonal skills training program?

Interpersonal skills are a major variable associated with the integration of handicapped students into mainstream settings (Gresham, 1981, 1982). Bryan (1974b), for example, used a sociometric technique to measure the social attraction and rejection of learning disabled children. Her results indicated that learning disabled students are more likely to be rejected by their peers. A one-year follow-up replicated these findings, demonstrating that peer relations are stable over time (Bryan, 1976). A related investigation by Bryan (1974a) indicated that learning disabled children are more likely to be rejected by their teachers. Furthermore, people who meet learning disabled students for a short time judge them less favorably than they judge nondisabled youngsters.

Several researchers have associated interpersonal skill deficits with depressed academic achievement. This relationship is attributed to the importance of student-to-student interactions during instruction and the observation that teachers interact more favorably with socially skillful students (Hops & Cobb, 1973, 1974). Procedures designed to alter the way learners interact in the learning environment (e.g., smiling, being attentive, and requesting assignments) have been associated with more favorable teacher evaluations and enhanced achievement (Foss & Peterson, 1981; H. M. Walker & Hops, 1976).

■ 1   With respect to the long-term effects of interpersonal skill deficits, the literature clearly demonstrates that a majority of mildly handicapped individuals adjust to community standards upon leaving school (Delp & Lorenz, 1953; Saenger, 1957). Mental age and school achievement do not appear to have a significant impact on adult adjustment, whereas social competence and interpersonal skills do appear to be associated with community adjustment (Domino & McGarty, 1972; Fiester & Gambria, 1972; Neuhaus, 1967; Sali & Amir, 1971). For example, Zigler and Harter (1969) have reported that interpersonal responses—including dependency, envy, aggression, and negative attitudes toward authority—are the major factors leading to work failure among handicapped persons.

A study of factors leading to the termination of handicapped employees adds further support to these views. Greenspan and Shoultz (1981) conducted structured interviews with former employers of 30 mildly and moderately handicapped workers who had been involuntarily terminated. Data from the interviews were coded within the social dimension—deficits in temperament, character, and social awareness—and the nonsocial dimension—production inefficiency, health problems, and economic layoff. The resulting data indicated that more than half of the subjects were terminated because of deficits within the social (interpersonal) dimension.

■ 2   These data emphasize the importance of interpersonal skills in school and work adjustment. Studies conducted in both school and work settings suggest that performance problems may be as much a function of interpersonal skill deficits as of the lack of academic or vocational competence. Recent reports, however, have emphasized that interpersonal skills training programs may have a favorable impact on handicapped learners (Schloss, Schloss, & Harris, 1984; Schloss, Smith, & Schloss, 1984; Smith, Schloss, & Schloss, 1984). The reports thus highlight the importance of integrating interpersonal skills training efforts into the school curriculum.

CONCEPTUALIZATION OF INTERPERSONAL SKILLS

General Definitions of Social Skills

■ **3** Libet and Lewinsohn (1973) have defined interpersonal or social skills as the ability to exhibit behaviors that consistently produce satisfying reactions from others and the inhibition of responses that are likely to produce unpleasant reactions. Similarly, Foster and Ritchey (1979) have identified interpersonal skills as "responses which, within a given situation... maximize the probability of producing, maintaining, or enhancing positive effects for the interactor" (p. 626). Finally, Bellack and Hersen (1977) have defined interpersonal skills as "an individual's ability to express both positive and negative feelings in an interpersonal context without suffering consequent loss of social reinforcement" (p. 145). Other theorists have offered related conceptualizations (Bates, 1980; Cartledge & Milburn, 1980; Gresham, 1981; Kelly, 1982; Schloss, 1984).

○ **1** Each of these definitions emphasizes the effect of interpersonal skills in producing reinforcing consequences. The first of several limitations, however, is that they do not provide the educator with sufficient information from which to identify curriculum objectives. Although they imply that there is a range of specific interpersonal skills—such as responding to criticism, complimenting others, or engaging in small talk—these discrete responses cannot be identified directly. In addition, the definitions fail to match interpersonal skills to specific environmental contexts. Socially skillful responses exhibited during one set of activities may vary from those exhibited during other events. For example, apologizing in response to criticism may be an appropriate interpersonal response in one situation (e.g., when addressed by the teacher regarding an incorrectly completed assignment), but precisely the same response may be inappropriate under other circumstances (e.g., when confronted by a peer about a failure to engage in disruptive behavior).

Besides failing to specify the contexts in which students should exhibit social skills, these definitions do not establish a criterion for the performance of interpersonal skills. There is little doubt that behaviors are not inherently skillful or unskillful; varying degrees of ability may be evident. One learner may be marginally adept at working through interpersonal situations and another may be adept to the extent that he or she is a strong candidate for a student body office. Although both may have limited needs for interpersonal skills training, the second learner clearly has a more refined interpersonal skills repertoire.

Finally, the definitions do not address the influence of age or developmental levels on interpersonal skills. Appropriate interpersonal responses for an 18-year-old are substantially different from those expected of an elementary-age child. The importance of age-sensitivity has been emphasized by research studies describing interpersonal skill deficits among various developmental groups. At the primary level, Hops and Cobb (1974), Cobb and Hops (1973), Foss and Peterson (1981), and Walker and Hops (1976) have identified a set of basic social "survival skills" that predict and promote achievement across subject matter. The interpersonal skills of greatest concern are eliciting assistance from the teacher, trying to answer questions, smiling, being attentive, and requesting assignments. At the secondary level, Rusch (1979) has identified responses, including "independently managing one's activities, minimal cleanliness and dress requirements, and communicating basic understanding of directives to continue or discontinue an activity" (p. 143).

Specific Definitions of Social Skills

Identifying specific interpersonal skills across age and environmental variables may overcome the limitations of the general definitions. For one applied treatment study, for example, Turner, Hersen, and Bellack (1978) defined interpersonal skills as the ratio of eye contact to speech duration, the number of words spoken, and appropriate intonation and affect. In similar studies, other interpersonal skills have been specified, including speech latency, posture, enunciation, speech content, loudness, and rate of speech (Bornstein, Bach, McFall, Friman, & Lyons, 1980); and social invisibility, social acceptance, social relationships, and social range and attentiveness (Edmonson, Leland, DeJung, & Leach, 1966). Other discrete response definitions have been proposed that address the function of the interpersonal responses: job interview skills (Kelly, Wildman, & Berler, 1980), conversational skills (Kelly, Furman, Phillips, Hathorn, & Wilson, 1979), and social greetings (Schloss, Schloss, & Harris, 1984).

■ 4   Specific definitions of social skills are clearly superior to general definitions for the purpose of classroom interventions. The general definitions, though useful in formulating broad goals, do not provide sufficient information for developing short-term objectives. For several reasons, specific definitions may be easily translated into objectives. First, they are associated with specific interpersonal contexts or conditions (e.g., responding to negative feedback in the classroom). Second, they account for the topography or appearance of a response in a manner that affords reliable observation. Finally, a criterion for performance can be established that ensures attainment of the objective.

CURRICULUM SEQUENCES

A limitation of the specific definitions of interpersonal skills is that they make no attempt to integrate the responses into a broader conceptual system. Without such a system, educators may be inclined to target isolated skills without considering the prioritization of skills, the interrelationships among skills, or the skill sequences that may be linked most effectively.

The preceding discussion emphasized the importance of social context, developmental level, and behavioral topography in defining interpersonal competencies. Recent literature has provided conceptual systems within which these factors may be used to integrate training objectives. Rinn and Markle (1979), for example, have proposed a taxonomy of interpersonal skills comprising four major components:

1. Self-Expressive Skills
   a. Expression of feeling (sadness and happiness)
   b. Expression of opinion
   c. Accepting compliments
   d. Stating positives about one's self

2. Other-Enhancing Skills
   a. Stating positives about a best friend
   b. Stating genuine agreement with another's opinion
   c. Praising others

3. Assertive Skills
   a. Making simple requests
   b. Disagreeing with another's opinion
   c. Denying unreasonable requests

4. Communication Skills
   a. Conversing
   b. Interpersonal problem solving. (pp. 110–111)

In a taxonomy of social skills that considers other factors, Bernstein (1981) has identified settings (e.g., residence, school, work, recreation, leisure, transportation, consumer, and others) and relationships (e.g., friend/same sex, friend/opposite sex, relative, authority figure, service provider, stranger, and others). The matrix shown in figure 14.1—based on the work of Rinn and Markle (1979) and Bernstein (1981)—may be useful in developing and integrating curriculum objectives. Specific entries in the matrix may be a function of the immediate environments in which the learner participates at his or her age. For example, exemplary objectives drawn from the matrix at the adolescent level might include the following:

1. Increased rate of self-expressive statements with peers in leisure settings.
2. Increased rate of other-enhancing statements with friends of the opposite sex in school.
3. Increased rate of assertive interactions with service providers in consumer settings.
4. Increased rate of interpersonal communications with authority figures in the work setting.

FIGURE 14.1   Matrix of Interpersonal Skill Competencies

Setting Variables

		Home		School		Work		Leisure/Play		Consumer	
		Adult	Peer	Adult	Peer	Adult	Peer	Adult	Peer	Adult	Peer
Self-Expressive	Feelings										
	Opinions										
	Responding to Compliments										
	Stating Positives about Self										
Other-Enhancing	Stating Positives about Others										
	Agreeing with Others										
	Praising Others										
Assertive	Making Requests										
	Disagreeing with Others										
	Denying Requests										
Communication	Conversing										
	Problem Solving										

Interpersonal Skills

Objectives at the child level might include the following:

1. Increased rate of self-expressive interactions with relatives at home.
2. Increased rate of other-enhancing responses with friends of the same sex in school.
3. Increased rate of assertive statements with authority figures in school.
4. Increased rate of interpersonal communications with unfamiliar people in leisure settings.

Developmental and Functional Considerations

■ 5   Use of the foregoing matrix relies on both developmental and functional considerations. Consistent with the curriculum philosophy discussed throughout this volume, mildly handicapped learners should be provided educational experiences that promote their adjustment in natural environments. This is a functional consideration. It is equally important, however, that those experiences be chained together in a pedagogically sound sequence. This, of course, is a developmental consideration. The matrix offers a range of potentially functional and developmentally sound objectives, but no attempt is made to prejudge which objectives are most important for a student or group of students. This tactic would violate the curriculum orientation discussed in chapter 2, whereby objectives are selected on the basis of an assessment of learner characteristics, future environments in which the learner is expected to participate, and the most efficient developmental sequence leading to the acquisition of skills. Therefore, the educator must address both developmental and functional concerns when selecting objectives from the matrix.

Developmental Concerns

Interpersonal skills develop among the general population through a fairly stable developmental progression. To demonstrate this progression, skills targeted for young children in applied treatment studies have included cooperative and competitive play (Knapczyk & Yoppi, 1975; Lancioni, 1982; Whitman, Mercurio, & Caponigri, 1970); social amenities (Lancioni, 1982); social play behaviors, such as taking turns and passing objects (Strain, 1975); and attending to others (Stoudenmire & Salter, 1975). Skills targeted for adolescents have included voice loudness (Jackson & Wallace, 1974), verbalizations about current events (Keilitz, Tucker, & Horner, 1973), conversational skills (C. Hall, Sheldon-Wildgen, & Sherman, 1980), job interview skills (Kelly et al., 1980), and verbal content (Matson, Kazdin, & Esveldt-Dawson, 1980). Finally, interpersonal skills targeted for development among adults have included small talk, asking for help, differing with others, and responding to criticism (Bates, 1980); and job interview skills (C. Hall et al., 1980; Hill, Wehman, & Pentecost, 1980).

The American Association on Mental Deficiency *Manual on Terminology and Classification in Mental Retardation* (Grossman, 1973) identifies adaptive behaviors, including interpersonal skills, by level and age. This literature provides a fairly descriptive analysis of developmentally sequenced interpersonal skills and related deficits that are associated with mildly handicapped persons. The chronological ages and associated social skills identified as characteristic of mildly handicapped persons are as follows:

> *3 years*—interacts with one or two other children in basic play activities unless guided into group activity; demonstrates a preference for interacting with some individuals more than others.
>
> *6 years*—participates in larger group activities and plays basic group games; engages in expressive activities, including art and dance; and interacts with other children in simple play activities, such as "store" and "house."
>
> *9 years*—is a spontaneous participant in group activities; participates in competitive games, such as dodge ball, tag, and races; may establish friendships that are sustained over weeks or months.
>
> *12 years*—interacts cooperatively and competitively with others.
>
> *15 years to adult*—along with cooperative and competitive interactions, initiates some group activities for social or recreational purposes; may belong to a local recreation group or church group.

These developmental guidelines are important in helping educators select objectives that are age-appropriate. In addition, they help teachers develop long-term goals that involve the chaining of several objectives. As has been argued throughout this book, however, they should not be used to establish objectives without reference to the function of the skill.

Functional Concerns

○ **2** Baer, Wolf, and Risley (1968), in the foundation paper underlying social development research, outlined the parameters of applied behavior analysis. Although their paper was concerned primarily with the experimental or scientific study of human behavior, it also provided a basis for the functional evaluation of interpersonal skills training. In effect, the same guidelines used to define applied behavior analysis are used here to describe functional aspects of interpersonal training procedures.

■ **6** *Applied* training involves the extent to which the interpersonal behaviors are important to people in the immediate social environment. Applied behaviors are viewed by society as important to adjustment in the immediate environment. Examples include actual response to an employer's criticism at work, complimenting a date on his or her appearance while eating at a restaurant, and asserting that insufficient change was given by a taxi-cab driver. Nonapplied behaviors are those that are typically measured to demonstrate or support a theory of social skills. Aside from the association of the behavior to the theory base, society assigns little value to these behaviors. Examples include responses on paper-and-pencil tests hypothesized to be associated with interpersonal competence; performance on projective tests; and responses on a cue sort.

Behaviors are not inherently applied or nonapplied. For example, providing polite social greetings, exchanging amenities, and engaging in small talk are applied skills only if the people in the immediate environment value these behaviors. It is reasonable that these would be applied responses in most consumer and work situations, but they might not be applied behaviors for workers in a public library.

It should be apparent that applied interpersonal skills have immediate and obvious utility for the learner in functional environments. Therefore, educators who direct their efforts at these objectives can be relatively certain of the benefits to the individual. Educators who focus on nonapplied measures of interpersonal skills may not be certain that the behavior being assessed (e.g., test taking) actually reflects a socially important change in behavior.

■ 7   *Behavioral* training again emphasizes the pragmatic nature of developing functional interpersonal skills. As with the term *applied*, *behavioral* suggests that the target of the intervention should be the same overt response identified as important for the person's social adjustment. Again, projective techniques, sociometric measures, self-reports, and so on, are seldom the actual outcomes expected of intervention. The term *behavioral* highlights the teacher's interest in evaluating and changing the actual target response, rather than events that, at best, reflect the response.

A second aspect of the term *behavioral* is that the response is amenable to reliable measurement. As discussed in chapter 6, a substantial amount of scholarly work has been devoted to the scientific study of students' responses. This literature has produced a range of recording procedures that produce reliable measures of the strength of student behaviors. A concern with behavioral factors requires that these techniques be used to ensure that the teacher's observations confirm a socially important change in student behavior, rather than a change in the teacher's perception of the behavior.

■ 8   *Analytic* training, as described by Baer et al. (1968), "requires a believable demonstration of the events that can be responsible for the occurrence or non-occurrence of behavior" (pp. 93–94). The authors suggest the use of two major single-case experimental designs to demonstrate control over behavior by a treatment: the reversal design and the multiple-baseline design. These designs rule out the effect of unrelated variables such as the student maturing, becoming familiar with the teacher and classroom, or observing others outside of the educational program. Behaviors that change as a result of these or other noninstructional variables may not be considered functional educational targets because they would have developed despite the teacher's efforts. Therefore, a reasonable amount of time and resources could have been saved by simply allowing nature to take its course. In addition, if the noneffective instruction were deleted from the school day, the student might have been available to participate in more important educational activities.

The terms *applied*, *behavioral*, and *analytic* highlight the functional orientation to interpersonal skill training promoted in this chapter. These terms establish criteria for selecting interpersonal skills objectives and procedures. Action Plan 14.1 summarizes these criteria.

Assessment of Interpersonal Skills

■ 9   From a developmental perspective, interpersonal skill deficits are recognized by a discrepancy between the learner's characteristics and the skills possessed by a chronological age-matched norm group. Assessment information ensures that target areas are actual deficiencies of the learner, not developmentally appropriate responses that offend the observer. From a functional perspective, assessment data are used to ensure that interpersonal problems are of sufficient severity to warrant intervention and that responses selected are important to the learner and to others in the immediate social environment. Target objectives are considered appropriate only if the learner or others recognize their importance in promoting adult adjustment.

ACTION PLAN 14.1   CRITERIA FOR SELECTING FUNCTIONAL SOCIAL SKILLS TRAINING OBJECTIVES

We believe that functional social skill training objectives should meet the following criteria:

1. They are viewed by significant persons in the immediate social environment as important to the learner's adjustment.
2. They are measured through direct observation; consequently, the extent of actual performance changes can be stated with reasonable confidence.
3. They can be influenced by systematic intervention procedures.

In the most comprehensive review of assessment procedures reported to date, Eisler (1976) identified four techniques commonly employed to evaluate interpersonal skills: (1) self-reports, (2) self-monitoring, (3) ratings by others, and (4) behavioral observations. Of these, self-reports and behavioral observations have been used most often.

Self-Reports

■ **10** ○ **3** Appendix 14A (at the end of this chapter) is a self-report inventory derived from the interpersonal skill competencies matrix presented earlier. The inventory may be completed independently by mature readers. Less adaptive learners may be asked the questions orally by the teacher, who also scores the sheet. Scoring of the inventory is best accomplished by looking at individual items scored as being deficient, rather than by computing an overall score. In this way, the teacher is able to pinpoint specific problem areas identified by the learner, and these areas may be studied more thoroughly as potential intervention targets. The overall score does little to isolate individual skill areas that might be the focus of interpersonal skills training activities.

Such self-report inventories have been described as the most frequently reported assessment device in the professional literature (Bellack, 1979). For example, Glassi and Glassi (1979) have identified 12 self-report measures of heterosexual interpersonal skills. Inventories such as the one presented here are intended primarily to identify potential goals and objectives. They may also be used along with other measures to determine students' perceptions of the influence of intervention on their quality of life.

As emphasized in the preceding section, self-report inventories are not suitable for evaluating the impact of interpersonal skills training programs. Empirical limitations of these inventories involve the limited extent to which a person's self-appraisal accurately reflects actual performance. Because of the complexity of social interactions, judgments regarding their quality are not easily made by handicapped students. Questions raised on the inventory and accompanying response options may not have the same meanings for the student as they have for the teacher. Also, it is likely that the teacher's or student's expectations may adversely affect the validity of resulting data. It is common for students' responses to more closely approximate their perceptions of ideal behavior.

Despite the widespread use of self-report inventories among the general population, they have seldom been reported in applied training demonstrations with handicapped persons. The limited cognitive and language abilities of handicapped persons may account for this finding. A notable exception to this observation is a report by Johnson and Bailey (1977), who orally administered a questionnaire designed to identify the frequency with which the mentally retarded subjects participated in 29 leisure activities.

The participants responded on a 5-point scale ranging from "never" to "daily." The authors reported that the questionnaire data concurred with the observations of staff members, supporting the reliability of the self-report measure.

Self-Monitoring

○ **4** Self-monitoring differs from the use of self-report inventories in that the student is encouraged to maintain a continuous, reliable count of the target behavior (e.g., number of social greetings per day, rate of appropriate reactions to criticism). Figure 14.2 illustrates a self-monitoring log kept by an adolescent to evaluate the frequency and nature of self-initiated interpersonal contacts. Similar self-recording logs could be kept for a range of behavioral objectives. Age differences can be accommodated by the format of the self-monitoring procedure. In a study by Holman and Baer (1979), young children were provided bracelets with red and white movable beads. The red beads and one white criterion bead represented the number of pages the children were expected to complete during the day. The children were told to move one bead around to the opposite side of the bracelet upon completing each page of work. The children's goal for the day was to move all of the red beads and the white criterion bead. Other self-monitoring devices, depending on the student's age and ability, are described in Action Plan 14.2.

Although professional interest in self-monitoring has increased over the past decade, there has been a relative absence of demonstrations in the interpersonal skill training literature. One major exception has been in the area of heterosexual social skills. Glassi and Glassi (1979) have emphasized the popularity of client-obtained information, including the number of dates, the number and range of interpersonal contacts, and the quality of interpersonal contacts.

FIGURE 14.2 Self-Monitoring Log Recording Interpersonal Interactions of an Adolescent

Activity	Time	Adults(A)	Friends(F)	RA	RF	IA	IF
				(Totals)			
Before School	8:00–8:30	RR	I	2	0	0	1
Student Lounge	9:30–9:50	R	I	1	0	0	1
Lunch	12:00–12:30	RR		2	0	0	
Physical Education	1:30–2:15	R	II	1	0	0	2
After School	3:30–4:00	R	IR	1	1	0	1
Totals				7	1	0	5

R = Responded to conversation
I = Initiated conversation

ACTION PLAN 14.2   SELF-MONITORING DEVICES

We recommend use of the following self-monitoring devices, depending on the student's age, ability, and training objectives:

An Abacus
The student moves one bead from the left to the right of the frame following the occurrence of each target behavior. More than one behavior at a time may be self-monitored by labeling each row of beads accordingly.

An Alka Seltzer Bottle
The student places one penny in the bottle following each target behavior. A piece of tape on the jar may be used to establish the criterion level.

Clown Ditto
The student colors one of the buttons on the ditto clown each time he or she completes the target behavior.

A Library or Money Counter
The student pushes the button on the counter each time he or she engages in the target behavior. The counter, unlike other devices, may be kept secretly in the student's pocket.

A Calendar
The student writes on the calendar the target behaviors performed throughout each day.

An Appointment Book
The student records behaviors exhibited during scheduled times each day.

Ratings and Reports by Others

○ **5**   The ratings and reports of teachers, parents, or peers regarding the student's interpersonal skills are also useful in identifying intervention targets. The most basic technique is to have a person familiar with the student use an instrument similar to the self-rating scale presented in Appendix 14A. Rather than obtaining the student's self-perception, however, the in-

ACTION PLAN 14.3   PROCEDURES FOR CONSTRUCTING A RATING SCALE

Tenbrink (1974) has recommended the following procedures for constructing a rating scale:

1. Specify the learning outcomes or objectives.
2. Determine specific behaviors that are characteristic of each outcome. For example, if the objective is for a student to be more extroverted, specific behaviors may include asking strangers for instructions, interacting in large groups, asking questions in class, requesting assistance from friends, and so forth.
3. Define a scale for each characteristic—a continuum used for judging the quality or quantity of the characteristic. Scales can utilize numeric ratings, as in the first example in figure 14.3; graphic ratings, as in the second example; or descriptive ratings, as in the third example.
4. Arrange the scales in a logical order (e.g., order of occurrence, order of importance).
5. Prepare instructions informing the rater how to use the instrument. Clear and complete instructions reduce the likelihood that error will occur because the evaluator does not understand how to complete the ratings. In general, the instructions should include (1) a description of the characteristics being measured, (2) directions on how to indicate choices, and (3) special instructions.

strument provides information on how others view the learner. Comparing the student's own ratings with the ratings of others may give a measure of consistency between the student's self-perceptions and the perceptions of significant others.

Tenbrink (1974) has suggested five procedures for constructing a rating scale. These are summarized in Action Plan 14.3 (see Figure 14.3).

A more elaborate rating system is the sociometric technique described by Moreno (1953). This procedure is designed to evaluate relationships between various students in a classroom. Figure 14.4, or a similar form, may be distributed to students in the classroom. It requests that they identify, in order, the two students with whom they would most like to engage in specific activities. Resulting data may be summarized in tabular or graphic

FIGURE 14.3 Numeric, Graphic, and Descriptive Ratings

Numeric Rating

Number of times the student initiates conversations with others during a class period:

_____	_____	_____	_____	_____
10 or more	7–9	4–6	1–3	0

Graphic Rating

Likelihood that the student will initiate conversations with unfamiliar students:

_____	_____	_____	_____	_____
highly likely	somewhat likely	neither likely nor unlikely	somewhat unlikely	highly unlikely

Descriptive Rating

Qualitative aspects of the students' interactions:

_____	_____	_____	_____	_____
initiates conversation to gain information, express feelings, and compliment others	initiates conversation to gain information, provide information, and express feelings	initiates conversation to gain information	initiates conversation only to gain necessary information	does not initiate interactions

form. Figure 14.5 illustrates a standard format for presenting such sociometric data. In the figure, arrows accompanied by the numbers 1 and 2 indicate students' first and second choices. Double-ended arrows indicate mutual associations. In the example shown, Bob is clearly indicated as the student with whom others would most like to play basketball, and Sharon is the least likely ball player.

Tenbrink (1974) has suggested four procedures for developing a sociometric device, as summarized in Action Plan 14.4.

A final rating procedure is the "Guess Who" device. With this technique, the teacher establishes a number of relevant social behaviors and de-

FIGURE 14.4 Sample Sociometric Scale Used With Elementary-Age Students

The students in our class are:

Bill George   Lisa Talbott
Sharon Smith   Sue Smothers
Mike Roberts   Bob Lyle
Sally Sands   Steve Spalding

Of these students, who would you like *most* and *second most* to do the following with:

Most	Second Most	
_____	_____	Play basketball at recess
_____	_____	Play a table game
_____	_____	Practice math flash cards
_____	_____	Read a book
_____	_____	Write letters
_____	_____	Sing in choir
_____	_____	Ride on the bus
_____	_____	Eat lunch
_____	_____	Play in the evening
_____	_____	Stay overnight

scribes them in a brief narrative, as shown in Figure 14.6. The students are then asked to identify the student who best matches each description. "Guess Who" questions can describe both positive and negative features of an individual. Also, they can be presented in pictorial form for young students. For example, the teacher may use pictures of people in various occupations and ask the children to label each picture with the name of a student in the class.

Behavioral Observations

○ **6** Direct observation has been used in virtually every applied interpersonal skills training program for handicapped students. The major advantage of direct observations in natural settings is their superior reliability and validity compared to other measurement techniques. As emphasized earlier, self-report and rating techniques are adversely influenced by students' inability to recall information objectively. Also, they may be biased by the students' selective perceptions of a limited range of incidents. Behavioral observations conducted throughout the day have the strongest potential of providing a reliable report of students' actual social functioning.

FIGURE 14.5 Standard Format for Recording Sociometric Data

Playing Basketball

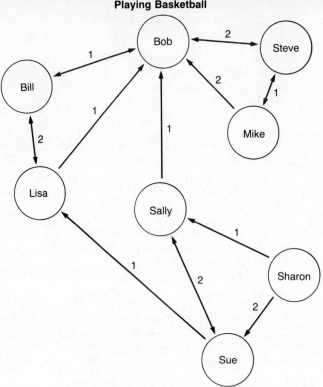

There are major practical and ethical limitations to observing a student through the entire day. Educational agencies seldom have the resources to monitor student behavior continually throughout the day. Also, one must question the morality of continued surveillance of an individual. To overcome these problems, writers in the field have suggested two alternatives: (1) observing students in vivo during a specified period of time (e.g., in the hall between class periods, at lunch, during math class); (2) developing analogue observations—primarily, situation performance tests.

■ 11   IN VIVO OBSERVATIONS   The most common approach to in vivo observations involve direct observation of student behavior following training sessions. Petersen, Austin, and Lang (1979) exemplified this approach by using a modified version of a social behavior recording procedure developed by Strain, Shores, and Kerr (1976). The assessment procedure was designed to quantify the motor-gestural and vocal-verbal responses of the students. The observation procedure was employed during a 15-minute training session

ACTION PLAN 14.4   PROCEDURES FOR DEVELOPING A SOCIOMETRIC DEVICE

Tenbrink (1974) has suggested the following procedures for developing a sociometric device:

1. Arrange the situation to reflect the interests and experiences of the students.
2. Specify the position to be filled or the task to be undertaken.
3. State the rules for nominating peers, including who and how many students may be chosen (e.g., four members of the class).
4. Decide how the students will respond. Options may include oral nominations during a private interview with the teacher or written nominations. In either case, make available a list of potential nominees so that the students do not overlook specific peers.

and later during a 15-minute free-play session with other students present. In a related example, Whitman et al. (1970) recorded social interactions of mentally retarded children during free-play activities in the classroom. The assessment procedure involved rating the number, length, and nature of interpersonal responses engaged in through two 15-minute observation sessions.

Some interpersonal behaviors occur only in uncommon situations. For example, self-corrective statements generally occur in response to criticism from others. Observing a person for 15 minutes a day may produce little usable data because it is not likely that the individual will be criticized during that time. To overcome this limitation, the teacher may expose the student to contrived incidents for the purpose of behavioral observation. Kelly, Wildman, Urey, and Thurman (1979), for example, arranged for mentally retarded participants in an interpersonal skills training program to interact for 8 minutes with another person. The conversations were preceded with the instruction that they should "get to know one another better." The contents of the discussion depended entirely on the two participants. The resulting conversations were rated on the basis of (1) questions asked by the participant, (2) self-disclosing statements, and (3) reinforcing or complimentary statements.

In a similar study, Schloss, Smith, and Schloss (1984) arranged for behaviorally disordered deaf students involved in an interpersonal skill

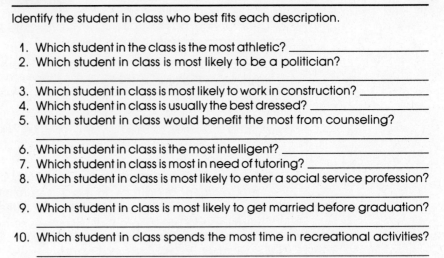

FIGURE 14.6 "Guess Who" Instrument Used with Secondary-Level Students

Identify the student in class who best fits each description.

1. Which student in the class is the most athletic? _____
2. Which student in class is most likely to be a politician?

   _____
3. Which student in class is most likely to work in construction? _____
4. Which student in class is usually the best dressed? _____
5. Which student in class would benefit the most from counseling?

   _____
6. Which student in class is the most intelligent? _____
7. Which student in class is most in need of tutoring? _____
8. Which student in class is most likely to enter a social service profession?

   _____
9. Which student in class is most likely to get married before graduation?

   _____
10. Which student in class spends the most time in recreational activities?

   _____

---

training program to encounter eight situations at a restaurant. Responses to these situations were obtained without the knowledge of the students. The situations included asking how long it will take to be served; arranging for the waitress to comment on an item ("The pizza sure looks good"), asking the student whether he or she would like anything else, and presenting the student with an incorrect bill. Untrained situations included asking the student whether he or she would like a salad bar, asking the price of a large pizza, arranging for the waitress to forget an ordered item, and arranging for the waitress to say, "Thank you for coming; come back again".

ANALOGUE OBSERVATIONS As discussed here, analogue observations are equivalent to situation performance tests. With this procedure, the researcher structures a testing setting so that the student is provided an opportunity to utilize an acquired interpersonal skill. The major advantage of such procedures is that the conditions expected to produce a response can be rigorously controlled and standardized. Unfortunately, there are several disadvantages to analogue procedures. First, the demand characteristics of the situations may produce reactive effects. The student who is participating in training may be more alert and more motivated to perform skills than he or she would be in natural situations. Second, unnatural cues may appear during the test that embellish the student's skill level (e.g., instructions for the situation role-plays serve as advanced organizers for the student). Finally, emotionally provoking aspects of the real-life situation may not be present under the analogue conditions. Bates (1980) confirmed these cautions when participants in his interpersonal skill training program failed to show the same level of performance in vivo assessment as in analogue observations. However, Schloss, Smith, and Schloss (1984) and Smith, Schloss, and Schloss (1984) demonstrated comparable effects for hearing impaired learners in analogue and in vivo observations.

Despite these cautions, analogue procedures may be very useful in evaluating interpersonal skills training programs. Turner et al. (1978) have reported the use of the Behavioral Assertiveness Test-Revised (Eisler, Hersen, Miller, & Blanchard, 1975) for evaluating the effects of an interpersonal skills training program for mentally retarded persons. Sixteen scenes depicting interpersonal contexts were presented to the subjects, including both pleasant and unpleasant interactions with men and women. The participants' responses to the situations were evaluated along five dimensions: ratio of eye contact to speech duration, number of words spoken, intonation, affect, and overall assertiveness.

Bornstein, Bach, McFall, Friman, and Lyons (1980) have reported the use of a similar analogue system. Twelve scenes based on common social interactions were modified from Goldsmith and McFall's (1975) Interpersonal Behavior Role-Playing Test. Equal numbers were provided for female and male role models. The response criteria used to evaluate the participants' skills were number of words spoken, speech latency, hand-to-face gestures, overall interpersonal effectiveness, posture, enunciation, speech content, loudness, hand movements, intonation, eye contact, and rate of speech.

Commercial Instruments

○ **7**   A number of rating scales have been developed and marketed through commercial publishers. In many cases, these instruments have the same characteristics and disadvantages as the teacher-made devices already discussed. Specifically, they require accurate self-appraisal or appraisal by others, but the accuracy is often limited by the cognitive abilities of the student who is completing a self-evaluation. Also, ratings by others are often limited by the frame of reference of the parents, professionals, or peers. In short, such devices provide a better measure of what the respondent says than of what he or she actually does. A more severe limitation in the case of commercial instruments is that they are not designed with reference to specific setting variables and assessment questions. Rather, they provide a sample of behavior that is very general in nature. For example, the Cain-Levine Social Competency Scale (Cain, Levine, & Elzey, 1963) includes only ten items intended to measure interpersonal skills. The educator may have limited confidence that such small samples of behavior will include specific responses that are important for the learner's social development.

An advantage of the commercial instruments is that, in some cases, a substantial amount of research and development work has supported their reliability and validity. For example, the Vineland Social Maturity Scale (Doll, 1953) was normed on ten male and ten female persons at each age level from birth to 30 years. Test–retest data were obtained by administering the scale to 250 persons at 1.7- to 1.9-year intervals. The resulting test–retest correlations were .98 for the sum of passing scores (social age).

With these assets and limitations in mind, the teacher may use selected commercial instruments as general screening devices. It is expected that more precise teacher-made rating scales and behavioral observations will be used to backup resulting assessment information. Selected commercial instruments that may be of use are described in the following sections.

Behavior Rating Profile

The Behavior Rating Profile (L. L. Brown & Hamill, 1983) provides an ecological assessment of social performance problems. It identifies (1) students who are likely to evidence behavior problems, (2) settings in which social performance problems are prevalent, and (3) persons with different expectations for the student's social behavior. The profile includes six independent measures and is used for students ranging in age from 6-6 through 18-6.

Vineland Social Maturity Scale

This scale (Doll, 1953) is probably the most frequently used measure of social competence among handicapped persons. It purports to assess eight clusters of social competence: Self-Help General, Self-Help Eating, Self-Help Dressing, Locomotion, Occupation, Communication, Self-Direction, and Socialization. The final cluster is the most relevant to interpersonal skill development. Items in this cluster relate to cooperative play.

AAMD Adaptive Behavior Scale: Public School Version

This instrument (Lambert, Windmiller, Cole, & Figueroa, 1975) is a modified version of the institutional instrument. Both were designed to assess the extent to which a retarded, disturbed, or developmentally disabled person "meets the social expectations of his or her environment" (Nihira, Foster, Shellhaas, & Leland, 1974, p. 5). The revised version, however, includes only items pertaining to and observable in school. This scale includes two parts. The first contains 56 items assessing skills in the following eight domains: physical development, economic activity, language development, numbers and time, vocational activity, self-direction, responsibility, and socialization. The second part contains 39 items within 12 domains: violent and destructive behavior, antisocial behavior, rebellious behavior, untrustworthy behavior, withdrawal, stereotyped behavior and odd

CASE FOR ACTION 14.1

> The social studies teacher has asked for your assistance in increasing the social acceptance of a learning disabled student in her class. You hypothesize that the youth's lack of acceptance is a result of his poor social skills. Specifically, he has difficulty interacting with his peers without saying things that are offensive. How would you assess the youth to determine the exact nature of the problem? How would you evaluate his actual status in the classroom?

mannerisms, inappropriate interpersonal manners, unacceptable vocal habits, unacceptable or eccentric habits, hyperactive tendencies, psychological disturbance, and use of medication.

Behavior Problem Checklist

This rating scale (Quay & Peterson, 1967) is based on the factor-analytic research of children's behavior disorders reported by Quay and his associates. It is designed for primary and middle-school-aged persons (K–8) and results in classification of behavior patterns as follows: conduct disordered, personality disordered, inadequacy or immaturity, and subcultural (socialized delinquency).

INTERPERSONAL SKILLS TRAINING PROCEDURES

Procedures used in empirical interpersonal skills training reports, as summarized by Turner, Hersen, and Bellack (1978), have included: (1) an emphasis on small component responses, (2) a substantial amount of attention given to each learner, (3) a socially reinforcing milieu, (4) frequent occasions to observe or model desirable behavior, and (5) numerous opportunities to practice new responses. Each of these will be discussed separately.

Component Responses

The early sections of this chapter provided a rationale and a methodology for selecting component skills of curriculum objectives. It was argued that handicapped learners are more likely to profit from instruction targeting discrete behaviors (e.g., social greetings, responding to compliments) as opposed to global responses (e.g., friendliness, extrovertedness). The use of precise behavioral objectives has three major advantages: (1) it reduces the demand for a large amount of change in the individual over a short period of time; (2) it restricts the range of situations in which newly acquired behaviors are expected to be used; and (3) it increases the extent to which the person can identify the satisfying consequences associated with the specific appropriate responses. Component behaviors may be trained individually and chained together so that more complex social responses can be formed. The response objectives can be based on the characteristics and needs of the learner.

Bates (1980) demonstrated this approach by teaching four component behaviors: (1) introduction and small talk, (2) asking for help, (3) differing with others, and (4) handling criticism. Rychtarik and Bornstein (1979) investigated social skills training across three component behaviors: (1) eye contact, (2) conversational questions, and (3) positive conversational feedback.

Attention

○ **8** The majority of social skills demonstrations reported in the literature involve small-group instruction. Through this format, instructors are able to focus a substantial amount of attention on the performance of each member in the group, from the identification of target behaviors to instructional and motivational procedures focused on the responses of individual group members. Several studies have utilized peer-delivered feedback and social reinforcement to further increase the amount of attention paid to each participant (Bates, 1980; Perry & Cerreto, 1977).

Social Reinforcement

○ **9** Verbal praise, gestures, and physical contact have been used to motivate performance in recent social skills demonstrations (Hersen & Ollendick, 1979; Spence & Marzillier, 1979). The use of social reinforcement is advocated because social interactions are the primary motivators of positive social behavior in natural settings. Parents, peers, employers, and others are more likely to respond to a student's socially skillful interpersonal behavior with social praise than with any other consequence. Therefore, it is reasonable for praise to be the primary reinforcer in artificial training settings. Action Plan 14.5 summarizes strategies for increasing the effectiveness of social reinforcement.

ACTION PLAN 14.5   PROCEDURES FOR INCREASING THE EFFECTIVENESS OF SOCIAL REINFORCEMENT

We recommend the following strategies for maximizing the effect of social reinforcement:

1. Label both process behaviors (e.g., "talked in a calm tone") and product behaviors (e.g., "avoided a confrontation").
2. Use the individual's name frequently.
3. Identify responses that are likely to produce social reinforcement.
4. Encourage relatives, peers, and others in natural environments to reinforce the individual socially when the target behavior occurs.
5. Once the target behavior occurs at an acceptable rate, reduce the rate of social reinforcement.
6. If social interactions are not sufficiently powerful to motivate performance, identify a more intrusive reinforcement procedure.

Modeling

○ **10**   Interpersonal skills training programs often include environmental conditions arranged so that participants learn new behaviors or strengthen existing behaviors by observing others. Interpersonal skills training demonstrations by Frederiksen, Jenkins, Foy, and Eisler (1976), Hersen and Ollendick (1979), and Spence and Marzillier (1979) have included two forms of modeling. In the first, the participants observe the trainer engaging in an appropriate response and are then asked to engage in a similar response. In the second, the participants observe a peer engaging in the target response and are then asked to imitate the response. Action Plan 14.6 summarizes procedures for increasing the effectiveness of modeling procedures.

Opportunities to Practice

○ **11**   Recent interpersonal skills training demonstrations have included components encouraging students to practice social competency behaviors under natural conditions or as close to natural conditions as possible. This procedure has three major advantages: (1) it limits the need for abstract thinking;

ACTION PLAN 14.6.   PROCEDURES FOR MAXIMIZING THE EFFECTIVENESS OF MODELING PROCEDURES

We recommend the following guidelines for maximizing the effects of observational learning:

1. Utilize models whom the participants are likely to want to emulate.
2. Utilize models whose performance is attainable by those involved in training.
3. Reinforce the model.
4. Verbally label the behavior of the model.
5. Prompt the observers to engage in the behavior demonstrated by the model.
6. Reinforce the observer for modeling the behavior.
7. Vary the models and the settings to enhance generalization of the learned behavior.

(2) by practicing in natural environments, the desired behavior is linked with the setting in which it should occur; and (3) it prompts adaptive responses that significant others can reinforce. Rusch and Menchetti (1981) increased the rate at which a moderately retarded man complied with requests of co-workers in a competitive work setting. The compliance training procedure involved rehearsing appropriate responses to supervisors' and co-workers' probable requests. A second component involved warning the subject of possible expulsion from the work setting for noncompliance.

Schloss, Smith, and Schloss (1984) arranged for hearing impaired participants to draw cards that described consumer-related situations. The participants were instructed to identify and act out appropriate social responses to the situations. If an inappropriate response was initiated, the instructor interrupted as quickly as possible and modeled a correct response. The participant was then asked to rehearse the appropriate response. Once the individual participant had rehearsed the appropriate social behavior, all group members were asked to rehearse the same behavior. Action Plan 14.7 identifies procedures for rehearsing positive social behaviors.

Another approach demonstrated in the literature that affords frequent opportunities to practice interpersonal skills in natural settings is *homework*. Homework may be loosely structured, as reported in studies by Smith, Schloss, and Schloss (1984) in which the regular classroom teachers were provided the training objectives and encouraged to provide feedback and social reinforcement for exhibiting the skill. During the group sessions, the students were asked to use the trained social skills in class and

ACTION PLAN 14.7   PROCEDURES FOR REHEARSING PROSOCIAL BEHAVIORS

We recommend the following strategies for practicing socially skillful behaviors:

1. Specify the social behavior to be practiced.
2. Identify situations in which the social skill should be used (e.g., when exchanging merchandise, when criticized by peers).
3. Identify the natural consequences of the social skill (e.g., obtaining a refund, peer approval).
4. Create a situation similar to the real-life conditions associated with the socially skillful behavior.
5. Model the prosocial behavior.
6. Ask the student to engage in the prosocial behavior.
7. Provide feedback.
8. Apply the natural consequences, if possible.
9. Encourage the student to use the socially skillful behavior in the natural environment.

report back to the group on their effects. Homework may also be tightly structured, as in the study by Bates (1980), in which, upon completion of each session, an index card was given to each participant identifying an interpersonal skill he or she should practice in the living environment. Houseparents were asked to sign the card, acknowledging the participant's completion of the assigned behavior rehearsal.

Feedback

○ **12**   A component that was not discussed by Turner, Hersen, and Bellack (1978) involves providing participants with evaluative feedback. As with social reinforcement, feedback may be provided by the group leader or by other group participants. Bates (1980) encouraged the use of peer feedback by distributing cue cards to participants. Each card contained one of six component responses expected to be developed during the training program. Following each behavior rehearsal, the group leader asked the participants to provide positive feedback. If a spontaneous feedback statement did not occur, the participant was asked to refer to the cue card. Cue cards were exchanged periodically between group members.

CASE FOR ACTION 14.2

A student in your class is socially isolated. He seldom interacts with others. When he does, he typically says the wrong things. You believe that the youth does not know how to talk with others and, therefore, that social skill training would be appropriate. Describe how you would develop and implement your social skill training program.

SUMMARY

This chapter has presented an orientation to interpersonal skills development that is directly applicable to handicapped learners' individualized education programs. Information presented early in the chapter emphasized the importance of interpersonal skill objectives. Evidence was presented to suggest that interpersonal skills may be a predominant factor influencing students' adjustment in mainstream educational settings. Furthermore, these skills are directly associated with work success in adult life. Consequently, it is likely that a majority of mildly handicapped learners will have IEP goals that address interpersonal skills.

Consistent with the direct instructional model proposed in chapter 4, interpersonal skills training programs are developed through several major instructional activities: determining learner characteristics; establishing goals, objectives, and task sequences; planning and implementing instruction; monitoring the effects of instruction; and revising the instructional plan or goal if necessary. Information presented in this chapter should assist in the development of interpersonal skills training programs within these dimensions.

Procedures suggested for identifying learner characteristics included self-reports, self-monitoring, ratings and reports by others, and behavioral observations. It was emphasized repeatedly that self-reports, self-monitoring, and ratings and reports by others may be of questionable reliability and validity. Consequently, they should be used in combination with other evaluation procedures. Also, although they are useful in identifying intervention goals, they are not sufficiently precise for use as program monitoring and evaluation instruments. Direct behavioral observations, as discussed in chapter 6, may provide substantially more reliable measures of the baseline rate of the target behaviors. Also, change resulting from intervention may be more accurately identified through direct observational measures.

This chapter also provided a rationale for using data on learner characteristics for establishing goals and objectives. Emphasis was placed on developing age-appropriate interpersonal competencies that will help the learner adjust in functional settings. A matrix that integrates learner behaviors (e.g., self-expressive, other-enhancing, assertive, and communication) with setting variables (e.g., home, school, work, leisure/play, and consumer) was suggested as a survey device for identifying specific objectives. Consistent with the discussion on establishing general goals and objectives in chapter 2, both developmental and functional aspects of goal selection were considered. In general, it was argued that goals should be matched to the chronological age expectations for the general population. In addition, emphasis was placed on three major functional criteria, including the extent to which they are *applied* (important to the learner and society), *behavioral* (characterized by overt skills that may be assessed through direct observation), and *analytic* (demonstrated to be influenced by educational interventions).

Finally, social development approaches commonly described in the literature were reviewed: focusing on small component skills rather than attempting to develop global characteristics of the individual; providing small-group instruction in which each participant receives a substantial amount of attention; structuring high levels of social reinforcement to motivate skill development and usage; providing frequent opportunities for students to model skills demonstrated by others; encouraging the students to practice interpersonal skills in a range of situations; and finally, providing learners with frequent, clear, and consistent feedback on their performance.

Appendix 14A
Self-Report Inventory
for Functional
Interpersonal Skills

This inventory is intended to identify possible objectives that may be included in an interpersonal skills training program. Your responses will be useful for identifying the type of instruction to be provided. Place a check in the space that best describes your skills in each situation.

1. Self-Expressive: Expressing feelings and opinions about myself and others to:

Adults at home

excellent	above average	average	below average	poor

Friends at home

excellent	above average	average	below average	poor

Adults at school

excellent	above average	average	below average	poor

Friends at school

excellent	above average	average	below average	poor

Adults at work

_____	_____	_____	_____	_____
excellent	above average	average	below average	poor

Friends at work

_____	_____	_____	_____	_____
excellent	above average	average	below average	poor

Adults when recreating/playing

_____	_____	_____	_____	_____
excellent	above average	average	below average	poor

Friends when recreating/playing

_____	_____	_____	_____	_____
excellent	above average	average	below average	poor

Adults when shopping

_____	_____	_____	_____	_____
excellent	above average	average	below average	poor

Friends when shopping

_____	_____	_____	_____	_____
excellent	above average	average	below average	poor

2. Other-Enhancing: Agreeing with, praising, or complimenting:

Adults at home

_____	_____	_____	_____	_____
excellent	above average	average	below average	poor

Friends at home

_____	_____	_____	_____	_____
excellent	above average	average	below average	poor

Adults at school

_____   _____   _____   _____   _____
excellent   above average   average   below average   poor

Friends at school

_____   _____   _____   _____   _____
excellent   above average   average   below average   poor

Adults at work

_____   _____   _____   _____   _____
excellent   above average   average   below average   poor

Friends at work

_____   _____   _____   _____   _____
excellent   above average   average   below average   poor

Adults when recreating/playing

_____   _____   _____   _____   _____
excellent   above average   average   below average   poor

Friends when recreating/playing

_____   _____   _____   _____   _____
excellent   above average   average   below average   poor

Adults when shopping

_____   _____   _____   _____   _____
excellent   above average   average   below average   poor

Friends when shopping

_____   _____   _____   _____   _____
excellent   above average   average   below average   poor

3. Assertive: Making requests, disagreeing with, or denying requests of:

Adults at home

| excellent | above average | average | below average | poor |

Friends at home

| excellent | above average | average | below average | poor |

Adults at school

| excellent | above average | average | below average | poor |

Friends at school

| excellent | above average | average | below average | poor |

Adults at work

| excellent | above average | average | below average | poor |

Friends at work

| excellent | above average | average | below average | poor |

Adults when recreating/playing

| excellent | above average | average | below average | poor |

Friends when recreating/playing

| excellent | above average | average | below average | poor |

Adults when shopping

_____   _____   _____   _____   _____
excellent   above average   average   below average   poor

Friends when shopping

_____   _____   _____   _____   _____
excellent   above average   average   below average   poor

4. Communication: Solving problems or engaging in conversation with:

Adults at home

_____   _____   _____   _____   _____
excellent   above average   average   below average   poor

Friends at home

_____   _____   _____   _____   _____
excellent   above average   average   below average   poor

Adults at school

_____   _____   _____   _____   _____
excellent   above average   average   below average   poor

Friends at school

_____   _____   _____   _____   _____
excellent   above average   average   below average   poor

Adults at work

_____   _____   _____   _____   _____
excellent   above average   average   below average   poor

Friends at work

_____   _____   _____   _____   _____
excellent   above average   average   below average   poor

Adults when recreating/playing

_____	_____	_____	_____	_____
excellent	above average	average	below average	poor

Friends when recreating/playing

_____	_____	_____	_____	_____
excellent	above average	average	below average	poor

Adults when shopping

_____	_____	_____	_____	_____
excellent	above average	average	below average	poor

Friends when shopping

_____	_____	_____	_____	_____
excellent	above average	average	below average	poor

References

Alberto, P. A., & Troutman, A. C. (1982). *Applied behavior analysis for teachers.* Columbus, OH: Merrill.

Altshuler, K. Z. (1974). The social and psychological development of the deaf child: Problems, their treatment and prevention. *Social and Psychological Development, 8,* 365–376.

American Speech and Hearing Association (ASHA). (1983). Social dialects: A position paper. *ASHA, 25*(9), 23–24.

Anastasi, A. (1976). *Psychological testing* (4th ed.). New York: Macmillan.

Anderson, L. M., Evertson, C. M., & Brophy, J. E. (1979). An experimental study of effective teaching in first-grade reading groups. *Elementary School Journal, 79,* 193–222.

Anderson, L. M., Evertson, C. M., & Brophy, J. E. (1982). *Principles of small-group instruction in elementary reading.* East Lansing: Michigan State University, Institute for Research on Teaching.

Applebaum, S. (1982). Challenges to traditional psychotherapy from the new therapies. *American Psychologist, 37,* 1002–1008.

Armstrong v. Kline, 476 F. Supp. 583 (E.D. Pa. 1979), *aff'd* CA 78-0172 (3d Cir. July 15, 1980).

Ashlock, R. B. (1976). *Error patterns in computation: A semi-programmed approach.* Columbus, OH: Merrill.

Baer, D. M., Wolfe, M. M., & Risley, T. R. (1968). Some current dimensions of applied behavior analysis. *Journal of Applied Behavior Analysis, 1,* 91–97.

Bagford, J. (1972). The role of teaching in reading. In W. H. Miller (Ed.), *Elementary reading today: Selected articles.* New York: Holt, Rinehart & Winston.

Bailey, J. S., Wolfe, M. M., Phillips, E. L. (1970). Home-based reinforcement and the modification of pre-delinquents' classroom behavior. *Journal of Applied Behavior Analysis, 3,* 223–233.

Baird, L. (1973). Teaching styles: An exploratory study of dimensions and effects. *Journal of Educational Psychology, 64,* 15–21.

Bandura, A. (1971a). Psychotherapy based on modeling principles. In A. E. Bergin & S. L. Garfield (Eds.), *Handbook of psychotherapy and behavior change* (pp. 653–709). New York: Wiley.

Bandura, A. (1971b). *Social learning therapy.* Morristown, NJ: General Learning Press.

Baratz, J. D., & Shuy, R. W. (Eds.). (1969). *Teaching black children to read.* Washington, DC: Center for Applied Linguistics.

Bartel, N. R., & Guskin, S. L. (1980). A handicap as a social phenomenon. In W. M. Cruickshank (Ed.), *Psychology of exceptional children and youth* (pp. 45–73). Englewood Cliffs, NJ: Prentice-Hall.

Bates, P. (1980). The effectiveness of interpersonal skills training on the social skill acquisition of moderately and mildly retarded adults. *Journal of Applied Behavior Analysis, 13,* 237–248.

Bates, P. E. (1983). *Social-interpersonal skill development.* Unpublished manuscript, Southern Illinois University, Carbondale.

Becker, W. C. (1977). Teaching reading and language to the disadvantaged: What we have learned from field research. *Harvard Educational Review, 47,* 518–543.

Bellack, A. S. (1979). Behavioral assessment of social skills. In A. S. Bellack & M. Hersen (Eds.), *Research and practice in social skills training* (pp. 75–104). New York: Plenum.

Bellack, A., & Hersen, M. (1977). *Behavior modification: An introductory textbook.* Baltimore: Williams & Wilkins.

Bellack, A., Kliebard, H. M., Hyman, R. T., & Smith, F. L., Jr. (1966). *The language of the classroom.* New York: Teachers College Press.

Bereiter, C., & Engelman, S. (1966). *Teaching disadvantaged children in the preschool.* Englewood Cliffs, NJ: Prentice-Hall.

Bernstein, G. S. (1981). Research issues in training interpersonal skills for the mentally retarded. *Education and Training of the Mentally Retarded, 1,* 70–74.

Bessant, H. P. (1972). *The effects of semantic familiarity and information load on the arithmetic verbal problem solving performance of children in special classes for the educable mentally retarded.* Unpublished doctoral dissertation, University of Connecticut.

Bialer, I. (1966). Conceptualization of success and failure in mentally retarded and normal children. *Journal of Personality, 29,* 303–320.

Blankenship, C. S., & Lovitt, T. C. (1976). Story problems: Merely confusing or downright befuddling? *Journal of Research in Mathematics Education, 7,* 290–298.

Bliesmer, E. P. (1969). Reading abilities of bright and dull children of comparable mental ages. In A. R. Binter, J. Dlabal, & L. K. Kise (Eds.), *Readings on reading* (pp. 189–198). Scranton, PA: International Textbook.

Bloom, B. (1956). *Taxonomy of education objectives: The classification of educational goals.* New York: Longmans.

Bloom, B., Hastings, J., & Madaus, G. (1971). *Handbook of formative and summative evaluation of student learning.* New York: McGraw-Hill.

Bloom, L., & Lahey, M. (1978). *Language development and language disorders.* New York: Wiley.

Bond, G. L., & Dykstra, R. (1967). *The first grade reading studies: Findings of individual investigations.* Newark, DE: International Reading Association.

Borko, H. (1978, April). *An examination of some factors contributing to teachers' preinstructional classroom organization and management decisions.* Paper presented at the annual meeting of the American Educational Research Association, Toronto.

Bornstein, P. H., Bach, P. J., McFall, M. G., Friman, P. C., & Lyons, P. D. (1980). Application of a social skills training program in the modification of interpersonal deficits among retarded adults: A clinical replication. *Journal of Applied Behavior Analysis, 13,* 171–176.

Brett, G. S. (1962). *History of psychology* (rev. ed.; R. S. Peters, ed. and abr.). New York: Macmillan.

Brigham, T., Graubard, P., & Stans, A. (1972). Analysis of the effects of sequential reinforcement contingencies on aspects of composition. *Journal of Applied Behavior Analysis, 5,* 421–429.

Broden, M., Beasley, A., & Hall, R. V. (1978). In-class spelling performance. *Behavior Modification, 2,* 511–529.

Brolin, D. (1976). *Vocational preparation of retarded citizens.* Columbus, OH: Merrill.

Brolin, D. E. (1977). Career development: A national priority. *Education and Training of Mentally Retarded, 12*(2), 154–156.

Bronfenbrenner, U. (1975). Is early intervention effective? In H. J. Leichter (Ed.), *The family as educator.* New York: Teachers College Press.

Brophy, J. (1983). Classroom organization and management. *Elementary School Journal, 83,* 265–287.

Brophy, J. E., & Evertson, C. M. (1976). *Learning from teaching: A developmental perspective.* Boston: Allyn & Bacon.

Brown, A. L., Campione, J. C., & Gilliard, D. M. (1974). Recency judgments in children: A production deficiency in the age of redundant background cues. *Developmental Psychology, 10,* 303.

Brown, L. L., & Hammill, D. D. (1983). *Behavior Rating Profile.* Austin, TX: Pro Ed.

Brown, L., Neitupski, J., & Hamre-Neitupski, S. (1976). The criterion of ultimate functioning and public school services for severely handicapped students. In M. A. Thomas (Ed.), *Hey, don't forget about me: Education's investment in the severely, profoundly, and multiply handicapped* (pp. 2–15). Reston, VA: Council for Exceptional Children.

Brown, V. (1975). Programs, materials, and techniques. *Journal of Learning Disabilities, 8,* 605–612.

Bruekner, L. J., & Bond, G. L. (1955). *Diagnosis and treatment of learning difficulties.* New York: Appleton-Century-Crofts.

Bruininks, R. H. & Rynders, J. E. (1971). Alternatives to special class placement for educable mentally retarded children. *Focus on Exceptional Children, 3,* 1–12.

Bryan, T. H. (1974a). An observational analysis of classroom behaviors of children with learning disabilities. *Journal of Learning Disabilities, 7,* 26–34.

Bryan, T. H. (1974b). Peer popularity of learning disabled children. *Journal of Learning Disabilities, 7,* 261–268.

Bryan, T. H. (1976). Peer popularity of learning disabled children: A replication. *Journal of Learning Disabilities, 9,* 49–53.

Burns, P., & Broman, B. (1975). *The language arts in childhood education.* Chicago: Rand McNally.

Buswell, G. T., & John, L. (1925). *Diagnostic chart for fundamental processes in arithmetic.* Indianapolis: Bobbs-Merrill.

Cahen, L. S., Craun, M. J., & Johnson, S. K. (1971). Spelling difficulty: A survey of the research. *Review of Educational Research, 41*(4), 281–301.

Cain, L., Levine, S., & Elzey, F. (1963). *Manual for the Cain-Levine Social Competency Scale.* Palo Alto, CA: Consulting Psychologists Press.

Campbell, J., & Willis, J. (1979). A behavioral program to teach creative writing in the regular classroom. *Education and Treatment of Children, 2*(1), 5–15.

Carlberg, C., & Kavale, K. (1980). The efficacy of special versus regular class placement for exceptional children: A meta-analysis. *Journal of Special Education, 14*, 295–306.

Carnine, D., & Silbert, J. (1979). *Direct instruction reading.* Columbus, OH: Merrill.

Carroll, J. B., Davies, P., & Richman, B. (1971). *The American Heritage word frequency book.* Boston: Houghton Mifflin.

Cartledge, G., & Milburn, J. F. (Eds.). (1980). *Teaching social skills to children: Innovative approaches.* New York: Pergamon Press.

Cartwright, C. A. (1981). Effective programs for parents of young handicapped children. *Topics in Early Childhood Special Education, 1*, 1–9.

Cartwright, G. G. (1968). Written language abilities of educable mentally retarded and normal children. *American Journal of Mental Deficiency, 16*, 312–319.

Cartwright, G. P. (1969). Written expression and spelling. In R. M. Smith (Ed.), *Teacher diagnosis of educational difficulties* (pp. 95–117). Columbus, OH: Merrill.

Cartwright, G. P., & Cartwright, C. A. (1972). Gilding the lily: Comments on the training based model for special education. *Exceptional Children, 39*, 231–234.

Cartwright, G. P., Cartwright, C. A. & Ward, M. E. (1985). *Educating special learners.* Belmont, CA: Wadsworth.

Cawley, J. F. (1978). An instructional design in mathematics. In L. Mann, L. Goodman, & J. L. Wiederhold (Eds.), *Teaching the learning-disabled adolescent* (pp. 201–234). Boston: Houghton Mifflin.

Cawley, J. F. (Ed.). (1984). *Developmental teaching of mathematics for the learning disabled.* Rockville, MD: Aspen Systems.

Cawley, J. F. (Ed.) (1985). *Secondary school mathematics for the learning disabled.* Rockville, MD: Aspen Systems.

Cawley, J. F. Calder, Cr. R., Mann, P. H., McClung, R. M., Ramanauskas, S., & Suiter, P. (1973). *Behavior resource guide.* Wallingford, CT: Educational Sciences.

Cawley, J. F., Goodstein, H. A., & Burrow, W. H. (1972). *The slow learner and the reading problem.* Springfield, IL: Thomas.

Cawley, J. F., Goodstein, H. A., Fitzmaurice, A. M., Lepore, A., Sedlak, R. A., & Althaus, V. (1976). *Project Math: Mathematics activities for teaching the handicapped: Levels I and II.* Tulsa: Educational Process.

Cawley, J. F., Goodstein, H. A., Fitzmaurice, A. M., Lepore, A., Sedlak, R. A., & Althaus, V. (1977). *Project Math: Mathematics activities for teaching the handicapped: Levels III and IV.* Tulsa: Educational Process Corp.

Chaffin, J., Maxwell, B., & Thompson, B. (1982). ARC-ED curriculum: The applications of videogames formats to educational software. *Exceptional Children, 49*(2), 173–180.

Christopolos, F., & Renz, P. (1969). A critical examination program. *Journal of Special Education, 3*, 371–374.

Clark, C. (1978). A new question for research on teaching. *Educational Research Quarterly, 3*, 53–58.

Clark, G. (1978). Mainstreaming for the secondary educable mentally retarded: Is it defensible? *Focus on Exceptional Children, 7,* 1–5.

Clark, H. B., Boyd, B. S., & Macrae, J. W. (1975). A classroom program teaching disadvantaged youth to write biographic information. *Journal of Applied Behavior Analysis, 8*(1), 67–75.

Cleland, C. C., & Swartz, J. D. (1982). *Exceptionalities through the life span: An introduction.* New York: Macmillan.

Cobb, J. A. & Hops, H. (1973). Effects of academic survival skill training on low achieving first graders. *Journal of Educational Research, 67,* 108–113.

Cohen, L. (1969). *Evaluating structural analysis methods in spelling books.* Unpublished doctoral dissertation, Boston University.

Cohen, S. B., & Plaskon, S. P. (1980). *Language arts for the mildly handicapped.* Columbus, OH: Merrill.

Cohen, S., & Stover, G. (1981). Effects of teaching sixth-grade students to modify format variables of math word problems. *Reading Research Quarterly, 16,* 175–200.

Cole, M. L., & Cole, J. T. (1981). *Effective intervention with the language impaired child.* Rockville, MD: Aspen Systems.

Conger, J. (1977). *Adolescence and youth: Psychological development in a changing world.* New York: Harper & Row.

Conners, R. D. (1978). *An analysis of teacher thought processes, beliefs, and principles during instruction.* Unpublished doctoral dissertation, University of Alberta.

Costin, F. & Grush, J. (1973). Personality correlates of teacher-student behavior in the college classroom. *Journal of Educational Psychology, 65,* 35–44.

Cronback, L. J. (1970). *Essentials of psychological testing* (3rd ed.). New York: Harper & Row.

Cronin, K. A., & Cuvo, A. J. (1979). Teaching mending skills to mentally retarded adolescents. *Journal of Applied Behavior Analysis, 12*(3), 401–406.

Cruickshank, W. M. (1982). *Psychology of exceptional children and youth.* Englewood Cliffs, NJ: Prentice-Hall.

Csapo, M. (1972). Peer models reverse the "one bad apple spoils the barrel" theory. *Teaching Exceptional Children, 5,* 20–25.

Cunningham, P. M. (1976). Teacher's correction responses to black-dialect miscues which are non-meaning-changing. *Reading Research Quarterly, 4,* 637–653.

Dale, E. (1965). The critical reader. *Ohio State University Newsletter, 30,* 1.

Darlington, R. B. (1980). Preschool programs and later school competence of children from low-income families. *Science, 208,* 202–204.

Delp, H. A., & Lorenz, M. (1953). Follow-up of 84 public school special class pupils with IQ's below 50. *American Journal of Mental Deficiency, 58,* 175–182.

Deno, E. (1970). Special education as developmental capital. *Exceptional Children, 37,* 229–237.

Deno, L. S., Mirkin, P. K., Lowry, L., & Kuehnle, K. (1980). *Relationship among simple measures of spelling and performance on standardized tests* (Research Report No. 21). Minneapolis: University of Minnesota, Institute for Research on Learning Disabilities.

Deno, L. S., Mirkin, P. K., & Wesson, C. (1984). How to write effective data-based IEP's. *Teaching Exceptional Children, 16,* 99–104.

Devard, A. J. C. (1972). *Oral reading of arithmetical problems by educable mentally retarded children.* Unpublished doctoral dissertation, University of Connecticut.

Diana v. State Board of Education, No. C-70-37 RFR (District Court of Northern California Feb. 1970).

Doll, E. A. (1953). *Measurement of social competence: A manual for the Vineland Social Maturity Scale.* Circle Pines, MN: American Guidance Service.

Domino, G., & McGarty, M. (1972). Personal and work adjustment of young retarded women. *American Journal of Mental Deficiency, 77,* 314–321.

Duke, D. (1978). How administrators view the crisis in school discipline. *Phi Delta Kappan, 59,* 325–330.

Dunn, L. M. (1954). A comparison of reading processes of mentally retarded boys of the same MA. In L. M. Dunn & R. J. Capabianco (Eds.), *Studies of reading and arithmetic in mentally retarded boys,* Monograph of the Society for Research in Child Development, *19,* 7–99.

Dunn, L. (1968). Special education for mildly retarded: Is much of it justifiable? *Exceptional Children, 35,* 5–22.

Durkin, D. (1978). What classroom observations reveal about reading comprehension instruction. *Reading Research Quarterly, 14,* 481–533.

Durkin, D. (1981). Reading comprehension instruction in five basal reading series. *Reading Research Quarterly, 4,* 515–544.

Durrell, D. D., & Sullivan, H. B. (1958). *Language achievements of mentally retarded children* (U.S.O.E. Cooperative Research Project No. 014). Boston: Boston University.

Edelstein, B. A., Elder, H. A., & Narick, M. N. (1979). Adolescent psychiatric patients modifying aggressive behavior with social skills training. *Behavior Modification, 3*(2), 161–179.

Edmonson, B., Leland, H., DeJung, J., & Leach, E. M. (1966). Increasing social cue interpretations (visual decoding) by retarded adolescents through training. *American Association on Mental Deficiency, 1,* 1017–1024.

Eisler, R. M. (1976). Behavioral assessment of social skills. In M. Hersen & A. S. Bellack (Eds.), *Behavioral assessment: A practical handbook* (pp. 369–397). New York: Pergamon Press.

Eisler, R. M., Herson, M., Miller, P. M., & Blanchard, E. B. (1975). Situational determinants of assertive behaviors. *Journal of Consulting and Clinical Psychology, 43,* 330–340.

Ekwall, E. E. (1976). *Diagnosis and remediation of the disabled reader.* Boston: Allyn & Bacon.

Ellis, A. E. (1963). *Reason and emotion in psychotherapy.* New York: Lyle Stuart.

Ellis, N. R. (1970). *International review of research in mental retardation* (Vol. 4). New York: Academic Press.

Elmore, P., & LaPointe, K. (1975). Effect of teaching sex, student sex, and teacher warmth on the evaluation of college instructors. *Journal of Educational Psychology, 67,* 368–374.

Emmer, E. T., Evertson, C. M., Sanford, J. & Clements, B. S. (1982). *Improving classroom management: An experimental study in junior high classrooms.* Austin: University of Texas, R&D Center for Teacher Education.

Ensher, G. L. (1980). Mainstreaming: The image of change. In J. W. Schifani, R. M. Anderson, & S. J. Odle (Eds.), *Implementing learning in the least re-*

strictive environment: Handicapped children in the mainstream. Baltimore: University Park Press.

Evertson, C. M., Emmer, E. T., & Brophy, J. E. (1980). Predictors of effective teaching in junior high mathematics classrooms. *Journal of Research in Mathematics Education, 11*, 167–178.

Evertson, C., Emmer, E. T., Sanford, J., & Clements, B. S. (1982). *Improving classroom management: An experimental study in elementary classrooms*. Austin: University of Texas, R&D Center for Teacher Education.

Faas, L. A. (1980). *Children with learning problems: A handbook for teachers*. Boston: Houghton Mifflin.

Faas, L. A. (1981). Learning disabled: A competency based approach. Boston: Houghton Mifflin.

Fafard, B. (1976). *The effects of instructions on verbal problem solving in learning disabled children*. Unpublished doctoral dissertation, University of Oregon.

Federal Register (1977, August 22) (1981, January 19). Washington, DC: U.S. Government Printing Office.

Fernald, G. M. (1943). *Remedial techniques in basic school subjects*. New York: McGraw-Hill.

Fiester, A. R., & Gambria, L. M. (1972). Language indices of vocational success in mentally retarded adults. *American Journal of Mental Deficiency, 77*, 332–337.

Finkel, L. (1985, March). Software copyright interpretation. *Computing Teacher*, pp. 13–14.

Fisher, C., Berliner, D., Filby, N., Marliave, R., Cahen, L., & Dishaw, M. (1980). Teaching behaviors, academic learning time, and student achievement: An overview. In C. Denham & A. Lieberman (Eds.), *Time to learn* (pp. 7–32). Washington, DC: National Institute of Education.

Flanders, N. (1970). *Analyzing teaching behavior*. Reading, PA: Addison-Wesley.

Foss, G., & Peterson, S. L. (1981). Social-interpersonal skills relevant to job tenure for mentally retarded adults. *Mental Retardation, 19*, 103–106.

Foster, S. L., & Ritchey, W. L. (1979). Issues in the assessment of social competence in children. *Journal of Applied Behavior Analysis, 12*, 626–638.

Foxx, R. M., & Jones, J. R. (1978). A remediation program for increasing the spelling achievement of elementary and junior high school students. *Behavior Modification, 2*(2), 211–230.

Franks, D. J. (1971). Ethnic and social status characteristics of children in EMR and LD classes. *Exceptional Children, 37*, 537–538.

Frederiksen, L. W., Jenkins, J. O., Foy, D. W., & Eisler, R. M. (1976). Social-skills training to modify abusive verbal outbursts in adults. *Journal of Applied Behavior Analysis, 9*, 117–125.

French, E. L. (1950). Reading disability and mental deficiency: A preliminary report. *Training School Bulletin, 47*, 47–57.

Gallagher, M. C., & Pearson, P. D. (1983). *Fourth grade students' acquisition of new information from text*. Austin, TX: NRC.

Galloway, E., & Gray, G. (1976, November). *Language experience: A reading approach*. Paper presented at the annual meeting of the Clemson Reading Conference, Clemson, SC.

Gallup, G. H. (1983). The 15th annual Gallup Poll of the public's attitudes toward the public schools. *Phi Delta Kappan, 65*, 33–47.

Gambrell, L., Wilson, R., & Gantt, W. (1981). Classroom observations of task-attending behaviors of good and poor readers. *Journal of Educational Research, 74,* 400–405.

Gardner, W. I. (1977). *Learning and behavior characteristics of exceptional children and youth: A humanistic behavioral approach.* Boston: Allyn & Bacon.

Gardner, W. I. (1978). *Children with learning and behavior problems* (2nd ed.). Boston: Allyn & Bacon.

Gates, A. I. (1930). *Interest and ability in reading.* New York: Macmillan.

Gearhart, B. R., & Weishahn, M. W. (1976). *The handicapped child in the regular classroom.* St. Louis: Mosby.

Gearhart, B. R., & Willenberg, E. P. (1980). *Application of pupil assessment information.* Denver: Love.

Gentry, J. R. (1984). Developmental aspects of learning to spell. *Academic Therapy, 20*(1), 11–19.

Gerber, M. M. (1984). Techniques to teach generalizable spelling skills. *Academic Therapy, 20*(1), 49–58.

Gersten, R. M., Carnine, D. W., & Williams, P. B. (1981). Measuring implementation of a structured educational model in an urban school district. *Educational Evaluation and Policy Analysis, 4,* 56–63.

Gillespie, P. H., & Johnson, L. E. (1974). *Teaching reading to the mildly retarded child.* Columbus, OH: Merrill.

Gillespie-Silver, P. (1979). *Teaching reading to children with special needs.* Columbus, OH: Merrill.

Gilliam, J. (1979). Contributions and status rankings of educational planning committee participants. *Exceptional Children, 45,* 466–467.

Gilliam, J., & Coleman, M. C. (1981). Who influences IEP committee decisions? *Exceptional Children, 47,* 642–644.

Gilliland, H. (1978). *A practical guide to remedial reading* (2nd ed.). Columbus, OH: Merrill.

Gillung, T., & Rucker, C. (1977). Labels and teacher expectations. *Exceptional Children, 43,* 464–465.

Glassi, J. P., & Glassi, M. D. (1979). Modification of heterosocial skills deficits. In A. S. Bellack & M. Hersen (Eds.), *Research and practice in social skills training* (pp. 131–187). New York: Plenum.

Goldsmith, J. B., & McFall, R. M. (1975). Development and evaluation of an interpersonal skill-training program for psychiatric inpatients. *Journal of Abnormal Psychology, 84,* 51–58.

Gollub, W. L., & Sloan, E. (1978). Teacher expectations, race, and socioeconomic status. *Urban Education, 13* (1), 96–106.

Good, T. L., & Grouws, D. A. (1979). The Missouri mathematics effectiveness project. *Journal of Educational Psychology, 71,* 355–362.

Goodman, K. (1965). A linguistic study of cues and miscues in reading. *Elementary English Review, 42,* 639–643.

Goodstein, H. A. (1981). Are the errors we see the true errors? Error analysis in verbal problem solving. *Topics in Learning and Learning Disabilities, 1* (3), 31–45.

Goodstein, H. A., Bessant, H., Thibodeau, G., Vitello, S., & Vlahakos, I. (1972). The effect of three variables on the verbal problem solving of educable mentally retarded children. *American Journal of Mental Deficiency, 76,* 703–709.

Goodstein, H. A., Cawley, J. F., Gordon, S., & Helfgott, J. (1971). Verbal problem solving among educable mentally retarded children. *American Journal of Mental Deficiency, 76,* 238–241.

Gottlieb, J. (1981). Mainstreaming: Fulfilling the promise? *American Journal of Mental Deficiency, 86,* 115–126.

Grabe, M., & Mann, S. (1984). A technique for the assessment and training of comprehensive monitoring skills. *Journal of Reading Behavior, 15,* 131–145.

Graham, S. (1985). Evaluating spelling programs and materials. *Teaching Exceptional Children, 17*(4), 299–303.

Graves, D. (1976). Research update: Spelling texts and structural analysis methods. *Language Arts, 54,* 86–90.

Greenspan, S., & Shoultz, B. (1981). Why mentally retarded adults lose their jobs: Social competence as a factor in work adjustment. *Applied Research in Mental Retardation, 2,* 23–38.

Gresham, F. M. (1981). Assessment of children's social skills. *Journal of School Psychology, 19,* 120–133.

Gresham, F. M. (1982). Misguided mainstreaming: The case for social skills training with handicapped children. *Exceptional Children, 48,* 422–433.

Gronlund, N. E. (1976). *Measurement and evaluation in teaching* (3rd ed.). New York: Macmillan.

Grossman, H. J. (Ed.). (1973). *Manual on terminology and classification in mental retardation: 1974 revision.* Washington, DC: American Association on Mental Deficiency.

Guskin, S. L., & Spicker, H. H. (1968). Educational research in mental retardation. In N. R. Ellis (Ed.), *International review of research in mental retardation* (Vol. 3, pp. 217–273). New York: Academic Press.

Guthrie, J. T., Seifert, M., Burnham, N. A. & Caplan, R. I. (1974). The maze technique to assess, monitor reading comprehension. *Reading Teacher, 28,* 161–168.

Gysbers, N., Miller, W., & Moore, E. (1973). *Developing careers in the elementary school.* Columbus, OH: Merrill.

Hagen, D. (1984). *Microcomputer resource book for special education.* Reston, VA: Reston.

Halderman v. Pennhurst State School and Hospital, No. 74-1345 (U.S. District Court, E.D. Pa. May 30, 1974).

Hall, C., Sheldon-Wildgen, J., & Sherman, J. A. (1980). Teaching job interview skills to retarded clients. *Journal of Applied Behavior Analysis, 13,* 433–442.

Hall, M. (1977). *The language experience approach for teaching reading: A research perspective* (2nd ed.). Newark, DE: International Reading Association.

Hallahan, D. P., & Kauffman, J. M. (1976). *Introduction to learning disabilities.* Englewood Cliffs, NJ: Prentice-Hall.

Hallahan, D. P., & Kauffman, J. M. (1982). *Exceptional children.* Englewood Cliffs, NJ: Prentice-Hall.

Hammill, D. D., & Bartel, M. R. (1978). *Teaching children with learning and behavior problems* (2nd ed.). Boston: Allyn & Bacon.

Hanna, P. R., Hanna, J. S., Hodges, R. E., & Peterson, D. J. (1971). *Power to spell*. Boston: Houghton Mifflin.

Hansen, C. L. (1973). Program slicing: A tool for individualizing instruction. *Education and Training of the Mentally Retarded, 8*, 153–158.

Hansen, C. L. (1978). Writing skills. In N. G.Haring, T.C. Lovitt, M. D. Eaton, & C. L. Hansen (Eds.), *The fourth R: Research in the classroom* (pp. 93–126). Columbus, OH: Merrill.

Hansen, C. L., & Eaton, M. D. (1978). Reading. In N. G. Haring, T. C. Lovitt, M. D. Eaton, & C. L. Hansen (Eds.), *The fourth R: Research in the classroom*. Columbus, OH: Merrill.

Hansen, C. L., & Lovitt, T. C. (1973). *Effects of feedback in content and mechanics of writing*. Paper presented at NIE Symposium, Seattle.

Hansen, J., & Pearson, P. D. (1983). An instructional study: Improving the inferential comprehension of fourth grade good and poor readers. *Journal of Educational Psychology, 75*, 821–829.

Haring, N. G., Lovitt, T. C., Eaton, M. D., & Hansen, C. L. (Eds.). (1978). *The fourth R: Research in the classroom*. Columbus, OH: Merrill.

Haring, N. G., & Phillips, E. L. (1962). *Educating emotionally disturbed children*. New York: McGraw-Hill.

Haring, N. G., & Schiefelbusch, R. L. (Eds.). (1976). *Teaching special children*. New York: McGraw-Hill.

Harris, A. J. (1970). *How to increase reading ability*. New York: McKay.

Harris, A., & Sipay, E. R. (1975). *How to increase your reading ability* (6th ed.). New York: McKay.

Harris, V. W. (1973). Effects of peer tutoring, homework, and consequences upon the academic performance of elementary school children. (Doctoral dissertation, University of Kansas, 1972). *Dissertation Abstracts International, 33*, 11-A, 6175.

Hasazi, J. E., & Hasazi, S. E. (1972). Effects of teacher attention on digit reversal behavior in an elementary school child. *Journal of Applied Behavior Analysis, 5*, 157–162.

Hatfield, E. M. (1975). Why are they blind? *Sight Saving Review, 45*(1), 3–22.

Heber, R., & Garber, H. (1975). The Milwaukee Project: A study of the use of family intervention to prevent cultural-familial mental retardation. In B. Friedlander, G. Sterritt, & G. Kirk (Eds.), *Exceptional infant*. New York: Brunner/Mazel.

Hefele, T. (1971). The effects of systematic human relations training upon student achievement. *Journal of Research and Development in Education, 4*, 52–69.

Hegge, T. G. (1934). Special reading disability with particular reference to the mentally deficient. *American Journal of Mental Deficiency, 39*, 224.

Heilman, A. W. (1972). *Principles and practices of teaching reading* (3rd ed.). Columbus, OH: Merrill.

Helfgott, J., & Voris, P. (1972). *The effects of training upon verbal problem solving for mentally retarded children*. Unpublished manuscript, University of Connecticut.

Helwig, J. J., Johns, J. C., Norman, J. E., & Cooper, J. O. (1976). The measurement of manuscript letter strokes. *Journal of Applied Behavior Analysis, 9*(2), 231–236.

Hendricksen, J., Roberts, M., & Shores, R. E. (1978). Antecedent and contingent modeling to teach basic sight vocabulary to learning disabled children. *Journal of Learning Disabilities, 11*(8), 524–528.

Hersen, M., & Bellack, A. S. (1977). Assessment of social skills. In A. R. Ciominero, K. S. Calhann, & H. E. Adams (Eds.), *Handbook for behavioral assessment*. New York: Wiley.

Hersen, M. & Ollendick, T. H. (1979). Social skills training for juvenile delinquents. *Behavior, Research, and Therapy, 17,* 547–554.

Hewett, F. M. (1967). Educational engineering with emotionally disturbed children. *Exceptional Children, 33,* 459–471.

Hewett, F. M. (1968). *The emotionally disturbed child in the classroom*. Boston: Allyn & Bacon.

Hill, J. W., Wehman, P., & Pentecost, J. (1980). Developing job interview skills in mentally retarded adults. *Education and Training of the Mentally Retarded, 15,* 179–186.

Hillerich, R. L. (1983). *The principal's guide to improving instruction*. Boston: Allyn & Bacon.

Holman, J., & Baer, D. M. (1979). Facilitating generalization of on-task behavior through self-monitoring of academic tasks. *Journal of Autism and Developmental Disorders, 9,* 429–445.

Hops, H., & Cobb, J. A. (1973). Survival behaviors in the educational setting: Their implications for research and intervention. In L. A. Hammerlynk, L. C. Handy, & E. J. Mash (Eds.), *Behavior change* (pp. 193–208). Champaign, IL: Research Press.

Hops, H. & Cobb, J. A. (1974). Initial investigations into academic survival skill training, direct instruction and first grade achievement. *Journal of Educational Psychology, 66,* 548–553.

Horn, E. A. (1926). A basic writing vocabulary of 10,000 most commonly used words in writing. *University of Iowa Monograph in Education*, (First Series, No. 4).

Hupp, S. C., & Mervis, C. B. (1981). Development of generalized concepts for severely handicapped students. *Journal of Association for the Severely Handicapped, 6*(1), 14–21.

Itard, J. M. G. (1932). *The wild boy of Aveyron* (G. Humphrey & M. Humphrey, Trans.). New York: Appleton-Century-Crofts.

Jackson, D. R., & Wallace, F. R. (1974). The modification and generalization of voice loudness in a fifteen year old retarded girl. *Journal of Applied Behavior Analysis, 7*(3), 461–471.

Jensen, A. R. (1969). How much can we boost I.Q. and scholastic achievement? *Harvard Educational Review, 39,* 1–123.

Johnson, C. W., & Katz, R. C. (1973). Using parents as change agents for their children: A review. *Journal of Child Psychology and Psychiatry, 14,* 181–200.

Johnson, G. O. (1963). *Education for the slow learners*. Englewood Cliffs, NJ: Prentice-Hall.

Johnson, M. S. (1966). Tracing and kinesthetic techniques. In J. Mory & G. Schiffman (Eds.), *The disabled reader* (pp. 147–160). Baltimore: Johns Hopkins Press.

Johnson, M. S., & Bailey, J. S. (1977). The modification of leisure behavior in a half-way house for retarded woman. *Journal of Applied Behavior Analysis, 10,* 275–282.

Jones, R. L. (1970, September). *New labels in old bags: Research on labeling blacks culturally disadvantaged, culturally deprived, and mentally retarded.* Paper presented at annual convention of Association of Black Psychologists, Miami Beach.

Jones, R. L. (1972). Labels and stigma in special education. *Exceptional Children, 38,* 553–564.

Jones, V. F., & Jones, L. S. (1981). *Responsible classroom discipline: Creating positive learning environments and solving problems.* Boston: Allyn & Bacon.

Jones, Y. D., McCormick, S., & Heward, W. L. (1980). Teaching reading disabled students to read and complete employment applications. *Journal of Reading Improvement, 16*(1), 28–31.

Joyce, B. (1978). Toward a theory of information processing in teaching. *Educational Research Quarterly, 3,* 66–67.

Kaluger, G., & Kolson, C. J. (1978). *Reading and learning disabilities* (2nd ed.). Columbus, OH: Merrill.

Kauffman, J. M (1981). *Characteristics of children's behavior disorders* (2nd ed.). Columbus, OH: Merrill.

Kauffman, J. M., Hallahan, D. P., Hass, K., Brame, T., & Boren, R. (1978). Imitating children's errors to improve their spelling performance. *Journal of Learning Disabilities, 11*(4), 217–222.

Kazdin, A. E. (1973). The effect of response cost and aversive stimulation in suppressing punished and nonpunished speech disfluences. *Behavior Therapy, 4,* 73–82a.

Kazdin, A. E. (1980). *Research design in clinical psychology.* New York: Harper & Row.

Kazdin, A. E., (1982). *Single-case research designs: Methods for clinical and applied settings.* New York: Oxford University Press.

Kazdin, A. E., & Matson, J. L. (1981). Social validation in mental retardation. *Applied Research in Mental Retardation, 2,* 39–53.

Keilitz, I., Tucker, D. J., & Horner, R. D. (1973). Increasing mentally retarded adolescents' verbalizations about current events. *Journal of Applied Behavior Analysis, 6,* 621–630.

Kelly, J. A. (1982). *Social-skills training: A practice guide for interventions.* New York: Springer.

Kelly, J. A., Furman, W., Phillips, J., Hathorn, S., & Wilson, T. (1979). Teaching conversational skills to retarded adolescents. *Child Behavior Therapy, 1,* 85–97.

Kelly, J. A., Wildman, B. G., & Berler, E. S. (1980). Small group behavioral training to improve the job interview skills repertoire of mildly retarded adolescents. *Journal of Applied Behavior Analysis, 13,* 461–471.

Kelly, J. A., Wildman, B. G., Urey, J. R., & Thurman, C. (1979). Group skills training to increase the conversational repertoire of retarded adolescents. *Child Behavior Therapy, 1,* 323–336.

Kimmel, T. H. (1973). *What critical reading skills are important in evaluating informative and persuasive writing, as represented by news, opinion, and advertisements in print.* Unpublished master's thesis, National College of Education, Evanston, IL.

Kirk, S. A., & Gallagher, J. J. (1983). *Educating exceptional children* (4th ed.). Boston: Houghton Mifflin.

Kirk, S. A., Kliebhan, S. J., & Lerner, J. S. (1978). *Teaching reading to slow and disabled learners.* Boston: Houghton Mifflin.

Knapczyk, D. R., & Yoppi, J. O. (1975). Development of cooperative and competitive play responses in developmentally disabled children. *American Journal of Mental Deficiency, 80*(3), 245–255.

Knoff, H. M. (1983). Investigating disproportionate influence and status in multidisciplinary child study teams. *Exceptional Children, 49,* 367–369.

Koenig, C. H. (1972). *Charting the future course of behavior.* Unpublished doctoral dissertation, University of Kansas.

Kounin, J. (1970). *Discipline and group management in classrooms.* New York: Holt, Rinehart & Winston.

Kroth, R. L., & Simpson, R. L. (1977). *Parent conferences as a teaching strategy.* Denver: Love.

Labov, W. (1966). *The social stratification of English in New York City.* Washington, DC: Center for Applied Linguistics.

Lambert, N., Windmiller, M., Cole, L., & Figueroa, R. (1975). *Manual for AAMD Adaptive Behavior Scale: Public School Version (1974) revision.* Washington, DC: American Association on Mental Deficiency.

Lamberts, F. (1978). *PL 94-142 and the IEP: A guide for teachers of children with special language needs.* De Kalb, IL: Northern Illinois University Press.

Lancioni, G. E. (1982). Normal children as tutors to teach social responses to withdrawn mentally retarded schoolmates: Training, maintenance, and generalization. *Journal of Applied Behavior Analysis, 15,* 17–40.

Larsen, S. C., Parker, R., & Trenholme, B. (1978). The effects of syntactic complexity upon arithmetic performance. *Learning Disability Quarterly, 1*(4), 80–85.

Lathrop, A. (1982). The terrible ten in educational programming. *Educational Computer Magazine, 2,* 34–36.

Libet, J. M., & Lewinsohn (1973). Social skills of depressed persons. *Journal of Consulting and Clinical Psychology, 40,* 301–312.

Lilly, M. S. (1979). *Children with exceptional needs: A survey of special education.* New York: Holt, Rinehart & Winston.

Lindsley, O. R (1964). Direct measurement and prosthesis of retarded behavior. *Journal of Education, 147,* 62–81.

Lindsley, O. R. (1968). Technical note: A reliable wrist counter for recording behavior rates. *Journal of Applied Behavior Analysis, 1,* 77–78.

Love, J. M., Nauta, M. J., Coelen, C. G., Hewett, K., & Ruopp, R. R. (1976, March). *National Home Start evaluation: Final report.* (Available from Abt Associates, 55 Wheeler Street, Cambridge, MA 02138, and High/Scope Educational Research Foundation, 600 N. River Street, Ypsilanti, MI 48197)

Lovitt, T. C. (1973). *Using applied behavior analysis procedures to evaluate spelling instructional techniques with learning disabled youngsters.* Unpublished manuscript, University of Washington, Seattle.

Lovitt, T. C. (1984). *Tactics for teaching.* Columbus, OH: Merrill.

Lovitt, T. C., & Curtiss, K. A. (1968). Effect of manipulating an antecedent event on mathematics response rate. *Journal of Applied Behavior Analysis, 1,* 329–333.

Lovitt, T., Eaton, M., Kirkwood, M., & Pelander, J. (1971). Effects of various reinforcement contingencies on oral reading rate. In E. Ramp & B. Hopkins

(Eds.), *A new direction for education: Behavior analysis.* Lawrence: University of Kansas.

Lucking, R. A. (1975). *Comprehension and a model for questioning.* ERIC #ED110 988.

Lundsteen, S. (1964). Teaching and testing critical listening skills in the fifth and sixth grades. *Elementary English, 41,* 743–747.

Lydiatt, S. (1984). Error detection and correction in spelling. *Academic Therapy, 20*(1), 33–40.

Lydra, W. J., & Church, R. S. (1964). Direct, practical arithmetic experiences and success in solving realistic verbal "reasoning" problems in arithmetic. *Journal of Educational Research, 57,* 530–533.

MacKay, A. (1977). The Alberta studies of teaching: A quinquereme in search of some sailors. *CSSE News, 3,* 14–17.

MacMillan, D. L. (1971). Special education for the mildly retarded: Servant or savant. *Focus on Exceptional Children, 2,* 1–11.

MacMillan, D. L. (1977). *Mental retardation in school and society.* Boston: Little, Brown.

MacMillan, D. L., Jones, R. L., & Aloia, G. F. (1974). The mentally retarded label: A theoretical analysis and review of research. *American Journal of Mental Deficiency, 79,* 241–261.

Madle, R. A. (1983). Mental retardation: General learning dysfunction. In R. M. Smith, J. T. Neisworth, & F. M. Hunt (Eds.), *The exceptional child: A functional approach.* New York: McGraw-Hill.

Mager, R. F. (1984). *Preparing instructional objectives.* Belmont, CA: Fearon.

Mager, R. F., & Pipe, P. (1984). *Analyzing performance problems or "you really oughta wanna."* Belmont, CA: Fearon.

Mahoney, M. J. (1974). *Cognition and behavior modification.* Cambridge, MA: Ballinger.

Maloney, K., & Hopkins, B. (1973). The modification of sentence structure and its relationship to subjective judgments of creativity in writing. *Journal of Applied Behavior Analysis, 6,* 425–433.

Marholin, D., II, & Steinman, W. M. (1977). Stimulus control in the classroom as a function of the behavior reinforced. *Journal of Applied Behavior Analysis, 10,* 465–478.

Marland, P. W. (1977). *A study of teachers' interactive thoughts.* Unpublished doctoral dissertation. University of Alberta.

Marlowe, R. H., Madsen, C. H., Jr., Bowen, C. E., Reardon, R. C., & Logue, P. E. (1978). Severe classroom behavior problems: Teachers or counselors. *Journal of Applied Behavior Analysis, 11,* 53–66.

Martin, G., & Pear, J. (1978). *Behavior modification: What it is and how to do it.* Englewood Cliffs, NJ: Prentice-Hall.

Matson, J. L., & DiLorenzo, T. M. (1984). *Punishment and its alternatives: A new perspective for behavior modification.* New York: Springer.

Matson, J. L., Kazdin, A. E., & Esveldt-Dawson, K. (1980). Training interpersonal skills among mentally retarded and socially dysfunctional children. *Behavior Research Therapy, 18,* 419–427.

McAfee, J. M., & Mann, L. (1982). The prognosis for mildly handicapped students. In T. L. Miller & E. Davis (Eds.), *The mildly handicapped student.* New York: Grune & Stratton.

McCarthy, W., & Oliver, J. (1965). Some tactile-kinesthetic procedures for teaching reading to slow-learning children. *Exceptional Children, 31,* 419–421.

McDonald, F. J. (1976). *Beginning teacher evaluation study, phase II: Executive summary.* Princeton, NJ: Educational Testing Service.

McGuigan, C. A. (1975). *The effects of a flowing words list vs. fixed words lists and the implementation of procedures in the add-a-word spelling program* (Working Paper No. 52). Seattle: University of Washington, Experimental Education Unit.

McKeachie, W., & Lin, Y. (1971). Sex differences in student responses to college teachers: Teacher warmth and teacher sex. *American Educational Research Journal, 8,* 221–226.

McLean, J. E., & Snyder-McLean, L. K. (1978). *Transactional approach to early language training.* Columbus, OH: Merrill.

Medley, D. M. (1977). *Teacher competence and teacher effectiveness: A review of process-product research.* Washington, DC: American Association of Colleges for Teacher Education.

Mercer, C. D. (1981). *Children and adolescents with learning disabilities.* Columbus, OH: Merrill.

Mercer, C. D., & Mercer, A. R. (1978). The development and use of self-correcting materials with exceptional children. *Teaching Exceptional Children, 11*(1), 6–11.

Mercer, J. R. (1973). *Labeling the mentally retarded.* Berkeley: University of California Press.

Miller, S. R., & Schloss, P. J. (1982). *Career-vocational education for handicapped youth.* Rockville, MD: Aspen Systems.

Miller, S. R., Schloss, P. J., & Sedlak, R. A. (1983). The effects of teachers' professional setting on expectancy of behaviorally disordered youth. *Journal for Special Educators, 20,* 59–63.

Mills v. Board of Education of the District of Columbia, 348 F. Supp. 866 (D.D.C. 1972).

Milone, M. N., & Wasylyk, T. M. (1981). Handwriting in special education. *Teaching Exceptional Children, 14*(2), 58–61.

Mintz, S. L. (1979, April). *Teacher planning: A simulation study.* Paper presented at the annual meeting of the American Educational Research Association, San Francisco.

Moffett, J. (1968). *A student-centered language arts curriculum grades 11–13: A handbook for teachers.* Boston: Houghton Mifflin.

Monroe, M. (1932). *Children who cannot read.* Chicago: University of Chicago Press.

Monteith, M. K. (1980). Implications of the Ann Arbor decision: Black English and the reading teacher. *Journal of Reading, 23,* 556–559.

Morine-Dershimer, G., & Vallance, E. (1975). *A study of teacher and pupil perceptions of classroom interaction* (Tech. Rep. No. 75-11-6). San Francisco: Far West Laboratory for Educational Research and Development.

Morris, J. (1958). Teaching children to read. *Educational Research, 1,* 38–39.

Moreno, J. L. (1953). *Who shall survive? Foundation of sociometry, group psychotherapy, and sociodrama* (2nd ed.). New York: Beacon House.

Myers, P., & Hammill, D. (1976). *Methods of learning disorders.* New York: Wiley.

Myklebust, H. R. (1960). *Psychology of deafness*. New York: Grune & Stratton.

Neef, N. A., Iwata, B. A., & Page, T. J. (1977). The effects of known-item interspersal on acquisition and retention of spelling and sight-reading words. *Journal of Applied Behavior Analysis, 10*, 738.

Neuhaus, E. E. (1967). Training the mentally retarded for competitive employment. *Exceptional Children, 33*, 625–628.

Niemeyer, J. H. (1965). The Bank Street readers: Support for movement toward an integrated society. *Reading Teacher, 17*, 542–545.

Nietupski, J., & Williams, W. (1974). Teaching severely handicapped students to use the telephone, to initiate selected recreational activities, and to respond appropriately to telephone requests to engage in selected recreation activities. In L. Brown et al. (Eds.), *A collection of papers and programs related to public school services for severely handicapped students* (Vol. 40). Madison, WI: Madison Public Schools System.

Nihira, K., Foster, R., Shellhaas, N., & Leland, H. (1969). *Adaptive Behavior Scales: Manual*. Washington, DC: American Association on Mental Deficiency.

Norwell, G. W. (1950). *The reading interests of young people*. Lexington, MA: Heath.

Palincsar, A. M., & Brown, A. L. (1984). Reciprocal teaching of comprehension fostering and comprehension monitoring activities. *Cognition and Instruction, 1*, 117–175.

PARC, Bowman, et al. v. Commonwealth of Pennsylvania, 334 F. Supp. 279 (1971).

Parker, S. L., Taylor, G. M., Hartman, W. T., Wong, R. O., Grigg, D. A., & Shay, D. E. (1976). *Improving occupational programs for the handicapped*. Report prepared for BEH under contract number OEC-0-72-5226 with Management Analysis Center, Washington, DC.

Patterson, G. R., Reid, J. B., Jones, R. R., & Conger, R. E. (1975). *A social learning approach to family intervention: Families with aggressive children* (Vol. 1). Eugene, OR: Castalia.

Payne, J. S., Patton, J. R., Kauffman, J. R., Brown, G. B., & Payne, R. A. (1983). *Exceptional children in focus*. Columbus, OH: Charles E. Merrill Publishing Co.

Pennsylvania Association for Retarded Children v. Commonwealth of Pennsylvania, 334 F. Supp. 1257 (E.D. Pa. 1971); 343 F. Supp. 279 (E.D. Pa. 1972).

Perry, M. A., & Cerreto, M. C. (1977). Structured learning training of social skills for the retarded. *Mental Retardation, 15*(2), 31–33.

Peter, L. J. (1965). *Prescriptive teaching*. New York: McGraw-Hill.

Petersen, G. A., Austin, G. J., & Lang, R. P. (1979). Use of teacher prompts to increase social behavior: Generalization effects with severely and profoundly retarded adolescents. *American Journal of Mental Deficiency, 1*, 82–86.

Peterson, L., Homer, A. L., & Wonderlich, S. A. (1982). The integrity of independent variables in behavior analysis. *Journal of Applied Behavior Analysis, 15*(4), 477–493.

Peterson, N. L., & Haralick, J. G. (1977). Integration of handicapped and non-handicapped preschoolers: An analysis of play behavior and social interaction. *Education and Training of the Mentally Retarded, 12*, 235–245.

Phelps, L. A., & Lutz, R. J. (1977). *Career exploration and preparation for the special needs learner*. Boston: Allyn & Bacon.

Phillips, E. L. (1968). Achievement place token reinforcement procedures in a home-style rehabilitation setting for pre-delinquent boys. *Journal of Applied Behavior Analysis, 1*, 213–223.

Phillips, L., Draguns, J. G., & Bartlett, D. P (1975). Classification of behavior disorders. In N. Hobbs (Ed.), *Issues in the classification of children* (Vol. I, pp. 26–55). San Francisco: Jossey-Bass.

Popham, W. J. (1978). *Criterion-referenced measurement*. Englewood Cliffs, NJ: Prentice-Hall.

Price, B. J. (1984, January). The tape recorder as an instructional aid in special education. *Educational Technology*, pp. 42–44.

Prinz, P. M., & Weiner, F. S. (in press). *Pragmatics screening test*. Columbus, OH: Merrill.

Quay, H. C., & Peterson, D. R. (1967). *Manual for the Behavior Problem Checklist*. Mimeographed, University of Illinois.

Quay, H. C., & Werry, J. S. (1979). *Psychopathological disorders of childhood* (2nd ed.). New York: Wiley.

Rankin, P. T. (1954). *Listening for learning*. Dubuque, IA: Brown.

Redding, S. F. (1979). Life adjustment patterns of retarded and non-retarded low functioning students. *Exceptional Children, 45*, 367–368.

Reynolds, M. C. (1962). A framework for considering some issues in special education. *Exceptional Children, 28*, 367–370.

Reynolds, M. C., & Balow, B. (1972). Categories and variables in special education. *Exceptional Children, 38*, 357–366.

Rhode, G., Morgan, D. P., & Young, K. R. (1983). Generalization and maintenance of treatment gains of behaviorally handicapped students from resource rooms to regular classrooms using self-evaluation procedures. *Journal of Applied Behavior Analysis, 16*(2), 171–188.

Rigg, P. (1978). Dialect and/in/for reading. *Language Arts, 55*, 285–290.

Rinn, R. C., & Markle, A. (1979). Modification of social skill deficits in children. In A. S. Bellack & M. Hersen (Eds.), *Research and practice in social skills training* (pp. 107–129). New York: Plenum.

Rivers, L. W., Henderson, D. M., Jones, R. L., Lodner, J. A., & Williams, R. L. (1975). Mosaic of labels for black children. In N. Hobbs (Ed.), *Issues in the classification of children* (Vol. 11, pp. 213–245). San Francisco: Jossey-Bass.

Robinson, N. M., & Robinson, H. B. (1976). *The mentally retarded child* (2nd ed.). New York: McGraw-Hill.

Robinson, P. C. (1980–81). The black English issue. *Education Leadership, 38*, 474–475.

Rogers, C. (1969). *Freedom to learn*. Columbus, OH: Merrill.

Rose, T. L. (1984). The effects of previewing on retarded learners' oral reading. *Education and Training of the Mentally Retarded, 19*(1), 49–53.

Rose, T. L., & Fur, P. M. (1984). Negative effects of illustrations as word cues. *Journal of Learning Disabilities, 17*, 334–337.

Rose, T. L., & Sherry, L. (1984). Effects of previewing on LD adolescents' oral reading performance. *Learning Disability Quarterly, 7*, 39–441.

Rosenshine, B. V. (1979). Content, time, and direct instruction. In P. L. Peterson & H. J. Walberg (Eds.), *Research on teaching: Concepts, findings and implications* (pp. 176–201). Berkeley, CA: McCutchan.

Rosenshine, B. (1983). Teaching functions in instructional programs. *Elementary School Journal, 83,* 335–352.

Rosenshine, B., & Stevens, R. (1984). Classroom instruction in reading. In P. David Pearson (Ed.), *Handbook of reading research* (pp. 745–798). New York: Longman.

Ross, D. M. (1970). Effect on learning of psychological attachment to a film model. *American Journal of Mental Deficiency, 74,* 701–707.

Ruhl, K. (1983). Mainstreaming. In R. E. Schmid & L. M. Nagata (Eds.), *Contemporary issues in special education* (pp. 2–26). New York: McGraw-Hill.

Rusch, F. R. (1979). Toward the validation of social vocational survival skills. *Mental Retardation, 17*(3), 143–145.

Rusch, F. R., & Menchetti, B. M. (1981). Increasing compliant work behaviors in a nonsheltered work setting. *Mental Retardation, 19,* 107–111.

Rusch, F. R., Schutz, R. P., Mithaug, D. E., Stewart, J. E., & Mar, D. K. (1982). *The vocational assessment and curriculum guide.* Seattle: Exceptional Education.

Russo, D. C., & Kuegel, R. L. (1977). A method for integrating an autistic child into a normal public school classroom. *Journal of Applied Behavior Analysis, 10,* 579–590.

Russo, N. A. (1978, April). *Capturing teachers' decision policies: An investigation of strategies for teaching reading and mathematics.* Paper presented at the annual meeting of the American Educational Research Association, Toronto.

Rychtarik, R. G., & Bornstein, P. H. (1979). Training conversational skills in mentally retarded adults: A multiple baseline analysis. *Mental Retardation, 17,* 289–293.

Sabatino, D. (1982). Prolog. In S. R. Miller & P. J. Schloss (Eds.), *Career-vocational education for handicapped youth* (pp. xiii–xxviii). Rockville, MD: Aspen Systems.

Saenger, G. (1957). *The adjustment of severely retarded adults in the community.* Albany, NY: Interdepartmental Health Resources Board.

Sali, J., & Amir, J. (1971). Personal factors influencing the retarded person's success at work: A report from Israel. *American Journal of Mental Deficiency, 76,* 42–47.

Salvia, J., & Seibel, P. (1983). Labeling and classification in special education. In R. M. Smith, J. T. Neisworth, & F. M. Hunt (Eds.), *The exceptional child: A functional approach* (pp. 34–50). New York: McGraw-Hill.

Salvia, J., & Ysseldyke, J. (1985). *Assessment in special and remedial education* (3rd ed.). Boston: Houghton Mifflin.

Sattler, J. M. (1974). *Assessment of children's intelligence.* Philadelphia: Saunders.

Scarr-Salapatek, S. (1975). Genetics and the development of intelligence. In F. D. Horowitz (Ed.), *Review of child development research* (Vol. 4). Chicago: University of Chicago Press.

Schenck, W. (1973). Pictures and the indefinite quantifier in verbal problem solving among EMR children. *American Journal of Mental Deficiency, 78,* 272–276.

Schloss, P. J. (1983). The prosocial response formation technique. *Elementary School Journal, 83*(3), 220–229.

Schloss, P. J. (1984). *Social development of handicapped children and adolescents.* Rockville, MD: Aspen Systems.

Schloss, P. J. (1984). Social development of handicapped children and adolescents.

Rockville, MD: Aspen Systems.

Schloss, P. J., Goldsmith, L., Sellinger, J., & Morrow L. (1983). Classroom based approaches to developing social competence among hearing impaired youth. *American Annals of the Deaf, 128*(6), 842–850.

Schloss, P. J., Harriman, N., & Pfiefer, K. (in press). Application of a sequential prompt reduction technique to the independent composition performance of behaviorally disordered youth. *Behavioral Disorders.*

Schloss, P. J., Kane, M. S., & Miller, S. R. (1981). Truancy intervention for behaviorally disordered adolescents. *Behavioral Disorders, 6*(3), 175–179.

Schloss, P. J. & Miller, S. R. (1982). The effects of the label "institutionalized" vs. "regular school student" on teacher expectation. *Exceptional Children, 48,* 263–264.

Schloss, P. J., Schloss, C. N., & Harris, L. (1984). A multiple baseline analysis of an interpersonal skill training program for depressed youth. *Behavioral Disorders, 9*(3), 182–188.

Schloss, P. J. Schloss, C. N., & Misra, A. (1985). Analysis of application forms used by special needs youth applying for entry level jobs. *Career Development for Exceptional Individuals, 8*(2), 80–90.

Schloss, P. J., Sedlak, R. A., Elliott, C., & Smothers, M. (1982). Application of the changing criterion design in special education. *Journal of Special Education, 16*(3), 359–367.

Schloss, P. J., Selinger, J., Goldsmith, L., & Morrow, L. (1983). Classroom based approaches to developing social competence among hearing impaired youth. *American Annals of the Deaf, 128*(6), 842–850.

Schloss, P. J., Smith, M. A., Goldsmith, L., & Selinger, J. (1984). Identifying current and relevant curricular sequences for multiply involved hearing impaired youth. *American Annals of the Deaf, 129*(4), 370–375.

Schloss, P. J., Smith, M. A., & Schloss, C. N. (1984). Empirical analysis of a card game designed to promote consumer-related social competence among hearing impaired youth. *American Annals of the Deaf, 129*(5), 417–423.

Schumaker, J. B., Hovell, M. F., & Sherman, J. A. (1977). An analysis of daily report cards and parent managed privileges in the improvement of adolescents' classroom performance. *Journal of Applied Behavior Analysis, 10*(3), 449–464.

Sedlak, R. A. (1974). Performance of good and poor problem solvers on arithmetic word problems presented in a modified cloze format. *Journal of Educational Research, 10,* 467–471.

Sedlak, R. A., & Cartwright, G. P. (1972). Written language abilities of EMR and nonretarded children with the same mental ages. *American Journal of Mental Deficiency, 77,* 95–99.

Sedlak, R. A., & Fitzmaurice, A. (1981). *Handbook of special education.* Englewood Cliffs, NJ: Prentice-Hall.

Sedlak, R. A., & Sedlak, D. M. (1985). *Teaching the educable mentally retarded.* Albany: State University of New York Press.

Sedlak, R. A., Steppe-Jones, C., & Sedlak, D. (1982). Informal assessment: Concepts and practices. In T. L. Miller and E. E. Davis (Eds.), *The mildly handicapped student* (pp. 263–282). New York: Grune & Stratton.

Sedlak, R. A., & Weener, P. (1973). Review of research on the Illinois Test of Psycholinguistic Abilities. In L. Mann and D. A. Sabatino (Eds.), *The first review of special education* (Vol. 1, pp. 113–156). Philadelphia: Journal of Special Education Press.

Sequin, E. (1866). *Idiocy: Its treatment by the physiological method*. New York: Teachers College Press.

Sharma, M. C. (1984). Mathematics in the real world. In J. F. Cawley (Ed.), *Developmental teaching of mathematics for the learning disabled* (pp. 204–224). Rockville, MD: Aspen Systems.

Shavelson, R. J. (1974). Methods for examining representations of a subject-matter structure in a student's memory. *Journal of Research in Scientific Teaching, 11,* 231–249.

Shavelson, R. J. (1981). Teaching mathematics: Contributions of cognitive research. *Educational Psychologist, 16,* 23–44.

Shavelson, R. J. (1983). Review of research on teachers' pedagogical judgments, plans, and decisions. *Elementary School Journal, 83*(4), 392–413.

Shavelson, R. J., & Borko, H. (1979). Research on teachers' decisions in planning instruction. *Educational Horizons, 57,* 183–189.

Shavelson, R. J., Cadwell, J., & Izu, T. (1977). Teachers' sensitivity to the reliability of information in making pedagogical decisions. *American Educational Research Journal, 14,* 83–97.

Shavelson, R. J., & Stern, P. (1981). Research on teachers' pedagogical thoughts, judgments, decisions, and behavior. *Review of Educational Research, 51,* 455–498.

Sidman, M. (1960). *Tactics of scientific research*. New York: Basic Books.

Silbert, J., Carnine, D., & Stein, M. (1981). *Direct instruction mathematics*. Columbus, OH: Merrill.

Sindelar, P. T. (1981). Operationalizing the concept of the least restrictive environment. *Education and Treatment of Children, 4*(3), 279–290.

Sindelar, P. T., & Deno, S. L. (1978). The effectiveness of resource programming. *Journal of Special Education, 12*(1), 17–28.

Sindelar, P. T., Smith, M. A., Harriman, N. E., Hale, R. L. & Wilson, R. J. (in press). Teacher effectiveness in special education programs. *Exceptional Children.*

Skeels, H. M. (1966). Adult status of children with contrasting early life experience. *Monographs of the Society for Research in Child Development, 31* (Serial No. 105).

Skeels, H. M., & Dye, H. B. (1939). A study of the effects of differential stimulation on mentally retarded children. *Convention Proceedings, American Association on Mental Deficiency, 44,* 114–136.

Skinner, B. F. (1968). *The technology of teaching*. New York: Appleton-Century-Crofts.

Smith, D. D., & Lovitt, T. C. (1975). The use of modeling techniques to influence the acquisition of computational arithmetic skills in learning disabled children. In E. Ramp & G. Semb (Eds.), *Behavior analysis: Area of research and application*. Englewood Cliffs, NJ: Prentice-Hall.

Smith, E. L., & Sendelbach, N. B. (1979, April). *Teacher intentions for science instruction and their antecedents in program materials*. Paper presented at the annual meeting of the American Educational Research Association, San Francisco.

Smith, M., Schloss, P. J., & Schloss, C. N. (1984). Empirical analysis of a social skills program used with hearing impaired youth. *Journal of Rehabilitation of the Deaf, 18*(2), 7–14.

Smith, R. M. (1968). *Clinical teaching: Methods of instruction for the retarded.* New York: McGraw-Hill.

Smith, R. M., Neisworth, J. T., & Hunt, F. M. (1983). *The exceptional child: A functional approach.* New York: McGraw-Hill.

Smitherman, G. (1981). "What go round come round": King in perspective. *Harvard Educational Review, 5,* 40–56.

Snyder, J. J., & White, M. J. (1979). The use of cognitive self-instruction in the treatment of behaviorally disturbed adolescents. *Behavior Therapy, 10,* 227–235.

Somervill, M. A. (1975). Dialect and reading: A review of alternative solutions. *Review of Educational Research, 45,* 247–262.

Spache, G. D., & Spache, E. B. (1977). *Reading in the elementary school* (4th ed.). Boston: Allyn & Bacon.

Speltz, M. L, Shimamura, J. W., & McReynolds, W. T. (1982). Procedural variations in group contingencies: Effects on children's academic and social behaviors. *Journal of Applied Behavior Analysis, 15,* 533–544.

Spence, S. H., & Marzillier, J. S. (1979). Social skills training with adolescent male offenders: Short-term effect. *Behavior, Research, and Therapy, 17,* 7–15.

Stallings, J. (1975). Implementation and child effects of teaching practices in follow through classrooms. *Monographs of the Society for Research in Child Development, 40*(Serial No. 163).

Starlin, C., & Starlin, A. (1973). *Guides for continuous decision making.* Bemidji, MN: Unique Curriculums.

Stauffer, R. G. (Ed.). (1967). *The first grade reading studies: Findings of individual investigations.* Newark, DE: International Reading Association.

Stern, P., & Shavelson, R. (1981, June). The relationship between teachers' grouping decisions and instructional behaviors: An ethnographic study of reading instruction. *Resources in Education* (ERIC #ED 201 971).

Sternberg, L. (1975). Pattern recognition training: A key to mathematics and language skill development. *Teaching Exceptional Children, 7,* 61–67.

Stevens, D. (1984). Individualized spelling technique. *Techniques: A Journal for Remedial Education and Counseling, 1,* 79–80.

Stevenson, H. W. (1972). *Children's learning.* New York: Appleton-Century-Crofts.

Stokes, T., & Baer, D. M. (1977). An implicit technology of generalization. *Journal of Applied Behavior Analysis, 10*(2), 349–367.

Stokes, T. F., Baer, D. M., & Jackson, R. L. (1974). Programming the generalization of a greeting response in four retarded children. *Journal of Applied Behavior Analysis, 7,* 599–610.

Stoudenmire, J., & Salter, L. (1975). Conditioning prosocial behaviors in a mentally retarded child without using instructions. *Journal of Behavior Therapy and Experimental Psychiatry, 6,* 39–42.

Strain, P. (1975). Increasing social play of severely retarded preschoolers with socio-dramatic activities. *Mental Retardation, 1,* 7–9.

Strain, P. S., Shores, R. E., & Kerr, M. M. (1976). An experimental analysis of "spill over" effects on the social interaction of behaviorally handicapped preschool children. *Journal of Applied Behavior Analysis, 9,* 31–40.

Sulzer-Azaroff, B., & Mayer, G. R. (1977). *Applying behavior-analysis procedures with children and youth.* New York: Holt, Rinehart & Winston.

Suran, B. G., & Rizzo, J. V. (1979). *Special children: An integrative approach.* Glenview, IL: Scott, Foresman.

Swanson, H. L., & Reinert, H. R. (1984). *Teaching strategies for children in conflict: Curriculum, methods, and materials.* St. Louis: Times Mirror/Mosby College.

Tarver, S. G., & Dawson, M. M. (1980). Modality preference and the teaching of reading: A review. *Journal of Learning Disabilities, 7,* 560–569.

Telford, C. W., & Sawrey, J. M. (1972). *The exceptional individual* (2nd ed.). Englewood Cliffs, NJ: Prentice-Hall.

Tenbrink, T. D. (1974). *Evaluation: A practical guide for teachers.* New York: McGraw-Hill.

Tharp, R. G. (1982). The effective instruction of comprehension: Results and description of the Kamehameha early education program. *Reading Research Quarterly, 17,* 503–527.

Thibodeau, G. (1974). Manipulation of numerical presentation in verbal problems and its effect on verbal solving among EMR children. *Education and Training of the Mentally Retarded, 9,* 9–14.

Thoday, J. M., & Gibson, J. B. (1970). Environmental and genetic contributions to class differences: A model experiment. *Science, 167,* 990–992.

Tickunoff, W., Berliner, D. C., & Rist, R. C. (1975). *An ethnographic study of the forty classrooms of the beginning teacher evaluation study known sample* (Tech. Rep. No. 75-10-5). San Francisco: Far West Laboratory for Educational Research and Development.

Titus, R. W., & Travis, J. T. (1973). Follow-up of EMR program graduates. *Mental Retardation, 11,* 24–26.

Tomaras, S. N. (1975). *Curriculum materials for individualized instruction: How to create rate sheets.* Unpublished manuscript, Tacoma Public Schools, Pupil Personnel Services.

Trap, J. J., Milner-Davis, P., Joseph, S., & Cooper, J. O. The effects of feedback and consequences on transitional cursive letter formation. *Journal of Applied Behavior Analysis, 11,* 381–394.

Travers, R. M. (1967). *Essentials of learning: An overview for students of education* (2nd ed.). New York: Macmillan.

Turnbull, A. P., Strickland, B. B., & Brantley, J. C. (1982). *Developing and implementing individualized education programs.* Columbus, OH: Merrill.

Turner, A. S., Hersen, M., & Bellack, A. S. (1978). Social skills training to teach prosocial behaviors in an organically impaired and retarded patient. *Journal of Behavior Therapy and Experimental Psychiatry, 9,* 253–258.

U.S. Bureau of the Census. (1982). *Labor force status and other characteristics of persons with a work disability.* Washington, DC: Author.

U.S. Commission on Civil Rights. (1983). *Accommodating the spectrum of disabilities.* Washington, DC: Author.

U.S. Department of Labor. (1977). *Sheltered workshop study.* Washington, DC: Author.

U.S. Department of Labor. (1979). *A study of handicapped clients in sheltered workshops.* Washington, DC: Author.

U.S. Department of Labor. (1982). *A study of accommodations provided to handicapped employees by federal contractors.* Washington, DC: Author.

U.S. Office of Education. (1977). Education of handicapped children: Implementation of Part B of the Education of the Handicapped Act. *Federal Register*, 42(163), 42480.

U.S. Public Law 93-112 (Rehabilitation Act of 1973), Sec. 504.

Van Houten, R., Hill, S., & Parson, M. (1975). An analysis of a performance feedback system: The effects of timing and feedback, public posting, and praise upon academic performance and peer interaction. *Journal of Applied Behavior Analysis, 8*, 449–457.

Van Houten, R., & MacLellan, P. (1981). A comparison of the effects of performance feedback and sentence combining instruction on student t-unit length. *Education and Treatment of Children, 4*(1), 17–33.

Van Houten, R., Morrison, E., Jarvis, R., & McDonald, M. (1974). The effect of explicit timing and feedback on compositional response rate in elementary school children. *Journal of Applied Behavior Analysis, 7*, 547–555.

Walker, D. F., & Schaffarzick, J. (1974). Comparing curricula. *Review of Educational Research, 44*(1), 83–111.

Walker, H. M., & Hops, H. (1976). Increasing academic achievement by reinforcing direct academic performance and/or facilitative nonacademic responses. *Journal of Educational Psychology, 68*, 218–225.

Walker, J. J. (1977). The gifted and talented. In E. L. Meyer (Ed.), *Exceptional children and youth: An introduction* (pp. 470–494). Denver: Love.

Wallace, C. & McLoughlin, J. A. (1975). *Learning disabilities: Concepts and characteristics.* Columbus, OH: Merrill.

Wallace, G. (1981). In J. M. Kauffman & D. P. Hallahan (Ed.), *Handbook of special education.* Englewood Cliffs, NJ: Prentice-Hall.

Wallace, G., & Kauffman, J. M. (1978). *Teaching children with learning problems* (2nd ed.). Columbus, OH: Merrill.

Warner, D. (1967). *Experimental phonetic reading programs for exceptional pupils.* Los Angeles: California University.

Wehman, P., Abramson, M., & Norman, C. (1977). Transfer of training in behavior modification: An evaluative review. *Journal of Special Education, 11*, 11–16.

Weisgerber, R. A., Dahl, P. R., Appleby, J. A. (1980). *Training the handicapped for productive employment.* Rockville, MD: Aspen Systems.

Weiss, C., & Lillywhite, H. (1976). *Communicative disorders.* St. Louis: Mosby.

White, O. R., & Haring, N. G. (1980). *Exceptional teaching* (2nd ed.). Columbus, OH: Merrill.

White, O. R., & Liberty, K. A. (1976). Behavioral assessment and precise educational measurement. In N. G. Haring & R. Schiefelbusch (Eds.), *Teaching special children* (pp. 31–71). New York: McGraw-Hill.

White, R. W. (1960). Competence and the psychosexual stages of development. In M. R. Jones (Ed.), *Nebraska Symposium on Motivation* (Vol. 8, pp. 97–144). Lincoln: University of Nebraska Press.

Whitman, R. L., Mercurio, J. R., & Caponigri, V. (1970). Development of social responses in two severely retarded children. *Journal of Applied Behavior Analysis, 3*, 133–138.

Wilhite, S. C. (1984). Hierarchial importance of pre-passage questions: Effects of cued recall. *Journal of Reading Behavior, 15*, 40–59.

Will, M. (1984, June). Bridges from school to working life. *Interchange*, pp. 2–6.

Wilson, R. M., & Hall, M. (1972). *Reading and the elementary school child: Theory and practice for teachers.* New York: Van Nostrand Reinhold.

Wolf, M. M. (1978). Social validity: The case for subjective measurement—or how applied behavior analysis is finding its heart. *Journal of Applied Behavior Analysis, 11,* 203–214.

Wood, F. H., & Lakin, C. K. (1978). *Punishment and aversive stimulation in special education: Legal, theoretical and practical issues in their use with emotionally disturbed children and youth.* Minneapolis: University of Minnesota, Department of Psychoeducational Studies.

Wyatt v. Stickney, 344 F. Supp. 387 (M.D. Ala. 1972).

Yinger, R. J. (1977). *A study of teacher planning: description and theory development using ethnographic and information processing methods.* Unpublished doctoral dissertation, Michigan State University.

Ysseldyke, J. E. (1973). Diagnostic-prescriptive teaching: The search for aptitude-treatment interaction. In L. Mann & D. A. Sabatino (Eds.), *The first review of special education* (pp. 5–33). Philadelphia: Journal of Special Education Press.

Ysseldyke, J. E., & Algozzine, B. (1982). *Critical issues in special and remedial education.* Boston: Houghton Mifflin.

Ysseldyke, J. E., & Foster, G. G. (1978). Bias in teacher observations of emotionally disabled children. *Exceptional Children, 45,* 18–26.

Ysseldyke, J. E., & Regan, R. E. (1980). Nondiscriminatory assessment: A formative model. *Exceptional Children, 46,* 465–458.

Zahorik, J. A. (1970). The effect of planning on teaching. *Elementary School Journal, 3,* 143–151.

Zeaman, D., & House, B. J. (1963). The role of attention in retardate discrimination learning. In N. R. Ellis (Ed.), *Handbook of mental deficiency.* New York: McGraw-Hill.

Zigler, E., Balla, D. A., & Butterfield, E. C. (1968). A longitudinal investigation of the relationship between preinstitutional social deprivation and social motivation in institutionalized retardates. *Journal of Personality and Social Psychology, 10,* 437–445.

Zigler, E., Butterfield, E. C., & Capobianco, F. (1970). Institutionalization and the effectiveness of social reinforcement: A five- and eight-year follow-up study. *Child Development, 3,* 253–263.

Zigler, E. F., & Harter, S. (1969). The socialization of the mentally retarded. In D. A. Goslin (Ed.), *Handbook of socialization theory and research* (pp. 1065–1102). Chicago: Rand McNally.

Zinzer, O. (1966, September). *Imitation, modeling and cross-cultural training.* Wright-Patterson Air Force Base, OH: Aerospace Medical Research Laboratories, Aerospace Medical Division.

Author Index

Subject Index

AAMD Adaptive Behavior Scale: Public
   School Version, 384–385
Academic learning time, 178
"Action zones," 174
Adaptive behavior scales, 64, 113
Age-appropriate, 100, 180, 390, 391
Allocated time, 175, 176
American Printing House for the Blind,
   199
American Speech and Hearing
   Association, 225
Antecedents, 12, 33, 179–183
Applied behavioral analysis, 80,
   371–373, 391
Arithmetic operations, 311–315
Assessment, 82, 112–116

Baseline, 160, 161, 260
Basal readers, 294–295
Behavior Problem Checklist, 385
Behavior Rating Profile, 384
Behavioral Assertiveness Test-Revised,
   383
Behavioral characteristics, 10, 12, 14,
   15, 25, 35, 37–38, 67, 82, 189

Calculators, 205, 310, 315, 320–322
Cascade of services, 50–53, 71
Chain, behavioral, 104
Chaining, 26, 386
   backward and forward, 43, 92–93,
      144–145
Chalkboard, 197
Characteristic-Specific Classification
   System, 26–27
Chronological age, 38–39
Classroom organization, 174, 298
Cloze procedure, 278, 291
Cognitive domain, 27–28, 70
Communication domain, 29, 36
Comprehension skills, 281–282, 285,
   289, 290
   categories of, 282–284
   instruction of, 282–283

Confidence intervals, 131
Consequences, 12, 33–35, 81, 101, 173,
   183, 187, 188
   application of, 103
   selection of, 103
Contingency contracting, 5, 188–191
Contingency plan, 86–87, 89
Cooperative Training/Placement
   Agreement, 346
Cover-Copy-Compare Method, 262,
   264
Criterion-referenced measures, 13, 30,
   67, 105, 114–115, 116
   development of, 117–134
Cue cards, 389
Cue words, 315
Cues, 12, 93, 223, 298, 299
   configuration, 276, 278
   contextual, 376, 378
   discrete, 344
   social, 12, 226, 227
   unnatural, 383
Curriculum:
   development of, 39–44, 305
   developmental, 15, 38–39, 305
   functional, 15, 38–39, 41, 100
   functional objectives of, 39
   vocational, 335, 341

Darley Tests of Articulation, 234
Data-based instruction, 6, 9, 13
Deaf, 19, 29, 381
Deaf-blind, 19–20, 29
Developmental sequence, 15, 36, 37,
   84, 371
Diagnostic teaching, 80
Dictionary, 255, 256
Dictionary of Occupational Titles
   (DOT), 337
Differential Reinforcement of
   Incompatable Behaviors, 187
Direct instruction, 80–82, 145, 178,
   297, 390
Discrimination deficits, 32–33

429